BRITAIN'S BEST EMPLOYERS

Britain's Best Employers
A guide to the 100 most
attractive companies to work for

Corporate Research Foundation UK

THE McGRAW-HILL COMPANIES

London • New York • St Louis • San Francisco • Auckland
Bogotá • Caracas • Lisbon • Madrid • Mexico • Milan
Montreal • New Delhi • Panama • Paris • San Juan • São Paulo
Singapore • Sydney • Tokyo • Toronto

Copyright © Corporate Research Foundation

Corporate Research Foundation UK
Standbrook House
2–5 Old Bond Street
London W1X 3TB
Tel: 0171 4934919
Fax: 0171 4932545

First published in Great Britain in 1997 by
McGraw-Hill Publishing Company
McGraw-Hill House
Shoppenhangers Road
Maidenhead
Berkshire SL6 2QL
Tel: 01628 502500
Fax: 01628 770224

A catalogue record for this book is available from the British Library

The right of the Corporate Research Foundation UK to be identified as the editor of
this work has been asserted in accordance with the Copyright, Designs and Patents
Act 1988.

McGraw-Hill
A Division of The McGraw-Hill Companies

Reprinted 1998

Printed and bound in Great Britain at The Basingstoke Press (75) Ltd.

Printed on permanent paper in compliance with ISO Standard 9706

FOREWORD

"Tell me the best company to work for", was a question I dreaded as a careers counsellor helping individuals find the organisation that would best match their interests, ambitions and values. I had quickly learnt that answering it on the basis of reading company recruitment literature was an inadequate response, and a prime reason for the early exiting of many talented professionals. The true answer is that there is no best company, but for each of us there are best companies. They are those who offer us what we need in order to feel we are contributing and who want what we most value in ourselves. While this book offers profiles of 100 UK organisations, only some will be best for you.

Reading through the book you will see that the focus is not on telling a detailed story of policies, procedures, remuneration packages and career development schemes, but on giving you a sense of how that organisation goes about its business. I welcome that approach because too often profiles of the 'best' describe those artifacts of the business which can be seen, measured and publicly presented. They can describe a world unrecognised by employees, who experience how they work in practice. More important is to know how it feels to be part of that company. What are the values which underpin its activities, how will you be expected to be if you are to be valued, and what are the challenges that you would face if you joined?

A year ago I co-wrote a book *New Deals*, which challenged organisations to consider the damage to the 'deal' between individuals and their employer that the business pressures of the 1990s had caused. We argued for the building of new deals as essential to delivering business differentiation. In subsequent workshops and seminars, employees have often told me that while the 'old deal' could not be sustained, it had given them a sense of connection to their organisation, and a belief that what their organisation did mattered. A conviction that one is involved with the best motivates performance, sparks creativity, and gives people the courage to do more than they thought possible. That can only be to the benefit of both the employee and the organisation.

The theme of the profiles is that of a changing relationship between employer and employee. All of the profiles describe excellence. In reading this book, I would encourage you to see yourself as a partner in the process and identify those things which are important to you. The writers are to be congratulated on giving the reader the information from which you can judge—it is up to you to decide which is 'best'.

Carole Pemberton
Career Matters

With many thanks to:

Sources and Advisers

Association of Graduate Careers Advisory Services
Association of Graduate Recruiters
Business in the Community
Dun & Bradstreet International
Investors in People
KPMG
People in Business
The Reward Group
Sanders and Sidney

Editor

Paul Donkersley

Writers

Simon Bain
Paul Donkersley
Gary Leboff
Bill Magee
Wilfrid Pickard
Helen Winnifrith
Tom Winnifrith

CONTENTS

Features

INTRODUCTION

There is more to a book than even a long descriptive like this can convey. The companies featured in this book are certainly excellent employers, in terms of their approach and attitude towards staff, whether formalised in policies or inherent in culture. They are also attractive companies to work for, and there are many different reasons for this: high rates of pay, excellent career prospects, a relaxed, friendly work environment, superb training, international opportunities, the chance to work with some of the most exciting products and brands, the chance to work with some of the brightest people.

It is difficult to make direct comparisons between the companies in this book. A design agency, a car manufacturer, a brand marketing company; all are different, and have unique characteristics which make them attractive companies to work for. The 100 companies chosen for the final publication will, almost certainly, be different to the ones you might list yourself. Ask 20 people for an opinion and you will get at least 20 different answers. But few would dispute that these 100 companies represent a superb list. Read each profile, and you will find 100 examples of being a leader, an innovator, a best practitioner.

The assessment criteria reveal our preferred emphasis of this book. There have been similar titles in different countries in the past, and there will be more in the future. Some projects have judged employers on shop floor practices and wage levels; others have evaluated companies on how they stack up against ethical measures. The subject of 'best employers' is really too big, and therefore some focus is appropriate. Unashamedly, we have targeted this book at a professional and executive readership. Graduates, young executives, professional job seekers, company analysts and watchers, management, human resources and personnel professionals.

The angle is "what makes this company an attractive one to work for, and what would it be like to be a part of it?" There is hopefully a logical flow to each company profile, telling a story beginning with that company's business, its markets, and its place in it; the company's culture, values and style are all-important, and a subject little-covered in business books. In considering human resource priorities, we were interested in how this function helps the company align its people resources with its business objectives. Specifics such as pay and benefits, career opportunity, and training and development all feature highly among the factors which employees hold in high regard. Finally, we recognised that no company has got it completely right nor is sitting on any laurels. Companies are always trying to make something better, are stretched somewhere, or find themselves in a process of constant change. In looking at 'The Future', we consider where each company will be placing priorities in the future and in so doing, hopefully give this book a reasonable shelf life.

How did the selection process work? Corporate Research Foundation first asked Dun & Bradstreet to undertake an initial screening of companies operating in the UK to produce a short list of 750 companies. Size was important, initially, and we wanted to at least consider the largest companies by turnover. We also looked for positive trends in financial growth—we wanted our selected companies to be still around in two years' time after all—and the number of people employed. CRF then added to and subtracted from this list on the basis of desk research and judgement.

An informal panel was formed of analysts, journalists, consultants and specialists in search, outplacement, reward and remuneration, training and human resources management, and various related associations. Some have kindly written a short feature on a specialist area which can be found towards the back of this book; others have remained anonymous. All were invited to submit names of companies which they thought might warrant consideration. I am grateful to them all for their respective contributions. This exercise aimed to identify areas of common opinion—the 'must have' companies. It also served to highlight any emerging companies which had somehow 'slipped the net'.

Necessarily, we considered most of the largest companies quoted on the London Stock Exchange. Not all of the top 20 companies by market capitalisation are in the final book. There might be many reasons for this, and are not to be gone into here on an individual basis. If anyone wants a personal view as to why some names are missing, I will be happy to discuss them. While a freelance editor, I can always be contacted through CRF's London office.

We appraised companies which were confident enough to come forward and stand up against our assessment criteria. We were sensitive to companies which requested not to be included in this edition, due to timing—perhaps surrounding major corporate restructuring, or processes of cultural change—or for matters of commercial confidentiality.

Any jurisdiction as editor was exercised towards the end of the project. It is one reason why some sectors have a stronger weighting than others: sectors of industry and commerce which are still strong in today's Britain—pharmaceuticals, financial services, information technology, energy, marketing, and brand management. Other sectors needed representation by the best companies in their field.

As the project unfolded, some common themes began to emerge among the most progressive organisations. The changing contract between employer and employee, 'jobs for life' being replaced by a commitment to providing individuals with greater employability through skills enhancement and training. Self-managed careers are the vogue, with people increasingly taking a share of the responsibility for their career development. The value placed on diversity in the work force is increasing—not just because it is a good thing, but because it can deliver real commercial advantages. Organisational structures are getting flatter, one implication being for horizontal career development in the absence of vertical promotion possibilities. Companies are expanding internationally, with emerging markets such as Eastern Europe and China as important for the future as the mature markets at home. Packages of benefits are increasingly 'flexible' in their composition. Pay is more often related to individual and team performance.

My thanks go to the team of writers, who endured with me the trials of researching and writing this project, and indeed, endured me. Often responding at short notice to analyse questionnaires, research information or conduct company interviews across the UK, their appetite for deadlines was tested to the full.

Paul Donkersley, Editorial Director
Corporate Research Foundation
11 November, 1996

BRITAIN'S BEST EMPLOYERS

3i

3i is the leading provider of investment capital to unquoted businesses in the UK. Since its beginnings over 50 years ago, 3i has invested close to £8 billion in more than 12,000 businesses. In 1995 3i invested £613 million in 554 businesses, with investments ranging from £100,000 to £20 million.

3i floated on the London Stock Exchange in 1994. Its 600 employees are located across 24 offices in the UK and continental Europe. Of this number, about half are involved in investment and supporting activities and half in professional services such as legal, tax and industrial advisers.

Biggest Plus: Fascinating, challenging work, sets your career up for life

Biggest Minus: A lot of pressure in getting investment deals done

3i plc
91 Waterloo Road
London SE1 8XP
Tel: 0171-928 3131
Fax: 0171-928 0058

The Business

"3i is a group whose business is investment", states chairman Sir George Russell. As the largest player in the investment capital market, 3i is often described as the 'university of venture capital', the training ground for many who go on to pursue successful careers elsewhere in the venture capital sector or sometimes in finance areas of industry. 3i is certainly *the* 'CV enhancer' in the industry.

An extensive regional office network ensures that 3i has good access to local communities and businesses. 3i focuses on providing investment capital to small- and medium-sized businesses and it is estimated that companies in which 3i has invested provide over one million jobs within the UK. Around 56% of total sums invested in 1996 were in management buy-ins and buy-outs, with the balance invested in growing companies and emerging businesses or start-ups. While its portfolio remains strongly oriented towards manufacturing businesses, the proportion of service industries is increasing, as is the number of new investments in technology companies.

A commitment to being a long-term partner differentiates 3i from many of its competitors, which often look for a shorter turnaround of funds. 3i follows the fortunes of its investee companies closely, but is not interested in running these companies as a hands-on investor. In the UK, in terms of numbers of investments, 3i has a 46% market share by volume and a 23% share by value. Around 900 companies supported by 3i have subsequently achieved a stock market listing.

Company Culture and Style

3i is very proud of the professionalism of its staff. "The people who work at 3i have to be good at analytical thinking, strong in terms of drive and resilience and have a high need to achieve. We employ bright, dynamic people and then give them a lot of scope to use initiative. They are technically very skilled, intellectually demanding and thrusting." says HR director Janet Gunn.

3i is organised into small semi-autonomous teams that interrelate across the business. Investment professionals are not sector specialists, but there are industry advisers—often ex-managing directors of businesses—who do specialise and are an important part of the deal-making process. "It is a knowledge-worker environment", says Janet Gunn. "You have bright capable people who need a high degree of autonomy and space, which they are given, provided they stay within corporate goals. They are expected to develop their own plans and programmes and come forward with new ideas."

If the spirit of innovation is one of 3i's core concepts, the thrill in 3i is deal-making, ensuring the incumbent management team achieves the transition to the next level of business development it is seeking. It is a work hard, play hard culture, featuring the highest standards of professionalism and integrity. Over the last three years, 3i has become more team focused. Cross-functional working groups and project teams working on a broad range of topics have given 3i a greater sense of openness and the contributions from staff across the company are increasingly valued.

Human Resource Priorities

3i's commitment to excellent people management is based around attracting and retaining the best and brightest people, as an integral part of keeping itself ahead of the competition. Providing competitive and attractive remuneration packages is only part of this task.

As chief executive Ewen Macpherson puts it: "3i is a major European business, although we employ just over 600 people. 3i's key asset is its people. We place a strong emphasis on the recruitment, training and retention of high quality and highly motivated staff for all functions within the Group."

In recruiting high quality people there are key things which 3i looks for. Analytical ability and commercial judgement represent the 'thinking' area; drive and resilience are important personal qualities that are required to 'get the deal done' and cope with inevitable pressure; and empathy is a behaviour that reflects the increasing importance 3i places on relationship-building skills. HR takes recruitment very seriously indeed, using best practice selection methods, and is clear on the personal qualities that will succeed and recruits specifically against them.

HR has a clear brief to develop policies that support its commitment to be fair and open with its people, including open communication and dialogue, which it follows up with staff attitude surveys and regular face-to-face meetings between senior management and staff at all levels in the organisation. Training its people to help them realise their full potential is another remit of the HR department.

Career Opportunity and Development

3i, as the 'university of venture capital', is a great place to learn the skills to succeed in the venture capital industry. 3i doesn't recruit graduates directly, but graduates with 3-5 years' experience from any industrial background, or with accountancy qualifications or MBAs, are hired frequently.

The company recognises the benefits in selecting people from a diversity of backgrounds, who can relate to the different types of businesses in which it invests. Personal skills are valued more highly than educational background, which has changed in recent years when an Oxbridge background might have been preferred.

Currently, only 18% of investment executive applicants are female, and 3i would welcome more women in management roles. Without discriminating positively, 3i is an equal opportunity employer of ethnic minorities and disabled people, and is considering in the future at least seeing every applicant from these groups.

All new recruits into the investment business go through 3i's one year investment skills training programme, during which they attend several courses and are coached in their office by a senior staff member. 3i also develops its people in management, supervisory and personal skills. The personal development workshops encourage participants to enhance their skills in interacting with colleagues and customers effectively.

As for career development, in this business it is competency and capacity to deliver that counts—3i does not have a hierarchical structure. Some opportunities are provided for secondments, lateral moves and promotions to larger management posts, but international postings are infrequent, as local people are employed and at 3i's level of business *very* good language skills are needed.

For those not finding their next career move in 3i, the high quality of intake, and subsequent development and experience gained, ensures that 3i's alumni rarely have problems finding attractive career opportunities on leaving the organisation.

Pay and Benefits

Pay is market-driven with different rates for different jobs. Investment bonuses can be up to 100% of basic salary. Most employees are company shareholders. All employees are eligible for annual profit sharing.

3i's benefits are single status. The biggest single benefit is the non-contributory pension scheme for every UK member of staff, which provides two-thirds salary after 25 years' service. Free private medical insurance is available for employees and spouses, together with health screening for all employees. 3i offers up to a £50,000 mortgage, subsidised at 5% interest. Employees at the two principal UK offices receive free lunches, refreshments and some sports facilities. Many employees also benefit from a flexible company car scheme, or a cash alternative.

The Future

After digressing into other business areas in the late 1980s, such as property and consultancy, 3i has now stripped out these peripherals and re-focused exclusively on its core business of investment.

3i has been developing the venture capital market in continental Europe for 15 years and is now firmly established in France, Germany, Spain and Italy.

"The UK remains our primary market place; we are committed to it and believe that we can continue to develop our leading position", says Ewen Macpherson. "Growth in Europe is a major challenge for us and a progressive portfolio expansion in our continental European businesses is an important feature of our medium-term plans. The venture capital market is evolving, so we are both creating the market and training suitable people. It takes up to five years to build a market and start doing deals, and management buy-ins and buy-outs were not familiar products on the continent before 3i put focus and energy into their development."

South East Asia is the next market 3i is planning to enter over the next few years, which will provide further opportunities and challenges for the talented professionals in the company.

3M UK PLC

3M manufactures more than 50,000 innovative products, ranging from Post-it Notes to pharmaceuticals, abrasives to adhesive tapes, reflective materials, respira-tors, and fabric protectors. 3M uses over 110 different technologies in 45 business units in the manufacture of products for a wide variety of industrial, commercial, health-care and consumer markets. The inventor of Scotch brand masking tape, the company now has world-wide sales of $13 billion, employing 70,000 people. In the UK and Ireland, 3M employs over 4,000 people in 16 locations and has a turnover exceeding £667 million.

Biggest Plus: A standard bearer for best practice and innovation

Biggest Minus: Cross allegiance between country and business units could be confusing

3M UK PLC
3M House
PO Box 1, Market Place
Bracknell
Berkshire RG12 1JU
Tel: 01344-858000
Fax: 01344-862367

The Business

"To find new ways to make things better" is 3M's credo. It has helped make 3M one of the most respected companies in the global business community and, according to *Fortune* magazine, one of the ten most admired corporations in America.

One of 3M's key philosophies is not only to interact with customers, but to stay at least a step or two ahead of their unarticulated needs. This approach has resulted in some of the company's most successful innovations, including the signature Scotch masking tape brand. The company looks to produce around 1,000 new products every two years and, typically, 30% of total sales are from products no more than four years old. 3M's management hopes that in the near future, around 10% of sales will come from products that have been in the market for just one year, an indication of the innovative nature of 3M's products and also their practi-cality and desirability.

3M is driven by success, and in the last ten years, sales per employee have increased by 100%. Yet 3M adopts a pragmatic, sometimes safe financial approach to business. When other companies were leveraging to the hilt in the 1980s, 3M was prudent, "like Midwest farmers," jokes chief executive Livio DeSimone, in reference to the company's global headquarters in St. Paul's, Minnesota.

Recent market changes have prompted major reshaping of 3M's European organisation, resulting in 11 new European Business Centres, which develop and manage a portfolio of products for customers in over 40 countries.

As a company that has kept ahead of the field for more than a century, innovation is crucial, and over the last five years, 3M has invested a massive £3.5 billion in research and development. Being truly innovative requires not being afraid of failure, and 3M accepts that attrition rates are high. For every 1,000 ideas, perhaps only 100 will make it to a formal proposal stage and of those, only a handful will reach the market as new products. When an idea works, however, success can be phenomenal; Post-it Notes, for example, are now one of the best-selling products in the office markets.

Company Culture and Style

Technology transfer gathers real momentum in the company when employees actively exchange ideas and information, which is a hallmark of the company. 3M's non-woven technology, developed in the 1950s, has spawned products as diverse as Buf-Puf facial sponges, 3M Nomad matting that stops dirt spreading through buildings, and 3M respirators to protect workers from air borne contamination.

'Bootlegging', is a highly productive culture somewhat peculiar to 3M. The company's scientists can spend up to 15% of their time on projects of their own choosing. Some have been known to spend more than 50% (and some less). The important message is that people have licence to be creative, and in encouraging risk-taking, 3M believes that it is better to ask forgiveness rather than permission.

This is how Scotch masking tape was invented. The scientist was told to leave his experiment, as it was consuming too much time and neglecting more pressing projects. He did this for a matter of hours. Ignoring orders and following a strong belief that he was onto a good thing, he went back to the laboratory and made his important discovery, from which 900 different tapes are marketed by 3M today.

On structure and working, HR director Ken Jackson says "As in other companies, organisational hierarchy naturally exists, but here the similarity ends. Hierarchy is only a problem when it leads to barriers. Any 'formal' organisation of 3M works with informal relationships and networking removing barriers. Innovation stems from secure employees feeling free to experiment and network."

People have to be responsible for their own actions and be prepared to help colleagues in a culture of co-operation, where managers listen to ideas from all employees. "Put fences around people and you get sheep," said William McKnight, one of the earliest chief executives, 70 years ago. The company may have transformed but the ethos remains the same.

3M's values extend to its comprehensive policy of making a contribution to the communities in which it operates and helping to preserve the environment. The company was among the first to make the environment a policy issue.

Human Resource Priorities

3M's spirit is one of learning, responsibility, independence yet interdependence, and individualism within a corporate framework. HR policies support this environment with a high regard for dignity and respect for the individual.

Also key is the employee-employer relationship. 3M undertakes an annual staff opinion survey of all UK employees, to identify current areas of concern with staff and provide a mandate for a focused and worthwhile response.

In addition, administration of the normal areas of recruitment, training and development and remuneration policy, fall under HR's ambit. In seeking to align its people resources to business objectives, human resources needs to address a 'matrix' structure of countries and business units.

All 3M staff are employed by the country in which they are located. Meanwhile, there are 11 different European business divisions. A sales manager, therefore, might be employed by 3M France, but his or her managing director employed by 3M UK; both work for the same European Business Centre and are accountable for sales and profit to that unit, but their employment contract, and human resources support, are held by their home country.

Those who do well at 3M tend to adapt to new situations easily. The company is very committed to equal opportunities and recognises that its management of diversity can be a key global competitive advantage.

Career Opportunity and Development

3M encourages the pursuit of long-term careers and it is rightly proud of its emphasis on promotion from within. Chief executive DeSimone champions long-term employment, believing that secure and happy employees are more likely to be productive at work. Average staff turnover is less than 3% a year, a remarkably low figure. Most promotion is internal and there is a sophisticated development process to equip people for new positions. An annual process identifies 'high fliers' with leadership potential.

Foreign postings are looked upon favourably indeed, experience in countries with different cultures and at different stages of economic development is viewed as an essential part of the development process for the future senior management of the company. Seventy per cent of 3M's top 135 executives have worked abroad for at least three years. Many senior managers outside the USA are local nationals.

There is a fundamental and substantial commitment to training at 3M. In addition to a range of work-related and competency/skills courses, further education is available for formal qualifications and 3M makes a generous contribution towards fees, allowance, and paid time off work. There is also an in-house graduate recruitment scheme and a student placement programme. An annual review process between employee and employer appraises past performance and focuses on long-term career development.

Pay and Benefits

3M's salary policy is to ensure that each employee is paid according to ability, performance, experience and individual contributions to the success of the company. 3M also conducts regular benchmarking with peer companies to ensure that salaries remain competitive.

3M offers a comprehensive benefits package, including contributory pension, free private health care (free for managers, discounted for other employees), company cars throughout sales, marketing and management functions. There is also a staff restaurant and extensive sports and social facilities.

There are no financial bonuses for innovation, which is considered 'part and parcel' of the job, but achievement is recognised and rewarded. For top scientists it could be election by their peers to the elite Carlton Society, or being recognised by promotion up a technical career path, carefully developed to allow scientists to remain in their field of expertise.

The Future

3M categorises its business opportunities into three markets—mature, developing and emerging. International growth is a priority placed on the last two, and the company is on track to establish more 3M international companies in the 1990s than ever before. If the company aims for the same level of market penetration in other countries as it has achieved in the USA, this will be some yardstick.

In Europe, the drive for greater market and customer focus will continue. As part of its efforts to serve customers better, 3M has realigned industrial businesses around markets and distribution channels. While modifying the way in which it delivers products to the market, 3M is retaining its long-standing entrepreneurial strengths. Individual 3M business units will continue to translate their understanding of customer needs into innovative solutions.

There is a genuine joy in innovation and invention at 3M. It has always been willing to invest in research for its own sake—"for the happy outcomes which emerge from the most unpromising of starts". That the company has increased revenues and profits in almost every single year since 1985 suggests that this innovative company knows precisely what it is doing.

ABBOTT MEAD VICKERS · BBDO LTD

Abbott Mead Vickers•BBDO Ltd.

Abbott Mead Vickers•BBDO is the number two advertising agency in the UK by billings (turnover) which stood at £260 million in 1995. Abbott Mead Vickers was created in 1977 by the three people in the company's name. In 1991 Abbott Mead Vickers bought BBDO London; at the same time, BBDO's parent Omnicom acquired a 25% share in Abbott Mead Vickers plc, which has been quoted on the London Stock Exchange since 1985.

Today the AMV Group is one of the largest marketing services companies in the UK, the result of a number of acquisitions. BBDO World-wide is the world's fourth largest agency network. In 1996 Abbott Mead Vickers•BBDO was named Agency of the Year by *Campaign* magazine and International Agency of the Year by *Advertising Age*. There are 320 people at Abbott Mead Vickers•BBDO, and another 650 in the AMV Group.

Biggest Plus: Creative, caring, fun, focused

Biggest Minus: All advertising agencies are relatively unstructured, if this is important to you

Abbott Mead Vickers · BBDO Ltd.
191 Old Marylebone Road
London NW1 5DW
Tel: 0171-402 4100
Fax: 0171-935 5883

The Business

That's enough about business, because Abbott Mead Vickers•BBDO (AMV) is all about *advertising* (although it does take very seriously the need to make a profit). In the advertising industry, an agency's reputation and track record of creative and effective advertising is everything. People aspiring to enter advertising are acutely interested in the professionalism and skills of the company they are joining. And its output. In advertising, there is an emotional commitment to the end product unlikely to be found in other manufacturing or service companies, therefore a company's reputation is a major attraction. AMV's is second to none.

AMV's impressive client list includes BT, The Economist, Gillette, Mars, Dulux, Pepsi-Cola, Pizza Hut, Sainsbury's, the BBC and the RSPCA. An agency with a conscience and discerning taste, it will not work for tobacco companies, and considers its compatibility with potential clients as much as the client judges AMV.

An important issue generally, because AMV is part of a group of related companies, linked by the businesses of persuasive communications. It seeks in its partners similarity in style and morality, a like-mindedness across different marketing skills. Business is easier and more enjoyable that way.

The relationship with BBDO has proved to be a fruitful one. Being part of an international agency grouping has significantly changed the balance of AMV's business. One-third of income is now international (defined as when working with at least three other BBDO offices outside the UK), with opportunities increasing all the time.

Company Culture and Style

AMV claims a unique culture, and of course others in the advertising business may do the same. But an environment free of back-stabbing, and glutted with nice, talented people living and breathing their work, is compellingly attractive. For this to happen, there must be unity at the top, and this is where AMV begins to stand out. David Abbott, Peter Mead and Adrian Vickers are still at the agency—in fact they're running the business. They knew each other as friends for 20 years before they started AMV.

"No room for disruptive geniuses," says deputy chairman Adrian Vickers. "We have no faith in creation through conflict." AMV far from discourages opinions, but it does look for a group effort to secure the end result. It wants bright, talented people to come to work, to enjoy it, and celebrate success together.

Queuing up to offer opinions on the agency's culture, "a meritocracy striving for excellence in all departments," suggests Jackie Boulter, planning director. "Intelligent consensus and respect for craftsmanship and civility," according to Cilla Snowball, head of client service, who adds that the "share of head principle" has a happy home at AMV, meaning that if you are absorbed by your work, and have no internal distractions or worries, success will follow.

In the words of chairman David Abbott: "You will almost certainly enjoy working at AMV•BBDO. You will sometimes put in unbelievably long hours, you will be frustrated by colleagues and clients alike; you will feel burdened by deadlines; but the exhilaration will always outweigh the exhaustion."

Human Resource Priorities

To ensure that AMV backs up what it says about caring for its people, agency managers are supported by an HR team of four, who have responsibility for pay, benefits and pensions administration.

AMV sets out to recruit the best talent—not necessarily graduates—but it does take on 5-6 of the latter each year. The agency also has a relatively novel and high-powered despatch department. A few graduates who might not have made the first cut at account management or planning are given a second 'bottom-up' chance; a number of people have made it through this way.

AMV does not expect 320 people to sense instinctively what is going on, so the agency makes an effort to communicate. 'Memos to all' are popular, reporting everything from the agency's results to celebrating pitch and campaign successes. The latter often spills over into the bar (AMV has its own bar with subsidised drinks and free breakfasts) which provides a vital social gathering place. In AMV's business, it is important that individuals frequently come into contact with their colleagues—the advertising industry would find it difficult to operate from remote locations.

As a wonderfully relaxed employer, any study of diversity at AMV is not really appropriate. To have full representation of all diversities among its work force, an agency would have to be cumbersomely large, and the idea is defeated by the economics of the business. But AMV needs no policy—it employs anyone who brings real talent to its business, and through natural forces, there is an increasing proportion of women in the business—at least at the 50% mark.

Career Opportunity and Development

In an industry characterised by volatility, where many young people and companies come and go, AMV takes the long view of its business. It takes very seriously the need to give its people the perspective of a possible long-term career, and regards all employees as potentially being there forever.

AMV seeks to talk to individuals about career development, and account managers and account planners have formal assessment ratings. The agency says it has learnt that it cannot spend too much time telling people how well they are doing and what the future might hold.

Training is a real and fundamental aspect of the way AMV treats staff; it has been practising it for so long that it is almost taken it for granted. Unlike many agencies, there is actually a budget for it. AMV contends that people derive satisfaction, but more importantly confidence from training.

The link with BBDO will bring opportunities to work abroad in other agencies, although this is not a selling point. But with 30% of AMV's business now international, people frequently find themselves showing their passports at the airport.

Should graduates be surprised that they are let loose on clients quite quickly? Not really. The advertising industry is one where you can do something 'useful' very early on, and this might as well be with clients as with your work mates. If there is one inherent characteristic of successful graduates who fight their way through the odds to join AMV, it is confidence (but without arrogance).

Pay and Benefits

AMV goes for the best talent and is prepared to pay for it; interestingly, in a country whose advertising and marketing industry is much revered, the agency believes that 'really good people' are few and far between.

There is no pay grading system, but managers have pay 'brackets' in their heads. Incentive schemes have been recently introduced for senior management, linked to the company's profitability and share price performance. AMV was one of the first companies to introduce PRP (Profit-Related-Pay), which everyone enjoys.

Bonus schemes are various, the spontaneous, spot or informal varieties as commonplace as annual ones. Benefits are numerous—premier medical insurance, life assurance, permanent health insurance, cars (be warned, Volvo is an important client) and the company pension scheme (another thing taken *very* seriously by the company—AMV doesn't just offer pensions to those who opt to opt in, it actively encourages its young people to understand them).

The Future

AMV's business challenges are now viewed in the international context. The dreaded word 'synergy' is being developed between Group companies and, more importantly, translated into value to clients. AMV observes a growing demand in recent years for integrated marketing communications services from fewer providers. If this is true, AMV has some terrific companies in the Group and its task will be to harness their power.

AMV is recognised and perceived as a good place to work, and probably retains its people, as it does clients, for above-average duration. But good people are constantly head-hunted in a business where curiosity and ambition reign supreme, and AMV like any agency, understands that it will not hang onto them unless it works hard at all aspects of communication and motivation.

Arguably unnecessarily, but certainly commendably, AMV tries to act in a way that offers its people the best job security possible, recognising that it has graduated from being a medium-sized operation to a large one. Intrinsically, this means continuing to give staff a sense of intimate involvement in the business and how this business is doing.

In communicating internally, AMV recognises it is a business that needs to achieve strong financial results but always puts advertising and creativity right at the centre. This priority of creative work first is noble and correct, because creative advertising is what AMV is all about; but it must keep delivering success, otherwise this order of priorities might appear indulgent or even arrogant.

As the lead part of the group, AMV is granted the option of deciding whether to absorb new areas of advertising and marketing, acquire them or ignore them. AMV the agency intends to focus on what it has always done—effective, creative above-the-line advertising.

14

AIR PRODUCTS

Air Products

Air Products supplies industrial gases, designs and manufactures gas processing equipment, has a chemicals business, and is also active in environmental and energy systems. World-wide revenues for the Group exceeded $4 billion in 1996. The Group employs 1,900 people in the UK, and 15,000 world-wide including joint ventures.

Biggest Plus: A fast-changing and dynamic organisation

Biggest Minus: No alternatives to hard work!

Air Products PLC
Hersham Place
Molesey Road
Walton on Thames
Surrey KT12 4RZ
Tel: 01932-249748
Fax: 01932-249893

The Business

Air Products in Europe is part of the world-wide operations of Air Products and Chemicals, Inc., a corporation founded in Detroit in 1940 to produce oxygen. To-day, the Group operates in 30 countries world-wide. Its European operations began in 1957 and now span the continent, with its European Support Centre based in Hersham, near London.

The Group has research and development facilities in the UK, Belgium, the Netherlands and Japan and a Group Research Centre in the USA. These extensive resources, backed by considerable investment, help keep the Group at the forefront of its rapidly changing businesses. The Group's diversity means that job opportuni-ties exist in engineering, sales, marketing, strategic planning, communications, hu-man resources, IT, research and development, manufacturing, finance and other areas. Talented people who want to work abroad also have considerable scope thanks to the international nature of the Group.

The influence of the Group's products is remarkably widespread. It is said that virtually everyone every day uses something produced with the aid of its industrial gases or chemicals: alarm clocks, razor blades, light bulbs, talcum powder, headache tablets, hamburgers, cars, calculators, glassware and many other products and appli-cations. The company itself has enjoyed enormous growth and continual change; nothing stays static in this technology-driven business. This rapid evolution has given its people an unusually strong opportunity to develop their careers, growing as the company grows.

Company Culture and Style

Leonard Broese van Groenou, vice president, HR & procurement, describes the company culture as "Open, frank, team-oriented, warm and friendly. It's a young, dynamic and creative company to work for. There's something about the company that's quite difficult to put into words but is immediately apparent to anyone coming in: there's a buzz about the place, a nice feel to it everywhere you go."

Part of this warmth and friendliness is undoubtedly due to the openness and sense of empowerment evident at Air Products. "I believe our people are far more empowered than ever before," Broese van Groenou says. "This process relies on trust; it's all about the confidence managers have in their people. We expect people to take more decisions than before, and earlier on in their careers. Undoubtedly we still have further to go, but this process is well on the way."

There's a refreshing informality about Air Products. Staff at Hersham meet together at the newly built Oasis coffee bar, and on Fridays even dress informally. All this helps promote a team spirit, a sharing of responsibility, a sense of moving forward together. A gymnasium, sports teams and clubs also flourish at many loca-tions. Indeed, there's a strong ethos of work hard, play hard at Air Products. Tal-ented and committed people are well rewarded here.

So what kind of person flourishes at Air Products? The company looks for results-oriented individuals with high levels of knowledge and skill: team players, good organisers, creative problem solvers. Broese van Groenou: "The company is all about outstanding people working together to high standards of ethics, safety and performance. People who enjoy hard work and thrive on challenge are likely to develop absorbing and rewarding careers here."

Human Resources Priorities

The company has a simple and straightforward policy when it comes to human resources: to be the first choice for its employees. But how does this work in practice?

At Air Products, there is a Human Resources Planning process. Each senior business manager looks at his or her own business plan and considers the human resources implications of that plan over the next two years. This involves considering existing teams and asking some searching questions: what is their potential? What can we do to develop them? Do we have all the skills we need or should we recruit externally? Who could succeed them? To what other positions could they aspire? Are they likely to leave? If so, how can we best persuade them to stay?

These and other questions are constantly considered as part of an ongoing human resource approach. Each business area prepares annually a plan of actions that are consolidated and implemented throughout the year. This, along with a number of other initiatives at Air Products, was created entirely in-house.

One factor that distinguishes Air Products is its desire to identify real talent. Although it offers all its staff attractive and rewarding careers, it is especially keen to spot and develop the stars of tomorrow. Young people of exceptional talent are fostered and helped to grow.

Air Products has a broad range of internal communications, from quarterly newsletters throughout Europe to twice-yearly meetings for all senior managers, as well as regular topical talks on technologies and other issues.

Staff turnover is currently just 4% a year and hardly ever rises above 7%. Every senior manager has been with the company for ten years or more. Many have risen through the ranks: the latest European president joined the company in 1964 as a trainee, and his example could be multiplied many times. All this supports Air Products' strong claims to be one of Britain's best employers.

Career Opportunity and Development

In 1996, Air Products sought to take on up to 25 graduate trainees: the number varies from 15 to 30, depending on the number of the previous year's intake. There are two graduate entry paths: the Career Development Programme, giving graduates experience in a number of areas, and Direct Entry, for those wanting to do a specific job.

Nicholas Gibbons graduated in management from Lancaster University in 1993 and joined the management information systems department through Direct Entry. "I was on familiar ground since I had spent my one-year industrial placement here as part of my degree. I came back because of the friendly working atmosphere and the company's commitment to training."

Alison Whitby read French and business at Aston University, graduating in 1979. "Being a mother of three children hasn't stopped me progressing my career with Air Products. Initially, I began with a market research assignment looking at developing new products for the welding group. Since 1985 I have held sales, marketing and general management posts and I have been marketing manager for the glass industries since 1995."

Graduates and other recruits can all look forward to excellent training. External training takes two forms: technical skills updates and a five-module leadership development course. The latter is a major investment, costing the Group world-wide over $12 million by 1999, of which a considerable proportion will go to the UK.

Career development is planned through the Human Resources Planning process, and through in-depth personal appraisals. Everyone's career is reviewed once a year where objectives are set and evaluated, and progress is monitored frequently throughout each year.

Pay and Benefits

Salaries at Air Products are very competitive and continually benchmarked against a peer group of companies.

Air Products also offers considerable benefits including bonuses for exceptional performance, Annual Performance Awards, stock option rights for all employees, cars for managers and essential users, a contributory final salary pension scheme, SAYE schemes in which over two-thirds of employees participate, BUPA health insurance, an excellent maternity leave facility, and subsidised sports. A tax-free pay scheme was launched in late 1996.

The Future

Air Products businesses are attractive, but the company works in an increasingly competitive environment, especially in the UK. There are more pressures on margins than ever before, while shareholders expect good returns on equity and capital investment.

Ron Sullam, president, Air Products Europe says: "The technological challenges are also becoming ever-greater. We're about to commission the world's biggest air separation plant in Rotterdam, which was designed and engineered in the UK, for instance. Bigger plants are increasingly the way of the future.

"The way to meet these competitive challenges is to ensure we recruit and retain the best people and give them the career opportunities they want. We must also continue to invest even more in research and development to retain our edge in the marketplace. These are great challenges—but we're confident that the company will succeed in both these areas."

Amerada Hess Limited

Amerada Hess Limited (AHL) is the wholly owned UK subsidiary of the Amerada Hess Corporation of the United States. AHL's principal activity is the exploration and production of oil and natural gas, and has been active in the UK since 1963 when the North Sea became the focus of a challenging era of oil and gas exploration and production. AHL is now the third largest operator in the North Sea, producing approximately 10% of the UK's oil needs, and controlling about 1% of total UK industrial investment.

AHL's turnover in 1995 increased to £765.7 million, on which it made a gross profit of £181.3 million. With over 600 employees (plus about 250 contractors) at its two offices in Central London and Aberdeen, AHL has an impressive profitability per employee ratio.

Biggest Plus: Positive, successful company, more set to follow

Biggest Minus: Must balance task-driven approach with the need to gear up for
                   rapid growth

Amerada Hess Limited
33 Grosvenor Place
London SW1X 7H
Tel: 0171-823 2626
Fax: 0171-887 2199

The Business

Amerada Hess is particularly good at seizing opportunities and has not been afraid to take risks over the years. Amerada Hess has earned a reputation as a successful explorer, but hard on its heels follows production. 1995 was an extremely busy year for oil and gas field developments, with seven major projects—often with Amerada Hess as operator—coming onstream.

In 1996, the company's wholly owned gas marketing subsidiary Amerada Hess Gas was not only one of the fastest growing independent marketers in the UK industrial and commercial gas market, but also the first company to announce its participation in the pilot scheme for the deregulation of the domestic gas market in the South West of England. While AHL is clearly nimble at the forefront of new commercial opportunities in gas supply, oil and gas exploration and production represent by far the bulk of the company's operations and income.

AHL emphasises safety, quality and integrity in all aspects of its business. Protecting its staff and the environment remain key priorities, and AHL has always been committed to the highest standards of safety in its offshore operations.

Company Culture and Style

Amerada Hess is sometimes perceived as being quite aggressive in its business style, but this probably has more to do with its willingness to take bold decisions and then make sure the job gets done. But the company is also good at striking up relationships with people, and a collaborative approach to strategic alliances and partnerships—with equity partners or with contractors—has delivered some notable commercial successes.

When the Scott field came onstream in 1993, AHL became the third largest operator of oil production in the North Sea. This achievement can in part be attributed to Amerada Hess's approach to date, which could be fairly described as task-focused, placing emphasis on results, achievement and delivery. These remain huge strengths, but there is now a desire for something more. The company is seeking to release and realise the full potential of its people, without losing the task discipline that has brought Amerada Hess its incredible success.

What might this mean? In a 1994 staff opinion survey, one comment which many AHL people allude to, was a picture of Amerada Hess as "a champagne bottle, with quality contents, passing through a narrow neck, but needing the cork released." The company wanted to go forward, but was conscious that it had attempted a form of cultural change before, which had led to some cynicism in the company. Maybe AHL was just guilty of simply floating a few words and mission statements, without implementing real cultural change, or more probably because the attempted impetus was 'outside-in', rather than the more successful formula of 'inside-out'.

So there is no new mission statement, nor any inclination to say "people are our greatest asset"—just a business vision in the broadest context. This is accompanied by a desire to create a shared sense of what Amerada Hess is about, what it is really trying to achieve in business terms, and how it should support that through new ways of working.

Amerada Hess people typically are very bright, performing to the highest levels not because of 'boss pressure', but because their colleagues expect it of them. Having competitive, ambitious people about the place may have a downside, in that people sometimes experience stress and feel a continuous need to perform, always searching for something new. However, the overall effect is very stimulating.

Human Resource Priorities

The HR department carries out the essential tasks of administering matters such as pay and benefits, training and recruitment, but it also has a prominent role in facilitating the ways of working in pursuit of the company's business vision. HR's real contribution is to fuel the business partnership concept, helping align people resources and aspirations with business objectives.

This remit embraces the putting in place of management development processes to coach people in acquiring new skills and behaviours; developing reward systems which value these behaviours; and better recruitment and selection policies to reinforce new values from the outset.

HR believes that any tensions between offices, departments and individuals are usually caused by a lack of appreciation among people about how others work. Consequently, it regards raising awareness of different ways of working as being very important, without saying to people that it *wants* them to work in a different way.

Some early successes have been recorded in putting together integrated teams and AHL is getting better at sequential ways of working. AHL can be a better-balanced company if it brings together its diverse functions, and it now assembles multi-disciplinary teams at the beginning of business projects.

Career Opportunity and Development

Amerada Hess recruits only the best and staff turnover is low. The company has a very high proportion of professional and qualified people in the areas you would expect—geology, geophysics, engineering, along with disciplines in commerce, law, trading, gas sales negotiation, information technology and planning.

Successful people at Amerada Hess might acquire both technical and commercial skills or instincts. This is not a one-way process of technical experts developing a commercial nose—commercial people are found in charge of AHL exploration and production in the North Sea without necessarily having a traditional technical background.

There are many functional forums that look specifically at individual development. Specialist forums, such as Petroleum Engineering, look across the entire company. Above that there are two major forums, Business and Technical, and beyond these, the Management Development and the Executive forums. These ensure that everyone's career development is discussed somewhere, opportunities are brought to the table, and development plans initiated.

Self-managed development is definitely encouraged in a deal based on partnership and shared responsibility. If the company was ever in the syndrome of 'develop me', it is not playing this game any more. Amerada Hess is still very much a people-focused organisation, one where people succeed for who they are and the skills they bring to bear. The company may have a rough outline of the parameters, but the person creates the role.

Pay and Benefits

The pay structure is relatively straightforward, essentially linked to market levels and trends. Benefits include PPP health insurance, a non-contributory pension for all employees, a share scheme, and an educational assistance programme.

The Future

Amerada Hess aims to achieve its business vision by unlocking potential in the organisation. It is self-challenged specifically to achieve consistency over 'what I say and what I do'. If the company concentrates on aligning cultural change with business objectives, recognising that it hasn't always delivered on this score in the past, it has a much better chance of doing so this time.

Setting cultural change aside, Amerada Hess is a highly successful company full of people who are ambitious achievers. And if all that the company is really saying is that it has yet to unlock the full potential of its people, it's a nice 'problem' to have. Exciting times may lie ahead.

ASDA

ASDA is the UK's third largest supermarket chain. With 210 stores, it has a total sales area of 8.4 million sq. ft. and its average store size of 41,000 sq. ft. is typically 60% larger than its competitors. The number of customers each week averages 5.6 million. Colleagues (employees) number 74,000, whose total work time equates to a full-time equivalent of 40,000. The group had a turnover of £6,042 million in 1996, and profit of £317 million.

Biggest Plus: Progressive retailer, dynamic but friendly culture

Biggest Minus: Image could be greater, but this is changing fast

ASDA PLC
Asda House
Southbank
Great Wilson Street
Leeds LS11 5AD
Tel: 0113-243 5435
Fax: 0113-241 8666

The Business

The pioneer of 'supermarketing' in the UK, based on low prices and good value, ASDA has regained its leading competitive position among supermarkets, after its rescue from almost certain bankruptcy in 1992. Its position had been dire, with outdated stores, a serious and continuing decline in its traditional working class customer base, and a crippling mountain of debt of £1 billion.

A new management under Archie Norman has transformed the business, refocusing strategy on high volume and good value trading. Norman's claim that "we have outperformed all our major competitors for the fourth year in succession" looks justifiable and ASDA has established a basis for sustained profit growth.

"The heart of our success depends on the colleagues who work for us, their motivation and involvement in improving the business. It is only by recruiting, motivating and involving the best people in the industry that we will deliver service with personality," says Archie Norman, chief executive, 1992–96, and chairman from December 1996.

With its very large stores and large buying power, ASDA is focused on being the country's best supplier of high volume, good value fresh food and also of clothing. The expansion of the 'George' range of clothing is proving very successful, and ASDA's reputation for good quality and value in wines and own brand products is also strengthening.

Progress has been impressive with weekly customers up by a dramatic 40% to 5.6 million. The rolling-out of a new bright and distinctive corporate appearance to its stores has been fully backed by a renewal of all the company's operations. The management structure was flattened to produce a more responsive business able to concentrate fully on customer service and satisfaction.

For anyone visiting ASDA House, the centre of operations in Leeds, the evidence of the group's purpose as a major retailer is inescapable. The entrance is deliberately laid-out like the entrance to a store, with regular changing of displays of toys, clothes ranges, cosmetics and other products, to reinforce to everyone that the company's business is based on sales and satisfying customer needs.

Company Culture and Style

One of the key features of the new ASDA culture is leadership from the front, aimed at establishing closeness to customers and colleagues. Behaviour is the acid test not words, and all colleagues are expected to have pride in selling their good quality and high value products. They should have a total commitment to providing service from the heart.

Some of Archie Norman's first instructions related to bringing back pride and self discipline and focusing on prompt delivery. This basic housekeeping and attention to detail is something that he continually reinforces by, for example, sticking up photographs he has taken himself touring the stores and highlighting such issues as broken notices, absent or poor labelling and other deficiencies.

Comradeship and partnership have been stressed with the abolition of reserved car spaces, monthly board meetings moving round the stores, and meticulously kept noticeboards posting staff promotions and moves. At ASDA House, and throughout the company, an open door policy saw partitions and offices torn down, with every manager, including the chief executive, openly on view and accessible.

The most graphic illustration of pulling the whole ASDA work force together to recognise the stores as the 'front line' of success is Team Christmas. ASDA House staff, including the directors, compete to spend as much time as possible helping in the stores during the whole of December at the crucial peak trading time of the year. Team Christmas involves military style organisation to ensure that every one of the 210 stores gets its share of head office reinforcements.

Human Resource Priorities

A determination to have the best people in retailing underlies the ASDA strategy and its human resources policies. Parallel to developing a real partnership of endeavour and achievement, decision making has been devolved to maintain the organisation's momentum and success. The group human resources manager, Jan Shaw, said that "At all levels we are recruiting the highest calibre staff. The key to our development is strong, professional management, who must have commitment and confidence in their own ability and potential."

Getting the best people with wide experience means, in the short term, external recruitment. But given the uniqueness of ASDA's business, identity and culture, the future emphasis will be to grow its own managers as far as possible.

The emphasis on personal excellence goes for all employees. Staff turnover has been reduced and is low for the sector, and there are many instances of people coming back to ASDA after finding work at competitors less satisfying.

ASDA adopts a more flexible and sympathetic attitude than many others in the sector to moving staff between stores. It operates in 15 regions throughout the country, and managers may ask for moves to be within a fairly tight regional area, rather than be sent to a store at the other end of the country.

Putting over the identity of the new ASDA requires considerable emphasis on communications at all levels, internal and external. Store managers have responsibility for local publicity and for establishing good relationships with the local press and media.

Career Opportunity and Development

ASDA has one of the most dynamic and innovative cultures of any UK company. In order to maintain the momentum achieved over four years, there is a drive to recruit and above all to train and promote people of high calibre. The setting up of a graduate recruitment programme illustrates how the new 'testing the boundaries' attitudes at ASDA are having an impact throughout the company.

Philip Horn, who runs the graduate training venture, said: "With little previous involvement in this area we decided we needed to stand out from the normal milk round approach. CVs and a covering letter only are requested from interested graduates; they are deliberately not asked to fill in an application form. The scheme was publicised through a combination of advertisements in the national press, the widely read by students, magazine *VIZ*, graduate head hunters and advertisements on the Internet.

The response and its quality was so good that in the first year, the number of graduates recruited was increased dramatically from the usual 20 to 106, then to 144 in year two (1996). A main feature of the scheme is practical experience, and the graduate trainee will be managing a team and will be given full sales and profit responsibility for a store department, such as fruit and vegetables, within six months of joining the scheme. "We want to make sure that they are able to contribute to the business with their enthusiastic fresh perspective right from the start," said Philip Horn.

Pay and Benefits

ASDA is very up-front that the basic pay for most of its workers is slightly below most of the competition. "However, taken in combination with the share options and other benefits, our people are on a par with the going rate," said Jan Shaw.

In its recruitment of top management, ASDA has had to set its remuneration package at an attractive level. As the company becomes increasingly profitable, general pay rates are likely to edge-up somewhat. But performance rewards will continue to be the main emphasis in providing a competitive overall package. A previously rigid salary structure has been made much more fluid, including scope for substantial bonus elements. Graduate trainees in 1995 started on £14,500, often rising to £17,000 within their first year. Store managers' salaries can vary from £25,000 a year to £50,000 or more.

The Future

The long-term challenge for ASDA is to keep up and intensify its performance improvement. It will need to apply the accelerator from time to time to maintain its momentum of improving performance—in customer numbers, in sales and profits.

The process of revitalising the organisation will need to be maintained into the future, and the culture to achieve that is in place. The message from ASDA's previous plunge to casualty status should serve as a reminder of the importance of always maintaining customer service; of the need to be competitive in every aspect of performance; and of the benefit of having unique advantages such as its present bias towards larger-than-average stores.

In the short term, the new chief executive Allan Leighton and his team will need to establish an alternative management identity to Archie Norman who, with his planned entry to national politics, will have to play a reduced role in the company's affairs. That may well see Mr Norman continuing to provide a public face to the group, while the management team strengthens its connections within the ASDA family of colleagues and customers.

AT&T

AT&T, established in 1885, is the oldest established telephone operator in the world. During this long and distinguished history it has recorded many firsts: the first transatlantic public telephone service, the first communication service to eastern Europe, the inventor of the free call service. Today, AT&T operates world-wide in competitive high technology communications markets. It has interests in 200 countries, nearly 30 in Europe alone, and in 1994 was awarded a UK Public Telephone Operator (PTO) licence.

In 1995, a global reorganisation spun-off Lucent Technologies, a communications systems and technology business, and NCR, the recently renamed computing business. The 'new' AT&T is a global company with revenues of £49 billion and approximately 110,000 people focused on providing 'anytime, anywhere' communication services in the world. The core businesses in the UK will concentrate on communications, value added, and outsourcing services. AT&T's growing UK work force numbered around 2,500 in October 1996.

Biggest Plus: Great opportunities as AT&T seeks to expand and develop in
                    the UK

Biggest Minus: Best reserved for the tough-minded and those with loads of en-
                    ergy at this stage of its growth

AT&T (UK) LTD.
Mitre House
160 Aldersgate Street
London EC1A 4DD
Tel: 0171-880 6500
Fax: 0171-880 6585

The Business

AT&T is probably *the* name in world telecommunications, but is relatively new to the UK. It has had a presence here for some years, but only a couple of years in terms of its communications business launch. Which is important—AT&T is a communications business, not just telecommunications.

AT&T offers tailored solutions to enhance business communication and to ensure cost-effective management of network resources to its customers, covering innovative services for all business, voice and data communication. Value added services develop network-based solutions, which may be proprietary or public works networks, but increasingly will be Internet-based. Outsourcing takes the concept a bit further, enabling business networks to connect more efficiently to suppliers and customers.

While AT&T is relatively new to the UK, it is here to stay, and the UK start-up is backed fully by its US parent. Under UK president Merrill Tutton, AT&T has aspirations in the main UK corporate market, as well as small/medium businesses and certain segments of the residential market, for example home working.

AT&T is growing rapidly and it intends to increase its employee population from 2,500 through 1997. Individuals will be joining a UK company, not a satellite of an international or American group. AT&T (UK) is very much a British organisation, recognising local market characteristics and dynamics, and the mindset of the consumer. Of course, there are excellent links between Europe and the USA, with many US people, including service contractors, based 'over here'. Already the second largest AT&T profit centre outside the USA, the strategic importance is obvious, with the UK being *the* strategic focus outside North America.

Company Culture and Style

Like any growing company, AT&T (UK) is finding its feet to a certain extent, and will shape its own culture in the months and years ahead. It is aware that it might be perceived as a US giant, with people wondering what it is doing in the UK. But the AT&T name does stand for a lot, beginning with credibility.

This credibility derives from its customer care reputation, and individuals joining AT&T must have an affinity to providing quality to the customer. This is the number one shared value. The customer coming first means asking them what they want, not presenting off-the-shelf answers, but tailoring services that add real value to their business.

All AT&T employees must commit to the Common Bond Values. 'Living Our Common Bond' is AT&T's world-wide formal code of conduct—both a public statement and a guide to ethical behaviour in business. Underpinning this is a legacy of maintaining the highest standards of integrity in anything AT&T does. The five values of the Common Bond are respect for individuals, dedication to helping customers, and the highest standards of integrity, innovation, and teamwork. Culture might be evolving at AT&T in the UK but every employee must sign-up to having read the Common Bond and to adhering to its values.

AT&T is a proud organisation—it has a lot to be proud of—but having been *the* name for so long, the extent of competition may have come as something of a revelation in Europe. AT&T will not dwell on its pedigree, however, and its projected rate of growth in the UK gives it every chance of fashioning a local culture that combines inherited strengths with a new dynamism needed to succeed in this rapidly evolving industry.

People who will thrive in AT&T are likely to be team workers, resilient, and quite tough. Start-ups and changing organisations require self-starters. People do have fun at work, but resilient people tend to see the fun side of working hard.

Human Resource Priorities

The UK is more flexible in response to HR issues than the USA, which is more process and procedure-driven. While some of the latter has been inherited, Martin Whitthread, AT&T's UK HR director believes strongly in 'driving HR down the line' and decentralising parts of the role.

One issue for AT&T's internal communications is that the UK organisation has multiple sites. The annual staff opinion survey picked up on the accessibility of the senior management team and the need to keep people informed on where the company is going. Senior managers responded to what staff were saying, and this triggered quarterly visits by the UK president and chief operating officer to each site, supported by videos and teleconferencing.

HR does have top-level support. Martin Whitthread operates at board level in the UK and the role is influential. One thing driven through quickly for introduction in 1997 was a senior management development training programme of seminars and workshops, the aim being to give managers skills in such areas as recruitment and selection; identifying stress in individuals; recognising performance in teams; and making appropriate reward. "Most people are so busy with their jobs" says Lynda Shattock, resourcing manager, "that we need to give them the skills to ensure that managing their people is not forgotten. The Board recognised this and signed up to the programme very quickly."

Some recruitment is handled through specialist agencies, but AT&T is happy to consider direct, written approaches. The company is keen to transmit one message in its recruitment, product and corporate advertising: 'one AT&T'. And if AT&T has one key HR goal, it is to be the 'Employer of Choice'.

Career Opportunity and Development

AT&T's big UK recruitment areas will be in sales/sales support, IT, operations engineers, and customer care specialists. Candidates are interviewed by line managers, and psychometric testing may feature. All jobs are advertised internally first. AT&T is starting to look at graduate recruitment across the UK, but it is difficult in start-up situations for managers to devote the necessary time to development, and hiring experience is often more expedient.

Many senior roles in the start-up arm of the business were filled from the USA initially, but opportunity is likely to increase as expatriates return home. There is a process for high fliers (who are nominated by their managers) when opportunities arise to take on a more senior role, or develop their expertise across the business.

Training is a business function led by HR encouraging a range of self-development, skills training and the opportunity to acquire a suite of highly developed business competency skills. AT&T also offers financial support for professional study.

Pay and Benefits

AT&T aims to pay competitively against the market in order to attract high calibre people. Most people also work towards individual and team objectives, against which they are paid a bonus; another bonus element depends on the performance of the business overall. A Reward and Recognition Programme allows managers and colleagues to recognise individuals for exceptional performance or achievement.

Other benefits include free private medical cover, company contributory pension and cars at the kick-in level. Share schemes are planned in the UK (AT&T stock is quoted on the NYSE), and management is looking at ways of introducing this tried and tested incentive into the UK.

The Future

AT&T's first business challenge is to communicate its position in the UK market, where customers are often confused by the many competitive choices available. And like all of its competitors, to reach that market its proposition must be understandable and believable. In particular, how AT&T can differentiate itself in a saturated market will be crucial.

The commitment of AT&T Corporation to supporting the development of its UK business is beyond question, but everyone involved will be keen to build revenue streams as quickly as possible.

In a business as fast-moving as telecommunications, there are retention issues. AT&T accepts that individuals today spend shorter duration's with any one employer, and so the balance between gaining individual's contributions, building the business, and helping people improve their CVs while they are in the company—maybe for just two years—needs to be struck. Providing challenges in a relatively flat-structured organisation is a challenge in itself and encouraging broader skills development, and facilitating lateral moves will help.

AT&T acknowledges that it will have to pay close and regular attention to morale. Starting, growing and accelerating a business can be exhilarating, rewarding—even fun; but while doing so, there is always a danger that people can feel undervalued and remote from the leadership. AT&T has recognised this early on, and has responded well to issues raised in staff opinion surveys.

AT&T is looking to recruit people who are highly marketable—people who others are looking to recruit too. The company has many advantages. The name AT&T has tremendous kudos in the business world, and that itself can instil a belief in its people that, "surely we cannot possibly fail". The company is likely to be highly attractive to tough, energetic people who relish the idea of working for a local start-up by one of the largest and most respected communications companies in the world that is already into its growth and development phase.

BAA plc

BAA is the world's largest commercial operator of airports. It owns and operates seven UK airports and also has facilities in the USA. Its operations include project management, retailing, property development and property management. In the year to 31 March 1996, its total revenue was £1,253 million. BAA employs over 8,000 employees, the vast majority of whom work in the UK.

Biggest Plus: A high-flying company with a bright future

Biggest Minus: Not for the faint-hearted or the easily tired!

BAA plc
130 Wilton Road
London SW1V 1LQ
Tel: 0171-834 9449
Fax: 0171-932 6699

The Business

BAA owns and operates seven UK airports: Heathrow, Gatwick, Stansted, Glasgow, Edinburgh, Aberdeen and Southampton. Together, these handle 71% of UK air passenger traffic and 81% of air cargo. Overseas, BAA manages the Indianapolis airport system and the shops and catering facilities at Pittsburgh airport.

The company has four distinct operational areas: airport management, projects, retail and property. Airport management covers all aspects of airport operations, from terminal security and customer services to snow clearers and fire services. The scale of projects to improve airport infrastructure—£4.4 billion over ten years—makes BAA one of the UK's largest clients for the construction industry. BAA also manages all the commercial facilities at its airports, and over 200 companies, many of them leading brands, have retail contracts within the company. And finally, BAA has a major property portfolio.

Company Culture and Style

The company has an ambitious mission: to become the most successful airport company in the world. Not surprisingly therefore, the culture at BAA is one of continuous improvement. Total customer focus is rapidly becoming the norm; whereas once complaints from customers were not uncommon, today they are rare—and those that are made are handled at the highest level. Every area seeks to enhance its efficiency and control its costs to benefit those customers.

Such a diversity of operations means a similarly wide span of jobs at BAA. Nevertheless, there is a profile of the person most likely to succeed within the company. He or she would ideally be intelligent, switched on, imaginative, able to understand the complexities of the business and see how the operations can be developed. The person who can deal with a multitude of interactions to the benefit of the company is also vital; there are over 100 airlines, all of which have different requirements. There are suppliers of equipment to liaise with, and customers to satisfy. There are environmental and local community issues to resolve. This is a complex network, but those who enjoy the buzz of high energy work thrive on it.

Inevitably, BAA has many sub-cultures. People who run airfields have their own disciplines and training. Fire services have a culture that places safety above all else and strongly emphasises teamwork. Retail stresses innovation and negotiation. Yet there is also a sense of pride and unity in BAA itself, and the company is doing its part to bring the sub-cultures together.

Internal communications are well handled at BAA. There is a Group-wide newspaper, and each location also has its own communications framework in place. Email is already an important means of communication and is set to become even more widely used as the company's Project Desktop standardises PCs throughout all the locations. Briefings, meetings, conferences and noticeboards are all put to good use, and senior managers epitomise the growing openness of style. Chief executive Sir John Egan meets staff directly and answers their questions at conferences, as do the MDs of the other businesses.

Human Resource Priorities

One of the company's critical success factors in achieving its mission relates to people. It promises to provide a good and safe working environment that attracts and retains committed employees, and through training and two-way communication allows them to fulfil their potential. Each airport company has its own HR department, looking after such issues as deployment, development and employee relations. Corporately, HR is also a considerable resource, with a Group Training and Management department and a centre for policy and strategy in people management.

BAA conducts surveys into many aspects of its operations, but HR is one of the most important. Every two years, a MORI survey commissioned by the company looks at employee satisfaction and opinions. The findings are cascaded down through the divisions. Where necessary, focus groups are set up after the survey to glean more information. So if problems are turned up, action follows quickly to correct the situation.

A demonstration of the importance of HR is given by BAA's huge project 'Freedom to Manage', headed by Christine Stewart who was formerly general manager of Heathrow's Terminal 3. The project, which is about customer service, empowerment, reducing bureaucracy and enhancing leadership style, is already improving working lives at BAA. Stewart: "Staff are much more interested in the business than they were before: they feel more a part of the business, and we give much more information to staff on how we're doing."

Career Opportunity and Development

Career advancement is on merit. All opportunities for promotion are openly advertised. As personnel operations director Ian Stewart says, "Internal job interviews are handled very constructively. Unsuccessful candidates get feedback and advice on what to do next, which puts them in a better position for their next attempt." This approach is reinforced at BAA's Development Centres: short events, normally a day, give people an insight into their strengths and weaknesses and help them develop the right attributes to move up.

The majority of promotions at BAA are from within, although the company will look outside if sufficient skills are not available. Promotions are decided, increasingly, by reference to a set of competencies required in the new job.

BAA has no graduate recruitment scheme, although from time to time it will recruit suitable people—particularly those who already have work experience. Indeed, it is probably true to say that some part of the organisation will be engaged in recruiting graduates at any one time.

Training is an important resource at BAA, where the emphasis is on helping individuals look at their personal development needs and then putting the required training in place. Training includes a mix of internal and external sources. Tony Ryan, training and management development director: "Development can be gained by such things as getting more experience in the company by shadowing work in another area. There is also considerable emphasis on leadership, which often starts before the individual has had a formal leadership role." Within two years of joining, most people will have had training in teamwork, communication skills and supervising others, and training increases with experience.

Within the company, there is a great deal of movement—a trend that is increasing rapidly. BAA's ethos of development means that traditional boundaries are less and less important. In particular, many people are moving from other areas into retail; but in general, there is widespread opportunity for people to develop by movement within BAA's operations.

Unusually in these times there have been no enforced redundancies in BAA. Even in 1991 when air traffic slumped due to the Gulf War, BAA scaled down operations entirely through voluntary redundancies. For anyone prepared to be flexible and learn new skills, the company offers excellent job security.

Pay and Benefits

The company regards itself as median to good upper quartile in terms of remuneration. This varies considerably between company and location, but across BAA, from the lowest to the highest grades, "Some are very well paid and none are badly paid," as Ian Stewart puts it. A graduate with three years' experience might expect to earn £25,000 or above; while accountants and financial services people can expect to keep pace with the best UK firms.

The idea of relating pay to performance is becoming more widespread. Senior managers receive a bonus that relates to BAA plc performance and the performance of their operating company. All employees have a profit-related pay scheme, a very good contributory pension plan and a share-save facility, and can take advantage of a good relocation scheme.

Other benefits tend to vary by location. For example, Heathrow has a Privilege Club that gives discounts at the retailers. It also has an excellent wholly owned sports club. Variations on these themes can be found at the other locations.

The Future

One challenge relates to the growing international aspirations of BAA, particularly in the USA and Australia as previously federally owned airports become privatised. Sir John Egan: "When customers see the good job we do here with such low landing fees, they will want to see that repeated elsewhere: and I would hope in future we would earn a good percentage of our profits overseas."

Another challenge is the need for a continuous upgrade of skills of people in every aspect of the business. This calls for a major investment in information technology and other areas.

Finally, BAA has to maintain and even improve its excellent customer service. This will include further infrastructure projects, such as the Heathrow express rail link that will be operating by 1998; also the proposed Terminal 5 at Heathrow, which if it goes ahead will be the first great building of the next century and create much new employment. The challenges for the future are great; but so too appears BAA's appetite to meet those challenges with confidence.

Bank of Scotland

Bank of Scotland was founded in 1695 and is still independent. Its 300 branches and 11,000 employees are mainly in Scotland, but the group provides financial services throughout the UK. Bank of Scotland has subsidiaries in Australia and New Zealand, as well as representative offices in Hong Kong and the USA.

UK banking has been through several waves of dramatic change. Bank of Scotland has expanded its customer base through home banking, telebanking, technology-driven services and direct marketing, while moving most 'back office' work out of the branches and into processing centres in the major cities.

Biggest Plus: A commitment to people at all levels

Biggest Minus: It takes time to chip away 300 years of hierarchical management structure

Bank of Scotland Plc
The Mound
Edinburgh EH1 1YZ
Tel: 0131-442 7777
Fax: 0131-243 7081

The Business

Bank of Scotland held its 300th annual general meeting in 1996 in the shadow of the sale of the 32% stake in the bank by its Edinburgh neighbour, the insurance giant Standard Life. The huge stake had made the bank virtually take-over-proof for the past 11 years. The shares were placed as long-term holdings with a range of institutions, and the threat of the bank losing its independence receded. But the upheaval highlighted how strongly the bank, and the wider Scottish financial and political community, valued the independence of an institution founded one year after the Bank of England, and how they are prepared to fight to hang onto it.

The bank decided in the early 1980s under a new young leader Bruce Pattullo (now Sir Bruce, the bank's governor) that it would expand into England not with bricks and mortar but with innovative financial services. It also kept a tight grip on its costs, and in so doing, has proved itself the best managed of all the UK banks. Compared with its main rival the Royal Bank of Scotland, its assets, advances, profit, earnings and number of employees have all increased at a faster rate in the past decade.

Most importantly for the organisation, the bank has managed to maintain its policy of no redundancies, at a time when most other UK banks have made sweeping cuts in numbers.

Company Culture and Style

When in 1996 the *Financial Times* called the bank 'boring', it was taken at the bank's headquarters as the City's finest compliment. The organisation prides itself on its distance from London and the financial markets, a distance that it believes lends perspective. It has not copied the mistakes of the big London-based banks in making expensive, mistimed and ill-judged forays into overseas markets, third world lending, and businesses such as estate agencies.

Avoiding compulsory redundancies has not been achieved by accident, it has been a cornerstone of the bank's philosophy. "That means we still offer careers," says Jim Morrison, assistant general manager for personnel, "and there is still an opportunity to get to the top."

Most executives and managers are home-grown. This enables the bank to pride itself on the closeness of its most senior executives to the problems, and the people, at the coal face.

The no-redundancy policy has meant there has been no wholesale removal of the over-50s, for instance, in order to create a younger work force and an instant culture change, as has happened in some other banks.

Instead, the culture is changing slowly, with tentative moves away from a hierarchical structure supporting the bank's preference for more localised decision making. For instance, the bank has maintained the local decision-making powers of branch managers, particularly for small businesses. Managers and staff are trained in proactively developing relationships with customers. Each division is slowly taking over more responsibility for its own affairs, notably personnel and recruitment. Staff are encouraged to participate in ideas schemes, which are frequently re-launched and offer generous rewards.

Human Resource Priorities

The personnel division's three main objectives are to reduce costs, remove hierarchical structures, and avoid redundancies, while maintaining the levels of training, career opportunity and staff motivation. The pace of change in the banking industry has meant constant reskilling and retraining, and an implicit commitment from the bank to create a multi-skilled and flexible work force.

The division has 100 people, headed by a general manager who has a seat on the bank's management board (although does not have a vote). Effectiveness of policies is measured through project management. The Scottish branch network and its card services division hold the Investors in People accreditation; the financial services division is working towards it.

The branch network has a communication and training hour from 9 a.m. to 10 a.m. one morning every week, and staff videos are used at least twice a year for top management to comment on the bank's results.

Career Opportunity and Development

Bank of Scotland views the professionalism of its staff as a key asset, and one-third of its staff and over 90% of management hold recognised professional qualifications or degrees, which it believes compares favourably with any other UK bank.

The governor began as a graduate trainee, treasurer Gavin Masterton joined the bank from school at 15, and although the bank has over the years drafted in a number of professionals such as chief executive Peter Burt, when they arrived they were no older than their late 20s.

Graduate recruitment varies according to manpower demands, but 44 graduates have joined the bank in a two-year period. The bank believes that its graduates will be very important to its future, and looks for "those who combine an analytical mind with a constructive approach so that they can bring a wider perspective." After five years, around 90% of trainees are still with the bank.

The bank has always encouraged a broad-based approach to developing people, which has been the key to flexibility and redeployment. "The bank recognises the wider value of learning—equipping you for a life in business," says recent graduate Clare Crosbie, now an executive assistant in the management team.

Now the group is responding to the present and likely future changes in the market place by bringing in a more formalised structure to a new management development programme. Almost every general manager has been sent on the Harvard Advanced Management Programme, which the bank has used for a number of years.

There are limited secondment opportunities in Australia, New Zealand, the USA, Bank of Wales, and in the NSW Bank in Chester.

Over 6,000 staff have been on training courses in the past three years in support of implementing a stronger sales and customer service focus, and as many again have completed training in technology, management and credit assessment. In 1996 the bank won a National Training Award for its procedural workbooks in the branch network.

Pay and Benefits

The bank has never prided itself on being a big payer, but says it is nevertheless highly competitive. The five supervisory grades run from around £15,000 to £27,000, while the five managerial grades start at £24,000 and go up to just under £45,000 for the manager of a fairly large branch. Two key benefits are fixed-rate mortgages, and a non-contributory pension scheme. Cars and BUPA membership are standard for managers, but the bank does not favour flexible benefits.

The arrangements for staff to hold shares in the bank are progressive. As many as 60% of staff, or 8,500 people, have at some time held shares, bought through a SAYE scheme that gives options to buy stock after three, five or seven years. The executive stock option scheme was first launched in 1985 and when renewed in 1995, it already complied with the recommendations of the Greenbury committee on executive pay, in that incentives and benefits were spread over a ten-year period and properly linked to company performance. More unusually, the executive scheme reaches down to include over 600 managers, and a proportion of the available shares each year are allocated to middle management grades.

There is also a profit-sharing scheme for all employees, which pays out in cash or shares, but is only triggered when the bank achieves a 12% return on proprietors' (shareholders') funds. In 1996 the scheme paid out the maximum, enabling all staff to enjoy an effective pay rise of 15%.

The Future

The traditional Bank of Scotland branch is rapidly disappearing from the high street, to be replaced by the smart new 'personal banking centre'. That means all staff have to be in the branch and customer-facing, or suitably skilled for the 'operational support units' which handle the processing of all transactions. With an annual labour turnover of 7-8%, the challenge for the bank is to maintain its no-redundancy policy by balancing people, skills, and tomorrow's jobs.

Phoneline, the 24-hour 365-day service which for many customers complements the branch service, and Centrebank, which sells mortgages and other products directly across the UK, are tomorrow's growth areas. When the bank reported in 1996 that its costs had risen from 49% to 52% of its income, still far below its rivals, it was accused of losing some management grip. But in fact it was an investment bulge, representing a commitment to information technology and branch redesign, as well as business opportunities in its finance house NWS Bank.

Resisting short-term pressures, continuing to invest, and defending its independence, will be the bank's key tasks. Sir Bruce Pattullo says it is an illusion to believe that size is, of itself, the panacea for commercial survival. "The most important qualities are flexibility, innovation, short lines of communication, a corporate culture to which staff subscribe, and an effective decision-making structure."

Continuity of management, and the role models it has offered, have been crucial in an organisation that has been sure-footed in its business strategy, admirably quick to innovate and seize market opportunities, but sensibly slow to embrace management fads in organisation or style. More of the same will be needed, and looks to be achievable.

B.A.T Industries plc

The B.A.T Industries Group is one of the UK's leading business enterprises with operations in more than 100 countries. The Group's principal interests are in tobacco and financial services. In 1995, B.A.T Industries' total revenue was £23 billion, while pre-tax profit was £2.4 billion. The Group employs 170,000 people world-wide, 15,000 in the UK.

Biggest Plus: A culture of growth, success and recognition

Biggest Minus: Competitiveness is a must!

B.A.T Industries plc
Windsor House
50 Victoria Street
London SW1H 0NL
Tel: 0171-222 7979
Fax: 0171-222 4515

The Business

The Imperial Tobacco Company (of Great Britain and Ireland) Ltd. was formed in 1901 by a number of British family-owned tobacco businesses, in response to an attempt by the founder of the American Tobacco Company to bid for the British tobacco market. After an intense and costly trade war, a truce was called in 1902. A new jointly owned company, British-American Tobacco Company Ltd, was founded to develop Imperial and American Tobacco's businesses outside the USA and the UK. This became a quoted company on the London Stock Exchange in 1911 when the American Tobacco Company divested its BAT shares. Ties with Imperial were cut in 1972 and the last equity link ended in 1980. A 1976 reorganisation restructured the Group into divisions and a new holding company called B.A.T Industries.

Since 1989, B.A.T Industries has focused on tobacco and financial services. British American Financial Services is the largest UK-based insurance group and one of the biggest in the world. The Group entered the financial services business with the acquisition of Eagle Star in 1984, Hambro Life (now Allied Dunbar) in 1985 and Farmers (which manages the sixth largest group of property and casualty insurers in the USA) in 1988. In 1994, Threadneedle Asset Management was launched by merging the investment operations of Eagle Star and Allied Dunbar to create one of the UK's largest international investment houses, managing funds of some £30 billion.

British American Tobacco is the world's most international tobacco manufacturer. With operations throughout the world it accounts for over 12% of the global market. The Group acquired American Tobacco in 1994 for $1 billion, strengthening its position in the US market and gaining world-wide ownership of *Lucky Strike* and *Pall Mall*. The Group also markets well-known brands in the other regions of the world and has the leading cigarette brand in over 30 markets.

Company Culture and Style

B.A.T Industries' principal operating companies both report to Group headquarters. These operating companies have considerable autonomy in the running of their operations, and not surprisingly have their own culture.

Having said that, there are elements of common culture. Each operating company is part of a fast-growing, fast-changing market place. Each is committed to growth. And each is dedicated to meeting customer needs through product and marketing innovation, continual improvement in its operations, and above all, first-class personal service.

Another shared factor is success. Each operating company is used to winning accolades and rising above its competitors. Allied Dunbar, for instance, is the UK's largest unit-linked life assurance and pensions company, while Farmers Group funds under management exceed £14 billion—and the organisation itself controls three US life companies.

Working in any part of B.A.T Industries' operations is all about dynamism, hard work, and rewarding challenge. People who do well at any of the companies tend to be highly committed to their company and its future growth, take on early responsibility and enjoy a demanding yet stimulating and absorbing environment.

Both financial services and tobacco are highly competitive industries with considerable amounts of pressure; yet BAT companies continue to forge ahead of their rivals through creative and original thinking and planning.

A final common aspect of culture is that all the Group's operations are active in their communities, supporting aid programmes appropriate to their circum-stances. Overall, the Group donated £8 million to charitable causes during 1995, of which £3 million was paid in the UK.

Human Resource Priorities

All B.A.T Industries' companies provide the strategies to attract, develop and motivate the highest calibre individuals for their businesses. They ensure that, at all levels within the company, their people have the right skills, experience and training to contribute effectively to the company's objectives. At the same time, each individual is encouraged to develop as a person through acquiring additional skills as well as fulfilling career potential.

In each company, the objective is to recruit and retain the most talented people. They achieve this goal by treating people fairly and equally, promoting from within wherever possible, ensuring that performance is the sole determinant of career development and advancement, and offering everyone as much responsibility as they can handle.

Career Opportunity and Development

A number of the operating companies have graduate recruitment schemes. These are seen as identifying and encouraging the leaders of tomorrow. To take the British-American Tobacco Company's scheme as an example, most graduate trainees join one of the production units to learn experience in both primary and secondary manufacturing.

The other route is to start in Technical Services, the company's world-wide equipment installation and servicing department that has a stronger electronic and mechanical engineering bias. Either way, graduates prepared for hard work and able to work closely with other people and business functions can look forward to rapid development.

Some of the operations have considerable opportunities for overseas movement and advancement. Eagle Star, for instance, writes business through associates and agents in 30 countries world-wide and offers a limited number of openings for working abroad. British-American Tobacco Company manufactures cigarettes in over 50 countries and has a greater number of openings for job transfer.

Training is taken very seriously throughout the Group. Allied Dunbar, for instance, has its own £20 million training centre, particularly valuable for the company's leading edge since most of its products are sold by its own direct salesforce. At British-American Tobacco Company, its 'Challenge Initiative' prepares new recruits for their first management role, bringing in business awareness, managerial development, self-evaluation and functional development. This runs for two years and is then backed up by ongoing training programmes to build specific skills.

Pay and Benefits

The scope of B.A.T Industries' business and the quality of its training and development are key to its attracting and retaining the best people. It also needs to ensure that the benefits it offers are consistent with those expected of a world-class, blue-chip employer. For example, in its tobacco business, each operating company takes responsibility for implementing its own remuneration policy to ensure that rewards are competitive at the upper quartile level among other local comparator companies—including companies in different sectors that also attract high calibre employees.

Pay relates to the performance of both the individual and of the operating company, and over time there is likely to be a greater shift to more variable pay packages. A wide range of benefits, which meet short-, medium- and long-term needs of employees, completes the reward package. These include pension schemes, profit-related and other share schemes, as well as profit-related pay where appropriate.

The Future

A number of challenges confront the Group in the area of human resources. It needs to continuously review its recruitment and selection strategies and tactics in order to hire optimum quality candidates in a highly competitive market place.

The Group is also required to provide its employees with significant career opportunities in order to develop and realise their full potential; and must ensure that they possess the knowledge and skills to progress the business in an environment of continuous change.

Bhs

Bhs is a leading high street fashion retailer in the UK, offering a wide range of stylish, quality, value for money fashions for the family and for the home. With turnover of £750 million generated from 138 stores in the UK and 52 franchised international stores, and some 14,000 full- and part-time employees, Bhs forms the major part of Storehouse, one of the UK's largest retailing groups.

Biggest Plus: Lots of early career opportunity

Biggest Minus: Managers have to do real hands-on work

Bhs PLC
Marylebone House
127-139 Marylebone Road
London NW1 5QD
Tel: 0171-262 3288
Fax: 0171-723 1115

The Business

Already a leading high street name, Bhs has undergone metamorphosis in the last five years, moving from a typical old style British retailer with a centrally driven hierarchical structure to a young company with a refreshingly open culture. A new management team decided to make radical changes, creating a modern, dynamic Bhs almost unrecognisable from the old.

The winners are both customers and employees (called associates), because these have been the focal areas of change. Bhs customers are typically a 'thirty-something' female and discerning, and the company endeavours to meet or exceed their expectations of purchases and 'the shopping experience' at Bhs.

Keith Edelman, chief executive: "Bhs is a highly successful business and the credit for that is down to each and every one of our associates. Without the effort, energy and dedication they demonstrate, we would not be the major force that we are in the High Street. Through significant investment in skills building and personal development programmes, we will ensure that our associates are equipped to support the growth of Bhs into the year 2000 and beyond."

Company Culture and Style

Change meant removing old layers of management and, with the full involvement of employees, creating a new team ethos. For this to work, a new spirit of openness is actively encouraged.

The complete area manager structure was stripped out. Old managers became new 'team leaders or captains'. Regional managers found themselves once again with store manager responsibilities for a major city centre store. By getting back in touch with the stores and the customers in this way, regional managers needed to develop their team and empower them, in order to free-up time for their wider responsibilities. This team principle has been implemented from the top to bottom of the organisation.

And while it might sound unusual to say that a retailer has become customer-focused, Bhs admits that perhaps in the 1980s, there was a 'we know best' attitude to the customer. That has all changed, and the management of the relationship between brand and customer is a key management skill for the Bhs executive of today.

Gone are the days when a planning change would be a process carried out behind closed doors and the consequences unveiled to the ranks. Recognising that people had a useful contribution to make on how to change, Bhs works with all people involved—from the outset.

Bhs deliberately recruits people who will speak up and challenge ideas, because these are the people who will grow the company and in turn grow with it. The result—a nimbler company that can identify and change methods, improve new business, strategy, and allow pioneering and quick decision making.

This cultural change has had a binding effect on the people who work at Bhs. Many cite 'the people' as the reason they like working there. Certainly the bright offices on Marylebone Road in London were full of people who seemed to be enjoying their day—a day where an important balance is maintained between work, home and social life.

Human Resource Priorities

While there is a streamlined human resources department at the head office (you won't find a dedicated HR manager in any of the stores), responsibility for this activity is put firmly in the hands of line management. If managers are responsible for their people, then the HR department sees its function being primarily to support them in this role.

Kevin Heald, human resources manager, (Stores) places great emphasis on recognition. "It is very important to recognise achievement in whatever form. 'Big' achievements—especially if they are customer related—are publicised across the organisation. Three store associates recently found themselves invited to the Bhs management conference to collect their promotional awards."

Another key strand of HR strategy is to be a 'First Choice Employer', achieving the 'best possible standards' as an employer. Kevin Heald admits "we are not quite there of course, but things are moving along nicely in the right direction." A cross-functional senior management team looks continuously at the ways to develop 'first choice employer' status, through a combination of recognition, work facilities and conditions, incentives and internal communication.

The latter is vital. There is an annual staff survey, and a monthly 'Team Briefing', cascading information from the board, is given to all employees. 'Bhs Business News' is a purely internal company newspaper distributed to all employees, also monthly, and there is a regularly distributed 'Bhs Video News'. Is there an open door policy? "There are no doors to open," answers Heald (all offices are open plan).

Career Opportunity and Development

One of Bhs' key objectives is to develop managers with a broad range of skills that can be brought into play at different times in different contexts beyond the confines of traditional business disciplines. People are prepared for real and early responsibility in functions diverse as buying, merchandising, marketing, store management or human resources.

The main career areas at head office are in buying and merchandising and career development allows for horizontal and vertical moves to acquire other skills and increase responsibility. In some of the other smaller teams, the HR function has to think more creatively about career development.

Career development in the stores progresses along a clear path from associate—department manager—store manager—regional manager—national retail manager—eventually to store operations director. Different store departments are of greater importance than others, and stores vary considerably in size and turnover (with even the smallest store taking in excess of £2m per annum), to offer plenty of scope for advancement.

Employees are encouraged to think about and steer their own career development in a two-way process—'Self-Managed Careers' is the phrase coined by Sue Oxley, human resources manager (head office). It seems to work—five out of nine Bhs main board members are internal promotions. Movement between Bhs and other key businesses in the Group, particularly Mothercare, is actively encouraged, as it is between the centre and the stores.

Bhs is making a substantial investment in training and education at all levels and much effort has gone into developing managerial and professional skills and in exploring more innovative ways of delivery. A learning centre equipped with the latest CD-ROMs, books and videos encourage individuals to take ownership of their personal development.

Pay and Benefits

At head office (around 650 people), Bhs keeps 'very close to the market place' to remain competitive and prevent specialist skills such as buying and merchandising from being head-hunted on a regular basis. A similar picture emerges in store management, where by remaining equally competitive, staff turnover is relatively low.

Bhs is proud of the various benefits it offers employees. Its profit-related pay scheme—called 'Profit From Success'—seems attractive enough, encouraging the company to meet its own profit forecasts, and enabling staff to gain 5–7% tax free pay in their basic pay and additional profit-related bonuses.

'Choices' is the company's flexible benefits scheme (Bhs was one of the first retailers to introduce such a bespoke arrangement) where employees can tailor their own individual package: big or cheap cars, one or two; private medical insurance can be upgraded, pensions and life insurance adapted for specific requirements. You can even buy more holiday!

There are various share schemes operating—SAYE schemes for everyone, and share option schemes for the senior manager group. To mark the millennium, everyone in Bhs will receive share option certificates—1,000 shares for full-time and 500 shares for part-time employees.

Private medical insurance is offered to all levels of management—which is a little unusual. And everyone benefits from 'Storehouse Selections', a range of negotiated purchases for all staff to buy (particularly) travel and insurance products at effectively corporate rates.

The Future

Heald views skill building among management and technical functions to be the biggest challenge facing Bhs. With the last few years devoted to organisational change and working towards philosophical beliefs, skill building is only now getting the prominence he wants. "It will take us 3–4 years to get where we want to be," admits Heald.

Job security is not seen as a major issue—on the part of employer or employee. Bhs practices the right values as an employer. Sue Oxley says "We are modern employers, openly aware that job stability goes hand-in-hand with business success, and that success in turn depends on employees making a contribution; if they do, they have a good future at Bhs."

While Bhs is rightly proud of the cultural and organisational change that it has implemented so successfully, it knows that this process must be a continuous one. In a highly competitive retailing market place, where other companies may be going through similar cultural change, Bhs is aware of the need to create new points of difference. It is starting from a strong position.

Birse

Birse

Birse Construction represents 98% of the group's turnover, and with five regional offices and five area offices, is a major national business. BPH Equipment (plant hire) has three area offices. There are small property and housing subsidiaries that are due to be phased out. Birse has 1,500 employees, with sub-contractors to the company employing another 2,000. Turnover in the year to April 1996 was £363 million, profits £1.1 million, and total assets £144 million.

Biggest Plus: Amazing revival story, based on trusting the commitment of people

Biggest Minus: Possible danger of developing people too well that they find employment elsewhere!

Birse Group plc
Humber Road
Barton-on-Humber
North Lincolnshire DN18 5BW
Tel: 01652-633222
Fax: 01652-633360

The Business

Started in 1972, Birse expanded rapidly to achieve a £100 million turnover by 1988, which then tripled to £300 million in little more than 18 months. This led to a London Stock Exchange flotation in 1990. A combination of the exceptional strains of fast track expansion and the impact of the early 1990s' recession then threw the company into substantial losses and facing the real danger of collapse.

Birse, though, is an amazing story of revival from near collapse. Instead of scaling back in the conventional way, the board pinned its faith on its 1,500 employees, committing very substantial resources to their development and focusing on building and reinforcing customer relationships and loyalty. Birse's introduction of an unconventional and non-confrontational management style has achieved a near miraculous improvement in performance, the business returning to profitability in 1996. Confidence is high that a more advanced programme of personal development for all staff will intensify the improvement in business operations and financial results.

The chairman, Peter Birse said: "We have again made great strides in improving business quality and the performance of managers. Our success is clearly evidenced by a 19% increase in turnover, very much in contrast to the general trend in the UK construction market."

Some staff were unfamiliar with the special internal and external culture that had been the foundation of Birse's original success and high reputation. But resolute action to get the whole company pulling together towards its full potential has been effective. The business has been repositioned with the disposal of the bulk of the housing business, the exclusion of high risk projects, and reduced exposure to the volatile major road market.

Company Culture and Style

Faced with the need to change or die, the board saw no merit in pulling back to its basic core activities. It determined that the company could recover, and build further on its enlarged size, if the Birse culture of positive internal and external relations was restored and enhanced.

To front this seemingly high risk strategy, the firm put its group safety manager, Steve French, in charge of the new culture and learning department to handle human relations functions, training and the re-building of employees' attitudes, and through them good relations with clients. Key measures were ominous. Morale was low with staff resignations, including some of the best people, running at 60 a month, against one or two previously; negotiated work had slumped from 60% of work to only 5%, and contractual disputes had risen alarmingly.

In 1994, employees were asked what they thought were Birse's dominant attributes. They said "Aggressive, Arrogant, Dynamic and Young". Steve French and the chief executive, Mike Wilson, identified that the key restructuring task was to create a more learning, supportive, dynamic and mature culture.

French initiated a two-year programme for re-training staff in non-confrontational management. Staff went through extensive training in residential sessions on 5DM. This is a philosophy that encourages individuals to extend their responsibility for management beyond themselves to include their superior, their subordinates, as well as internal and external colleagues.

In mid-1996 a more advanced programme of personal development was launched—the Transformation Programme which involves five or more weeks of intensive residential workshops, about which Sheila Whelan a manager in the culture department said "It has been one of the most exciting events in my life. The objective of the programme is to encourage staff to become fully developed as people, and to maximise the effectiveness of their abilities, fully accepting that they will be well equipped to move on to other jobs elsewhere with their newly developed skills."

One senior staff member going to another job after seven years at Birse said: "The decision to leave the company was not easy, although I had reached my career potential at Birse. The Transformation Programme helped me to realise the need to be true to myself and to take the opportunity on offer." He described Birse as a good place to work, progressive and good for people, and that he would like to return to the firm if the right job was on offer.

Human Resource Priorities

Optimum development of personal and corporate effectiveness is the central driving force that is given full backing by the chairman and all directors. Leading by example, they have been the first to undertake the full rigour of the Transformation Programme modules. The key role of the six-strong culture department has been recognised by Steve French's appointment to the board.

All aspects of HR and personnel administration are carried out at regional level, with all members of the regional boards playing a full part. HR co-ordination and development is carried out by a team of 32 regional directors and key people, led and co-ordinated by the culture department.

Career Opportunity and Development

Any women with the appropriate qualifications should get a sympathetic response from Birse, which has a commitment to increase the number of women it employs, and it has many valued staff members from ethnic minority groups.

A full range of technical training is carried out in all regions. The extent has been stepped-up to reinforce the effectiveness of the 5D and Transformation Programmes. Every encouragement is given for people at all levels to widen their experience and take on additional responsibilities. Colleagues assume responsibility for each other and are encouraged to obtain first-hand knowledge of as wide a range of jobs and relevant disciplines as possible.

All these elements link in to Birse's policy to promote from within wherever possible, and provide greater than usual scope for promotion and advancement. But, as Paul Fox, the learning manager underlined, "If someone believes that their best contribution can be made at the level they have achieved, and want to continue there, they will not lose out in salary or benefits." Birse takes on 15 graduates a year as part of a well-established recruitment and training scheme.

Pay and Benefits

Birse pays competitive salaries, and benefits are frequently generous. Rapid promotion gives scope for fast movement up the pay scale. Pay levels are set taking account of the person's contribution to the company, with reward given for good achievement. An important element in this judgement is derived from an all-perspectives range of assessments made by colleagues, subordinates and superiors, as well as the individual's own views.

Graduates started on £12,000 in 1995, but typically after 4–5 years, they could be earning £25,000 equivalent or more. The pension is rated good by industry standards, and most people are provided with health insurance. Company cars are considered essential for a majority of employees, with some 800 cars provided for the 1,500 work force, with pool cars also available. Good work by a team, or office, is recognised by outings or vouchers for a night out for employees and partners.

The Future

For the sceptic, and many outsiders, Birse looks to be dabbling in fantasy. As a central plank of its Transformation Programme, it tells employees that 'Birse builds dreams', at first sight a highly improbable approach for down-to-earth Northerners, construction folk and the financial gnomes of the City.

Birse, however, through its radical motivation techniques, has made giant strides. It has liberated its people, encouraging them to realise their dreams and ambitions, and providing a challenging climate, encouraging and assisting success.

The greatest challenge will be to maintain the novelty and inspiration of its Transformation Programme on a continuing basis to realise the synergy benefits of personal and organisational development for all its stakeholders. Any faltering could lead to an accelerated reverse and an exodus of its most talented people. Steve French said: "Our people said with amazement that we are equipping them to go out and succeed in many other jobs at other companies."

The work force indicated that it wanted the directors to adopt a more active leadership role. They responded by completing the core of the Transformation Programme in a period of three months, and they are benefiting greatly from applying the tenets of absolute truth and trust. Peter Birse said: "Our meetings now take one quarter of the previous time and are much more effective. Excuses for non-fulfilment are out. Realistic assessments are made of assignments taken on since everyone is honour-bound to take full responsibility for their commitments."

Such attitudes fit well with a company where open door means that every employee has the chairman's home phone number and can contact him at any time if the situation requires it.

THE BOC GROUP

The BOC Group

The BOC Group is a portfolio of four businesses—industrial and special gases, health care, vacuum technology and distribution services. Based in the UK, BOC is a truly global company. The company manufactures in 60 countries and sells its products in more than 100. Around 11,000 of the Group's 40,000 employees are in the UK.

BOC is a powerful business, and a highly successful one at that, boasting an intrinsically good track record in terms of profit and return on capital. Probably best-known for its gases business, BOC produces 20,000 different gas mixtures for use in the manufacture of just about everything produced by man and machine. The scope for new applications appears to be almost limitless. This is a growing industry.

Biggest Plus: Rewarding, challenging careers on an international plane

Biggest Minus: You may never leave

The BOC Group
Chertsey Road
Windlesham
Surrey GU20 6HJ
Tel: 01276-477222
Fax: 01276-471333
http://www.boc.com

The Business

Many companies claim to be global, but BOC can document impressive evidence. Its British origins gave the company a strong presence in the parts of the world 'once coloured pink', but the acquisition of Airco (BOC's equivalent in the USA) in 1981 really opened up the world market. Airco's CEO Richard Giordano, who was soon to become BOC's long-serving and recently retired chairman and chief executive, had both influence and foresight in the North Pacific market, and BOC's early entry to this region including China is a major success story.

Succeeding Giordano, new chairman David John added, "I was attracted by the geographic spread of the Group's businesses almost equally throughout Asia/Pacific, Europe and the Americas. It's also been in a lot of these countries for a long time." North America, Europe and the Pacific each account for roughly 30% of BOC's revenues.

Dominant positions characterise BOC's portfolio of businesses. BOC has 16% of the world industrial gases market, and is particularly strong in the rapidly growing North Pacific region. In health care, BOC is a world leader in inhaled anaesthetics, having invented and developed many of the pharmaceuticals used. BOC is a major player in vacuum pumping technology, being the preferred supplier to seven of the top ten semiconductor manufacturers. And not so many people know that the lesser-known BOC Distribution business handles most of Marks & Spencer's fresh food business.

Company Culture and Style

The international culture of BOC is high in chairman David John's thoughts. "I was struck when I joined the board by the number of different nationalities represented in its senior management and this is true right through the Group."

Senior management turnover is extremely low—perhaps as little as 3–4% per annum. That suggests continuity and the statistics talk for themselves—the average length of service of the senior management team is 20 years; two-thirds of the top 150 managers joined the company before 1986. BOC also enjoys a high graduate retention rate.

Don Beattie became head of human resources at BOC Group early in 1996. "I was particularly impressed by the professionalism and classiness of the managers, and the quality in depth. A relaxed style—but not a laid back one. People are very results-oriented, with a positive outlook on the opportunities for the Group." Yet BOC is a very open, informal business, and a relaxed working atmosphere reflects a non-hierarchical, sensitive and caring company.

BOC's style is entrepreneurial for a large, global business, and this permeates down to all levels of the organisation. "It allows businessmen to be businessmen," suggests head of public relations, Nigel Abbott. "The level of responsibility on each individual is quite high, but they are recognised for their achievements."

Just as well, because BOC expects achievement. Chief executive Danny Rosenkranz believes, "If you want to be a top class company or team and you are relaxed about coming second or third, you will fail. It's not always necessary to be number one in size. It's being number one in results that's important. Giving your shareholders a good and constant return is the ultimate goal."

Human Resource Priorities

HR forms an integral part of BOC's strategic business planning process. But each of BOC's four businesses are different, and HR policy is developed primarily at the individual business level—there is little 'off-the-shelf' corporate packages. The central HR function supports the executive management board and acts where coherence in policy across the businesses is needed.

A relentless drive to improve financial performance has put increased pressure on employees to revitalise and reshape their contribution to the business. HR's role supports this process and, avoiding popular jargon and buzzwords, places great emphasis on communication and alignment of culture, so that all employees know intuitively what has to be done.

Internal communication includes employee surveys, briefings, cascade techniques, while the BOC message exploits various media such as BOC Video News and the excellent 'BOC World', which has a circulation of 20,000 reaching at least half of the Group's 40,000 employees. There is also a 'Fast News' service and BOC's E-Mail net has more than 10,000 users.

Career Opportunity and Development

BOC recognises the difference between growing tomorrow's general and line managers, and developing the depth of technical skills it needs to remain supreme in technology-driven markets. The company invests in making experts and creating the right environment for them to flourish. While grooming its leaders requires exposure to a range of company operations, cultures and managerial situations.

BOC has one tremendous advantage—the company is growing, and can offer such development opportunities. Capable young people are given 'stretch' responsibility at an early stage in their careers with the Group, and this pays off in terms of personal growth and development in later years. BOC believes that this 'exposure for experience' formula works best.

Paul Espitalier-Noel was sponsored by BOC at university, and after 12 years with the company is in his seventh job. "I was fortunate enough to spend three years in New Jersey, USA, which gave me superb insights into a different country's business culture and also a network of excellent contacts, which I still use. I travel a lot in my current job in the electronics sector. Customers like TI, Samsung and Intel are global, and we need to manage them on a global basis."

International assignments play a major part in career development—there are 300 or so at present, and not just UK expatriates abroad. People can expect to have genuinely international careers. Two-way benefits accrue, in the form of personal development, exposure to different international business styles, and the transfer of technology, where experts are expected to leave behind three or four more 'new' experts after the assignment.

BOC acknowledges there is a shortage in some countries of skilled managers, and expatriates are relied upon until local managers can be developed. BOC has created a 'Chinese MBA programme', an in-house MBA programme devised using Western modules, and aimed at growing a cadre of Chinese managers groomed in both Western and BOC business methods. This has evolved into the virtual concept of the 'BOC North Pacific College'—a four-week programme for other prospective managers.

BOC enjoys a high standing in the graduate recruitment market place. Taking great care in the selection process—many senior executives are actively involved—Don Beattie says "the company has an unusually high acceptance rate; it is very rare that people turn us down."

Pay and Benefits

BOC is competitive on pay, judging the 60th percentile to be appropriate. It does not enter into pay 'shoot-outs', preferring instead to emphasise other factors like job challenge, personal development, the people you work with, and the ability to employ your skills.

There are various employee share schemes, with everyone in the UK eligible for the SAYE scheme. Around 350–400 managers are in the company share option scheme.

BOC offers the usual market-competitive package of benefits, but is particularly proud of its company pension scheme.

The Future

The need to accelerate the development of managers through the organisation is a priority, as BOC expects to be 'management hungry' in the next decade. Matching managerial resource to the company's rate of growth in the North Pacific region is a real challenge, but one that is not exclusive to this region.

BOC's successful operations are likely to become increasingly competitive, and BOC aims to move much closer to being 'world class' in everything that it does. That means honing the performance management systems so that everything is running 'like a Swiss clock'. BOC also expects to do a tremendous amount of work in the area of 'change management'.

As in any growth or 'stretch' situation, some logistics lag behind developments at the cutting edge. Beattie intends to improve the HR information systems, and recognises that the scale of international assignments will demand improved processes, particularly for expatriate movements between countries other than the UK.

While leaner than a few years ago, BOC has not had to endure any dramatic downsizing, and is not a 'hire and fire' organisation. Work patterns have changed, but job security is not a 'top of mind' issue for BOC employees, who are subscribed to a culture of reality. People have also taken on board that responsibility for career development is a shared one, and not a process dependent on managers. Employees know that they are not in a cross country walk—the competitive international market is more akin to the Olympic Games—and they realise that everyone has to be fit, fast and flexible to succeed.

BOC claims to be more international than most UK-based multinationals, and the evidence would support this. A highly professional approach married to an informal relaxed style has delivered business success, and personal achievement and satisfaction for the many people who have pursued rewarding careers in this quality company.

THE BOOTS COMPANY

The Boots Company

The Boots Company includes Boots the Chemists, Halfords, Do It All, Homestyle, FADS and Boots Opticians, making it one of the UK's leading retailers. Other businesses in the group; Boots Contract Manufacturing, Boots Healthcare International and Boots Properties contribute to a turnover of over £4 billion. Boots the Chemists is the largest of the retail businesses, with some 1,200 stores and over 57,000 staff. Almost two-thirds of the population shop at Boots the Chemists at least once every month.

Biggest Plus: Huge range of opportunities with a caring company

Biggest Minus: Environment and culture still rather formal

The Boots Company PLC
Group Head Office
Nottingham NG2 3AA
Tel: 0115-950 6111
Fax: 0115-968 7151

The Business

The Boots Group offers careers in retailing, pharmacy, optometry, product development, manufacturing and marketing, property management and a wide range of support functions. Since it was founded by Jesse Boot in 1877 it has maintained a tradition of being a caring company with high standards, both for its products and its work force.

Sir Michael Angus, Group chairman, said "The value of our people continues to grow with their skills, knowledge, experience and dedication. It is no coincidence that our businesses won no less than three new Investors in People awards during the year for the quality of their training and communication. Nor is it any coincidence that we can confidently put forward the expertise of our store staff as a key differentiator for our businesses."

Company Culture and Style

The Victorian paternalism of the founder has been modernised to give a strong culture of a caring, open, ethical organisation valuing discipline above flair; however, the importance of flair and an entrepreneurial attitude has now been recognised and greater importance will in future be attached to this quality.

Boots is an open organisation valuing the exchange of views and opinions among its staff. Some policies and procedures are determined centrally in consultation with the individual businesses. Great importance is attached to the creation of a good working environment for staff that the company believes will be translated into high standards of customer service. A recent profile by external consultants showed that employees see Boots as a listening organisation with clear expectations for each staff member, but that they want to see more importance attached to flair and fun.

Human Resource Priorities

Equal opportunities and effective training are two main planks in HR policy—though Boots doesn't use the term 'HR', preferring 'Personnel'. 80% of Boots the Chemists' staff are female and gender and race equality opportunities policies have been thoughtfully worked out. The company is a founder member of Opportunity 2000. A high proportion of women return to Boots after maternity leave. There are term-time contracts and family-friendly schemes—such as a summer play scheme in Nottingham, where Boots is the city's largest employer.

Competency related training is a high priority, with the total training cost running at £25m annually. Boots has been involved with NVQs from the start, and with some 21,000 employees registered for NVQs in 1995–96, it is the largest NVQ user in the country. The group is proud that four of its eight subsidiary companies have achieved the Investors in People award, pioneered by Boots the Chemists that has recently got through the tough re-assessment procedure.

Effective communication is an important strand of HR practice: the group staff magazine 'Blueprint' is published monthly; Boots the Chemists publishes its 'Quality Times' three times a year and each staff member receives an annual group performance review. Every week staff participate in a team meeting where information cascades down, while the Staff Council gives ample opportunity for bottom-up ideas and information.

The group is one of the largest employers still to have an in-house welfare organisation, dating back to the days when the wife of the founder provided breakfast drinks for badly fed employees in Victorian times. It is a well-respected scheme, using some nursing trained staff to provide a variety of help from post-incident trauma to financial and social problems.

Career Opportunity and Development

With eight companies covering different sectors and professions, the group offers a wide range of career opportunities—sales assistants (who have a more challenging job than in most high street stores as they need to understand health, beauty and other products in depth), opticians, pharmacists as well as the underpinning careers in finance, marketing, logistics, personnel, etc.

The graduate recruitment scheme takes about 60 people each year and puts them through a two-year development programme on a starting salary of £16,000. There are group-wide schemes to give breadth of experience, as shown by Alan Alcock's history. Alan joined three years ago in logistics providing an employee relations advisory service to distribution managers. He has progressed to become a senior personnel officer with Boots the Chemists and says "One of the great attractions of working for Boots is that you get such a good structured development. I was given responsibility from day one, but there's a comprehensive support network. I've now moved into information systems and I'm getting involved with the more strategic issues."

Specialist programmes also exist—for instance, 350 graduate pharmacists join Boots the Chemists every year and achieve a high pass rate in their final exams of 90%.

Each employee has an annual performance review that determines their pay. A separate development review takes place 2–3 months later, which leads to a personal development plan for each staff member. Assessment centres and psychometric tests are used as part of the promotion procedure to try to achieve objectivity.

A career guidance review may be brought in soon, to encourage people to learn about other opportunities within the group. The top 200 managers work for the group, not an individual company, and their development is carefully planned. 50% of this senior cadre have worked their way up within the company, while 50% are recruited externally, either because of new needs, such as expansion into European markets, or to bring in external experience. An example of a successful in-company career is that of the group personnel director who sits on the board. He joined as a graduate and has worked in finance, merchandising and property as well as personnel.

Training is not confined to NVQs and at the top level includes the company's own Executive Development programme and participation in an MBA programme at Nottingham University.

Quality leadership is the aim, to give people a clear understanding of management's expectations, combined with the motivation needed to fulfil them.

Change in the retail sector takes place constantly and rapidly, and a constant challenge for Boots is to manage this change effectively. When change affects job security, vigorous efforts are made to redeploy staff or find them alternative employment, including the use of external outplacement. John Wykes, director of personnel for group and retail, says he sees "No incompatibility between a culture that demands high performance and a caring company—we try to support people to perform better."

Pay and Benefits

Boots the Chemists aims to offer competitive salaries at sales assistant level in the knowledge that the satisfaction of working as specialists in the areas of health and beauty is also an important motivator. A profit-related bonus scheme can increase total remuneration by 8% if company targets are met and generous staff discounts—from 12.5 to 22.5%—apply to merchandise sold by all the group's retail chains.

The company encourages staff share ownership through its SAYE scheme, giving an option to purchase at 80% of the market price, and is expecting the current 12% take-up by group employees to continue rising.

The Future

The toughest challenge is, in the words of John Wykes, "To continue and maintain the level of our people's competence throughout the organisation." The competitive advantage of the group depends on the quality of its people.

A further challenge is to manage the accelerating pace of change effectively and, in the tradition of the company, to do this sensitively. Also for this traditional company, it must meet the challenge of developing new flexible ways of working, moving away from the hierarchical structure of the past to project-based teams, forming and reforming as the business demands.

In line with this, decision making is being shifted down as people are empowered within the limits of their tasks. Staff do not lack bright ideas of developing the business, as was shown by the employee who earned £10,000 from a suggestion scheme within the manufacturing business. The company acknowledges that it must develop new ways of letting its staff demonstrate their flair.

THE BOSTON CONSULTING GROUP

The Boston Consulting Group

The Boston Consulting Group (BCG) are genuine pioneers. Established in 1963, BCG founded the industry of strategy consulting, originating concepts that are now part of the management lexicon: experience curves, cash cows, stars and time-based competition.

Employing 1,500 consultants in 38 offices across the globe, BCG continues to grow at a rate in excess of 25% year-on-year, with two-thirds of its clients ranked among the world's largest 500 corporations.

Biggest Plus: Stimulating working environment, outstanding opportunities for secondment all over the world

Biggest Minus: Only the strong survive

The Boston Consulting Group Limited
Devonshire House
Mayfair Place
London W1X 5FH
Tel: 0171-753 5353
Fax: 0171-753 5750

The Business

The Boston Consulting Group is driven by a crystal clear mission—to be the consultant of choice for senior management at the top of organisations. Its success is phenomenal. While others downsized during the recession, BCG continued to expand, cementing its innovative reputation at the head of the consulting pack.

BCG are strategy specialists, not generic consultants offering functional aid on management issues. Those seeking advice on computer systems or methods of improving internal communications are advised to look elsewhere.

Seventy consultants are employed in the London office, working alongside FTSE-100 organisations on issues of strategy and corporate advantage. BCG prides itself on staff diversity: 27 nationalities are represented in London, a pallet of consultants encompassing ex-poets, art students as well as scientists, and even one member of the Swiss yachting team.

Company Culture and Style

A challenging, collegiate, non-hierarchical, intellectually rigorous organisation, BCG has historically recruited predominantly young staff. Such thinking speaks volumes for organisational attitudes. While old heads carry pre-set ideas and outdated prejudices, consultants untainted by history are more likely to think 'outside the box', pushing back conventional boundaries to achieve fresh solutions.

The office atmosphere is creative and nourishing. Consultants are actively encouraged to contribute from day one and those displaying the requisite qualities are rewarded with promotion irrespective of vacancies. All staff are continually given as much responsibility as they can handle, while fun at work is a daily imperative.

"The people we're recruiting," observes Paul Mitchell, managing partner of the London office, "are in huge demand from head-hunters. All the top head-hunters have complete CVs of everyone in the firm. For that reason alone, the work has to be good and people must have a sense of enjoyment or they wouldn't stay.

"As for the issue of job security, when all the competition was downsizing, we continued to recruit. There probably is some measure of insecurity around—'have I got what it takes to be successful in this business?'—but not 'will my job still be here tomorrow?'."

Secure employment, absorbing work, stimulating colleagues—no wonder BCG ranked second in a survey among European graduates in the *Financial Times* List of the 50 Most Desirable Companies to Work for in Europe.

Human Resource Priorities

The Boston Consulting Group has no discrete HR departments. Although a set of HR mechanisms exists to determine pay and rations, the function is devolved to Career Management Committees charged with one central task: supporting individuals and teams to ensure that careers are as fulfilling as possible. Career Management Committees are staffed by consultants dedicated to the cause of individual development. Half of all BCG partners double-up as career managers, devoting 15–25% of their professional time to the task.

The arguments against a dedicated HR division are twofold. The Boston Consulting Group believes that career development is too important to be hived-off to a separate function. Moreover, the prime objective of HR is to attract the best people, and facilitating their rapid ascent through the organisation. BCG maintains that off-loading such responsibility to a separate department is less likely to build mutual understanding than widen chasms between senior staff and those lower down the pecking order.

On an informal level, each office operates a committee comprising representatives from individual peer groups and designed to air significant issues. Female members of staff in BCG's London office recently staged a dinner to highlight problems that might not be addressed by a mixed audience.

Career Opportunity and Development

"People who join from university," posits Charmian Caines, manager, London office, "are expected to work as an associate for two years. If both parties then have a mutual interest in their staying with BCG, we either sponsor them to go to Business School or place them in industry for a period of personal development before returning as a consultant."

Career progression at BCG is clear and divides into four stages—associate, consultant, manager, partner. Steadfast proponents of equal opportunity, 50% of the 1995 intake in London were women.

Consultants are expected to become partners in a further seven years. While some get on a faster track than others, those falling short of partner material are encouraged to seek fresh careers, a process that calls for sensitive handling. "It's important for people to remember their time at BCG positively," Paul Mitchell observes. "We want them to feel good about themselves and those they worked with when they were here." BCG maintains contact with ex-colleagues by holding alumni dinners and parties. Not only does this underpin a continuing bond, it can also provide a useful source of fresh business.

Secondment goes with the turf. New recruits are warned they can expect to spend 4–6 months abroad every year. BCG's Paris and London offices operate an 'Ambassador' staff-exchange programme, while bulletin boards regularly advertise openings in Washington, Hong Kong or Bombay.

No one is excluded from training. All fresh recruits attend a 1–3 week course covering BCG techniques, the basic tools of financial analysis and accounting procedures. Two days off-site training are provided every six months, a core curriculum marshalled by external facilitators. One Friday every month is also set aside for training sessions conducted in-house, while practice group meetings debate outstanding issues.

External qualifications are actively supported. The Boston Consulting Group are major sponsors of MBA courses for high-performing associates—six full-time sabbaticals are awarded each year by the London office alone.

Pay and Benefits

Like John Lewis, The Boston Consulting Group insist they are 'never undersold'. "BCG pays as well as the best names in the business," declares Caines. "Everyone is competing for a relatively small number of people from the same pool. All those people have a detailed understanding of the market and a 1–2% differential in the package being offered will not go unnoticed."

Pay increases at BCG are merit-based and determined by career management committees focusing on rate of career progression, performance in the job, and contribution to the office.

Senior staff (partners and managers) are rewarded with bonuses from a profit share scheme. Assessments are governed by levels of new business generated, individual performance and overall contribution to BCG's welfare.

A broad range of other benefits are also provided. Staff and their families are covered by medical insurance, and medical facilities in the London office are second to none—two of the staff are ex-GPs! All employees are covered by the corporate pension scheme, five weeks' holiday entitlement is standard after two years (four weeks for new entrants), while maternity leave of 12 weeks on full pay is twice the statutory norm. Paternity leave is offered on an ad hoc basis but proud fathers (who can stand the noise) are encouraged to take a week off.

The Future

The Boston Consulting Group refuses to look back. Far from generating a mood of complacency, three decades of unparalleled achievement have merely set the standard for future growth. It won't be easy. As the competition strives to make up ground, Paul Mitchell pinpoints recruitment as an area requiring special attention, "Our single greatest challenge is going to be attracting and retaining enough of the genuinely brightest and most able people. We're in an era when there are more consulting organisations than ever before and the UK industry is starting to attract and pay for talent in a way that historically it has not.

"We see a continuing demand from the most exciting companies for advice on issues of strategy and competitive advantage, driven by a range of factors including global markets and deregulation. Meeting that demand—and at the moment we are turning business away—will to a very large degree depend on our ability to recruit the best and the brightest."

No effort is spared in doing so. Maintaining a visible presence at Oxford and Cambridge, BCG actively encourages applications from university graduates. 1,000 CVs are received each year by the London office, 100 candidates interviewed and perhaps 10–15 jobs are offered.

One other significant hurdle has yet to be overcome—Paul Mitchell concedes that the lines of communication between subsidiaries need to be streamlined in order to take advantage of cumulative experience. "Although solutions must be tailored to each client," he muses, "it's infuriating to discover you've invented the same wheel as someone in Sydney or Stockholm."

Many would be glad of such problems. The Boston Consulting Group appears well set on a path of enduring prosperity, providing generous levels of job satisfaction and financial rewards for a highly motivated work force.

The BP Group

The British Petroleum Company is one of the world's largest petroleum and petrochemical companies. BP has major operations in Europe, the USA, Australia and parts of Africa, and is expanding in South East Asia, South America and Eastern Europe. The Group has 56,500 employees, 16,500 of them in the UK.

The BP Group, whose corporate headquarters is in London, consists of three core businesses: BP Exploration (oil and gas exploration, field developments and production); BP Oil (refining, marketing, trading, shipping and supply); and BP Chemicals (petrochemicals, plastics and speciality products).

Biggest Plus: The company has really got its act together

Biggest Minus: Have to be comfortable with continuous change

The BP Group
Britannic House
Finsbury Circus
London EC2M 7BA
Tel: 0171-469 4000
Fax: 0171-496 4630

The Business

BP has come a long way since it discovered the Middle East's first commercial oil field in 1908, which led to its founding. While truly international, the company is the most British of the world's oil majors.

The company has turned itself around in the last three years—it needed to because the company was unprofitable, over-borrowed and in trouble. It has been quite some achievement, surpassing demanding targets set in terms of profits, debt, and effective use of capital. BP focused on core activities, outsourced many functions, and reduced staff numbers. £2.2 billion profit in 1995 is testimony to these efforts, and BP is perhaps the most admired oil company in Britain today.

The modern BP places great emphasis on performance. Every asset must earn its keep, and must be in the top quartile of comparable assets world-wide, to avoid radical surgery or disposal. The whole company is viewed as a series of assets or business units.

From its origins as an oil producer, the upstream sector is still a source of great strength (around two-thirds of operating profits). It was once said that "a Shell man couldn't discover oil if it was spilling over the top of his boots, and a BP man couldn't sell oil even if the customer had *his* foot halfway through the door with a blank cheque in his hand." Neither statement is true, and certainly BP has become increasingly hard-nosed and successful in the downstream area.

Company Culture and Style

BP has shed many jobs over the last few years, removing intermediary layers of management, and focusing upon the factors deemed essential to sustained growth. Technology, relationships and people figure prominently. In terms of cultural change, BP has come a long way.

Much effort has been put into instilling teamwork in the minds of employees. It is no good being a loner in BP—you must work well with others in order to get on. Part of this is a willingness to share information and empower individuals, and this starts at the very top.

BP encourages flexibility and innovation in its business approach, and is at the forefront of the oil sector in breaking the mould and finding new ways of doing things. Much store is held by relationships—with colleagues, customers, communities and suppliers. Building a good climate of understanding is good for business, or creating a 'win win situation' as BP describes it.

One surviving value is integrity. BP's strict code of business conduct contends that accountability in business means keeping your nose clean. High environmental standards are cherished by BP. The company is very open, honest and communicative on its excellent record, believing this creates a more understanding climate if anything ever does go wrong.

What kind of person fits into today's BP? With so much emphasis on 'the people' in the organisation, good communication skills are vital. Individuals will know how to build and use networks, seek out information and use it effectively and profitably. People are encouraged to expose their business flair by taking calculated risks and responsibility for their own decisions.

With half the number of total employees from eight years ago, no one believes in the BP 'career for life' any more, although many people still carve out long, successful and rewarding careers in the Group. Of the staff numbers lost, 50% was due to businesses sold, while another 25% was attributed to job outsourcing. Of the remainder, 80% of people who wanted another job found one within six months. The BP name on your CV is hard currency.

Human Resource Priorities

BP's management of people has a series of enduring themes that form the strands of HR policies. There are no tablets of stone—they are regarded more as working drafts. There are five of them that drive people management within BP.

One important theme is motivation and communication. Recognising that if business is to be done, people must be motivated; 'conversation' is a popular word, and is an important part of the team leader's role.

This in turn entails creating first class leadership at all levels, and an important HR task is to work with line managers to identify long-term leaders of the organisation. Excellent management development and training will follow.

High standards of recruitment are essential. BP once recruited around 600 graduates world-wide each year, but that figure is now between 100–200. This number is never fixed—graduates must be top quality, or the company simply doesn't recruit. BP has drawn its top management almost entirely from its cadre of graduates.

Skill enhancement is another popular theme, recognising that BP has every chance of remaining a superbly efficient organisation if it has highly skilled people capable of dealing with rapid change.

BP, like any international Group with decentralised operations, seeks both a balance between local empowerment and the need to have control mechanisms and common standards, and the sharing of good practice across all parts of the Group. It calls this 'integration'. Several UK sites have attained the Investors in People recognition

Career Opportunity and Development

There is still a dazzling range of rewarding careers to be had in BP, despite the recent downsizing. People take on real jobs from day one and, through early development programmes in their first 2–3 years, are exposed to a range of disciplines, and have ample opportunity to move across functions and businesses.

In all areas, there is a commitment to building up the collective bank of technical and commercial skills, through acquiring a set of 'competencies' in four areas. 'Technical masters' are a pre-requisite of a high technology industry; business skills are less Harvard and more commercial awareness and style in emphasis, while the honing of behavioural skills focuses on BP's values of openness, teamworking, responsibility and networking. Leadership is the fourth category that takes on more importance as an individual rises through the organisation.

BP advertises all jobs below middle management electronically. The nature of BP's business and the ease of global communications ensure that there is an international dimension to many jobs in BP.

BP people are often posted abroad, if not at the same levels of previous years, and the company's accelerated growth into many new regions of the world should allow an accumulation of stamps in your passport.

Pay and Benefits

BP seeks to attract its people through the excitement and challenge of jobs in the oil industry, but recognises that it must be broadly competitive on pay and benefits compared with its peer group of the top industrial companies in the UK.

In the 1995 annual report, chairman David Simon said "Great efforts are made to ensure that our employees, wherever they work in the world, receive competitive rewards. This is vital to retain our best people and secure their loyalty... as well as being competitive, the packages are intended to reward distinctive business achievement. BP does not merely expect to reward employees for good performance: it wishes to do so."

Pay typically comprises base salary, individual and team bonuses, share schemes and allowances (London and regional). Pay increases are decided principally by individual appraisal, although there are some market-driven special categories such as traders, lawyers and tax experts. Other benefits also add up and the company pension scheme is very attractive.

BP's various employee share ownership schemes (participation, SAYE, and options) operate in 16 countries and enjoy an impressive level of participation by eligible employees: 80% of UK employees owning more than 1,000 BP shares is proof of this.

The Future

The petroleum industry is no longer a 'comfy zone'—unsympathetic rulers such as the oil price and global competition guarantee this—and there is constant pressure to enhance performance and reduce costs by finding new ways of doing things.

BP recognises the need to re-address career development in a period of change. Perhaps vertical promotion is not what it used to be and a more creative approach, involving horizontal career development, is where progress is being made.

As one of the best, open communicators, BP recognises that these dynamics will inevitably impinge upon morale. Change has been positive, but people have been put under more pressure. Horizontal skill development is fine in principle, but it requires individuals to accept new challenges and drop some old habits. The calibre of BP people is high and they have responded well to these changes.

The pointers and statistics show that BP is doing extremely well, and is a good place to work even if this work is sometimes hard. BP cares desperately about its people, and intends to find ways of balancing new demands, values and rewards. The company needs quality work from its people, and accepts that there is life outside the work place. As BP is effectively doing today what it did five years ago with half the staff, it will take time to find this new equilibrium. The company is incredibly realistic and purposeful, which should guarantee its success.

BR▲NN

Brann

Brann's business is communications and its purpose clear: "Helping our clients create loyal customers". Brann offers an exceptionally wide range of marketing services to an impressive client list, including advertising and direct marketing; communications consultancy; customer databases and data analysis; and call centre services.

This private company has grown considerably since its management buy-out in 1994. Turnover has risen 90% over two years to stand at nearly £40 million in 1995. Brann has 683 employees, based at the company's two main locations of Bristol and Cirencester, and a London office opened in 1997.

Biggest Plus: One of the innovative 'Academies' of British marketing

Biggest Minus: Need to work hard to understand Brann and how it fits into the marketing communications process

Brann Limited
Phoenix Way
Cirencester
Gloucestershire GL7 1RY
Tel: 01285-644744
Fax: 01285-654952

The Business

While delivering this impressive growth, Brann has changed its business emphasis dramatically. No longer described as a direct marketing company, its three main activities of a year ago (communications, systems and call centre) do not adequately describe the business today. Brann has identified a unique position in the market, by bringing all three aspects together into an integrated marketing proposition.

It is hard to decide who to compare Brann with. Brann employs more people than any UK advertising agency; it ranks third in the direct marketing league tables; it has one of the largest call centres in the UK; it has built three of the largest customer databases in the country; its data analysis software is a world-beater in terms of speed, capacity and functionality; and Brann's creative department is one of the UK's largest.

Much of Brann's vision and innovative marketing thinking revolves around understanding brands and understanding customers. Brands are usually thought to be created through image, but chief executive Chris Gater argues that there is too much dissidence between image and the experience a customer goes through in buying products. Brann seeks to help its clients understand this process, providing help and services at whichever stages are required. Brann now counsels in 'The Contact Zone' between clients and customers. In contending that it is customers, not producers, that own brands, Gater is in tune with marketers who think they need a better way of selling their products beyond funding the TV advertising industry.

Brann, in staking out the future of marketing communications, needed a vision, or 'flag on the hill', and has done much work over the last year to develop this integrated proposition. 1996 is likely to be a year of slower growth, as the company absorbs this change, invests heavily in the business, and concentrates on doing more for its largest, key clients.

Company Culture and Style

Most people have responded enthusiastically to what is seen as a pioneering approach. "Brann could do with a period of consolidation," says Chris Gater, "but I'm not sure that the market will let us." Brann's style is not to advertise its dreams, but prefers instead to emphasise the business value it has brought to its clients, and quantifies money earned whenever it can.

In 1995, there were three sub-cultures in the communications, systems and call centre operations. While sub-cultures may still exist discretely, there is now one company battle cry. Brann has still hung onto some of its positive characteristics though—the business, a bit of the 'family' value, and innovative or 'can do' attitudes. Success itself becomes cultural.

Brann is really a diverse culture of 700 individuals, according to personnel director, Jon Parsons. Providing every aspect of marketing communications, including its own printing operation, Brann has every kind of 'culture' as creatives, print, IT/systems experts, telemarketers, call centre operators and, of course, client handlers.

Most senior Brann people have not grown up in rigid, large companies, although a few are refugees from them. With many young people recruited into the organisation, there are not too many people aspiring to be just managers, although there will be people good at their functions who will become leaders and assume responsibilities.

Inevitably, the client service culture is extremely strong. A high proportion of jobs are client-facing, and there is a very strong feeling of 'wanting to do the best for the client'. Creative juices flow freely too. While the creative department won more gold awards in the top three competitions than any other agency in 1995, Brann is very strong in encouraging all of its people to come up with ideas.

Two people suggested in mid-1995 that Brann might have an interactive media business. It now has 20 people, is contributing profit, and developed with Microsoft the highly successful Euro '96 web site, which drew an unprecedented 18 million visits during the 1996 European Football Championships.

Another is 'Viper', a marketing information analysis system designed by Brann, but when it realised it had also invented a powerful data mining tool, it formed Brann Software as a spin-off business. Yet another example is an interactive touch screen kiosk Brann has designed for use in medical locations such as doctors' waiting rooms—certainly non-core activities, but typical of the company's willingness to back 'sparky' ideas that its employees might have.

Human Resource Priorities

Brann has done a lot of 'people work', equipping staff to have conversations with clients on the 'bigger picture', presenting integrated components of the marketing process rather than separate services. Like most people, Brann found change required hard work and was not for everyone, but the company is not changing for 'now', it is looking into the next decade.

The personnel department hardly ever sends out pieces of paper (although it has them if wanted). It has appraisal forms, but concentrates on supporting the processes of discussion and agreement. Brann has a strong attitude against judging people in boxes.

Each person has their own dedicated personnel professional to talk to when they want, and managers are encouraged to come to personnel on a quarterly basis with 'People Planning' to discuss their team members' performance, training and development, pay and promotion; this is the main area where personnel comes together in any formal sense.

Recruitment is very respected in Brann. "We find our people from all over the place, and also allow them to find us," says Jon Parsons. Brann doesn't do too badly in retaining its people, considering its reputation as a 'Marketing Academy' and the obvious dangers of losing staff regularly to other agencies. Brann creates in its people's minds the cross-functional opportunities, the ability to operate absolute best practice in specialist areas, and the chance to learn at the frontier of marketing communications.

Career Opportunity and Development

Brann's personnel department views development as part of a continuous process of employment, through recruitment, induction, training, remuneration and career development. Training is particularly important.

Managers are expected to encourage the wider development of their staff, identify talented people and urge them forward in their careers. By working in teams, individuals cannot help but come to the notice of others in the company, and so the informal network plays its part too.

Brann's is a fast-moving business, and people do move across the organisation and across functions, free of barriers. People have moved from client service to creative; from systems to planning. Generally Brann does this well, but recognises that at times, presenting opportunities to individuals could be construed as applying coercion!

In two years of massive growth, more than 170 people have enjoyed promotions. Brann also promotes by encouraging the growth of each individual's job.

Pay and Benefits

Pay levels are around upper quartile levels, although this varies function by function. Profit-related pay applies to everyone. There is no annual pay round—each person effectively has their own financial year starting from whenever they join Brann. Recognition (and appropriate reward) is both formal and informal, for exceptional performance or noteworthy effort.

Brann offers 'big company' benefits—a company pension, life insurance, 25 days' annual leave; benefits are fairly flexible, and company parties are twice a year.

The Future

Chris Gater knows that Brann is only beginning its journey, that any process of change is far from over, and that many hills remain to be climbed. He identifies many future opportunities with clients, and is encouraged by his conversations with them which recognise that the nature of the marketing business could be quite different in three or four years' time. The marketing services industry is decreasingly aligning itself to traditional boxes, and Brann is setting its stall out where it wants to be in the new era.

While Brann cannot point to specific client pressure, the international dimension is becoming increasingly important. Particularly in the call centre business, incoming customer service operations are being aggregated to serve international markets. With the telephone contact point of customer service playing such a vital part of the delivery of the brand, Brann has some important choices to make. One only needs to look at the phenomenal growth of the call centre business in the USA to realise that Brann must get this right, and quickly.

Interactive has gatecrashed the communications scene at speed. This new media has made life more complicated and more exciting. With several interactive points of the buying process, Gater sees it as an area in which Brann will be doing much more. "I am convinced that it is an area Brann will develop. Currently, there are many small boutique providers, but clients will realise that it is a vital part of the presentation of its brands to customers, and must control it in the same way."

Bristol & West Building Society

Britain's ninth largest building society, Bristol & West is the leading financial institution in the West Country. At a time of increasing diversity in the financial services sector, Bristol & West focuses on a trio of core business activities—mortgages, savings and investments—achieving national market penetration through a wide variety of direct sales channels.

In April 1996, Bristol & West and Bank of Ireland announced that they had reached agreement on the terms under which Bristol and West will join the Bank of Ireland group, creating a major new force in the British personal finance market.

Biggest Plus: Culture places a premium on relationships, empowering and involving staff

Biggest Minus: Lack of formal management development programmes

Bristol & West Building Society
Broad Quay
Bristol BS99 7AY
Tel: 0117-9792222
Fax: 0117-9432522

The Business

Bristol & West offers a branded range of competitive products throughout the UK and offshore, marketed through a network of distribution channels including mortgage brokers and financial institutions.

Founded in the mid-19th century, B&W currently operates through 159 branches nationwide, and has 182,000 mortgage accounts and 1.2 million savings or investment accounts. B&W broke fresh ground in 1994 by launching a 24-hour remote savings account for customers preferring to deal by phone.

After a brief flirtation with the estate agency business—Hamptons was sold in February 1996—Bristol & West now concentrates on sectors where the company enjoys major player status. B&W has a gross asset base of £8.6 billion, reporting pre-tax profits in 1995 of £77.1 million.

John Burke, chief executive, comments, "We have chosen to concentrate on our core businesses: mortgages, savings and investments. This has meant stripping away non-core activities such as the estate agency business, travellers cheques and private health insurance. This strategy will allow Bristol & West to achieve the highest possible levels of customer service and a very wide choice of accounts and distribution channels within these core areas."

Corporate Company and Style

Bristol & West has returned to traditional strengths, moving away from a hierarchical culture towards an atmosphere that values performance and teamwork. Bristol & West actively seeks to involve, consult and generate staff commitment in pursuit of organisational goals, releasing their potential in the process.

B&W's corporate values are refreshingly direct. Seeking to create a style of behaviour based on mutuality, honesty and responsibility, tenets include telling staff what to expect and delivering results; being straight with good news and with bad; and emphasising that values are as important as results.

Those at the top regularly 'walk the talk'. Chief executive John Burke likes to hold coffee mornings with staff and other directors arrange gatherings of their own, allowing employees to set the agenda.

Bristol & West is fully committed to two-way communication. Team briefing processes stress the value of team listening, Partners' Councils provide staff opportunity for HR input, while employee surveys are carried out on a quarterly basis, supplemented by training and communications audits. 'Awaydays' and Team Building days bring an element of fun to the business, while involvement is also encouraged in external activities such as Duke of Edinburgh Award schemes.

Human Resource Priorities

Bristol and West's HR team is dedicated to fulfilling people-related goals specified in the mission, for example realising employee potential and open management styles. Bristol & West takes pride in having gained Investors In People recognition.

Acknowledging that the era of 'cradle to grave' employment is over, B&W pursues a policy of continuous learning, enhancing staff CVs through a broad array of training programmes. Every employee enjoys an average of 14 days training per year—not only higher than the industry standard, but a level set to increase to 18 days in 1997. Training is offered regardless of seniority or divisional status. All employees benefit from staff development programmes, many designed in conjunction with the West of England University.

John Paice, administrator, observes, "It is refreshing to work for an organisation which actively encourages staff development. I have been able to take advantage of training opportunities at Bristol & West that would not have been available at many other companies."

Change management is important. A research student from the local university is currently working alongside the change management team, studying problems associated with managing staff through organisational transformation.

Significant resources are devoted to the HR function, while the director of Group Services sits on the main board. Forty professionals are assigned to the HR department, supported by a network of staff in regional training teams.

Career Opportunity and Development

Bristol & West takes the view that employees are more talented than even they believe, and encourages staff to seek the highest standards of achievement while taking responsibility for their own careers. All posts are advertised internally, and 80% of promotions at B&W are made to internal candidates.

Although Bristol & West does not operate a formal management development programme, staff can choose from a substantial menu of courses and development events. Career management workshops called 'Lifeskills' have been developed with an external organisation. Aimed at helping staff understand their own talents and aspirations, the workshops are open to all employees. At management level, Bristol & West calls on a team of business psychologists to carry out assessments on senior managers, providing feedback on current performance. An annual training plan—developed bottom-up—details the purpose of training for each individual.

Many employees have risen through the ranks. training and development manager Steve Aumayer joined as a junior HR officer, rising no fewer than four grades in six years. Richard Brown was recruited as a programmer/analyst in 1991 and is currently head of non-retail business units. The most notable example is that of John Burke, who joined Bristol & West in 1964 as a branch assistant in Plymouth and worked his way up the ladder to become chief executive in September 1993.

Secondments are sometimes available. Jennie Barton was seconded to UNHCR in Geneva, while Mike Hughes is helping a local consortium bid for a Performing Arts Centre on the Bristol waterfront.

External qualifications are actively encouraged. All fees are paid for, and study leave is provided, where possible, for relevant courses. 93 members of staff are currently studying for Level 3 customer service NVQ, a figure typifying Bristol & West's commitment in this area.

The company abandoned its graduate recruitment programme in 1991—another policy under review—and B&W has commenced a fast-track intake to provide a fresh supply of quality branch managers.

Pay and Benefits

B&W aims to offer median levels of base salary with heightened rewards for those delivering superior performance. Benchmarks are provided by Hay market data, with B&W participating in surveys of the top 13 building societies. Bristol & West has awarded average pay increases of 3.5% over the last two years. Rises are determined by reference to a performance-related matrix, the range of increases spanning 0–10%.

Employees determine objectives with their line managers at the start of each calendar year. Targets are negotiated rather than imposed, with quarterly objectives providing the basis for performance ratings and subsequent input into the salary mechanism. PFMs (personal finance managers) occupy a category of their own. The corporate sales force works purely on a commission basis with the potential for highly competitive earnings.

In 1996, salaries at Bristol & West ranged from £100–120,000 for executive directors, £15–73,000 for managerial and professional staff, and around £8–20,000 for administrative staff.

There are no share option schemes, but all members of staff participate in a profit-related pay scheme, however, with targets communicated in advance. B&W pays up to 10% of base salaries if profit objectives are achieved, with staff receiving a 9.5% bonus in 1995 and 11.5% in 1994.

Benefits are sometimes flexible. Staff can opt for either a final salary or money purchase pension scheme, with varying levels of contribution. Bristol & West maintains a fleet of 400 vehicles, ranging from Golfs to Audi A6s; cars are offered at managerial level and above, with a cash option. Medical insurance arrangements divide into three strata. Executives and their families are fully covered, other grades of manager pay 50% towards dependents, while non-management grades pay 50% towards their own policies. Bristol & West offers an enhanced maternity scheme and three days' paternity leave as of right.

Relocation packages are provided for staff moving due to work-related factors, but subsidised mortgages were phased out in 1991. Subsidised meals are available in the staff restaurant and Bristol & West runs a highly active sports club. Teams competing in local leagues include both men's and women's football XIs.

The Future

Bristol & West has good cause for satisfaction. Having obtained Investors in People recognition in under three years, the company appears to have struck a sensitive balance between managing by objectives and taking heed of individual needs. Even so, significant hurdles have yet to be overcome. Ian Beveridge, head of HR management, pinpoints the principal challenge: "We want," he suggests, "to be regarded as a great place to work. The goal is to provide a challenging environment where people have the opportunity to achieve, and be rewarded for achievement, and to release the potential that is latent in everyone. Turning that potential into a reality is absolutely essential."

The future appears bright for Bristol & West. A friendly, enterprising organisation that genuinely values staff contribution, Bristol and West is set fair for the new millennium.

BT

BT is one of the world's leading providers of telecommunications services. Its main products and services are local, long distance and international calls (with direct dial connections to more than 230 countries); telephone lines, equipment and private circuits for homes and businesses; providing and managing private networks; and supplying mobile communications services.

In the UK, BT has 20.5 million domestic and 6.8 million business exchange lines. BT handles about 100 million local, national and international calls every day. BT employs around 130,000 people and for the year ended 31 March 1996 made pre-tax profits of £3,019 million on turnover of £14,446 million.

Biggest Plus: Industrial giant in growth industry of telecommunications

Biggest Minus: Continuous change in response to massive competitive pressure

British Telecommunications plc
BT Centre
81 Newgate Street
London EC1A 7AJ
Tel: 0171-356 5000
Fax: 0171-356 5520

The Business

BT's vision is to become the most successful world-wide telecommunications group. It is one of the few companies in the world that could even aspire to such a goal, for BT is a giant by any standards.

Since its privatisation in 1994, which brought it a quote on the London Stock Exchange and some 2.4 million shareholders, BT has rarely been out of the public eye. In the UK it operates under licence and is regulated (as are its competitors) by watchdog OFTEL, with the express intention of stimulating greater domestic competition and protecting the consumer. The UK is one of the most open and competitive markets in the world, with more than 150 licensed operators.

By and large, BT has responded extremely well to this environment and is widely regarded as one of the better successes of privatisation. BT genuinely puts its customers first, and is recognised as providing the highest quality of service.

Telecommunications is one of the most rapidly changing industries in the world. In addition to developing and growing its UK business, BT's strategy is to expand into new services such as interactive TV and multimedia, and to expand overseas, through partnerships and in its own right. The just announced take-over of the US telecommunications giant, MCI for £13 billion shows the level of clout that BT has.

While BT's main market is obviously the UK (where it is obliged to provide and maintain a telephone network), BT has many international interests, including a 20% stake in MCI Communications Corporation in the USA, including a joint venture company Concert. In Europe, it has joint ventures with Banco Santander in Spain, VIAG in Germany, and Banca Nazionale del Lavoro in Italy. Cellnet, the company jointly owned by BT and Securicor, has almost 2.4 million customers.

Company Culture and Style

Any company that has downsized to the extent that BT has must work that bit harder on the motivation, morale and aspirations of those who remain. Certainly the financial performance of the company has been impressive, and there is nothing like success to instil belief.

BT has been very successful in creating a customer-focused culture. This is fairly vital, for few other industries are as much a part of the social fabric as telecommunications; few companies touch so many lives or offer such opportunities for the UK as a whole.

BT's values are solid ones for successful business—putting customers first, taking pride in professionalism, earning the respect of colleagues, and working as part of an ever-improving team. Teamwork is an important concept at BT, and an approach encouraged in every employee.

Successful BT people are likely to have excellent communication and interpersonal skills, and be good motivators. Even within the most technical roles there is a need for good communication skills, and outside the technical areas, people should feel comfortable with technology.

Creativity and the ability to generate new ideas and solutions to customers' needs are highly valued skills at BT. So too is a sense of humour and perspective in the work place, to help cope with a fast-changing and sometimes high pressure working environment.

BT believes strongly in contributing to the community. BT's programme of community involvement remains the largest of its kind in the UK, focusing increasingly on areas that relate to BT's business and the particular contribution its technology can make. In 1995/96 it contributed £15 million through its Community Partnership Programme, targeted at people with disabilities, people in need, economic regeneration, education, environment and the arts.

Human Resource Priorities

BT has made a major reduction in the number of people working for the group—from around 227,000 five years ago to 130,000 early in 1996. BT prides itself on the fact that this reduction in numbers has been achieved on a voluntary basis. Severance packages were particularly attractive. 1996 is intended as the last year of the company-wide voluntary redundancy programme.

The company remains committed to providing equal opportunities for all its people and actively encourages the employment, training and development of disabled people. BT has emphasised its commitment to equal opportunities by registering under the UK government's Two Ticks disability scheme for organisations that can demonstrate a positive approach towards people with disabilities. Diversity in all areas is encouraged, BT welcoming ethnic minorities, women seeking a career in engineering, and mature students.

Employees' opinions are actively sought and an annual company-wide attitude survey gives people full scope to air their views. As well as providing a range of publications and briefings, BT operates a formal team meeting system, broadcast news services and a business TV channel.

BT continues to consult and negotiate with recognised trade unions. Building on its platform of good employee relations in the UK, it has established, with the support of the UK unions, the BT European Consultative Council, with the inaugural meeting in the middle of 1996.

Career Opportunity and Development

A career at BT offers opportunities and responsibilities. BT rewards merit and ability, and so opportunities are what individuals make of them. Necessarily, the company hires a lot of people for engineering and technical roles, but BT offers virtually every type of career, including business management, customer service, sales and marketing, IT and systems, finance, personnel and operator services.

BT puts great emphasis on training and development. For the 130,000 people who have stayed with the company, there are many training and development opportunities, averaging three days each year per person, and a similar amount of time spent on 'in job training' and other activities to equip people with the skills required by the BT of the future.

Career planning is a two-way process. In reducing its work force by around 40%, structures necessarily flattened out, and horizontal development into different work areas is often a better route to personal advancement than a modest vertical move in an existing business area. The graduate programme ensures that while graduates perform real jobs from day one, wider experiences are gained through project assignments. BT managers are very supportive, but graduates are expected to take an active role in their own future.

Pay and Benefits

Benchmark pay levels are competitive and BT believes in rewarding performance. If individual contributions are above average, pay will be too. BT's executive remuneration policy is to reward senior executives competitively, benchmarking against the largest companies by market capitalisation, particularly those organisations where the complexity of roles, of the business and the extent of international scope are comparable.

Other benefits include a save-as-you-earn share option plan, profit sharing, product discounts and the chance to join one of Britain's biggest pension schemes. Some job packages include a car, and many BT locations have excellent fitness facilities.

The Future

According to Chairman Sir Ian Vallance, "BT's long-run trading prospects are very good, but susceptible to short-term turbulence in the regulatory environment, overseas as well as in the UK."

In pursuing BT's vision of becoming the most successful world-wide telecommunications group, new chief executive Sir Peter Bonfield says, "We will need to be more focused on customer requirements, more committed, innovative and flexible, and quicker to market. But we also have to do new things in new ways. BT is a company in transition—from a telecommunications company to a communications company."

Clearly there is a world of opportunity for BT. There is still much scope to grow the domestic UK market and provide advanced services, and new technology is making possible new ways of accessing and interacting with information. And as telecoms markets around the world liberalise, major opportunities will be created for those companies that are fastest on their feet.

Of course in this arena, BT will have the opportunity to pit its expertise against the big international players, including many from the USA and Japan. While the termination of merger discussions with Cable & Wireless will not have changed BT's basic strategy to become a global player, it will need to find and attract, in competition, the right suitors to join its 'family'.

Sir Peter Bonfield believes that BT will have to focus more on the people, resources, skills and systems needed to become more flexible, more decisive, and more accountable. "I am introducing trading units, with individual managers having much greater responsibility and accountability for their profit and loss performance."

H.P. Bulmer

H.P. Bulmer is the world's leading cider company. Based in Hereford, it has three manufacturing sites in the UK and subsidiaries in Australia and Belgium. It has remained a family firm since its foundation in 1887 but has grown to hold 52% of the UK cider market and over 80% of the UK's cider exports. Its turnover in 1995 was £259 million and it has approximately 1,250 employees world-wide, of whom over 1,000 are based in the UK, mostly in Hereford.

Biggest Plus: No-threat culture, true commitment to career development

Biggest Minus: Comparatively unprogressive in attitude and style, for example still no female senior managers

H.P. Bulmer Holdings PLC
The Cider Mills
Plough Lane
Hereford HR4 0LE
Tel: 01432-352000
Fax: 01432-352084

The Business

The Bulmer family retains a 51% shareholding and there is still a strong family ethos to the business. It has gone through a major strategic reinvigoration since 1989, spearheading sustained growth in the UK cider market in spite of the recession and the generally depressed drinks market.

Within the local area it is a major employer with a strong commitment to local training, environmental and charitable concerns. Chairman, Esmond Bulmer, says "Consolidation, competition and investment to improve productivity all impact on employment. The drive to reduce costs has generated insecurity in some industries on a scale not felt since the Depression. No company today can offer a job for life but we have to do all that we can to ensure that those who work in our companies keep their skills up to date and acquire new ones."

Company Culture and Style

Bulmer's culture is "striving to retain the more positive aspects of paternalism while becoming more professional and commercially focused," in the words of Rob Garner, Group personnel director.

There have been aggressive cost reductions and the company has taken huge strides forward in efficiency, customer service and brand marketing. Inherent in its culture is 'fairness in dealing' and this has implications for all employees. A 'no threat' culture values progressive, non-confrontational working relations that contribute to its excellent reputation locally as a good employer. People are proud to work for H.P. Bulmer and the company values their loyalty.

The company contract with its employees is now more based on employability with a strong emphasis on acquiring new skills for new working challenges. Over the last two years, 300 jobs have been lost, mostly through volunteers and early retirement, but there have been some redundancies. This has caused much pain among the work force, which was eased through the use of external outplacement consultants and efforts to prepare survivors to cope with altered jobs as well as emotions of guilt and extra pressure.

These redundancies have caused "an understandable overreaction" among the work force, to use Rob Garner's expression, and the company is trying to rebuild people's confidence in their future with Bulmer—provided they are willing to adapt and learn new skills as needed. There is now a stress policy and a stress consultant is available.

The culture hasn't deliberately emphasised fun at work, but it is now recognised that this is a valid part of work culture.

There is a strong tradition of consultation and co-operation with union and employees. Statistics on absence (just above 3%) and staff turnover (just under 3%) show that people have a positive attitude to their work and this is borne out by the average length of service—an impressive 17 years.

Human Resource Priorities

Bulmer's HR policies focus on reskilling, developing more positive attitudes to change, a more international approach, and building a culture appropriate for a creative, entrepreneurial and customer-focused business.

Openness is an important part of the company's approach to its staff—Rob Garner says, "I believe we are as open with our employees as far as our status as a PLC allows." As well as a general open attitude, there are many channels of communication designed to achieve openness.

These include a twice-yearly magazine *Newsline*, sent to all employees and shareholders; a monthly publication *Newsbrief* for all employees; monthly team meetings, when each department manager cascades down information in the briefing notes, adds departmental news and feeds any questions or comments back to the personnel director; the Employee Council, which meets four times a year; the employees' AGM; and annual lunches when Employee Councillors meet members of the Holdings Board.

A recent Business Processes Review exercise was carried out along participative lines, with small groups reviewing their work and how their time was used. 3,000 suggestions came in as a result, and a new scheme will encourage everyone to submit ideas and challenge current thinking, with awards for the best ideas from individuals or teams.

The company is aiming for single status for all staff. The trade union has played a major part in this type of development and Rob Garner is proud or the co-operative approach. Bob Hardwick, convenor of the Transport and General Workers Union, has been with Bulmer for over 20 years and shares this pride. He also stresses the positive role of the Employee Council. Bob believes, "Our best attribute as company and union is that we never fail to talk."

The fruits of the Council's work show that it is far more than a talking shop. A recent extension of the participative role of the Employee Council has been the creation of a joint union/management working party. "This is founded on a desire to generate change through joint discussion and agreement, not enforcement or conflict," said Bob Hardwick. "Unions nationally have changed their approach to the introduction of new working practices and management techniques. The TGWU has recognised these trends and at Bulmer we are seeking to develop a positive approach."

Career Opportunity and Development

Bulmer's language talks about employee development as opposed to management development, underlining its belief that every employee has development potential. The company's employee development policy challenges all staff to update and improve their skills, while emphasising the link between employability and adaptability. The aim is for everyone to have an individual development plan, based on the existing annual review—the emphasis is on 'self-driven learning'. These plans are essentially an agreed contract between the individual and his or her manager, with the HR department acting as a facilitator rather than interfering in the individual/manager relationship.

Development centres are used to explore people's suitability for promotion into management. Internal promotion is the norm, an excellent example being the chief executive, who joined as a salesman.

The comparatively small work force means that Bulmer has no graduate trainee scheme, but people with high flying potential can join a one year fast-track development scheme. Graduates often join as their second job after university, and tend to stay with the company and enjoy promotion. There are possibilities of spending a year abroad in Belgium or Australia.

Bulmer is extremely committed to learning rather than training, focusing on the range of ways in which competence and skills can be developed and applied. It has achieved Investors in People recognition and is energetically pursuing an NVQ program for engineers, packaging staff, secretaries, warehousing operatives and HR staff.

The physical expression of this commitment is its very attractive Learning Centre, opened in May 1996 in a converted warehouse opposite the head office building. Personnel manager Richard Thomas explains that, "the Learning Centre facilities give employees the opportunity to release their untapped potential by learning in their own time and at their own pace." Up-to-date equipment includes a soundproof language room to avoid embarrassment when people are improving their foreign accents. Learning Centre staff are on hand to help and the centre is open 24 hours a day, so night shift staff can also use the facilities. At present, over 160 staff are using the facilities and the company is delighted with the early success of its new venture.

Pay and Benefits

Pay levels are good, both in terms of local rates of pay for packing operatives and nationally comparable packages for senior staff. Bulmer is in the upper quartile of FMCG companies for managers' and directors' pay. 'Flexibens' allows managers to choose their benefits in a cafeteria approach, perhaps taking a smaller car to upgrade other benefits. All employees can join a medical care scheme, and the company pays 50% of the costs. There are two schemes to promote Gainsharing among employees and all staff participate in the deferred profit share scheme. Over the last two years, 7–9% of pay has come from the combination of these schemes. The company is proud of these schemes and all staff are treated as shareholders.

The Future

Rob Garner believes that the main challenge facing Bulmer is that it must increase the rate at which it meets change. Given the embedded family character of the business and its situation in rural Herefordshire, it is not surprising that it is a challenge for this business to make the leap into the 21st century. Rather like the Red Queen in Alice in Wonderland, it wants to go ever faster and constantly drive up to the rate of change.

Its aim is to be world class in everything it does, from the sharpest cost base to the most creative and innovative customer service. As Garner says, "the only way to deliver our aspiration is through people," so a major challenge is to ensure the work force is equipped with the necessary skills.

Given the enormous potential international market for cider, there is the possibility of an exponential increase in demand. Current plans aim to triple the volume of cider produced to satisfy demand, so Bulmer seems set to continue its expansion and success.

CABLE & WIRELESS

Cable & Wireless

Cable & Wireless is one of the world's leading providers of international telecommunications services. It provides over 10 million customers in over 50 countries with a complete range of international, domestic and mobile communications. It is the world's third largest carrier of international traffic, operates a mobile network in 30 countries, as well as the world's largest, most advanced cableship fleet.

Biggest Plus: Its new UK company could provide a great leap forward

Biggest Minus: Mercury shows that without the right touch and timing, there can be big leaps backward too

Cable & Wireless plc
124 Theobalds Road
London WC1X 8RX
Tel: 0171-315 4000
Fax: 0171-315 5000

The Business

Cable & Wireless (C&W) is one of the 20 largest companies by market capitalisation on the London Stock Exchange. Its shares are also listed in New York, Tokyo, Hong Kong, Frankfurt, Geneva, Basle and Zurich.

Its 1996 profits were £1.34 billion on a turnover of £5.5 billion, demonstrating strong financial performance. When news leaked out in the summer that C&W had held talks with BT about a merger that would have created a £33 billion group to rival the US's biggest, the City was expectant. Market sentiment had focused on the dependence for the bulk of C&W's profits on its 57.5% owned subsidiary Hongkong Telecom. The talks came to an end, but in October 1996, under a new chief executive Richard Brown, C&W announced a spectacular deal to create the UK's leading provider of integrated telecommunications, information and entertainment services.

Mercury, as such, will disappear and a new company will emerge called Cable & Wireless Communications, formed through a merger of Mercury with Nynex CableComms Group, Bell Cablemedia, and Videotron. It will be the first UK company to be able to offer multichannel television and Internet services alongside the full range of telecommunications services. It is also strategically positioned to offer new products such as interactive digital services and multimedia products as they emerge.

Richard Brown hailed the deal as a "tremendous breakthrough", giving customers the best of telecommunications and the best of information and entertainment services from a single source. Cable & Wireless would be the only UK company offering a combination of telecoms, broadband, data transmission, video shopping and Internet access. The merger deal aims to "build on common and complementary strengths to create a unified customer-driven and marketing-led organisation". The new company is expected to increase revenues, reduce costs, and improve services.

Cable & Wireless already provides advanced integrated services in Hong Kong, where interactive multimedia services are scheduled for launch in 1997. It is a major shareholder in Australia's second carrier Optus, which is building a cable TV network, and was also a founder member of Japan's second international carrier IDC. In the USA, Cable & Wireless Inc. is a leading long-distance carrier specialising in business communications, and the group provides telecommunications in 14 countries in the Caribbean.

Mercury in the UK has created Europe's first all-digital national network. In continental Europe, the group has businesses in nine countries and an alliance with VEBA of Germany aimed at developing even more.

Brown says: "Cable & Wireless is big enough to be successful but small enough to be nimble. I think the winners of the future in this industry will not be the bigger players but the better players."

Company Culture and Style

Cable & Wireless is concentrating on growth, efficiency and identity. Brown says speed of action and quality of response are essential, performance must be measured in enhanced value to shareholders, and the Cable & Wireless identity is an important asset. He also sets a tone and style for the group in saying: "I understand the value of strategic plans, but too many times people labour over the strategy to get it picture perfect, while failing on the execution. I admire intelligence, but believe the world has more smart people than effective people."

And when he talks in business terms about "the ones who can move quickly, the ones who are tuned into their markets, the ones who can perform", he is also reflecting the values of the organisation.

At Mercury, there is a strong emphasis on individual contribution. Mercury's head of benefits Russ Watling says: "It is a fast-changing industry, and it is not possible to predict what we will look like in five years' time." That means a constant need to focus individuals on what they want to do, where they are going, and what skills they will need to get there.

Human Resource Priorities

C&W says that it is constantly seeking innovative approaches to manage and develop its people in a way that facilitates organisational change, enhances career planning for the individual, and contributes to the success of the group.

In 1996 there was a significant development in management philosophy, moving the group from the previous consensus-based approach to one in which the central HR function provides a strong lead to group businesses on people-related issues.

That is expected to produce greater cohesion world-wide, especially in areas such as international training and the development of senior management. It also aims to make it easier for the group to deploy top people in areas most suited to their skills and development.

Individual businesses implement group policy as appropriate within their own geographical markets.

At Mercury, there is a strong emphasis on 'contribution management', an appraisal system which the company says "allows individuals to put together career portfolios and get input from whatever source they need". This means seeking feedback on their performance and style not only from their manager but from colleagues or subordinates.

Career Opportunity and Development

"Encouraging employees to take responsibility for their own careers is fundamental to the nature of career development in Cable & Wireless," the group says. To further this it has set up a service known as Career Action Centres. They offer a range of tools to help employees take responsibility for their own career progress, and to become more effective in the international working environment. The centres were used to help redeploy many of the people made redundant when Mercury was faced with major retrenchment in early 1995.

The group has set up an International Executive Development programme "for the individual with long-term potential", while there is a year-long personal development experience called the 'Leaders of Tomorrow' programme for those already identified as future top managers. The Leadership Workshop launched in 1996 involves the whole senior management population and is led by group directors.

Cable & Wireless is increasingly looking across business boundaries to fill key positions, and needs more managers with international experience. "Mobility is of prime importance," says the company. "Not only does it benefit the individual, it also supports start-up businesses and aids the sharing of knowledge round the group." During 1995–96 more than 500 employees spent all or part of the year working outside their home base.

The purpose-built Cable & Wireless College in Coventry is the main training establishment for the group, and is able to draw in academic expertise. It delivers. It provides technical, sales and management training, develops the skills of a wide range of people from trainee engineers to senior directors, and its work also supports partners and other organisations world-wide.

In the UK, Mercury has taken in around 20 graduates a year.

Pay and Benefits

Pay is geared strongly to individual contribution. Mercury, for instance, has no job grades. Reward is based on market worth, and the individual's contribution. In some areas there is an element of team-based reward, including customer services.

Mercury has a save-as-you-earn share scheme with C&W shares, with five and seven year option periods and a 15% discount. There is also an executive share option scheme that extends down to senior management and administrative staff.

The Mercury flexible benefits scheme is indicative of the group style, producing individual choice and flexibility. Watling says: "Staff can put more money towards pension accrual, have cash instead of healthcare for themselves or their partner, or purchase more health care to a higher level, and can grade up or down on life cover." The standard five weeks' holiday can be traded down to four or up to six, and the scheme is open to all employees.

The Future

The group suffered a highly public disagreement at the top in 1995–96, with major changes at the top of both C&W and Mercury. It now moving even more strongly to imbue its businesses with a strong sense of common purpose, and is one of the few companies to dedicate a page in its annual report to talking directly about its people.

In being so highly geared to individual needs, Cable & Wireless will have to ensure that its HR management really is able to support businesses that are making constantly changing demands of individuals.

Cadbury Schweppes

Cadbury Schweppes

Employing nearly 42,000 members of staff world-wide, Cadbury Schweppes is a major global company, producing and selling beverages and confectionery products. Committed to profitable growth, strengthening its portfolio of outstanding brands and investing in new markets, Cadbury Schweppes' products are enjoyed in over 190 countries around the world.

Biggest Plus: Devolved international structure offers scope for individual managerial responsibility

Biggest Minus: Achieving synergy as the company continues to grow

Cadbury Schweppes plc
25 Berkeley Square
London W1X 6HT
Tel: 0171-409 1313
Fax: 0171-830 5137

The Business

Cadbury Schweppes' origins date back to 1783 when Jacob Schweppe perfected his process for manufacturing mineral water. John Cadbury began selling tea and coffee in 1824. Cocoa and chocolate, although initially incidental, quickly became the founder's main business. The two companies merged to form Cadbury Schweppes in 1969, initiating a programme of expansion world-wide.

Cadbury Schweppes' current pre-eminence stems from a strategy instigated over a decade ago. In 1984, the company bucked the trend towards diversification, choosing to focus on two core strengths—beverages and confectionery.

The company subsequently embarked on a stream of acquisitions within the beverage and confectionery fields. The most notable acquisition in recent times being Dr. Pepper/Seven Up, which Cadbury Schweppes bought in 1995 at a cost of £1.5 billion. This acquisition has proved to be an enormous success, transforming the company's competitive position in the US soft drinks market.

UK sales totalled £4.7 billion in 1995, when pre-tax profits soared 17% to £561 million. Cadbury Schweppes is disposing of its 51% interest in Coca-Cola Schweppes Beverages, a move that will reduce its UK work force to 10,000.

The company's group headquarters recently received Investors in People recognition, and Cadbury Schweppes was paid perhaps the ultimate compliment in 1995, when it was voted the UK's Most Admired Company in a survey conducted by *Management Today* magazine.

Company Culture and Style

Cadbury Schweppes is a highly devolved organisation. Since its transformation during the mid-1980s, the company has crystallised from a mainly UK-focused corporation into an organisation with a truly international personality.

Centralised controls are kept to a minimum in a non-bureaucratic, non-hierarchical structure, providing significant scope for personal creativity. Cadbury Schweppes welcomes ideas from all members of staff in an open, collegiate, non-political environment.

The atmosphere at head office is warm and friendly. New recruits sitting down to lunch may find themselves joined by the chairman, chief executive or members of the board, everyone addressing each other on first name terms.

Communication is the cornerstone of autonomy. A two-way flow of information enables local managers to operate independently, reporting successes and failures in a spirit of mutual interdependence.

Cadbury Schweppes has never yet mounted a hostile take-over bid, tending to make agreed acquisitions of organisations with similar credos. On some occasions, the company has even won the day despite being outbid by a third party, with the target company more attracted by the better cultural fit with Cadbury Schweppes.

Human Resource Priorities

The task confronting Cadbury Schweppes' team of HR professionals appears straightforward—recruiting, developing and motivating the best people. However, that policy is merely the starting point for a series of strategies relating to key business initiatives.

As profits increasingly stem from beyond the UK, cultural beliefs must be disseminated throughout the international community and appropriate training and recruitment vehicles put in place. For example, Cadbury Schweppes is strongly committed to continuous learning across all levels of the organisation, a philosophy stretching from the factory floor to the boardroom. Over recent years, Cadbury Schweppes has rolled-out a development programme aimed at its top 150 executives world-wide, combining conceptual learning with practical applications—effectively how to improve the business on a day-to-day basis.

'Best practice' ideas must also be taken across the group. Cadbury Schweppes' HR team strives to take advantage of local successes, applying any valuable lessons learned throughout the organisation.

Charged with integrating a range of companies acquired around the world over the last 10 years, Cadbury Schweppes' HR function has been proactive in assisting operating executives to blend the new companies in with the rest of the group.

The HR function (and budget) is relatively decentralised, with all business units receiving an appropriate level of support. Teams range in size from two specialists in single-location facilities, to 25 specialists serving multi-location, fully integrated sites.

Career Opportunity and Development

Cadbury Schweppes recognises the need for all employees to receive a continuous programme of training and development. Responsibility is shared, and individuals must provide the drive and initiative, with the company responding by providing the tools for growth.

Career opportunity at Cadbury Schweppes can be seen in three dimensions: functions, businesses and locations. In order to give future business heads a broad range of experiences, Cadbury Schweppes increasingly moves key people across organisational boundaries.

"I want our management," says John Sunderland, group chief executive, "to reflect the core values of our major brands—quality, consistency, reliability, performance and value for money. A vital factor will be the quality of our people, so developing the right capabilities is going to be an ongoing theme."

Employees kick-start their training process by first sitting down with their line manager to initiate a personal development plan. Once that is established, agreement is then reached about how individual and company will take the plan forward over the forthcoming 12 months.

Training can be specific, and each business unit provides training systems and programmes that meet the learning needs of its employees and the business; obviously, needs will vary considerably from one unit to the next.

As the group expands internationally, training assumes an important role. In South Africa, for example, an Adult Basic Education programme is available to help employees improve standards of literacy. Before starting a new business in China, Cadbury Schweppes provided intensive training for 250 employees, with courses ranging from chocolate manufacture to management training.

Secondments across businesses, locations and functions are increasingly regarded as crucial. Over 140 managers are currently on secondment across the globe—a figure that has more than doubled since 1992.

"Within my first three years," recalls marketing manager Liz Wilkinson, "I had two secondments abroad, in France and the USA, and experience of sales and marketing as well as engineering. The time spent in these different cultures was really an eye-opener."

Cadbury Schweppes sometimes sponsors MBA studies, providing financial support rather than sabbaticals. Increasingly, potential managers are encouraged to develop a broad range of skills in a flat organisational structure.

Pay and Benefits

Cadbury Schweppes offers rates of pay approaching the upper quartile. Increases averaged 4.5% in 1996, and the pay process is tied in with appraisals. All employees are evaluated twice each year, objectives are set down in writing, and are reviewed on an ongoing basis. Appraisals encompass an overall rating linked to a merit scheme for individual performance.

Cadbury Schweppes operates a generous Share Save scheme, open to all employees, allowing shares to be purchased at a 20% discount in three, five or seven year options.

Cadbury Schweppes provides medical insurance for senior managers and their families, associates must contribute 50% towards subscriptions. Senior executives, middle managers and sales staff also receive cars from a corporate pool of some 2,000 vehicles. The company employs a full-time medical officer and offers health screenings and physiotherapy services at the Bournville location. Other perks include a defined benefit pension scheme, discounted staff shops and a range of sports facilities.

The Future

Cadbury Schweppes has a balancing act to perform. Determined to sustain the pace of corporate growth, the company is seeking to retain a devolved structure while taking advantage of productive synergy.

Committed to proactively moving staff across boundaries, Cadbury Schweppes aims to recognise and reward managers who develop people effectively. The company is also intent upon building closer customer relationships, gaining an increasingly detailed understanding of the competitive dynamics of retailing.

Group HR director Bob Stack: "We need to continue innovating in all areas of the business. This includes our products, how we manage our brands, and policies towards people. We must also foster an environment of continuous learning, spreading best practice information. None of these challenges will get any easier as the company continues to spread round the globe."

Cadbury Schweppes appears well equipped to meet all these challenges and more. Quality management, marketing expertise and contented employees create a blend that is widely envied throughout British industry, a world-class company primed to succeed on the international stage.

CHARTERHOUSE

Charterhouse

Charterhouse plc is a holding company co-ordinating the activities of three subsidiaries that provide investment banking, development capital and stockbroking services. Charterhouse has £200 million of capital and employs 400 people in London. It is backed by £70 billion of assets and £3 billion of capital from its joint owners.

Formerly owned by the Royal Bank of Scotland plc, Charterhouse was sold in 1993. Two substantial European players bought equal shares in the operation: BHF-BANK, one of the ten largest private commercial banks in Germany, and Crédit Commerciale de France (CCF), a leading French retail and investment bank.

Biggest Plus: A niche investment bank with a friendly, human face

Biggest Minus: No place for macho bankers with red braces!

Charterhouse plc
1 Paternoster Row
St Paul's
London   EC4M 7DH
Tel: 0171-248 4000
Fax: 0171-334 3501

The Business

The change of ownership had far-reaching consequences. Charterhouse now has a new set of corporate cultures, a pan-European remit, and a determination to excel in its market niches. Chief executive Michael Hepher: "I believe that we have the basis on which to build a group which will be a compelling choice for corporates wanting to do business in Europe. After all, we have banks where other people have branches."

So Charterhouse now has the vision of building something unique in Europe: a medium-sized European investment bank that specialises in certain key areas of expertise. Those areas are corporate finance, structured finance, development capital and agency stockbroking. Hepher: "Charterhouse...cannot be good at everything. What is needed is focus. We want designated areas of excellence." This process is already well under way.

Company Culture and Style

People who joined one of Charterhouse's subsidiaries—Charterhouse Bank Limited, Charterhouse Development Capital or Charterhouse Tilney Securities—before 1993 speak of a friendly and warm but slightly old-fashioned organisation. Some felt that it lacked a certain impetus and discipline. Following the sale, the organisation has become more dynamic without losing its friendly atmosphere.

Empowerment and responsibility within working groups is fostered by the company's fairly flat structure. But, although Charterhouse people work hard, there's a reassuring lack of the cut-throat, backstabbing culture sometimes encountered in investment banking. The relatively small size undoubtedly helps here. In quiet periods, no one is expected to sit at a desk into the small hours. Nor is there anything macho about not taking holidays; staff are encouraged to take their full allowance.

The new European aspect of the operations is undoubtedly the most important cultural change for Charterhouse. It was always a meritocracy where talent was the only requirement for advancement, but it retained a British character. Now the place is far more cosmopolitan, with French, German, American and even Bulgarian accents to be heard. Any 'traditional' barriers that may have existed are fast disappearing under this influence.

Group personnel director Keith Robinson points out an interesting aspect of the new Charterhouse: "Having two shareholders rather than one gives us a unique quality. It results in much more of a partnership. For instance, decision making increasingly involves all three players. Obviously Charterhouse itself is the smaller partner with 400 staff compared to BHF-BANK's 3,100 and CCF's 10,700. But we have our own centres of excellence and definitely have a part to play."

The next task on the cultural front is to integrate the disparate styles. This has already advanced some way within Charterhouse, with committees made up of all parts of the organisation. *Grapevine,* a frequent and chatty newsheet, reports on promotions, departures, and other personnel matters. There's also an annual briefing by the chief executive that brings everyone together. The next stage is to streamline cultures right across the European group, which will be more difficult but also highly rewarding.

In London, Charterhouse has a charitable committee that encourages people to get involved in good causes. These include working with a hostel that aims to get homeless people back into employment. Charterhouse staff not only raise funds and donate equipment but also provide hands-on help such as assistance with interview techniques.

Human Resource Priorities

HR takes a high priority at Charterhouse. The company is committed to fair and equal payment policy, and to enabling its employees to realise their full potential. This is done by providing training and development opportunities wherever required, and by promoting entirely on merit and performance.

All senior management are involved in succession planning, salary reviews, and staff development and training. All HR policy decisions must be approved by the Charterhouse plc board. And the effectiveness of these HR policies are monitored through structured frameworks and processes.

Charterhouse's size is an advantage here: it's small enough to care, but large enough to put the right resources in place. The HR department is accessible to all staff, and sees itself as existing to help and represent staff as well as management.

An Attitude Survey in 1991 confirmed that HR policy was on the right track. As Robinson says, "These surveys don't usually tell you things you didn't know, but they do make it easier to quantify information."

Career Opportunity and Development

One disadvantage of being relatively small-scale is that succession planning is difficult. Now, as part of a European consortium and with a presence in New York, this disadvantage is a thing of the past for Charterhouse. There is now much greater career diversity, coupled with an organisation and structure that allows people to progress.

A graduate recruitment programme was formerly in place at Charterhouse but was abolished in 1989. The reason was that, in investment banking, graduates are often of little use until they have acquired basic skills. It was also costly, since 65% of graduates change companies within their first 18 months. Charterhouse now prefers to take graduates after they've built up some expertise—and decided where their future lies.

Career development can be rapid at Charterhouse. People identified through the succession planning process as having strong potential can enter a fast-track. The current group finance director, also a plc board member, joined as an accountant in 1980 and rose through the ranks, and a number of other staff rose swiftly to director level. Where possible, promotion is internal.

There is an extensive range of external training courses designed to build up competencies as the staff progress in their careers. Internal courses supplement these competencies with language training and presentation skills. A recently developed modular training programme is now in place. Employees are also sponsored to further their qualifications: these may include Institute of Banking courses or MBAs. Sabbaticals are also permitted, and several staff have taken a year off to travel the world and then returned to their positions.

The new group structure inevitably led to some job losses where duplication of operations existed. For instance, Charterhouse formerly had quite a large derivatives department, but CCF had a far larger operation. Overall, 100 redundancies were made in the last three years, almost all as a result of such changes. Compensation included ex gratia payments and outplacement counselling according to individual circumstances.

Pay and Benefits

The sharp end of banking is all about risk and reward. For those who perform, the rewards are high—but so are the risks if performance falls off. In support areas, this equation does not apply and so a more typical reward structure is in place. The average salary for administrative staff at Charterhouse is £20,800, rising to £42,000 at the top end. Managers could be looking at £50,000 while the average executive director salary is over £80,000. These are within the median and higher quartile levels of the industry. A significant element of compensation is variable through a discretionary bonus scheme.

Pay increases are assessed by an annual appraisal process that takes into account both individual and group performance; teamworking is vital at Charterhouse.

Benefits include a profit-related pay scheme, private medical insurance for all employees (and dependants if they wish), cars for managers and above (with a cash alternative), a non-contributory final salary pension scheme and a senior executive pension scheme, a mortgage subsidy for all employees, free meals, season ticket loans, a sports and social club and a ball every 18 months. Staff also enjoy discounts of anything up to 20% in a range of London shops: the scheme includes clothing, foreign currency, cosmetics, luxury gifts and jewellery.

The Future

Charterhouse has consciously decided not to attempt to offer full investment banking services but to concentrate on certain quality areas. Before the 'Big Bang', big was definitely beautiful: if that attitude returned, the stance of the bank could be difficult to maintain. Nevertheless, in today's cost-conscious world, expertise in selective areas looks like a sensible proposition.

Investment banking is a rapidly changing market. To keep pace with the competition, Charterhouse needs to maintain and increase research and development spending to offer the right products at the right time. But banking is and always will be a people business; personalities and the confidence that they engender are vital.

This is where the business and HR goals of Charterhouse overlap. As Robinson says, "People represent 70% of our fixed cost base. Some banks indulge heavily in the transfer market, but our policy is to retain our own top people. This won't be easy with much bigger competitors around, but we will aim to achieve it by giving our people more challenges, more opportunities and a more satisfying working environment. Being part of a powerful continental consortium should give our people the best of both worlds: friendly atmosphere and scope for development across Europe."

Christian Salvesen

Christian Salvesen PLC

Christian Salvesen is a tightly focused truly international business with turnover in excess of £600 million; 50% of its operating profits is generated overseas. Three key business areas are concentrated on—logistics distribution, Aggreko specialist hire, and food services. Together the group employs around 14,500 people. The company constantly reviews ways in which it can achieve further strong and consistent growth.

Biggest Plus: Separate divisions pull together towards common goals

Biggest Minus: Profit-related pay only operates in some parts of the business

Christian Salvesen PLC
50 East Fettes Avenue
Edinburgh EH4 1EQ
Tel: 0131-559 3600
Fax: 0131-559 3655

The Business

Ask anyone what the name Christian Salvesen means to them and they will probably conjure up a picture of a company with roots in shipping and fishing, stemming from the nineteenth century. Certainly everyone within Salvesen is proud of the company's 150-year-old history and traditions. They provide a thread of continuity as the group continues to commit substantial investment in training and development to provide for the future of the Salvesen name.

Christian Salvesen has established a reputation as a leading player in each of its operational activities—where each of its three businesses and the group as a whole are financially strong. The strength of the group lies in its proven ability to continuously evolve in line with changes in the market place.

Dr Chris Masters, group chief executive, said: "We have a very clear strategy and have indicated to our shareholders that we are willing and able to examine all methods which could be used to enhance shareholder value."

Salvesen will embark on any of these, only if the company is convinced it is in the best interests of its shareholders. "None of the current areas under examination is one which is new to us," he added.

Company Culture and Style

Salvesen continues to recognise that its culture is directly related to maintaining the company's competitive edge. As Richard Coles, head of human resources and member of the management board, puts it: "It is recognition that if we are to be successful, we must have the right culture, and all employees must understand the value of it."

His HR colleague, Louise Clarkson, recruitment and development manager, described the company's cultural style as fair but firm, and one that achieves an atmosphere of integrity and openness. "This is a very hard-working business and personal expectations are equally high."

Salvesen is not a company to work for if you do not expect to put in extra effort. The company is both demanding and challenging and these two attributes are fed through from customers' own requirements.

Salvesen likes to keep its structures of daily working practices flat. This means that the company's decision makers keep very close to the point of action. Senior managers are both visible and accessible in the work place. In the past, management style has been more paternalistic, but this has changed for ever.

Coles said they discovered recently from employees' comments that in one certain part of the group, communications could be better. "Two links in the chain were therefore removed, leading to a more open channel."

Salvesen places great weight on its employees' opinion survey, conducted every two years on an independent basis by specialists SIA, and in consultation with other companies which Salvesen rates. It checks out its style of management and whether, as Coles described it, "the system works".

"The survey is not about pushing out platitudes. It represents the real method of discovering whether best use is made of our people's skills. Employees tell us what they really think and that is perhaps its greatest strength."

Each of the group's three businesses is considered to have its own distinctive culture, reflecting both the history and individual market place. Yet an atmosphere of openness continues to be generated within the group as a whole. This augers well as Salvesen implements its strategy for the future.

Human Resource Priorities

HR strategy has changed fairly dramatically in recent years. Now in place is a more tailor-made and proactive human resources policy for each business sector within the group. The company believes that it has recognised the importance of developing people properly. It has therefore established a series of fundamental principles and a more decentralised system of implementing them. Line management holds the primary HR responsibility and decisions are taken through an interface with those involved, rather than by any far-off head office dictum.

Works Councils give employees an enhanced opportunity to voice their opinions. Head of HR Richard Coles says the councils have been established in parts of the group for some years. "We had briefing groups since the 1970s but felt we had to go a stage further. Now employees feel sufficiently empowered to raise issues, within properly elected councils which meet regularly."

Chief executive Chris Masters briefs head office staff monthly, encouraging them to be open and to ask questions whatever the subject matter. In all, Salvesen's HR strategy is centred around building teams to create the climate so that the group's business strategy can be achieved.

Part of the HR strategy is to encourage Salvesen people to be curious. "If our people want to know what is happening and why, this leads to good communications," Coles said. Self-development is a process shared between company and individual.

Career Opportunity and Development

All parts of the company are committed to training, but type and level varies depending upon the area of business involved. One section can be involved in NVQs/SVQs work through trained assessors, while others can be found working towards Investors in People.

Salvesen recognises that to be a market leader or at least in the top three in each of its businesses, it needs the best people. Salvesen used to run a central graduate recruitment scheme. This was decentralised in 1995 and the various businesses now recruit their own, from those universities with which they have built good working relationships over the years. This decentralised approach represents what Salvesen describes as a "degree of ownership" and is aimed at improving retention of graduate employees.

The linkages are clear: "To meet growth targets we need to grow people and improve productivity," said Louise Clarkson.

Expenditure on training is regularly monitored in the Salvesen businesses and on a quarterly basis group-wide. Within an evolving strategy, a regular management development audit monitors the effectiveness of training and development of key people.

In addition to end-of-course evaluation, subsequent follow-up is mandatory. Achievements of a particular training course are measured against objectives established by both supervisor and subordinate.

The Salvesen opinion survey includes questions on both adequacy and effectiveness of training. Chief executive Chris Masters regularly attends in-house training courses, a move viewed by the company as having a positive impact on employees.

Richard Coles: "Unfortunately, we live in a world where employment for life cannot be guaranteed. Our training and development, however, equips employees not only for their current tasks within Salvesen, but also for their future careers."

Pay and Benefits

Salvesen says it pays at least the median rates of pay set against the market place and aims to pay at the upper quartile for appropriate performance. Structures are flexible and reflect an individual's personal contribution.

No upper limits to earning potential are imposed, nor are there any rigid salary scales in place. Each job is evaluated on a consistent basis. The average graduate starting salary in 1996 was set at £15,500.

An SAYE scheme is in operation and 25% of employees are also shareholders. Each subsidiary business operates bonus schemes directly linked to profitability. All permanent employees are offered company pension scheme membership. A system of profit-related pay is operated within some parts of the group's businesses.

Private medical insurance is offered, at management discretion, to employees above a certain salary minimum. 'Job status' company cars are offered to senior employees. 'Job need' cars are allocated where travel is involved in the region of 15,000 miles per annum. Cash alternatives may be offered at 25% list price. Staff discounts are available on personal travel.

The Future

Chief executive Chris Masters believes that strong and consistent growth represents the real key towards developing lasting shareholder value. He is convinced that Salvesen will deliver.

The company believes that employees' values and awareness will help Salvesen meet future objectives and that an ongoing process of open communication within its organisation has helped greatly.

The challenge now and in the foreseeable future is one of achieving consolidation on the significant progress made throughout the Salvesen business. The group is, according to its chief executive, well placed to return to the path of profitable growth.

Churchill Insurance Company

Churchill is the second largest direct response insurance company in the UK and one of the fastest-growing insurers in Europe. This £200 million business is wholly owned by the Winterthur Group, Europe's fourth largest insurance organisation: this association provides financial strength and support but Churchill retains its operational autonomy. The company employs 1,080 people in the UK and a further 20 in New Delhi, India.

Biggest Plus: Great fun to work for

Biggest Minus: Difficult to join if you've already worked in insurance!

Churchill Insurance Company Limited
Churchill House
17 London Road
Bromley
Kent BR1 1DE
Tel: 0181-313 3030
Fax: 0181-313 5361

The Business

Churchill is a great British success story. The company is very much the brainchild of chairman and chief executive Martin Long, whose thorough-going experience with UK mainstream insurers convinced him that British customers would respond well to genuinely excellent service. As a result, he asked Swiss giant Winterthur to fund a new company. Interestingly, even the name of the company was chosen because it embodies so many of its attributes: Britishness, trust, strength and perseverance.

The company began life in June 1989 with 88 employees selling car insurance policies, and added home insurance products the following year. Today, Churchill has nearly 900,000 customers and its employees have burgeoned to 1,100. Exceptional service underlies that growth rate. Indeed, the company's vision is to deliver the unquestioned, publicly acknowledged, best customer service in the insurance industry world-wide. Martin Long believes that the company is already on the way to achieving that, and is probably already number one in Europe.

He is not alone in that opinion. A third of new business comes from recommendations and 85% of existing business is renewed. (Most competitors can only marvel at the renewal rate, as the industry average is below 60%.) Customers send in 150,000 comment forms a year without any incentive to do so—and over 99% of those customers are highly satisfied. Third-party endorsements are also not uncommon. The Halifax Building Society chose Churchill to sell motor insurance after a rigorous evaluation of the top 20 such insurers in the UK. In their words, "We felt that our customers deserved to have the highest standards of service." Furthermore, companies such as Shell have visited Churchill to study its approach.

Company Culture and Style

The company is characterised by a flat and remarkably open structure. The attitude is one of continuous improvement, and everyone is encouraged to make suggestions. From January to mid-October 1996 the tally was already 5,600. Team leaders and managers must respond to a suggestion within five days, or the person has the right to take it to the next level. This enthusiasm for improvement is partly due to the rewards on offer (anyone whose suggestion earns the company £500,000 or more will receive a free flat in Bromley!) but more to the fact that people feel empowered and part of the company's future. Churchill is going places fast and making waves in the industry. The team spirit and sense of togetherness in place at Churchill is unusual and perhaps unique in its industry.

The company has an impressive record of innovation. The firsts already include service guarantees, wholly owned garages to ensure the highest standards of repair work, courtesy cars for customers when there own are off the road, a customer loyalty programme, and much more. In a typical move, the company opened an IT software subsidiary in India in February 1996 linked to Britain by satellite. At a stroke this confirmed Churchill as having the best software in the industry, capable of handling 18 million transactions a day; gave it a source of excellent, well-educated programmers; and allowed it to process work round the clock thanks to the time overlaps.

The company demands hard work and commitment from its people; but it is also highly supportive. It is both fun and rewarding to work for: long-service awards of £150 after three years (!), Top Dog awards for good performers, Star Performers and a Hall of Fame for outstanding performance (with rewards of weekend breaks), Silly Hat days and much more go to prove this point. Employees are actually exhorted to have fun and enjoy their work in the company's values.

A striking aspect of the company's style is its openness. Martin Long meets all new recruits when they begin their training. Even more surprising is the concept of the In Touch days. Martin and his fellow executives such as HR director Michael Raywood will do other people's jobs for a day. As Michael says, "This not only makes us more accessible, we learn a tremendous amount ourselves—and we can often make people's jobs easier as a result." Clearly, Churchill is an unusual insurance company. It is also unusually successful. At a time when other insurers and brokerages are losing direction and being swallowed up, this company knows exactly where it's going.

Human Resource Priorities

Martin Long: "Most people have tremendous energy and talent—but they never use it at work. We try to harness this, so that people want to come to work. This is all about empowerment. Bureaucracy frustrates people, so we have as little as possible. Instead, everyone is encouraged to develop and grow."

In short, HR has high priority—and this attitude can be seen throughout Churchill's operations. After training, new recruits have mentors, people not in their chain of command, who can help them. Development Centres for managers help keep them on top of HR issues. The company is the sole UK insurer to have both Investors in People and ISO 9002 (the only recognised quality award for service companies).

Employees are regularly quizzed on their opinions. The questions are often quite trenchant: "What would you change about your job? What would you change about the company?" Half-yearly questionnaires are supplemented by constant feedback and two-way communication.

Career Opportunity and Development

Churchill staff are recruited on personality. Previous insurance experience is almost a disadvantage in all but technical areas such as underwriting. Far more important are confidence, enthusiasm, intelligence and the ability to learn. Those who answer the company's recruitment adverts are given telephone interviews and the successful candidates invited for an array of intelligence, keyboard skills and personality tests. On average, one in three ends up joining Churchill—and often decides to stay there.

Once on board, employees can expect excellent training. For three weeks, recruits do nothing but absorb knowledge—and demonstrate their understanding through regular written, telephone and customer care tests. They are then 'buddied' for perhaps four weeks, eased into full-time work through close contact and support from an experienced member of staff. Given that many other insurers put new recruits to work almost immediately, Churchill's reputation for outstanding customer service becomes easier to understand.

Development is ongoing after this initial period. Training and development contracts with each staff member identify the next step forward. Language training, MBAs, professional qualifications: the company will support people throughout extra training wherever appropriate.

Employees also develop through a multi-skills approach. Once competent in one skill, for example sales, an employee can move on to learn another, say claims. Awards are given, rising to Gold (and £500) for three-skill employees. This is great news for staff and also for customers, who are far less likely to be shunted around when ringing with questions.

Pay and Benefits

The company sees itself as an above-average payer for its sector. Pay rises are determined solely on performance, as measured by the review procedure. As a result of the reviews, pay rises can be from 0% to 15%—although a zero increase would indicate serious performance problems. Pay can also be considerably enhanced through productivity. For instance, one employee has sold over 16,000 policies.

Benefits include an excellent money purchase pension scheme with company contributions as a percentage of salary rising from 5% to 10% with service (7% to 12% for managers). There is also a profit-related pay scheme, although not for anyone with a record of excessive sickness or bad discipline. Other benefits are private medical cover that can be expanded to include family members, life cover, a car or cash alternative for managers, and great working conditions for everyone.

The Future

The first challenge for Churchill is to maintain its profitable growth in a mature, deregulated market. It will be aided here by its powerful parent, but even more by its care for customers and staff. "Quality of customer service represents the only long-term competitive advantage," says Martin Long. "Products, IT and strategy can all be copied, but outstanding customer service cannot be replicated overnight. We've worked hard for seven years putting ours in place."

Of course, other companies will try to match Churchill's impressive customer service; but while they do so, Churchill will continue to innovate. It has an array of services lined up for introduction. For instance, the company already has a guarantee whereby it approves a repair within an hour of being informed of it. If it fails to do so, it gives the customer £20 back. In Martin Long's opinion, Churchill is not far off being able to offer customers all their money back—a guarantee that will give its competitors further headaches!

Although Churchill's market place will continue to remain highly competitive, the company does seem to have a genuine edge based on a radical vision, a deep commitment to customer care and staff development, and a refreshingly different way of operating. All these attributes combine to make Churchill one of Britain's best employers.

CLIFFORD CHANCE

Clifford Chance

Clifford Chance is a European-based, international law firm offering a full range of legal services to businesses, financiers and governments. Clifford Chance is firmly positioned as one of the leading law firms in the City of London, Clifford Chance employs 2,000 people in the UK, 3,300 world-wide.

Biggest Plus: Excellent rewards and superb overseas career development openings

Biggest Minus: Certainly not a nine-to-five job

Clifford Chance
200 Aldersgate Street
London EC1A 4JJ
Tel: 0171-600 1000
Fax: 0171-600 5555

The Business

A 1987 merger between the firms Clifford Turner and Coward Chance created Clifford Chance. Immediately following the formation, the firm employed 1,200 people. In less than ten years the total has nearly trebled—despite severe recessions in the interim. Today, the firm is recognised as a leader in its field. The *Legal 500* says of it: "Clifford Chance will often be the firm that introduces change, with other City law firms content to sit on the sidelines and watch."

Clifford Chance is the largest firm within the UK legal profession. It also has the largest network of overseas offices, with 24 locations. These cover all the main European centres from Spain to Russia but also include offices in the USA, the Middle East and the Far East. Firmly convinced that the demand for legal services will become ever more international, the firm intends to expand this network even further in the future. As a result, opportunities for working overseas are excellent for Clifford Chance lawyers.

Size is less important than quality. Clifford Chance is totally committed to delivering the highest quality professional service to its clients. In fact, Clifford Chance's size is a result of its quality.

Company Culture and Style

The culture at Clifford Chance is extremely professional, yet is unusually friendly and informal for a law firm. The feeling is one of openness, team working and good communications. Although it is the largest City law firm and one of the most successful, Clifford Chance is keen to avoid complacency. As a result, it has a reputation for dynamism, innovation and creativity.

Interestingly, no fewer than 40% of Clifford Chance lawyers have non-law degrees. The firm sees this as an advantage in two ways, as head of personnel Alistair Dawson confirms: "This policy allows us to obtain a greater number of top-class people. It also provides our people a wider pool of experience. Engineering can give a useful insight into intellectual property cases as can medicine into product liability. Chemistry, economics and languages all have their value here. And of course even an unrelated degree can be evidence of sound training and a willingness to learn."

Because of the nature of its clients and their requirements, working for Clifford Chance can be demanding. The London office never closes, with shifts of secretaries working round the clock to support the lawyers—some of whom will be at the office at any given time. It is better to think of the lifestyle in terms of a merchant bank than of a high-street solicitor's. Or perhaps the lifestyle of a hospital doctor may be a better analogy, since when transactions are being handled lawyers at the firm may find themselves working for 36 hours non-stop! This hard work is, however, offset by excellent rewards, outstanding facilities, absorbing career prospects and a strong sense of camaraderie.

Simon Davis, recruitment partner, sums up what it takes to flourish at the firm. "There are certain qualities you must have to succeed here: dedication to the job, an imaginative approach to problem solving, the ability to get on with other people and masses of energy." However, there is a great deal of support available as people learn the job and become more experienced. People are not criticised for making mistakes but for not seeking guidance.

Internal communications takes the form of an informal weekly publication *Clifford Chance News*, a glossy quarterly called *The Link*, and much use of noticeboards, meetings and email. Nevertheless, the firm is eager to improve on this even further and is upweighting and professionalising its whole internal communications function.

Human Resource Priorities

As Alistair Dawson puts it, "This organisation has only one resource: its people. We don't have a product as such, and we don't physically manufacture anything. We succeed or fail by the quality and professionalism of our people." Not surprisingly therefore, the firm is deeply committed to human resources and to the welfare and development of its individuals.

A major survey among all Clifford Chance staff canvassed their opinions on a whole range of human resources-related issues. The findings of this survey was taken very seriously by senior management, and a number of initiatives now in place at the firm are the direct result of the survey.

This process still continues today with HR initiatives being debated. Many legal firms have perhaps the flattest structure of any British businesses, with just three levels: trainees, lawyers and partners. Whether this is appropriate for the future, or whether there is a better career and development structure, is currently being debated within the firm. This and other HR issues will continue to be discussed at Clifford Chance as part of its drive to produce ever more effective HR policies.

Career Opportunity and Development

Graduates who join Clifford Chance as trainee lawyers receive an outstanding training package which includes considerable responsibility from the outset. The two-year training period comprises four six-month periods in different areas within the firm, working with senior lawyers on a day-to-day basis.

About 50% of trainees spend one of their training periods abroad. Responsibility is also very much up to them. If an individual wants more responsibility and is capable of handling it, there are very few barriers.

Following the training period, trainees become qualified as lawyers. No fewer than 97% of the most recent generation of trainees were offered jobs with the firm on qualification.

Once qualified, lawyers take on increasing responsibilities. Progress thereafter depends entirely on performance. Those who demonstrate outstanding technical and personal qualities may be invited to join the partnership, in effect share ownership of the business. The ratio of lawyers to partners at Clifford Chance is 4:1. Some individuals have achieved partnership within six years of qualifying. By their mid-thirties, it is usually apparent who will or will not reach partner level.

Not becoming a partner is not always a criticism; in some business areas, for instance, no new partners may be required. In this situation, some people move into different areas of the firm and achieve partnership there. Others prefer to move to other legal firms or indeed to clients or other companies. Thanks to the reputation of Clifford Chance, this is usually not difficult.

One of the factors underlying that reputation is the sheer quality of the training, recognised even by rival firms as excellent. Training takes two forms: technical and non-technical skills. Most courses, co-designed by the firm and external training consultants, take place in-house or at residential training centres. The remainder would be purely external.

Pay and Benefits

The firm regards itself as being towards the top of its market place in terms of remuneration. Employees rise through pay scales according to their experience. In 1996 trainees earned £19,000 in their first year and £21,500 in their second; qualified lawyers started at £28,000 and after 18 months qualified experience move onto scales. One constant factor in remuneration policy for all staff is that the firm rewards performance. Already competitive in the market place, individuals are reviewed on merit annually, and bonuses are paid for outstanding performance or unusually demanding work.

Benefits include a minimum of 22 days' holiday, a profit-related pay scheme, an interest-free season ticket scheme or staff loan facility, private health insurance, a nurse on site and a firm's doctor, a subsidised restaurant, life assurance and permanent health insurance. Employees in the modern London office also have an impressive array of additional benefits including a swimming pool, a gymnasium, squash courts and a fitness centre. There is also a choice of final salary and money purchase pension schemes.

Performance is encouraged even before joining! Clifford Chance pays a prize of £600 to anyone who achieves an all-important first class honours degree after accepting an offer from the firm, and a similar prize for achieving an overall distinction in the Legal Practice Course.

The Future

The international ambit of the firm creates its own challenges. For instance, its international offices are growing faster than the London operation. As a result, management structures, personnel and training must continue to develop internationally.

A permanent challenge—and of most relevance to an expanding firm like Clifford Chance—is to maintain the highest standards of client service and professional quality. Clifford Chance believes that if it gets the issue of quality right—in the calibre of its staff; by instilling customer service as an instinct; by encouraging team work; and in the way the firm treats its staff, then the quality of the product will be easy to deliver.

The market place is increasingly competitive. US firms are tending to set up operations in London, while accountancy firms are offering their own legal services. In facing these competitive challenges, Clifford Chance will need to be responsive and sustain its reputation for excellence if the firm is to continue to grow as quickly as it has.

Coca-Cola Great Britain and Ireland

Coca-Cola was first sold in 1886. Since then, Coca-Cola has become the world's premier soft drink, with the Coca-Cola Company selling nearly half of all soft drinks consumed around the world. These drinks include Fanta, Sprite, Five Alive and other well-known names as well as Coca-Cola itself. Coca-Cola is the most successful product ever marketed—and with 94% of the world population recognising the name, it is said to be the most widely understood word after "OK". The Coca-Cola Company is also the second most valuable in the world; any predator interested in mounting a take-over would have to find $100 billion. The company employs 30,000 people world-wide, 275 in the UK.

Biggest Plus: Outstanding international career opportunities

Biggest Minus: Difficult to decide where to move next; Coca-Cola is available in nearly every country!

Coca-Cola Great Britain and Ireland
1 Queen Caroline Street
London   W6 9HQ
Tel: 0181-237 3000
Fax: 0181-237 3700

The Business

The Coca-Cola Company began building its global empire in the 1920s. Today the product is available in all but a few countries world-wide and its drinks are enjoyed 873 million times every day. In the UK, Coca-Cola Great Britain and Ireland supplies syrup or concentrate to independent bottlers who add the carbonated water and sugar. The company itself is responsible for marketing throughout the UK; and the resources, advertising spend and brand awareness make marketing posts at the company highly sought-after. Indeed, a survey in *Marketing Week* three years ago confirmed that the company is clearly first choice among marketeers.

The UK is the second most important market in Europe for Coca-Cola and the other corporate brands. It is also a highly fragmented market. The big three names of Coca-Cola, Pepsi and Cadbury Schweppes together account for only 55% of the market place, while the figure for the USA would be 91%. The British Soft Drinks Association still has just under 100 members, so there remains plenty of challenge when it comes to local market share.

Company Culture and Style

There are two aspects to consider when it comes to company culture: the purely UK aspect and the global 'Coca-Cola family' one. The UK company is young, dynamic and lively: it's a fun business with all parts of the marketing mix handled. The company's main target market comprises teenagers and those in their early 20s, so youthful flair certainly helps—although increasingly people who grew up with Coca-Cola are taking their soft drink habit with them into later life. Anti drink-driving legislation, and even the current spate of hot summers, are also broadening demand!

Sally Hurley, HR manager, describes the UK culture as one where people work hard and play hard. "This is very much a can-do culture. People have lots of responsibility and know they can make a difference. We have a flat structure which means little bureaucracy. There's a real buzz, a sense of excitement about working here." The company is also noticeably professional, both in terms of the marketeers and the other employees who include finance people and technical engineers. People come in and take immediate responsibility, and are therefore highly empowered.

The work-hard side is easy to see, with employees from all functions working long hours. They are also required to be contactable at weekends and even on occasions on holiday. But the play-hard side matches this level of commitment: a Sports and Social Committee organises team challenges between the company and advertising agencies, and there is also an in-house gym. There's also a Summer Ball, a Christmas Ball, a day out at Ascot, and other events to look forward to. Last year's included a hoe-down on America's Independence Day, for example.

The other aspect of the culture is driven by the global nature of the corporation. Manager of external affairs Ian Muir joined in 1966 as a travelling auditor and spent over six years visiting over 30 countries where Coca-Cola had a presence. Many people who join the corporation in the UK go on to develop their careers by moving abroad. Expertise garnered in the UK is always required in other markets, particularly those that are less developed in terms of marketing and promotion. Mobile staff often find that the sky is the limit when it comes to their careers: four British people currently hold senior posts in the corporation's Atlanta head office.

Internal communications are well-handled. A quarterly UK publication, *Well Red*, goes to all staff: this is a superbly produced glossy with lots of news about staff and promotional campaigns. *Journey*, a quarterly produced for employees world-wide, discusses strategic issues and also reports from around the globe. Team briefings, press cuttings and noticeboards also play their part, a representative group called 'Red Cats' feeds suggestions to management, and the North West European president holds quarterly meetings on where the business is and where it's going, which are well-attended. The open-plan structure in the UK also fosters good communications, while email links everyone in the company's world.

Human Resource Priorities

Meeting the needs of employees is vital for Coca-Cola. As an example of how seriously HR issues are taken, the chief executive of the company world-wide has raised the focus of people even higher recently. His challenge is for everyone in the group to double their skills by the year 2000.

In addition, many efforts are being made to make Coca-Cola a leading organisation in people terms. This is being done through initiatives relating to knowledge sharing, as well as encouraging employees to take responsibility for their own training and development.

A Personnel Development Review sets objectives for everyone in the UK company at the beginning of each year. Here as elsewhere, the idea is to challenge people to go beyond the usual, to become more effective, and to get more out of working life.

Career Opportunity and Development

Ian Muir: "Every annual review contains a Learning Contract, which encourages people to add to their skills. These can range from presentation skills to full-scale career development. They don't even have to be work-related; anything which adds to self-confidence and motivation could be supported by the company. More academic courses such as MBAs are of course also considered."

Brighter and more talented individuals with the desire to learn, the ability to react to change and work as part of a team are sought out for rapid development. A senior vice president, currently number four in the entire organisation, started work only 25 years ago as a junior accountant. Indeed, lots of senior people are young: the head of North West Europe attained his current office around the age of 35, while his female predecessor made head of Great Britain and Ireland by 32.

For those prepared to work abroad, Coca-Cola offers a truly outstanding set of career opportunities. In fact there are so many opportunities, it can be a problem deciding where to move next! Development is aided by a blend of internal and external training, which at higher levels might take individuals from the UK to Atlanta for courses.

The company has no graduate recruitment programme with formal induction and training, since virtually all employees come on board trained in their field to a high level. Employees are likely to be either graduates or of graduate calibre, reinforcing the professionalism of the company.

Pay and Benefits

Pay is reviewed on the anniversary of either joining or being promoted. Pay increases are determined by personal performance and with reference to an employee's place in the pay grade structure. Overall the company sees itself as an upper quartile payer.

Benefits include a company pension, a private health scheme, life cover, and a share option scheme. Since July 1991, UK personnel have been able to join an excellent share save scheme: they can invest 3% of their salary into Coca-Cola shares and the company will also contribute 3%—the equivalent of a 3% salary rise. Free travel cards, a subsidised restaurant, free use of the gym and a free case of Coca-Cola a month are also part of the package. Furthermore, employees can buy extra supplies of the company's drinks at wholesale rates.

The Future

A key challenge for the company is to find and keep the best people. All this growth creates special problems for the UK company. Sally Hurley: "Resourcing our expansion, particularly in Eastern Europe and the Far East, sucks people out of the UK company and from other sophisticated countries. We are currently exporting a lot of very good people. The way to meet this challenge is to continue to recruit only the best, but perhaps widen the geographic base. We still want the best UK marketeers, but now also consider hiring from across Europe and even further afield."

World-wide, opportunities remain almost infinite for the group. Its products still account for only 5% of the world's liquid consumption. In Mexico, per capita consumption of Coca-Cola products is 300 cans a year; in China, it is currently only five. The challenge is to grow world market share while fending off similar efforts from the competition, which again requires excellent marketeers and other specialists.

COMMERCIAL UNION

Commercial Union

Commercial Union is one of the UK's leading international insurance companies with major operations in Europe and in 80 countries around the world. 22,000 staff work for the company—8,600 in the UK—handling annual premium income which reached £9,608 million in 1995. Total world-wide assets stand at £56 billion. Commercial Union shares are quoted on the London Stock Exchange and the Paris Bourse.

The group conducts life and general assurance, and offers other financial services products, including pensions, unit trust and investment management. The biggest part of the business is in the UK, but major contributions come from the USA, France (Groupe Victoire), Holland (Delta Lloyd) and Australia.

Biggest Plus: Enlightened financial services company; real empowerment of individuals

Biggest Minus: Much change to grapple with, policies still evolving

Commercial Union plc
St. Helen's
1 Undershaft
London EC3P 3DQ
Tel: 0171-283 7500
Fax: 0171-662 8140

The Business

Commercial Union (CU) has strong traditions. The Hand-in-Hand Fire and Life Insurance Society, the oldest surviving British fire insurance society, celebrated its 300th birthday in 1996. The Hand-in-Hand was merged with Commercial Union in 1905. But it is hard to find a more progressive insurance company today than Commercial Union.

The company is global and is organised along territorial lines, although it is exploring which entities of its business might be international. Chief executive, John Carter and his team focus strategy on balancing the global businesses to offset downturns in any one area, by expanding CU's life business internationally and improving the quality of its general insurance business. The UK might still be the 'pump' of the business, but the acquisition of Groupe Victoire in 1994 reveals the company's international aspirations.

In the UK, the four main business areas are Investment Management, Life, General Insurance and Marine. The company's goal in the UK is pre-eminence, and it seeks to achieve a proper balance between the needs of key stakeholders—CU's owners, customers and employees/business partners. Realising that it needs to pay more attention to employees, CU has embarked on a cultural journey which will lead the company towards 'Best Place to Work'.

Company Culture and Style

'Best Place to Work' has become the brand name for cultural change. Having 'printed the label', the company then asked its staff what they understood it to mean. CU approached 770 employees in a matter of two weeks, through 110 focus groups, and asked "What would it be like if CU was 'Best Place to Work'? What would you keep and what would you want to start doing? What would you stop and what would you continue?"

A year later, the company revisited employees through a survey to see how it had stacked up against what it had said. 420 delegates were voted from around the business, and assembled along with 80 senior managers at the 1995 'Fast Forward' conference, held at the NEC in Birmingham. Tony Clarry, UK divisional director: "The level of energy was incredible. 'Stop tolerating mediocrity' and 'get rid of passengers' were some of the cries from the floor. There was flag-waving like the Last Night of the Proms. But we were only just beginning..."

CU believes that the danger in so-called business process engineering is in throwing the baby out with the bath water, which it decided not to do. Instead, a low-key approach was preferred, involving working out better ways to do things. For example, in its General Insurance business, 'Bubble' was born. At a few designated sites CU, in co-operation with the union, suspended all rules and gave staff the freedom to change any aspect of any job. Everything was up for grabs. The response was enthusiastic, and the process has begun to accelerate. CU stressed that the objective was not just to lose jobs, but to create new ways of doing things. This includes changing the way jobs are designed, changing systems and processes, planning and control systems, technology and human resource practices.

Some cultural direction also emerged from the company's recognition that the people want to be successful; people prefer to win rather than lose; have fun rather than not; and want to feel valued rather than unrecognised. CU is seeking to unleash these talents, and avoid changing people from the moment they walk through the corporate door.

Human Resource Priorities

In 1995, Commercial Union 'deconstructed' its UK personnel department. HR holds the key to delivering cultural change, and in turn, supports the company's strategy. CU set up five HR teams to support the business through their market-driven change programmes.

Training and development activities were focused on equipping managers and staff with a competency set which CU believes will be required for future success. Many courses and programmes are run at CU's impressive in-house training centre at its own country house in Kent. Education sought to encourage and develop an organisation built on a wider education base, including distance learning and qualifications.

Elsewhere, HR professionals considered the ideal relationship between the organisation and the people within it. The processes and systems to support change are an integral part, which includes matching reward schemes. Finally HR, as an 'internal consultancy', recognised that now that it has all these processes it is how they are introduced to management teams that will pay the rent.

CU recruits around 50 graduates each year, regardless of business conditions. The company is beginning to beam out to this audience what the modern CU is about: belonging, contributing, growing, being fairly rewarded, and fun. The message is 'Don't join if you don't subscribe'. Recruiting and getting the best from talented people is vitally important as CU strives for pre-eminence, competitive advantage and the Best Place to Work. The graduate recruitment programme supports this by providing a key input to the future pool of senior management talent and in contributing to the resourcing of key management and technical roles.

The onset of technology in the financial services industry represented a fork in the road. It could lead to a de-skilling of the work force but CU instead has opted for the other route, using IT to create bigger, better jobs, and enable richer decision making.

In remuneration policy, HR has decided to extend the variable component of pay as far as it can, so that people can see their value or contribution to the business. CU regards pay to be not just about reward, but about opportunity.

Career Opportunity and Development

Until recently, CU territorial businesses stayed within the limits of those territories. The company is now beginning to move its talent around. It has established mechanisms for developing talent and creating shared experiences for its top country managers, which feed through to succession planning.

The graduate recruitment programme has been restructured, and there is now a comprehensive management development programme in place across all its UK businesses. CU's goal is to have a development plan for every employee by the end of 1997. Development is increasingly linked to performance and competencies. Ensuring 'peak performance' has been a cornerstone of a number of programmes, particularly in the Life and Marine businesses, where all managers have been assessed against a strategic set of competencies. An understanding of the company's 'talent pool' is vital to its development portfolio and programmes.

360 degree feedback is taking hold incredibly quickly—directors were among the first to experience it—and in a feedback-rich environment, people cannot get enough of it, providing as it does objective feedback and the scope for real personal development.

Pay and Benefits

CU ranks highly in the financial services industry for pay and benefits for front line staff, although it realised sometimes for the wrong reasons. Now the company's pay levels are best described as median for base pay, and top quartile for better performers. A strong correlation is made between company and team performance and reward. Pay policy aims to be seen as 'fair', and other important considerations are merit, transparency and choice.

The company doesn't always match the top rates in the market, preferring to attract a person who wants to *do*, as opposed to be something at Commercial Union. "We don't want to buy them by the yard," says John McBrien, human resources manager, "and it is not always sensible to be the highest payer."

The Future

CU faces a number of business challenges. With many new competitors, CU continues to build its own brand. It expects to invest in the business, make it work, and harness technology. In distribution, it must continually find out what its customers want and how to reach them. And the expense base will require constant attention, as someone else will always strive to be cheaper.

Among implications for people, the overarching one is the need for adaptability. While sometimes linked to clichés like 'the learning environment', CU believes that you cannot tell people what to do under every set of circumstances. CU wants the right people in the right place, properly equipped and prepared to do the right thing for their customers. That's responsibility where it matters, at the front line.

CU also expects to become a company with greater throughput of talent—in, through, out, in again—and not the conventional in, then to the top. The company recognises that people leave at all levels of the organisation, and they also join at all levels. This creates a breeze of change, new thoughts, and opportunities for everyone. CU regards the old system of 'keep people' as the worst model of opportunity and one that serves people who worry too much about control.

CU is creating an HR system that treats its employees consistent with the way it treats its customers. The company is committed to rebuilding every HR policy within two years, and then adapting them as needed. In growing employees' competencies, CU regards technology as allowing enormous strides to be taken 'to get the place heaving'. It's heaving already, and in the right direction.

Data Connection Ltd.

Data Connection Ltd. is a world-class software development company with a unique reputation for designing complex, high quality products. Employing over 150 members of staff in the UK, Data Connection maintains offices in Enfield, Chester, Edinburgh and Washington DC.

Biggest Plus: Friendly, collegiate working environment

Biggest Minus: 'Ordinary' performance levels unacceptable

Data Connection Ltd.
100 Church Street
Enfield
Middlesex EN2 6BQ
Tel: 0181-366 1177
Fax: 0181 367 8501

The Business

Founded in 1981, Data Connection has grown from an original team of seven founders into an organisation comprising 150 (predominantly young) staff. Turnover has risen from approximately £2 million in 1983/84 to £13 million in 1995/96, with profits soaring from £250,000 to £4 million over the same period.

Data Connection is a major provider of technology at virtually all levels of communication networks, such as high performance asynchronous transfer mode switching products, complex routing protocols and complete corporate directory solutions. Customers include the development laboratories of IBM, Hewlett Packard, ICL, Hitachi, Lotus and Microsoft, as well as sophisticated end-user organisations including Barclays Bank, Citicorp and the US Library of Congress.

As the bias towards the Internet continues to gather pace, application areas addressed by the company include real-time data conferencing, email, client-server connectivity to legacy mainframes and audio access to the World Wide Web.

In the retail sector, Data Connection's area of expertise extends to hand-held scanner technology and point-of-sale applications for large retail chains.

Company Culture and Style

In an industry notorious for poor quality, project overruns and slipshod product design, Data Connection has prospered by offering customers a refreshing alternative.

Encouraging creativity, versatility and enthusiasm from all members of staff, Data Connection stresses the importance of communicating ideas, actively nurturing the desire for personal growth.

The company is organised into small development teams within a highly disciplined management structure. The office is open-plan, with areas of floor-space sectioned off for each team. Data Connection propounds the benefits of free and open communication, exchanging ideas and mutual help.

Formal and informal components blend together in a challenging environment. On a formal level, Data Connection's commitment to quality demands intellectual rigour and a disciplined approach. On an informal level, the corporate dress code imposes few restrictions.

New members of staff are assigned to tasks of genuine value at the earliest opportunity, emphasising Data Connection's commitment to stretching employees: "The atmosphere at Data Connection," proclaims software engineer David McWalter, "is a brilliant combination of professionalism and fun. The management is not a clumsy bureaucracy, but a source of genuine guidance and support. We are organised in teams typically consisting of 3–5 'techies' and a manager, which form centres of informal discussion as well as crucibles of technical development and debate. The atmosphere is relaxed enough to encourage this discussion but professional enough to allow concentration."

"At each stage," confirms development manager Conor Foley, "you're given as much responsibility as you are willing and able to take on. In my case, this meant that within a few weeks I was writing code which was soon shipping in a real product. Within a few months, I was given responsibility for designing and implementing a core component for our next project."

Human Resource Priorities

Data Connection seeks to recruit outstanding people, developing staff to the limits of their abilities, and retaining and motivating employees with challenging work and financial incentives.

Personnel issues are a boardroom priority, the drive to match HR aspirations originating from MD Ian Ferguson. Executives entering the management training programme are left in no doubt that the needs of their people are a prime responsibility.

Managers hold Status Meetings once a week with every member of their team to monitor matters of concern. Performance reviews at nine month intervals provide another invaluable source of HR feedback.

Recruitment is the dominant activity for HR professionals as the vast majority of staff join direct from university. Attracting high-calibre graduates is vital to long-term prosperity and Data Connection employs a sophisticated system to filter around a dozen entrants from some 2,000 applications per annum.

The other prime responsibility for HR staff is to provide administrative support and policy to line managers responsible for virtually all aspects of people care (pay, training, personal development).

Career Opportunity and Development

Training and development at Data Connection is woven into the fabric of the company.

Each graduate has their own training profile tailored to meet individual needs and objectives. Training is underpinned by a high level of support from mentors and managers, who can devote up to 50 days to each recruit in the first year alone.

On-the-job training and personal mentoring is supported in several significant ways. In-house seminars are specifically tailored for new recruits, covering every aspect of corporate operations; detailed technical seminars outline specific projects and business areas; exercises are designed to improve individuals' presentation and communication skills; and external conferences and courses are aimed to encourage management development and technical skills.

"As my Mum used to say," observes company director Graeme MacArthur who joined Data Connection as a graduate in 1985, "a rolling stone gathers no moss.

"My career has taken me through almost all aspects of software engineering—developing code...testing...management of code, maintenance, customers, projects and, most importantly, people. I have also started to broaden into other areas of company business—marketing, recruitment and tax evasion (just kidding)."

Individual progress is governed by personal ambition rather than any formal or restraining career structure. Virtually all promotion at Data Connection is internal, and six out of 13 members of the current board joined as graduates.

Data Connection offers excellent opportunities for secondments to the USA and travel abroad. Overseas performance is so strong (almost 90% of revenue) that the company boasts a Queen's Award For Export.

Pay and Benefits

Data Corporation is at the top of the software development industry pay league. Most graduates increase their pay levels by over 50% in fewer than two years (some more than double it). Remuneration is made up of several components:

Data Connection are firm believers in rewarding staff in accordance with contribution, and salaries may be revised on the basis of performance during nine-monthly reviews. Graduate starting salaries are kept deliberately high at £20,000 in order to attract outstanding candidates. Offers may even be increased for applicants with a relevant PhD or DPhil.

Profit share is distributed to employees according to performance. Ownership of the company is vested in the Data Connection Employee Benefit Trust, and virtually all the profits accumulated each year are transferred to the trust for distribution.

All employees enjoy a range of supplementary benefits. These include a non-contributory pension scheme, life assurance and private medical insurance schemes; corporate accommodation for new members of staff; subsidised canteens; and a flexible company car scheme which kicks-in after nine months' service.

There is also a company outing every 18 months; in 1995, this was four days' skiing in the chic French resort of Courchevel. There is an active sports scene, the company providing corporate membership of tennis, golf, squash and health clubs.

The Future

With ownership vested in the Employee Benefit Trust, Data Connection appears to have a solid framework for continued success unhindered by the whims of shareholders or stock market fluctuations.

However, the areas of software technology in which Data Connection specialises remain fast-moving and the company must stay alert to market-place developments such as the Internet and multimedia. The challenge is to create radically fresh products in short time frames without compromising Data Connection's reputation for quality. Only by extending current activities, researching fresh business and product areas while constantly embracing new technologies (for example, object-orientation, JAVA, and network computers) can the company remain competitive.

In terms of people challenges, Data Connection's plans necessitate developing managers, mentors and business unit managers at a higher rate than in the past. The company intends to redouble its efforts to foster excellent relations with UK universities, ensuring quality candidates continue to apply, helping the company remain at the forefront of software technology.

DAVIES ARNOLD COOPER

SOLICITORS

Davies Arnold Cooper

Davies Arnold Cooper (DAC) is a leading UK commercial law firm with expertise in many fields, but with an international reputation in litigation, insurance and reinsurance. Its client base includes all sizes of British and international public and private companies in the manufacturing and service industries, with particular strengths in the insurance, pharmaceutical, construction and property sectors. Based in the City, DAC has 49 partners and over 400 staff.

DAC has two City offices and another in Manchester, while overseas there is an office in Madrid and associate offices in Brussels and Hong Kong. The firm has delivered strong organic growth—fee income has increased by 31% in the last four years. The firm is very profitable. DAC's mission statement describes 'quality people in a quality business providing excellence for future success'.

Biggest Plus: A pioneering law firm, opportunities for anyone with talent

Biggest Minus: Don't expect the ways and structures of a traditional practice

Davies Arnold Cooper
8 Bouverie Street
London   EC4Y 8DD
Tel: 0171-936 2222
Fax: 0171-936 2020

The Business

Davies Arnold Cooper (DAC) has built its professional reputation on a practical and commercial approach, but it is also a pioneering firm, setting the pace for others in its profession. DAC distinguishes itself from its peers by its open culture, married to self-styled corporate values, in what is still largely a traditional profession.

The *Financial Times* Datamonitor Survey commented: "Davies Arnold Cooper differs markedly in its determination to run itself like a business rather than a traditional firm of solicitors. During the boom time of the 1980s, many firms forgot (if they ever knew) that they were indeed businesses, and failed to stick to some of the standard rules of commercial enterprises. These included open and reasonable prices, restraint in expanding staff numbers, efficient procedures and preserving unity within the organisation, and Davies Arnold Cooper's strategy can be explained by its strong and unified culture which permeates through the whole organisation."

David McIntosh, who happens to be the longest serving senior partner of any UK commercial law firm, believes that the legal profession "is terrified of change. The biggest problem is seeing change as a threat." David McIntosh doesn't, and DAC has emphasised a number of points of difference—value for money, real client service, a transparent menu of prices, and the encouragement of non-solicitors to progress to the highest levels in the firm.

Company Culture and Style

DAC is refreshingly different from other firms of solicitors. It has an entrepreneurial, creative culture, and human resources structures and policies offering real career opportunities for *all* levels of staff.

The first clue to DAC's style lies in its continuity of management. Many DAC solicitors were articled at the firm or joined as young solicitors, ensuring that DAC's pragmatic culture is imbued within. Although DAC was formed in 1927, it is the last ten years that have witnessed the fastest growth, and it has probably coped better than most in maintaining the essential camaraderie and intimacy of a small firm in this transition to becoming a larger practice.

DAC does not restrict itself in its search for 'modern brain power', combining graduates with varied academic backgrounds whichever universities they derive from, with a high proportion of school leavers who started at the bottom and came up through less traditional routes.

If clients are to receive a value-for-money service, DAC contends that legal practices need to offer a tiering of abilities to deliver the appropriate mix of expertise at optimal costs. In assembling comprehensive but nimble teams of people who can relate to diverse clients, work types and levels of responsibility, DAC encourages skilled practitioners other than partners. This paves the road of opportunity for trainees, junior solicitors, legal executives—all are client handlers at DAC.

This commitment to diversity extends beyond fee earners. While senior people in non-solicitor disciplines such as finance, marketing, human resources, and strategy planning cannot become equity partners, DAC believes quite strongly that they are equally important to the business.

DAC is a hard-working, highly professional firm, but it very much has a 'human face'. The satirical in-house magazine *Hazlitt* is an avid read, as is the excellent *DAC Reports*, the firm's annual external magazine. Written by its own law-yers, *DAC Reports* previews current legal and business issues in a lively, plain-talking, and informative style. And the firm has a great band—a rock and roll band that is—whose seven members include two partners, a legal executive and a secretary on lead vocals.

Human Resource Priorities

Led by Catherine Williams, human resources director, HR's main role is to recruit, retain, train and develop the high quality people DAC needs to achieve its business objective of servicing clients. In providing professional support to the practice, the department is broadening the firm's understanding of the business contribution that the HR function can make. By challenging partners and staff to contribute to their full potential, HR delivers a positive impact on profits.

DAC's HR initiatives enjoy a high level and visible commitment from the senior partner. David McIntosh considers that his main job is to motivate and enthuse others, which he asserts is difficult unless you are enjoying your work yourself. It would appear that he is.

DAC's approach to finding out what staff expected from their career and from DAC was simple. McIntosh asked them. This 'asking' came in the guise of the 'Conquering the Future' survey, involving individual one-hour interviews with around 60 senior managers and partners. This survey revealed that if DAC did have a weak spot, it was in communicating with and involving everyone in the strategic planning process for the business. To follow-up, all partners were then interviewed individually by Manchester Business School consultants in a search for shared aspirations and values. From this process emerged the firm's future strategy and the structural changes needed to fashion career opportunities for everyone.

Catherine Williams: "We are working to create a trusting and open environment where all talented people can flourish, grow with the firm, and grow the firm simultaneously. Our starting point is not a structural business model, rather the talents of our people and a strong entrepreneurial culture. From this base, strategic directions are developed and adjusted to ensure the continued success of DAC."

HR devotes much effort to developing the firm's own lawyers, but also recruits external specialists, and the best ones at that. DAC has a well-honed graduate recruitment programme—around 18 join each year.

Career Opportunity and Development

Career development is planned with each individual through informal review processes, and by individuals themselves through strong career orientation. A number of alternative career paths can be pursued, assisted by a career development structure that includes client and project exposure, and a management development programme.

The development programme aims to give individuals good technical legal skills through case work, careful supervision, mentoring and formal training. It also provides an introduction to the operation of a legal business, with a particular emphasis on developing effective personal and interpersonal skills vital in a client-focused business.

A key role of the senior partners is to manage the needs of the partnership now, and to initiate changes in structure and methods to meet and resource the future demands of an increasingly sophisticated market place. DAC does not want to fall into the trap of selecting only academics, but presents real opportunities for people with a diversity of talent and qualifications.

This encourages people who enter through the legal executive route; people who might be businessmen as much as lawyers, and who may well be more streetwise and communicative to clients. You can be a legal executive at DAC and thrive—the firm has five senior legal executives treated on a par with partners of the firm.

Pay and Benefits

Pay rates are on a par for City firms of solicitors, and pay increases reflect market value adjustments, performance, and value to the firm. DAC believes that it is 'refreshing' that its reward and recognition system allows nothing to get in the way of meeting the future needs of the firm.

The way in which DAC structures pay is related to the contribution of the individual whatever their position or title. All staff are in the profit-related pay scheme. Benefit packages are attractive and flexible, eligible employees are able to opt into the car, pension and health schemes, or take cash alternatives.

The Future

Specialist firms of solicitors are being threatened by multi-discipline practices serving global corporations. If 'one-stop shopping' in professional services is somewhat unproven, it still forms the challenge of tomorrow. Specialists need to excel, and in hiring the best lawyers, DAC looks not only for an ability to attract business, but also excellent business handling skills. It then aims to create an environment where individuals are happy to stay. Motivation, enthusiasm and openness are hard currencies in this area.

Within the firm, DAC needs to manage in parallel the expectations of its staff and the continued expansion of the firm. Further organisational restructuring and cultural shift may be needed to provide a better business focus for the firm— understanding clients' businesses and the changes that are taking place within those businesses remains the overriding objective.

And DAC is already taking up the challenge of recognising the value of different types of contribution, refining new career path opportunities, and encouraging the development and progress of its most talented people—whatever their discipline or qualification.

DAC does have the genuine feel of a 'different' type of practice. If the firm itself sometimes wonders why it has been allowed to claim—and substantiate— uniqueness in a number of business areas, you are still left with the feeling that if other firms do catch up, DAC will find something else to do first.

Dixons Group plc

Dixons Group plc

Dixons is a UK retailing group specialising in the sale of high technology con-sumer electronics, personal computers, photographic equipment, communication products and domestic appliances. Divided into four chains—Dixons, Currys, PC World and The Link—the Group also provides after sales service for electrical goods through its 'Mastercare' organisation.

Biggest Plus: Individuals recognised and rewarded for achievement

Biggest Minus: You need to be energetic, hardworking and prepared to react quickly to changing circumstances—only a minus if you don't fit the culture!

Dixons Group plc
Marylands Avenue
Hemel Hempstead
Herts HP2 7TG
Tel: 01442-353000
Fax: 01442-233218

The Business

Across the spectrum of contemporary business, few success stories compare with Dixons Group plc ('Dixons'). When Stanley Kalms joined Dixons in 1948, it had a turnover of £105 per week. In July 1996, Dixons reported pre-tax profits of £135.2 million and turnover approaching £2 billion.

With retail sales showing a 23% increase, over 2,200 new jobs created and further expansion planned in subsidiaries encompassing Currys, PC World and The Link, Dixons' upward momentum seems set to continue.

Company Culture and Style

John Clare, chief executive, describes Dixons as "dynamic, fast-moving, competitive and ambitious."

As the high-tech product range is constantly evolving, staff need to be adaptable, quick-thinking and eager to learn fresh skills. Such an approach dovetails with chairman Sir Stanley Kalms' vocational philosophies, maintaining that employees in the 1990s need a basket of skills to survive and flourish. If the business changes (which it will), staff must change too.

Dixons is perceived as a highly secure employer. Not only did the company ride out a recession that ultimately accounted for several competitors (Rumbelows, for example) but rapidly entered a period of growth once the recovery got underway.

Fun at work is actively encouraged. "We like to think," confirms personnel director Peter Cox, "that people enjoy working for Dixons. There's a buzz about being part of a fast-moving, exciting company that doesn't have the historical constraints of some other top organisations."

Communication is a lynchpin of the corporate ethos. Once a week, staff have the opportunity to talk to their managers, swap ideas and find fresh ways of strengthening performance in Branch Training Hours. Most new initiatives are kick-started with focus groups at the coal face.

Human Resource Priorities

Dixons' HR department is committed to meeting the needs of the business by providing sufficiently skilled staff. Behind that simple statement lies a variety of complex issues, including offering an unsurpassed level of service to customers; locating individuals with requisite capabilities; and motivating staff—with the right reward packages, quality of management and equality of treatment.

Dixons' commitment to HR is manifest. David Longbottom, group director of human resources, heads a department over 100 strong, and significant resources are set aside to meet HR requirements.

One member of Longbottom's team takes specific (and full-time) responsibility for employee relations, running a helpline that staff can ring to talk about stress, discrimination or other issues that may be of concern.

A separate team is dedicated to PC training. 6,000 employees have come under its auspices so far, resulting in a high degree of computer literacy.

The needs of the customer remain paramount. Dixons has launched a campaign entitled 'My Customer, My Responsibility' devoted to improving customer service. Dixons has put in place a range of projects that will measure the capability of the staff and the organisation in delivering better service. Monitoring is regarded as essential. Dixons assesses the effectiveness of HR initiatives through attitude surveys, polling every member of staff at least once a year.

Career Opportunity and Development

It starts right away. Every sales assistant joining Dixons Group is sent on a residential course, called 'Career Start', during their first fortnight with the company.

Seven Career Start centres have been established around the country, all equipped with mini-shops. Top managers on six-month secondment share their expertise with the latest intake and the programme leads to a Certificate of Retail Experience recognised by NVQ.

Further down the line, the Retail Management Development Programme (RMDP) is available to employees satisfying assessment criteria. 500 members of staff pass through the RMDP scheme each year.

20 graduates come on board each year. While Peter Cox has no time for "high-faluting graduate schemes that tag one particular group of employees, burdening them with unrealistic expectations," Dixons is eager to attract those prepared to adapt their special skills to the needs of the business. Cox is also uneasy with talk of 'fast trackers'.

"I prefer to talk about people progressing on merit," he says. "We have 30-year-olds who are directors and there's a constant process of appraisal to spot potential high fliers."

Evidence from the stores backs up Cox's claims. Jisvinder Phagiiram is a branch manager in Victoria: "Within seven weeks of joining I was made branch manager of our Lewisham store. Now I am being given the chance to create fresh history of my own by opening a brand new store in Victoria. There's nothing holding you back."

19 year old Ruth Ramsey is a deputy manager in Kendal: "I was attracted to Dixons after 'A' levels because I'd heard the training was brilliant. It was definitely the right decision. I had very strong training on sales and procedures along with some great residential training courses. Both prepared me for my promotion to deputy manager—after just nine months! Support and encouragement has been incredible all the way."

The challenge is summed up by David du-Barry Payne, deputy manager of Dixons in Oxford Street, London: "You're driving the business from within, staying abreast of the latest technology and keeping the focus firmly on customer service. Change is the only constant here. If you thrive on pressure, the opportunities are fantastic."

Dixons has a high proportion of ethnic minority staff and actively encourages female employees to take responsibility. The current director of business planning, advertising director and Currys marketing director are all women.

Pay and Benefits

Peter Cox: "Our sales assistants are incredibly important to the health of our company and are treated as such."

While Dixons offers rates of basic pay comparable to rivals, sales staff enjoy a heightened bonus opportunity. Top sales people—accounting for a scarcely credible £1.7m sales each per annum—can not only reap up to £14,000 in bonuses (£31,000 total including basic salary), but are also invited to an overnight prize-giving seminar at a luxury venue. Commission lies at the very heart of Dixons' operations, reflecting the importance placed on individual performance. Graduates could expect to start with Dixons on around £14,000 in 1996.

Performance-related pay is crucial. 20% of earnings directly relate to corporate performance while annual increases take account of profits, inflation, the state of the job market and individual performance.

Staff offered a company car may choose from an array of 100 models, all equipped with airbags and extra security features. None, however, will be black. "25% of twilight accidents involve black cars," shrugs Cox, "so we don't buy them."

Medical insurance is offered to all senior managers (and, in most cases, their families), while 25% of employees have now opted-in to the corporate pension scheme. Dixons is so committed to this scheme that audiotapes containing details are available to staff on request.

Other benefits include 10% discounts on all goods and occasional 50% discounts on products given special focus in-store. Nothing beats hands-on experience and staff using products at home can sell with greater confidence to customers.

The Future

Dixons' performance appears set to continue. Around 15 Currys Superstores and 10 PC Worlds are scheduled to open over the next 12 months, while the programme of upgrading Dixons stores to meet the new millennium continues apace.

Staff have reason to be pleased. Building on the success of 'My Customer, My Responsibility' and the introduction of profit-related pay, Dixons has now extended the share option scheme to cover all employees (including part-timers) registering five years' service with the company.

Yet much still remains to be done. Refusing to rest on their collective laurels, Dixons has identified three barriers to corporate vision. First, importing and developing the people needed to adapt to a changing market place and rate of growth. Secondly, maintaining proximity to customers. A challenge facing every retail organisation, the ability to meet customer needs has become paramount. Thirdly, engendering product knowledge. With developing technological advancements, the product knowledge of sales staff will be key to achieving mass market share.

The opportunity is obvious. Dixons may place high demands on its staff but, as the payroll continues to expand, those with the ambition, focus and intelligence will rise to the challenge. Those that do so can expect to enjoy significant recognition and financial rewards from an organisation committed to sharing the fruits of success.

East Midlands Electricity

East Midlands Electricity's core businesses are the distribution and supply of electricity covering an area of over 16,000 sq. km in the East Midlands. It distributes to over 2.2 million customers within its region and to businesses across the country. The company's turnover was £1.3 billion in 1995, and it has over 4,000 employees. East Midlands also supplies gas to business customers, has an electrical contracting arm, and energy consultancy and small generation businesses.

Biggest Plus: A utility company determined to prosper in the private sector

Biggest Minus: HR practices not yet totally up to date

East Midlands Electricity
PO Box 444
Wollaton
Nottingham NG8 1EZ
Tel: 0115-901 0101
Fax: 0115-901 8200

The Business

In common with other privatised utilities, East Midlands Electricity has been going through a period of dramatic change, which continues to be a major feature.

In recent years, after a period of diversification, its strategy has been to concentrate on its core businesses. It distributed over 25.1 billion units of electricity in 1995 through a distribution network of more than 67,000 km of overhead lines and underground cables. The company has focused on customer care, reducing the number of disconnections by over 60% until there were only 56 in 1995.

East Midlands Electricity has three key objectives: to keep prices down (which competition assists), to provide its customers with good service, and to create value for its shareholders.

Company Culture and Style

Historically, people joined East Midlands Electricity and other public sector utilities expecting a job for life. The changes that have stopped this from being a reality have affected the style of the company and the attitudes of those working for it—but not always negatively. There is now more encouragement of an entrepreneurial attitude, with more opportunities for those willing to challenge management and come up with new ideas.

Parallel with this breath of fresh air, the strong public service ethos of the previous culture has survived, exemplified in the number of employees actively involved in community ventures and volunteering.

There is also a culture of flexibility in moving people around different functional areas, presenting opportunities for people to broaden their careers without the rigidity found in some companies.

An example of this is Duncan Sedgwick, customer service director in the company's supply business, who has also worked in the company secretarial area, internal audit and general management. He says, "I was given active encouragement to develop with significant challenges at an early age. I have received opportunities across different functions in general management that many of my friends in other companies do not appear to have."

Strong emphasis is laid on the importance of good communications throughout the company. There is a regular team briefing system on a monthly basis, and managers often hold extra briefings when they are needed. The monthly company newspaper is sent to all employees' home addresses, and also to pensioners. Every year, all employees receive an 'at a glance' booklet containing information such as company values, objectives, and stakeholders.

Periodically, the chief executive, Norman Askew, holds road shows when he and board members visit business units and deliver informal presentations with question and answer sessions. This open style encourages questions on any topic, and has been very successful in giving people direct access to top management. There may be a need for better bottom-up communication, which is being explored through focus groups.

The company culture maintains a strong concern for health and safety, as one would expect in a business where much work is still 'up the poles and down the holes', and where safety is paramount. There is a full-time company doctor and two occupational health nurses who carry out many health campaigns for all staff to participate in if they wish. Confidential counselling is available through external counsellors for staff and their families.

The general style is to move forward into team working and project-based assignments, and as Sally Smedley, the human resources director puts it, "There is a hunger to find smarter ways of doing things." Because of this, she says the people who will flourish within the company are those "who deliver in terms of doing their job effectively and are prepared to challenge management and the status quo." So people are encouraged to feel confident and credible, and to take responsibility for their ideas even if this may involve taking a risk in coming out into the open with their ideas.

There are many sports and social clubs, a general spirit of informality and first name use; the chief executive queues in the staff restaurant for his lunch along with all other staff, and a relaxed atmosphere prevails at business meetings. This is in marked contrast to the more formal and hierarchical style of working before the company was privatised in 1990.

Human Resource Priorities

Sally Smedley's appointment early in 1996 as HR director was the first time this post had existed. Since then she has been reviewing and developing policies and practices. The five main areas on which she is focusing are: refining succession planning; formalising management development systems; examining the company's internal communications; a complete overhaul of salaries and rewards; and bringing in a more focused performance management system. There is strong board commitment to this updating of key HR practices.

East Midlands Electricity has an excellent record on training, allocating a generous level of resources to it. Training is seen as a fundamental business need, not an add-on, and it will remain a HR priority.

The business has shed nearly 3,000 employees since privatisation, a necessary task that the company has handled sensitively and generously, involving external outplacement consultants and pre-retirement courses run internally.

Equal opportunity is taken seriously, as one would expect of an organisation subscribing to Opportunity 2000. Women are being promoted to senior positions; there is a generous maternity programme and paternity leave; flexible hours are encouraged wherever possible; and a childcare allowance is available for lower-paid staff, together with special rates for local nurseries.

Career Opportunity and Development

There is a healthy blend of internal promotion and people joining from outside, especially with a view to bringing specific private sector experience to the company. The performance management system is being upgraded and will feed into training and succession planning.

Training has always been a strong point and East Midlands Electricity owns two training centres; both have achieved Investors in People recognition. Inter-nally provided training includes technical and engineering skills, usually linked to NVQs, along with other topics including team building and supervisory and man-agement training. Approximately 20 new technical apprentices are taken on each year. There are opportunities for staff to be sponsored for MBAs and DMS at local universities.

Graduate training schemes are run when needed. The company anticipates taking on average about 10 graduates each year, mainly in engineering and finance. Graduate entrants can take further professional qualifications and their development programme includes different work around the company, with the guidance of a mentor. Secondment within the organisation takes place to encourage breadth of experience, a process that benefits both individual and company.

Pay and Benefits

The level of remuneration packages across the company is very good, including typical benefits of a company pension, special rates for private healthcare, and a staff sharesave scheme; this has a high take-up, with 73% of all employees currently saving to purchase shares in the business. Employees are seen as one of seven groups of stakeholders in the business, along with customers, shareholders, suppliers, the community, government and the electricity regulator.

The Future

East Midland Electricity's main challenge is to prosper in a highly competitive market place, and this implies the need to take the work force successfully through continuing fast and dramatic changes. In Sally Smedley's words, the business has to "harness all the positive attributes of existing staff and focus them so we can win in this new environment."

It is this challenge that underpins all current strategy on management development, training, and communications. As Norman Askew, chief executive explains, "Change is essential for companies to survive and move forward and our people have seen a lot of change in recent years. Directors and managers must recognise the changes that are required before they become obvious and articulate this vision to all people who work in the business, so that change is effected before it is required. At times we have asked a lot; we have certainly stretched the elastic, but people have responded magnificently. The company attracts the right people."

Part of the challenge is to improve managers' ability to tackle problems of unsatisfactory performance head-on at review time and on other occasions. Simultaneously, there is a different need to reassure a work force that has gone through a period of insecurity and which needs help with rebuilding expectations and reassurance that there is a good future for people who are achievement centred.

An external challenge comes from the regulator, whose powers create extra pressure. Customers' expectations of excellent service increase and customer care challenges must also be met convincingly.

The Edinburgh Woollen Mill

'...the home of __Natural__ value.'

The Edinburgh Woollen Mill Ltd.

Edinburgh Woollen Mill is a speciality retailer. It trades under a number of different formats, and each store is uniquely different in style, attitude and market profile. The company has grown considerably in the last five years, the number of stores in the UK increasing from around 90 to nearer 220, and turnover has risen from approximately £50 million to in excess of £120 million. Edinburgh Woollen Mill employs around 2,500 people, allowing for seasonal variations.

Biggest Plus: Expanding niche retailer, great emphasis on quality of people

Biggest Minus: Pace of change in retailing only gets faster

The Edinburgh Woollen Mill Ltd.
Waverley Mills
Langholm
Dumfrieshire DG13 0EB
Tel: 013873 80611
Fax: 013873 80920

The Business

EWM started as a retail operation in 1970, when its first shop opened in Randolph Place, Edinburgh. The head office of Edinburgh Woollen Mill (EWM) is found in an idyllic setting in the Scottish Borders. Behind this serenity and traditional mill heritage lies an ambitious company driven by a high quality, modern management team.

EWM's natural wool product is relatively unique. The company has few direct competitors, yet its products are characterised by value for money. It is a compelling combination, with a clever retailing mix that includes formats such as Pitlochry Knitwear, James Pringle Weavers, and The Golf Shop, which also operates concessions in some of the larger EWM stores. Many of its stores are located in the high street and in market towns, and EWM also has a number of specialist theme stores, including visitor and tourist centres. EWM's business strategy has allowed it to open new stores at a healthy rate for the last five years

Quality and value are important watchwords. Retailing is the essential dynamic of the business, but EWM also takes a close involvement in specifying only the finest natural woollen product, from processing of raw materials through to production and design of garments. Much of EWM's products are made by Scottish Woollens Worsted Group—wholly owned by EWM, but a quite separate business, to which EWM stores are major customers.

Company Culture and Style

The quality of the people it employs is a fundamental strength of Edinburgh Woollen Mill, and the company is committed totally to their development, regarded as key to the pursuit of the company's business objectives. In turn, each member of staff is constantly reminded that they work for a retail business where customer service is paramount.

During this period of strong organic growth, Edinburgh Woollen Mill has retained the close-knit community spirit that permeates throughout the business. The contribution of each and every employee is valued, and everyone is regarded as an important stakeholder in the business. Trust is at the heart of the business.

EWM's culture is very open, honest and one that encourages the sharing of knowledge and information between departments. This helps create an environment and atmosphere where everyone can enjoy their work, and job satisfaction is high. EWM believes that work can—and should—be innovative, exciting and fun; it also believes that individual opinions should be respected and appreciated.

Much of EWM's culture is natural and spontaneous. But much is down to an enlightened management board, which in 1991, articulated company values and missions that may have been latent in the organisation, but needed leadership to instil to the day-to-day business environment.

Human Resource Priorities

With EWM so fast-growing, human resources has a main priority to recruit and develop the people resource needed to meet the expansion plans of the business. Recruitment is held to be crucial, and EWM's staff selection process is rigorous. Staff need to have a strong belief in, and commitment to, the company they work for, and a valuable HR skill is to be able to identify qualities such as enthusiasm and loyalty at the interview stage.

EWM likes to recruit people ahead of vacancies appearing. It can do this with a certain confidence during a phase of growth, but the advance building of a 'talent bank' reveals an intrinsic belief in taking on good people when they are available.

One innovative policy, which helps engender the customer service philosophy, encourages all staff from every function to spend some time—even just one day—in one of the stores to experience first hand the all-important interface with customers. Meanwhile, store and branch managers spend time in head office for short familiarisation courses that cover the company's wider business perspective. EWM believes that this two-way 'exchange' is well worth the time, effort and investment.

The open culture at Edinburgh Woollen Mill also embraces a personal touch, and the company's directors are very communicative and accessible. Newly appointed managers—many of whom are home-grown—are invited to meet and mix with the directors at Langholm, a management style that reveals a genuine interest in the progress of the individual and one which can be highly motivational.

Career Opportunity and Development

Edinburgh Woollen Mill provides excellent scope for rewarding careers. The rate of growth of the business has created great opportunities for people to come through the business, and also for new people to join. The company has to position itself going into the millenium and beyond, and requires also for external talent and expertise to be recruited. This adds up to a matter of balance, and the location of the head office in the Borders, away from the main population centres, is an additional consideration.

Everyone at EWM has the opportunity to develop their career and skills. There are training programmes at all levels. For some staff this might involve NVQs, or the Scottish-equivalent SVQs; for others it could be tailored management development courses. Extended training programmes go beyond initial induction and development after joining the business, and EWM's training department is central to the growth of the business.

It would be fair to describe EWM's approach to development as careful and measured. The company has adopted a pragmatic approach to Investors in People, for example, electing to study first how appropriate and effective IiP could be for its business before considering going for formal recognition.

Pay and Benefits

Edinburgh Woollen Mill aims for its pay levels to be competitive with market rates. In benchmarking against appropriate retail companies with similar turnover, EWM eschews the use of the likes of Hay, preferring instead to commission specialist consultants to provide tailored information that is more relevant for its purposes.

Remuneration packages place more emphasis on pay, rather than non-cash benefits, although the usual range of benefits apply at eligible management levels. EWM does have annual and performance bonus schemes, and employees will shortly be able to join the company's SAYE share scheme. Non-financial benefits include comprehensive sports and leisure facilities at Langholm.

The Future

Although there is no equivalent, national competitor, Edinburgh Woollen Mill's still faces competition, often in the form of independent or one-off operations. It takes competition seriously. EWM's emphasis in the immediate future will be to maintain and resource its expansion. The company is well placed in the tourist/ visitor centre market segment but one particular variable that can affect this business is the weather. EWM looks well positioned to deliver its divisional strategy of opening around 20 stores, mostly in the high street, year-on-year.

Arguably, the greater challenges are those which EWM poses to itself—to keep its store-opening programme at a brisk but manageable pace, including the development of existing stores, and to explore and expand its range of retailing concepts. The business continues to improve efficiency and productivity, with IT and systems playing an important part.

The strength of the company is always likely to reflect the quality of the people it employs. That in itself is a major challenge for the HR function. EWM has already succeeded in reducing its staff turnover from 35% to a relatively low figure of 15% in 1995. Given Edinburgh Woollen Mill's accelerated growth, recruiting and retaining talented people will remain a top priority.

Ericsson

Ericsson Limited is one of the major operations in the Ericsson Group. Ericsson is one of the world's leading telecommunications companies, recognised for its advanced systems and products for wired and mobile telecommunications used in public and private networks. It is the world leader in cellular systems with a market share of 41%. The Group's activities span across 100 countries and turnover exceeds £10 billion. Ericsson employs 86,000 people world-wide, including 3,500 in the UK.

Biggest Plus: Dynamic, fast-moving, exciting—and lots of opportunities

Biggest Minus: Only for those who thrive on pressure!

Ericsson Limited
Telecommunications Centre
Ericsson Way
Burgess Hill
West Sussex RH15 9UB
Tel: 01444-234567
Fax: 01444-234234

The Business

Ericsson was founded in Sweden in 1876 and began selling telephone sets in the UK through an agent in 1880. By 1897, Britain accounted for 28% of the company's telephone sales, so it was a logical move to set up its own office in London in 1898. Today, Ericsson is one of the largest telecommunications suppliers in the UK, with all the established public network operators, fixed and mobile, as customers along with businesses of all sizes. Ericsson exchanges carry 90% of all international traffic in the UK. The UK remains Ericsson's fourth largest market after the USA, Sweden and China.

Impressive though this progress was, the 1990s have seen even more rapid growth for Ericsson Limited thanks to deregulation and liberalisation of telecoms markets, and to Global Ericsson's own research and development: 20% of turnover goes on R&D. Ericsson now leads the market in the wireless office environment using DECT technology, its mobile phones are available for all cellular standards and all networks in the UK, and its business networking technology is in service with businesses, governments and universities.

Growth has been particularly strong over the last three years; no less than 60% of Ericsson's turnover in 1995 came from products not even available in 1992, and 45% of Ericsson customers in the UK have been added since then. Net sales rose from £233.7 million in 1992 to £534.9 million in 1995.

Company Culture and Style

The typical Ericsson person is a self-starter who takes the initiative. The culture is open, stretching and challenging, an environment where individual contributions are expected—but also recognised. This is definitely not an organisation where managers take credit for the achievements of their staff, nor is it hierarchical or bureaucratic. Rather, Ericsson has an unusual degree of consensus in its operations.

At the heart of the culture is customer service. Ericsson people take on challenges to deliver a demonstrable result to the customer. This makes them entrepreneurial, enthusiastic, team-oriented and highly professional in everything they do. The work is often pressurised; but then Ericsson people tend to thrive on pressure. Pushing standards forward and producing results that go beyond customer expectations make the effort more than worthwhile.

Group chief executive officer Dr Lars Ramqvist: "All our activities are based on Ericsson's shared values: professionalism, respect and perseverance." These attributes are key to achieving its mission of offering its customers communications solutions better adapted to their needs than those offered by its competitors. Naturally, delivering on this promise means that the company and its people must be highly responsive to change. As a result, Ericsson is a flexible organisation; but it also acts in a co-ordinated way to provide the best possible solutions.

This co-ordination often includes working with other parts of the Group worldwide. Indeed, everyone at Ericsson UK will liaise with colleagues elsewhere in the Group at some stage, while many do so on a daily basis. There are also frequent trips abroad or visits to the UK by overseas colleagues. These bring home the fact that Ericsson Limited is part of a truly global company at the forefront of the world's fastest-changing market.

Internal communications at Ericsson Limited include an excellent company magazine, divisional newsheets, an Ericsson Group newspaper, a highly professional Ericsson Group glossy magazine, posters, news screens, wide angle view, communication days, lunchtime addresses and Intranet communication. Suffice it to say that no one is ever in the dark at this company!

Human Resource Priorities

Ericsson's aim is to be an excellent employer. Ericsson Limited HR director Margaret Brooks: "We want to ensure that people are both excited and challenged by their jobs. It's a demanding environment. I believe we can all meet that challenge." HR policies are worked out for the Group as a whole, but—in line with the attribute of flexibility—local companies work within this framework and develop their own initiatives.

There is a very strong commitment to HR in Ericsson. The objectives are to offer all staff excellent training, facilities and scope for development. An excellent appraisal system is in place. There is also an emphasis on developing future managers, with the company continually striving to improve model management techniques.

There are regular employee opinion surveys on a wide range of themes, including a world-wide employee opinion survey called Compass which in the UK is run every two years. Each country has the opportunity to add its own questions. Response rates are regularly above 80%. Each UK division has its own results, which in turn are fed back to staff through management briefings. Smaller scale surveys are also used, to focus on issues arising in local areas.

Career Opportunity and Development

Ericsson signed up five modern apprenticeships in June 1996—the UK's first in telecommunications. A further six joined in September. Of the rest of its workforce, no less than 65% have had further education, and 41% have university degrees.

Graduates can expect first-class training and early responsibility. Louise Barnes read European Business Studies: "It's incredibly dynamic. I'm out a lot talking to customers, doing presentations and meeting suppliers. I was actually in Sweden on my second day!" Vikas Arora, who has a BSc in Business Studies: "It's an exciting place. You get a real buzz working in a team against tight deadlines, and you're part of that from day one." Elicia Pendlebury (MSc in Communication Engineering): "It's really satisfying to see work I've done in my first year actually being used in the latest Ericsson phones."

Once on board, career development can be rapid. Given the global nature of the Group, development is often overseas for those with the right skills and commitment. All vacancies are advertised internally, and 140 Ericsson Limited employees are currently working abroad. This would typically be a 2–5 year contract, although six-monthly projects also arise. Wherever employees work within the Group, they remain supported by the common social welfare package.

There is clearly a feeling that there is always something new to do; fresh challenges are the norm, not the exception. Ericsson is a complex organisation with a wide range of sophisticated and fast-changing technology. Matrix management encourages people to develop new skills as their careers progress. As a result, turnover is low at Ericsson. Furthermore, a number of those who do move outside the Group find themselves returning!

Despite the youthful, dynamic nature of the company (75% of the workforce is under 50), there are many examples of people rising through the ranks. A typical case is that of Jonathan Smith. "I have worked for Ericsson now for 12 years. I started off as a trainee and I now report to the MD. So I see that Ericsson has developed me, empowered me and trusted me."

Training is a high priority at the company. Last year, Ericsson Limited ran over 500 training courses—11,500 training days. These range from soft skills to highly technical training. Everyone is encouraged to develop his or her own career, which can include secondment to other areas as well as professional or higher academic qualification sponsored by Ericsson.

Pay and Benefits

Ericsson sees itself as a good payer in the median of its market range. Annual pay reviews are related to individual performance and merit. The company sets objectives for itself and its divisions, which in turn are cascaded down to individual targets each year.

Benefits include flexible working hours at most locations (except for managers), subsidised meals at all sites, healthcare schemes, maternity provision (including incentives to return and support for childcare), a final salary pension scheme, cars for managers, sales force and essential users with a cash alternative and a trade up or down facility—and a range of events at each site such as a formal ball or a beach barbecue.

The Future

Margaret Brooks: "Our biggest challenge is to ensure we are flexible, adaptive and responsive given that the business is evolving so rapidly. We do our best to predict those trends, but surprises are inevitable! As a result, we need to help people feel confident about this environment and help them see changes as opportunities rather than threats."

The UK market has grown phenomenally over the last few years. This means that Ericsson Limited has its own challenges, among them that of ensuring that all UK staff, especially the many new starters, feel as well-treated as others elsewhere in the Group.

Despite these issues, Ericsson looks well-placed to handle whatever the future of telecommunications may bring. Its strategic plan, updated every two years, covers everything from finance and HR to the business areas. This plan, which is cascaded to everyone in the Group, is particularly good at considering strategic competencies. This type of thinking is typical of a forward-looking, dynamic and fast-growing Group at the forefront of cutting-edge technology.

☰⫻ ERNST & YOUNG

Ernst & Young

Ernst & Young is one of the world's leading firms of business advisors. Its core areas are audit, tax, corporate finance, corporate recovery and consultancy. It audits nearly one in five of the world's top 1,000 companies, and has 70,000 people based in 670 offices in 130 countries, including 6,700 in the UK operating from 26 offices.

Biggest Plus: Looks like a winning team in a range of growing management disciplines

Biggest Minus: Possible future loss of grip in traditional areas could mean job uncertainties

Ernst & Young
Becket House
1 Lambeth Palace Road
London SE1 7EU
Tel: 0171-928 2000
Fax: 0171-928 1345

The Business

Seen as one of the 'big six' accountancy firms in the UK, Ernst & Young (E&Y) is also one of the top three firms in over 60 countries, it is the world number one in tax, and number two in management consultancy.

In mid-1996, E&Y announced the appointment of 33 new UK partners, taking the total to 435, and a net increase of 5%. Between 1992 and 1995, partner numbers had dropped from 411 to 386. Senior partner Nick Land said it was a response to increased demand for the partnership's services. "Management consultancy, corporate finance and taxation are the most buoyant areas. We think we can take more market share if we have the right number of partners."

This followed a comprehensive structural reorganisation in London that began in early 1995, which created four market-focused offices: financial services; industrial, consumer and public services; media and resources; and entrepreneurial services. The firm has national coverage in the UK through a total of 24 business units.

Ernst & Young was due in December 1996 to publish financial results, in a format more akin to plcs than partnerships, for the first time. The firm's last reported UK revenues for 1995 were £401 million, and its world-wide revenues for 1995 grew by 14% to a record $6.87 billion.The increase matched the increase of the previous four years put together, and was well above the growth due purely to economic factors.

Company Culture and Style

The firm's aims are entirely client and market focused. "By helping our clients achieve success in their aims, and distinguishing our ability to do so from that of other professional advisers, we will ensure our own success," says Nick Land.

"We are in the middle of major cultural change and organisation transformation," says US-born human resources director Barry Leskin.

Like its rivals, E&Y is having to evolve and grow away from the traditional dependence on audit to become a provider of a comprehensive set of consulting services to clients. These cover areas such as strategy, performance improvement, process re-engineering, information technology, acting as lead adviser on deals and innovative tax advisers. It means more of a sales culture, where partners and staff are able to persuade clients that the firm has a broad range of services to offer.

The view from within is that the firm now has the most people-oriented culture of any of the big six. "People will come here even if they might make more money elsewhere," says Leskin, "because of the internal quality of work life. It is not a ruthless environment, we work hard, but it is a non-bureaucratic, informal, first-name, personable culture, and that is critical to people who have choice of employers. That view is reinforced by clients who describe their working relationship with Ernst & Young in a similar way."

Teamworking has always been an integral feature, as offices collaborate to supply clients with project teams hand-picked from a wide range of specialists.

The rise in business achieved by the management consulting group in 1996 was seen as partly due to the new style of high-performance teamworking, putting people from different disciplines together to form consulting teams.

Human Resource Priorities

Ernst & Young has introduced a radical reorganisation of its human resources function, to reflect the critical importance of change management and employee development within the group. It believes there are two HR functions that really matter in a professional service firm: staffing, and development.

It is appointing within each business unit a head of human resources whose primary expertise is in change management and developing people. The other less strategic functions are hived-off to specialists who report to the head of HR.

The group believes its competitive edge lies in "better harnessing the talents of all of our people", which depends on putting in high quality HR professional experts partnered with line management, where the business is being done.

Senior partner Nick Land takes personal responsibility for being the HR leader in the firm. There is a commitment to a minimum number of days of personal development work for every executive. Although Investors in People is not considered appropriate, the group target is to provide every professional in the firm with at least ten days' structured development and learning a year.

Career Opportunity and Development

UK managing partner Andrew Jones says, "Use of new technology combined with a commitment to research and development means a constant upgrading of the delivery of ideas and services to clients. It means that while graduates and other recruits still need extensive training in core areas, they are freed to provide the higher levels of consultancy and general business advice our clients demand."

While most graduates are recruited with qualifications as chartered accountants at a career milestone, some are recruited directly as business analysts, a career path which can be linked to qualification as a member of the Chartered Institute of Management Accountants, and a small number take a direct route into management consultancy through a comprehensive training and business experience programme.

Audit trainees in the four largest offices (London, Manchester, Birmingham and Glasgow) join a trainee development group that is relatively unique among accountancy firms and ensures that trainees in a large office have the same variety and depth of experience as colleagues in smaller offices.

The firm says: "There are four key elements to learning and development at E&Y: the performance development system, training for professional exams, in-house training and on-the-job learning."

A typical career path for a qualified accountant in the firm might be supervisor within 18 months and senior manager within another 4–5 years. From audit or tax there are many routes, e.g. transferring to corporate finance, corporate recovery or consultancy, transferring between audit and tax, or joining a specialist team in knowledge management or training.

Exchange programmes and secondment schemes offer the chance to work overseas for varying periods, often linked to serving a particular client, or to work abroad permanently.

Kailesh Karavadra, a senior manager recently on secondment to San Francisco, says: "Throughout my career I have been very impressed with the level of training and support I have received. The firm does require commitment in return, but I certainly feel that success and hard work are rewarded."

Brian Turner, tax partner in the London office, says: "After 40 years the thing that most pleases me is that I haven't had a boring day yet."

Pay and Benefits

"On pay, overall we aim to remain competitive with the leading players in each of our markets," says Barry Leskin. Ernst & Young is also competitive with its rivals in conventional benefits such as pensions, cars, holidays and health care.

The first of the big six firms to reveal more of its internal financial workings was KPMG, and observations here give clues to elsewhere. Partners received an average £180,000 in 1995, made up of £125,000 in salary, £31,000 in profit share and £24,000 in pension payments. The senior partner received a total package of £740,000. Nick Land commented: "We have a much flatter pay structure, with nobody over £500,000." His own package was reported as being under £400,000, while average partner earnings are similar to KPMG's.

Among the partners there is an open information system on pay, and the ruling principle is one-firm compensation: bonuses are allocated on the basis of the profitability of the firm as a whole. The performance management system, the framework used right across the firm, is used for mutual evaluation of individual performance.

The Future

E&Y freely admits that its present challenge is to produce enough home-grown partners and senior staff to meet the opportunities that it believes are out there. It is bringing in partners from outside, and investing in the professional support staff that each partner needs.

Senior partner Nick Land says: "As well as technical excellence, we look for people who are flexible and adaptable, who have excellent interpersonal skills and who can react quickly and effectively under pressure."

The significant rise in business, particularly in the fundamental but highly competitive area of management consulting, looks to be vindicating a strategy that gives HR management a clear and central role. The numbers so far visibly suggest the strategy is working. In a new reporting era, in which the big six will reveal far more about their real strengths, E&Y has already positioned itself to achieve more than its 'fair share' of growth.

Federal Express

Federal Express

Federal Express (FedEx) is the world's largest express transportation company, offering rapid and reliable services, delivering nearly 2.5 million parcels in 211 countries each day. The company has over 124,000 employees and uses over 560 planes and 37,000 vehicles. It has operations in 325 airports world-wide. During the fiscal year ending 31 May 1996, FedEx reported revenues of $10.3 billion.

The UK/Ireland business is part of the Europe, Middle East & Africa (EMEA) region, whose headquarters are in Brussels. The UK hub is at Stansted Airport, and FedEx also has ground operations and offices throughout the UK and Ireland. There are around 1,200 employees in the UK/Ireland district.

Biggest Plus: People come first

Biggest Minus: A unique style and culture, in which not everyone excels

Federal Express Europe, Inc
35–37 Amersham Hill
High Wycombe
Bucks HP13 6NU
Tel: 01494-464555
Fax: 01494-462045

The Business

The idea of an overnight delivery business was conceived by Frederick W Smith while an undergraduate at Yale University. He founded Federal Express Corporation in 1973 and has never looked back since. Ten years after start-up, FedEx reached $1 billion in revenues. That figure today stands in excess of $10 billion. Smith stands as an American business legend, and still heads up this exceptional company. The nerve centre of the system is the SuperHub at Memphis, Tennessee, which is also FedEx's world-wide headquarters.

Boeing's 1996 World Air Cargo Forecast estimates that the world's air cargo market will grow at a compounded annual rate of nearly 7% between 1995 and 2015, with the international express segment averaging 18% growth during that period. FedEx is uniquely positioned to profit from that growth.

FedEx invests $1 billion annually in customer-serving, productivity-enhancing technologies that enable the company to manage a complex system of thousands of vehicles, packages, routes and all possible weather scenarios.

Company Culture and Style

Describing the culture of FedEx conjures up many descriptions—people-oriented, diverse, dedicated to open communications, energised, the encouragement of creativity, accessible top management, and a 'do' rather than 'say' attitude.

From the outset, Fred Smith, chairman and chief executive, set about creating a model work place, putting in place progressive personnel policies. "From its inception, Federal Express has put its people first because it is the right thing to do and is good business as well. Our company philosophy is People-Service-Profit."

Everything that FedEx attempts and accomplishes is premised by People-Service-Profit (P-S-P), contending that if it takes care of its employees, they will in turn deliver impeccable service to customers, who will reward the company with the profitability necessary to secure its future. Commitment in terms of contribution and 'going the extra mile' is visible across the business.

The company's structure is not very hierarchical. Amazingly, there is a maximum of five layers of management between the CEO and any employee, in an organisation that numbers more than 124,000. Much effort goes into teams, seen as a fundamental way of working, and there is some experimentation and current research into self-directed teams.

People who enjoy working for FedEx, and who do well, are likely to be creative, be prepared to challenge and air their own views; increasingly they should be comfortable with the latest technology. With the market changing dramatically, people need to be very flexible, and 'think outside the box'. This environment encourages people to excel.

Human Resources Priorities

The central thrust of FedEx's HR policy and objectives is to meet the spirit and intention behind its P-S-P philosophy. This is understood to mean fair and equitable treatment for all; reward achievement and performance; and ensure that everyone can fully utilise their talents. HR is represented at all levels and plays a key role in pursuing the company's business objectives. There is also an organisational effectiveness department in Memphis.

FedEx proliferates in open communication. FX TV broadcasts world-wide to every station. VPs and MDs are encouraged to visit each station in their district once every quarter. 'Skip' meetings, missing out a layer of management, are held to ensure that communication is relayed to the appropriate people. Team briefing sessions are held every day in order to re-emphasise operational plans, set future objectives, and most importantly, solicit feedback from the team. Senior managers must hold two meetings a year with the entire station to measure performance against original plans.

That's not it—there are Quality Action Teams, a European communication task force, and Employee Consultation Forums. One could question if any work is done with all this communication going on, but FedEx's open communications culture is *highly* successful. So much so, that there are no formal union recognition agreements needed in the UK business.

At the root of FedEx corporate philosophy is Survey, Feedback, Action, or SFA. This 360 degree process has been used in the UK for 10 years, but has been well founded and supported in the USA for nearer 15 years. SFA surveys all employees' concerns each year, generating productive feedback, making managers aware and providing a process for continuous improvement. Importantly, a manager's action plan must be clear, achievable and recorded.

UK/IRL personnel manager Kevin Dunkeld says: "Although completion of the survey is voluntary, the company has enjoyed a 98% employee participation rate; in my opinion this underpins the importance and high regard that employees place on this process. SFA is very beneficial and supports our people first policy."

One purpose of SFA is to make sure that managers are people-oriented. If managers don't achieve a certain level on the SFA score, they get support from personnel. SFA is at the heart of FedEx, and trust is at the heart of SFA. Managers don't get involved in the 'Survey' stage—that is handled by personnel—'Feedback' is when managers get involved. Managers need to pay close attention to their action plans—compensation interacts with SFA scores.

FedEx can boast having a personnel policy and procedure for just about everything, enshrined in the People Manual. One of its more unusual policies is the Guaranteed Fair Treatment, or GFT. This enables the employee to have the right to appeal on any eligible issue—a problem or complaint—through a process of systematic review by progressively higher levels of management. GFT enables employees' concerns to be heard by management and to ensure fair evaluations of those concerns without fear of retaliation. Another unusual challenge for FedEx managers.

And is there an open door policy? Of course, in Section 5.30 of the People Manual.

Career Opportunity and Development

An annual Performance Review encourages a frank and open discussion between manager and employee and also provides a platform for possible career and personal development. All vacancies are advertised internally on the Bulletin Board via email. FedEx believes that one of the most challenging positions to secure is that of first line manager position. The Leadership Evaluation and Awareness Process (LEAP) was developed as a personal management development programme to identify employees with the leadership skills necessary for management at FedEx. LEAP is optional; but you must do it if you want to bid for a management vacancy.

Every job function is supported by training, with the HR department committed to delivering a comprehensive training schedule each year. Some training requirements are mandatory for certain job positions. New management appointees are required to visit the Leadership Institute in Memphis within three months of their appointment to have orange and purple blood pumped into them.

Pay and Benefits

FedEx provides a market-competitive package of benefits that is comprehensive and flexible. FedEx aims to reward exceptional individual or group performance through its Bravo Zulu, Star, Superstar Golden Falcon, Team Sharing and Pay Exception programmes. Managers and professionals are incentivised to achieve objectives through Management by Objectives (MBO) and Professionals by Objectives (PBO) schemes.

Depending on the job position, other benefits may include company cars, a contributory pension scheme, and private medical and personal accident insurance. More alfresco benefits include the 'healthy lifestyle' programme, Early Years childcare, and 'jump seating'—free travel in FedEx freight planes.

The Future

FedEx has a nice problem in needing to resource and meet the profitable growth of the business—all the trends have been upwards in the last few years. But the company is wary that it must avoid any complacency that could settle during times of profitability, and needs to retain that vital urgency.

In meeting this challenge, FedEx UK believes that it will have to constantly review its recruitment and selection methods, and keep a close eye on management ratios to maintain its effective communications. The company believes that it is closer to its people, and this open understanding allows it to empathise with their hopes and fears for the future.

F·I·GROUP PLC

FI Group

FI Group is an information technology group, focused on applications management, and has become a market leader in this fast-growing sector. Founded as the UK's first computing services and training company in 1962, it became a pioneer of the distributed office concept and telecommuting. The company has grown from 100 women working at home to 750 salaried staff and the same number of freelancers, in a network of nine IT centres. FI was floated on the London Stock Exchange in April 1996.

Biggest Plus: You know who you are in a group that means business

Biggest Minus: Could also feel more like being self-employed

FI Group
Campus 300
Marylands Avenue
Hemel Hempstead
Herts HP2 7TQ
Tel: 01442-233339
Fax: 01442-238400

The Business

When the group's founder and major shareholder Steve Shirley OBE decided to hand the company on in the early 1990s, it was believed an employee buy-out would be the best route to continuing success. It worked, and employee shareholders who achieved 51% of the voting power in 1991 saw their stakes rise ten-fold in five years.

Since 1985 FI has focused on a small number of specialist IT services where it can be the market leader, notably applications management and IT training and recruitment. Pre-tax profits have risen from £1 million in 1991/92 to an expected £4.6 million in 1995/96 when turnover is expected to reach £78.8 million.

A key strategy has been to grow long-term partnerships with customers, and in 1996 it signed or renewed deals with Thames Water, Eagle Star, Legal & General and Barclays Bank. Other major partners include BT, the Scottish Office, Cooperative Bank and Tesco.

Subsidiaries FI Recruitment and FI Training are growing strongly. The order bank has grown from £9 million to £72 million in four years, and divides into three roughly equal parts: services, finance and retail. Three sector divisions focusing on each of these areas were created in 1996.

"Flotation was a launch pad for future expansion," says chief executive Hilary Cropper. "Driven by the IT outsourcing trends, computer services is a high growth sector, but competition continues to intensify especially from the large global players." The group is using the capital raised in the flotation to finance its bigger outsourcing deals and start up new ventures.

Company Culture and Style

FI has one of the most distinctive cultures of any UK company. "What differentiates FI is the dual commitment to customer service and group performance that comes from collective ownership," says Cropper.

Half the shares are still owned by employees, half the staff and most of the directors are women, and the flexible working which was the original hallmark of the group has been maintained and formalised.

FI was one of the sponsors of the Royal Society of Arts' Tomorrow's Company project, and it is seen as a model of the more inclusive, stakeholder-oriented, corporate philosophy. It believes employee ownership can remove much of the potential conflict between shareholders and employees, particularly as decision making involves intensive communication and consultation. Staff not only vote on strategic issues at annual meetings, they also discuss the daily decisions affecting the company.

But Hilary Cropper says: "The fact you have workforce control doesn't mean you are going soft." She says democracy, equality and flexibility help, not hinder, speed and competitiveness in a highly aggressive market place.

Sir John Harvey-Jones has said of the group: "The key to their philosophy and I'm sure to their success is a belief in decentralisation, in delegation, in releasing energy rather than in control."

The open culture is also expressed in FI's dealings with business partners, where negotiations include open book accounting, independent audits and agreed procedures for arbitration.

Human Resource Priorities

Although 50% of FI's 1,500 workforce are women, recruitment and selection is strictly on merit, with no positive discrimination in favour of women.

The group believes in trying to maintain the strength of workforce ownership as a means of achieving maximum motivation and results. Employee investment is encouraged through a web of share options, internal share dealing and share-related profit schemes, in an attempt to keep the workforce's stake above 20%. At the floatation, a Quest (qualifying employee share ownership trust) was set up to buy shares from employees.

An unusual feature of the group's share option scheme, aimed at heightening employee identification with the company, is that employees are assigned options, giving them the right to buy more shares in the future, if they buy shares now. And the number of options granted to an individual depends on how many shares he or she buys in relation to their salary.

Employees are offered choice in their way of working. FI has introduced an innovative Flexible Employment Contract for people who want flexible hours and working patterns. By mid-1996 the group had recruited 70 people on the new contracts.

FI designates its self-employed contractors as associate suppliers, and has produced a charter that sets out the relationship between both sides and the mu-tual benefits.

The group's commitment to innovation includes finding "new ways of keeping our workforce motivated...this is vital to our continued success in support of our customers' businesses."

Career Opportunity and Development

In 1996 the workforce grew by 260 people, most of whom were salaried employees, including 60 new graduates, who were given an intensive initial training programme. Training and development have remained a high priority following the flotation. The main focus is on a strategic development programme for senior management, and advanced training for project managers.

The creation of three sector groups, the establishment of two applications management centres in 1996–97, and the planned extension of the range of FI services, has provided new opportunities for development and promotion within the group.

Although there is no sex bias, one aim is now to attract more female graduates by recruiting from the arts and science disciplines as well as from computer sciences.

Staff are encouraged to further their own development through voluntary community activities, with FI's support.

Pay and Benefits

"We offer competitive reward levels which are performance based," says the group. In addition, share ownership gives staff the opportunity to build up significant capital stakes.

A new profit-sharing scheme is intended to bring enhanced opportunities to buy shares in a tax-efficient way, with employees' entitlement linked to "the achievement of challenging profit targets". Bonuses of up to 10% of salary can be paid in shares and locked into the share trust for three years. But if the bonus is paid in cash, it is worth only half as much. In 1996–97 the bonus level, if taken in shares, was 6.45%. To qualify for the Option Scheme, an employee has to own and hold shares for three years.

FI designs its overall pay and benefits levels to be competitive, but makes the benefits package as relevant as possible to the individual. A discretionary flexible benefits scheme was introduced in 1996, which offers not only a choice of the mix of cash and conventional benefits, but a choice of pensions: personal, money purchase, or final salary. The package is equally available to staff opting for a flexible employment contract. The move is said to be strategic, in that it helps the group more easily absorb people transferring from other organisations.

FI gives preference to its associate suppliers over other freelance workers, by offering longer term contracts wherever possible and at least four weeks' notice.

The Future

After three years of rapid growth and the pressures of a new raft of institutional shareholders, it would be easy for FI to become one of those technology companies that began to disappoint the City.

It has demonstrated that workforce ownership does not have to be soft and cuddly, and that flexibility for staff can mean a more flexible response to customers. It now needs to invest as much in developing its workforce skills as it does in growing its vital long-term partnerships.

FI chairman Sir Peter Thompson is better-placed than most to see the obvious pitfall ahead. As chairman of NFC, he saw the company that was the first model of a successful employee-owned business first lose its way and then lose most of its worker-shareholders, being left with under 10%. Hilary Cropper, who is 55, has said she would not worry even if FI employee ownership halved to 25% or less.

Perhaps more critical will be successful handling of senior management development and succession issues, to give FI a chance of continuing to outrun and outsmart its massively bigger rivals in an expanding but dangerous IT universe.

First Choice

First Choice Holidays

First Choice is a leading high-quality, mass-market package holiday business in the UK and North America. Turnover now exceeds £1 billion, with the Group employing 4,500 people world-wide, 2,500 in the UK.

Biggest Plus: Knows where it's going and cares about its people

Biggest Minus: Not for you if you want a quiet, challenge-free life!

First Choice Holidays PLC
First Choice House
London Road
Crawley
West Sussex RH10 2GX
Tel: 01293-560777
Fax: 01293-588081

The Business

Until August 1994, First Choice was called Owners Abroad. In this form the organisation had many strengths, not least the ability to expand into one of the leading mass-market holiday companies and the possession of highly experienced personnel. Unfortunately, its weaknesses had begun to outweigh those strengths. The company name was a liability; it didn't reflect the nature of the business. Market share had fallen to below 10%. Owners Abroad had just fended-off a hostile takeover bid by Airtours. Brands and brochures proliferated confusingly.

The result was a continual weakening of staff morale, to the point where the corporate culture could be described as a culture of dependency. In 1994, however, the company decided to overhaul its entire operations. The changes were dramatic, and inevitably involved some tough decisions: 10% of the workforce was lost through compulsory redundancy, for instance. Nevertheless, the effects of the reorganisation were rapid and impressive.

Six months after the reorganisation, the company's market share had risen from 9% to 16%. Company name awareness had risen from 0% to 56%—making it one of the most successful launches ever. Most importantly, morale had changed out of all recognition. Existing staff were motivated and recruits eager to join. This was as much due to the open and frank handling of the reorganisation as the changes themselves; everyone felt part of the new set-up and believed their opinions counted. There was, and continues to be, a strong sense that the company is serious about its future and determined to succeed: good news for customers and staff alike.

Company Culture and Style

First Choice now has four operating divisions. These comprise First Choice Holidays and Flights, covering its UK and Irish mass-market tour operations; Air 2000, the company's own airline which serves its three tour operating divisions, selling unused capacity to other companies; Signature, a Canadian mass-market tour operator; and Skibound, a skiing, lakes and mountains tour operator.

This aspect of the reorganisation represents a considerable streamlining on what had gone before. But this is just the beginning. There is now a far greater merging of the divisions: people are First Choice employees. An example of how this works in practice is the fact that UK employees now wear the same uniform as those based abroad to welcome holidaymakers.

Tony Coleman, First Choice's Group human resources director: "I really believe that people have a sense of our moving in the right direction. It's not all in place yet, but we're getting there. You can see that in the way people feel able to criticise what the organisation is doing, with the confidence that their critiques will be listened to and acted upon."

So what is the main change in culture since the relaunch? Coleman: "The culture is now one of pride, of achievement, of professionalism. First Choice employees, I believe, see themselves as professionals in the travel business—in other words, that they can deliver the company's promises. They're typically innovative, customer-centred and market-driven—and they're very proud of those things.

"Air 2000 employees are more operationally focused, but the same qualities describe them. Airline ethos and professionalism, an excellent safety and punctuality record, and so on. For instance, Air 2000 has consistently maintained its position as the leading charter airline, and in 1995 we were once again voted Best Charter Airline in the Travel Weekly Globe Awards. Everyone who works for Air 2000 is proud of this, and determined to build on it in the future."

Overall, it's a young company. The average age is just 28. The company looks for people with good interpersonal skills who like to work as team members, have an enquiring and challenging approach, and are flexible when it comes to moving around geographically. The majority of employees don't work in the UK, so this last factor is important. There is also cross-movement between the divisions, particularly as careers advance.

What's it like to work for First Choice? "It's exciting, and it can be hectic and pressurised, particularly at seasonally busy times," Tony Coleman says. "If you like that sort of challenge and the chance for early responsibility, this could be for you. Everyone works as a team and there's always a friendly atmosphere."

Human Resource Priorities

"It's unusual for a company to embody its human resources policy into its mission statement, but that's what First Choice does," says Coleman. "That's how important our people are to us. We can't change the aeroplanes, the destinations, the resorts or the hotels, but we can recruit and retain the best people. In turn, they can help customers make the right decisions, both through innovative packages and through excellent service.

"Many people spend more on their annual holiday than on any other single purchase. If we can make that product easier to buy and more enjoyable, then hopefully they'll come back to us. For that, we need the best people in all of our operations, which is why we're serious about our staff."

Part of that seriousness is seen in the open management approach. At the time of the relaunch, the company produced explanatory videos, newsletters and brochures, and held seminars. But communication is continuous. Videos are produced several times a year, there are excellent newsletters with a good blend of company and personnel news, attractively presented media news digests, and a roadshow twice a year.

Career Opportunity and Development

Much new blood was injected into the company leading up to the relaunch. The objective was to build on the success and experience of many individuals by adding new perspectives from outside. This remains the objective today, but over the medium to long term, First Choice is keen to develop its own talent.

In the past, Owners Abroad recruited graduates—over 250 work for First Choice—but had no special career path. This changed in 1995 with the launch of a graduate programme. This is a two year route that can lead on to MBA qualification and a fast track to senior management. Tony Coleman is proud of the fact that all 15 of the 1995 intake are still with First Choice. The company plans to recruit 15 or more graduates each year.

Alison Knapman, graduate trainee, worked for customer services and Air 2000 in Manchester and in human resources in Crawley in her first year. "I've had a thorough grounding and varied insight into the tour operating and airline industry. The job has been all that I expected it to be."

Alun Williams has an MSc in Tourism Management and entered the 1995 programme. "I wanted to join a company which was young and which allowed people to make a difference. First Choice certainly lived up to my expectations! I have learned enormously over the past year—the experience I have gained has been invaluable."

As well as graduate courses, the company is committed to in-depth training. Managers can expect two weeks a year of formal external training. At less senior levels there is even more: about three weeks of specific skills training and product familiarisation.

Pay and Benefits

The average salary at First Choice is around £20,000. Lowest salaries, for seasonal, part of the year jobs, would be £7,500, while the top salary is currently £320,000. Salaries vary considerably within the organisation, given its need for specialists in finance, marketing, HR and IT, and of course airline crew. Altogether, such professionals account for 40% of First Choice personnel. Coleman: "We expect generally to be in the mid to upper-quartile for pay. We must be, to compete with the top 250 companies for staff."

Pay is entirely performance-related—another far cry from the Owners Abroad days! All staff, from directors down, have an in-depth review process. Each commits to a series of goals during the next operating cycle, some of which are financial, others more qualitative. But all goals are specific, measurable, achievable, relevant and time-bound. The review also has a questionnaire, allowing staff to comment on their colleagues—and on their bosses!

First Choice has a contributory money-purchase pension scheme and a share option savings scheme. In addition, share options are used as incentives and rewards: managers can recommend that individual employees are given share options for outstanding performance.

The Future

Tony Coleman: "The toughest challenge we face is to develop brand equity with the customer in a traditionally price-led industry; to develop the clearly powerful economics of repeat business; to deliver a product which surpasses the customer's expectations; and to offer consistency of service at all times.

"I believe that the way to do all that is to create innovative products and maintain a service edge. Innovative products will be imitated and replicated elsewhere—but truly great service is inimitable. That is the key element that will keep us ahead of the competition."

Fitch plc

One of the world's leading design and brand development consultancies, Fitch plc operates offices in London, Columbus, Boston and San Francisco. Employing over 300 members of staff with significant expertise in the fields of product, graphic and environmental design, Fitch's client base includes leading-edge corporations all over the globe, including Apple Computers, Microsoft, Reebok International, Coca-Cola, Disney Development Corporation and BT.

Biggest Plus: Highly creative working environment

Biggest Minus: Stock option scheme limited to associate directors, directors and senior directors

Fitch plc
Commonwealth House
1 New Oxford Street
London WC1A 1WW
Tel: 0171-208 8000
Fax: 0171-208 0200

The Business

Fitch is a global consultancy. Working with over 200 clients in 24 countries, Fitch has built an envied reputation for design expertise since the early-1960s, blending excellence in its chosen field with an innovative approach towards research and strategy, software development and business administration.

The company focuses on three principal areas of activity: developing consumer environments—from retail stores to high street banks and multiplex cinemas, Fitch is renowned for redefining and reshaping commercial locations; consumer communications—enhancing clients' relationships with their own customers through effective communication and delivery of brand values at every point of contact; product development—conceiving, developing and designing products, identifying market opportunities and bringing designs to fruition. In several industry surveys, Fitch achieved the highest ratings for product development consultancy, balancing clients' strategic ambitions with informed anticipation of end-user needs.

The design industry was badly hit by the recession in the 1990s. From a pre-tax loss of £7 million in 1992, Fitch recovered to post pre-tax profits of £1.7 million in 1995 and recently declared 1996 interim profits up 89%. The recession experience was not without value, with exposure to commercial realities providing insights subsequently utilised to solve client problems.

All Fitch's endeavours are driven by a passion to improve the bottom line. Superior design is not regarded as an end in itself, but a means to producing measureable improvements in sales, margins and customer loyalty.

Company Culture and Style

Fitch offers a highly creative working environment, an upbeat atmosphere that is energetic, resourceful and commercially focused. Such an environment tends to suit entrepreneurial individuals, employees with a passion for creative thought, capable of thinking 'outside the box' and unfettered by international boundaries.

Change is constant. Not only does Fitch constantly seek fresh business opportunities, but commissions tend to emanate from organisations seeking to undergo some form of change process.

"Questioning what's happening in our clients' businesses," notes senior director Zuilmah Wallis, "makes us question what is happening in our own. We're constantly striving for excellence and a better way of doing things."

Designers operate by a process of personal interaction so fun at work is essential. All members of staff, however junior, are encouraged to take the initiative even if specific tasks fall outside their job description.

Although the corporate lattice may appear unstructured, at the heart of Fitch's day-to-day operations is a string of multi-disciplinary teams. Blending product, graphics and design expertise, such units mirror relationships with clients by developing solutions together. Each team is also allocated a small budget to reward special performance with a night-out or weekend break in the country.

Once a year, Fitch stages an off-site review reflecting on achievements over the last 12 months. Esprit de corps is further engendered by softball fixtures (Fitch's team competes against clients and rival consultancies), go-kart evenings, and winding-down sessions at a local pub each Friday night.

"Inquisitive, sociable, challenging and enthusiastic, from brainstorming to pub crawls, brand building to go-karting, Fitch has a clear and common direction," according to Nick Richardson, senior designer.

Human Resource Priorities

Human resources attitudes at Fitch plc were transformed by the arrival of Jean-Francois Bentz as managing director in 1994. Pressure of work had previously diverted attention elsewhere but Mr Bentz wasted no time promoting staff care up the corporate agenda.

25% of weekly management meetings is now spent discussing people-related issues, for example improving the quality of the working environment. Only lack of time prevents that level of commitment rising still further. Although not formally stated (in contrast with US affiliates), Fitch's HR policy is aimed at fostering an environment enabling the company to recruit high-quality staff, develop employees, retain workforce loyalty and fulfil client briefs by encouraging creative thinking.

Everyone joining the company is provided with a clear job description, placed in teams best suited to their skills, and given the opportunity to discuss any problems at weekly meetings monitoring work in progress.

"Our whole business," suggests Zuilmah Wallis, "is about people working with people. Although we don't have dedicated HR specialists, it's impossible to extract HR from the day-to-day business of managing the company. In a sense, everybody is involved in HR."

Career Opportunity and Development

"Being at Fitch is about learning something new every day and being given the opportunity to do something with the knowledge," says John Fillingham, associate director.

In a fast-moving design organisation, training requirements change from year to year. Fitch sets aside £20,000 for training in 1996, subsidising a variety of external courses and placing the emphasis firmly on high technology. By the end of the year, all staff will have enjoyed some form of computer training, ranging from basic courses in Excel to advanced courses in 3D modelling.

Project team leaders are specifically charged with facilitating, supporting and training members of the hub. On-the-job training is an essential part of the learning process, Fitch pursuing a philosophy of giving junior people meaningful responsibilities, interfacing with clients at the first opportunity.

"The brilliant thing about working at Fitch," suggests researcher Frances Marty, "is being able to speak to anyone at any level and having the scope for creativity irrespective of your position."

Multi-disciplinary teams form a vital plank in the learning process. Pairing junior members of staff with senior designers provides new recruits with alternative problem-solving strategies, and also encourages cross-fertilisation of ideas.

Fitch recruits 12–15 design students each year and promotes internally wherever possible. Outsiders are recruited only where specific skills are unavailable in-house and there have been several outstanding examples of employees rising through the ranks. Neil Whitehead joined Fitch as a junior designer 15 years ago and is now a senior director.

Opportunities are available for secondments across the Atlantic. Seven members of the London staff are currently in the USA on open contracts, a further seven are currently seconded for the duration of specific projects.

Pay and Benefits

Rates of pay at Fitch are competitive within the industry and based on individual reviews. An innovative feature of this process is that if an individual enjoys a less than harmonious relationship with their line manager, they can invite along any member of staff to safeguard fair play.

A bonus scheme was introduced in 1995 covering all senior members of staff. Bonuses are paid on a quarterly basis and amounted to 12% of base salary for the period ending June 1996. In 1994, an Equity Participation Plan was introduced giving stock options to 70 managers and senior managers across the business.

Only two members of staff still drive company cars (the scheme has virtually been phased out); medical insurance is provided for associate directors, senior directors and their families through BUPA, although in-house medical facilities fail to extend beyond a first-aid kit. Any employee can contract into the corporate pension scheme, where a 5% contribution by employees will be matched by a varying company contribution dependent on seniority.

The Future

Having survived the recession with reputation (and business) intact, Fitch continues to cement its position as design industry leaders. Emerging back into profit may have pleased City analysts, but insiders remain under no illusions about the challenges that still lie ahead:

Retaining staff loyalty—and indeed staff—remains an ongoing challenge. Competitors (and headhunters) are continually trying to poach key Fitch employees. "It's a nightmare and a compliment at the same time," suggests Zuilmah Wallis.

Maintaining the knowledge base of staff in order to keep pace with business, design and technological progress is another task that needs to be addressed continuously. Keeping up with change presents sufficient problems for most organisations but Fitch's renaissance depends on staying *ahead* of the game.

As staff numbers continue to grow, the company has to work harder at spreading understanding and gaining acceptance for corporate philosophies. A programme entitled 'Fitchness' is already in place. Building individuals' understanding of its vision and values, spelling out central credos and disseminating a common vocabulary, Fitch is determined to set standards of uniform excellence all over the globe.

Friends Provident

Friends Provident is one of the UK's leading providers of insurance and investment services. It has more than 2½ million policies in force and assets under management exceed £15 billion. The company's 3,600 employees are spread across four main offices in the UK. Friends Provident is also a member of the Eureko Alliance in Europe

The company's main activities are organised into two groups—Business Operations handles all customer activities, from sales and marketing through to customer service, and includes direct insurance. Asset Management embraces all of Friends Provident's investment management activities, with an increasing presence in the unit trust, PEP and institutional markets.

The company says: 'Our mission is to flourish as a leading provider of quality financial products, offering customers the best possible service and above-average performance backed by high standards of ethics and integrity.'

Biggest Plus: A real hands-on, 'just do it' business

Biggest Minus: Regulation in the financial services industry dictates frequent change

Friends Provident
Pixham End
Dorking
Surrey RH4 1QA
Tel: 01306-740123
Fax: 01306-740150

The Business

With Quaker traditions dating back to 1832, and being a mutual, Friends Provident has inbred business values of integrity, ethics and fair play. Treating the customer fairly is uppermost in mind, requiring a careful balance between the interests of customers, employees and other stakeholders. These values look like serving the company well as the financial services industry races through unprecedented change.

With imposing regulation in the industry coupled to greater sophistication on the part of the customer, chairman Lord Jenkin of Roding says that "the prizes will go to the companies which can match (these changes) with product innovation, a really well-trained sales force, backed by the best technology and high standards of service."

The acquisition of NM Financial Management in 1993 reveals Friends Provident (FP) as a growing company, while its international activities are crystallised in Eureko, a pan-European alliance owned by FP, Achmea of the Netherlands, Topdanmark from Denmark, WASA of Sweden, Ocidental in Portugal and Gothaer in Germany.

Company Culture and Style

'Rising through the ranks' is certainly a characteristic of Friends Provident. Many people boast careers of 25–40 years' duration, revealing a genuine affection for the company. Chief executive Michael Doerr, the MD of Business Operations, and the head of customer services all joined as 'A' level students or actuarial trainees.

Why do people stay so long? If you remain optimistic, enthusiastic, and flexible, FP offers excellent opportunities to develop your own career ideas on route. This continuity has helped imbue a solid trust in the capabilities of senior management. Actuarial expertise provides a solid foundation, giving management full control and a genuine feel for what is going on at all levels of the business at any time.

FP has adapted well in acknowledging that its main resource, people, is a flexible one. People increasingly take their professional discipline as their career rather than one specific company, and if this makes it difficult to move people around different functions, it is worth remembering that a company like FP is an aggregation of a wide range of specialists—actuaries, fund managers, functions in sales and marketing, legal, finance, and (increasingly) in information technology. FP is particularly innovative in the use of IT and has, over the years, been recognised in Europe as one of the industry leaders.

Inevitably, work culture varies across functions. Sensibly, the company observes rather than creates cultural values, and reacts to them accordingly. This is a tenet of a very practical organisation—one that looks forward, continually identifying opportunities, but possessing few thrills. If others have more razzmatazz, Friends Provident just gets on with it. When it had to create a direct sales force, the actioning request came on a single piece of paper; 10,000 applications were processed, 230 people were recruited and started work, in less than a year. This 'just do it' attitude simultaneously reveals the 'we trust you' factor which exists between people in the company.

Human Resource Priorities

The HR function provides the support and guidance to management normally associated with this activity, in the areas of staff appraisals, personal and management development, training, and pay and benefits.

At the operational level, HR is a service function to line managers. The agenda is to help the divisions develop their business by using people effectively, with HR acting as a 'consulting function', offering a toolbox of different skills. At the heart of the appraisal system is the responsibility of monitoring and managing the dialogue between manager and employee.

Successes can generate certain strains on the agenda for overall corporate development of people resources. For example, the management development programme is highly focused for each division, but the best features of any one are lifted out and deployed in other divisions' programmes. And in developing competencies, an initiative that started in various divisions now forms part of a programme for nearly everyone.

Another HR responsibility is to sit at forums and seminars such as the strategic planning forum, and to contribute and initiate programmes as a result. This underpins FP's commitment to the role of HR as a real enabler of business strategy.

Career Opportunity and Development

FP believes quite firmly in the concept of managing your own career. "You can count on us, but don't rely on us," as the assistant general manager, HR puts it. Employees are considered to be best-placed to judge, identify and manage their own aspirations and requirements. This is fundamental to FP's development philosophy, and translates right across all training.

If specialists do hold greater allegiance to their profession, then FP is happy to support this and encourages the development of excellence, including the pursuit of professional qualifications. Meanwhile, development consultants help people acquire key practical skills such as team-building, time management, as well as advice on how to really learn through experience. The company runs three in-house Learning Centres and, realising that providing Learning Centres is one thing but getting employees to use them is another, markets them positively and staffs them with controllers to help dinosaurs through the IT interface.

Pay and Benefits

The HR department has expansive and well thought-out views on pay, contending that pay is as much about perceptions as absolutes. Their view is that you move pay structures at your peril unless you are absolutely clear about what you are doing and why, and that it is crucial that any pay system should not get ahead of senior management's commitment. Many well-intended elaborations and ideas have died a quick death.

Pay policy also needs to reflect other messages, and FP believes that people must see that the way in which pay is allocated is 'fair'. Personnel departments sometimes deal in 'bad news' in matters of pay, but while people may not always like the message, they are entitled to know why it is being given.

This puts the onus on the pay system to be well-structured and openly understood, which seems to be the case—the system is fairly traditional but very carefully thought through and managed. A sophisticated matrix incorporates scales and pay bands, negotiations with the unions, the use of consultants such as Hay, own surveys, and also checks that any rose-tinted managers do not over-reward their own people disproportionately—not everyone in the company is likely to have performed 'brilliantly' at the same time.

Sometimes the system comes under strain in certain professional groups, particularly where the external market—or individuals' perceptions of it—can throw up distortions. The remuneration unit is always fully aware of market pay levels for all functions, which sounds like the Secret Service but reflects a tremendous commitment to know exactly where these levels are so that the company can take decisions on 'special cases' accordingly. Friends Provident is willing to pay people for what they do or can do, less so for what that person thinks he or she *might* be capable of doing.

The Future

Friends Provident faces many challenges in harnessing its people resources effectively in support of its business strategy. 'Find clients, not a job' can be traced back to Charles Handy's work, which finds supporters in FP's HR department.

The changes in the financial services industry have seen people leave and people join. FP is working hard to manage this transition, involving some inevitable restructuring, particularly of its various sales operations. It has already laid down markers on how to handle redundancy situations, in a genuine rather than any self-interest wish to avoid a 'black bag' syndrome. "They are our people and we cannot just tip someone out onto the street. The impact upon people still in the company is important, who are bound to ask 'what happened to my friend'."

FP is a little concerned over the fracturing of pay structures. While not in the vanguard of appreciating competency-based pay ideas, it recognises that the company must address the question of how fast to move on evolving its own pay systems.

And while FP's job training or professional development is good, it wants to work much harder in the area of management development. Aware that people can climb the technical or professional hierarchies and, somewhat inadvertently, step into positions with serious people management responsibilities, HR needs to supplement this progress by helping individuals develop real, purposeful, management skills.

Friends Provident agrees that tremendous demands are placed on all employees in Britain today, and views it as 'remarkable' that people respond and deliver so well. Motivation is at the heart of this dynamic, resting somewhere between putting pressure on employees and creating an open environment where nothing is expected. Motivation is not regarded as a precious commodity that should come in expensive bottles. Instead, its deep-thinking HR department uses its range of ideas and policies, along with the knowledge that individual line managers often know best how to unlock motivation, to release this crucial element of future success.

GKN plc

GKN is a world leader in many of its operations, including the design, development and manufacture of automotive and agricultural components, aerospace and defence products, and industrial services. The company's operations span five continents and around 35 countries. GKN has an annual turnover of over £3 billion. It employs 30,000 people in subsidiaries world-wide, 14,000 in the UK; and a further 10,000 in joint venture companies around the world.

Biggest Plus: A dynamic company at the cutting edge of engineering

Biggest Minus: A seriously demanding environment!

GKN plc
PO Box 55
Redditch
Worcestershire B98 0TL
Tel: 01527-517715
Fax: 01527-517700

The Business

GKN is a top 100 UK company renowned for its sound financial planning, forward-looking management and outstanding engineering skills. GKN driveline systems and components are found throughout the automotive industry: in Western Europe, Japan, the USA, Poland, Brazil, China and India. BMW, Fiat, Ford, Jaguar, Nissan, Toyota and VW are among the well-known companies that rely on GKN components.

Although well known for its automotive business, this represents only half of what GKN does. Another aspect of its operations is GKN Westland, a company at the leading edge of civil and defence aerospace technology. This company designs and manufactures helicopters as well as a range of products for the aerospace industry. Among its famous products are the Apache, Sea King and Lynx helicopters.

GKN Special Vehicles Division is the UK's leading supplier of light armoured vehicles—and 60% of such vehicles used by the British army were made by GKN. The Warrior is an infantry vehicle first deployed in the Gulf War, while the Piranha is a rapid deployment vehicle now on operational duty in the Middle East. The company has also added to its range through acquisition: this now includes the Tactica family of 4x4s and Aquatrack fully amphibious tracked carriers.

Other areas of GKN deliver dedicated logistics, pallet and container hire. The Chep group of companies is the world leader in pallet-pooling services and is the fastest growing area of GKN's business. In Europe and the USA Chep is a joint venture with Brambles Industries of Australia. Cleanaway is also a joint venture with Brambles, and is one of the UK's leading solid waste collection, municipal waste collection and street cleaning companies. It also has an incinerator for the disposal of chemical and industrial waste. All in all, GKN is a diverse, dynamic and fast-growing group.

Company Culture and Style

Although made up of a range of companies with very different products, services and market places, there is definitely a GKN culture. This is based on a common goal of wanting to produce the best products and to deliver increasing performance to its customers. All its businesses share a culture of challenge, toughness and competitiveness. In turn, this means that working for GKN is rewarding and exciting. For anyone who thrives in a demanding environment, this is an ideal place to work.

So who is likely to do well at GKN? The company looks for adventurous, imaginative and intelligent people who are self-starters and self-motivating and can also work as part of a team. Confidence and enthusiasm are vital attributes, but so too is open-mindedness; employees must have the ability to listen and learn.

The culture is also one of self-development. In building a career, GKN provides the framework and building blocks but employees themselves structure, guide and define that career path. They also tend to be responsible for their personal development, taking ownership of their learning by studying and attending seminars even in areas outside their career brief.

Internal communications include a video twice a year that reports on results from around the Group. Most internal communications are handled on a cascade basis with considerable use of two-way meetings and discussions. These tend to be site-specific in the main, but also put local issues into the Group context.

GKN plays an active part in its communities, partly by assisting education through providing scholarships and giving financial assistance to literacy and numeracy courses. It also makes substantial charitable donations and contributes to community activities in the UK. Fund raising by employees is also at a high level. In the USA, for instance, GKN Automotive employees raised $125,000 for local communities.

Human Resource Priorities

GKN's reputation for excellence depends on the ability to recruit, develop and retain people of the highest quality. To this end, sustained and targeted investment in training is seen as a strategic priority.

Training throughout the Group has two clear aims: to improve the performance of the businesses, and to encourage and enable individuals to achieve their full potential. Throughout the world, GKN supports the principle of equal opportunity irrespective of sex, race, colour or creed. Full and fair consideration is given to employment applications from people with disabilities. The Group has demonstrated its commitment to the principles of the Investors in People programme, and all GKN companies in the UK are dedicated to achieving this quality standard.

Career Opportunity and Development

GKN has a graduate recruitment and development programme designed to provide the company with its future leaders. The programme has three paths: engineering, finance and commercial. Once on board, the graduate trainee develops through a series of placements. Each last from four to six months and one is overseas. This practical work is supported by off-the-job training, individual mentoring and the Scheme Management team which helps trainees plan and guide their development. Most graduates take from two to two and a half years to complete the programme.

Robert Starr read Engineering, Design and Manufacture at Hull and entered the engineering path. "The Graduate Development Scheme is structured to provide as much assistance as required in developing your true professional and managerial potential. The Scheme not only provides training to become proficient as an engineer but also allows you to develop those skills necessary for a future senior position with the company."

Around half of the company's manufacturing operations are outside the UK, so there are plenty of opportunities to develop careers overseas. Language, personal and management training is provided, and people working abroad are able to develop their cross-cultural understanding as they mix and work with nationals of other companies.

GKN's graduate recruitment and development policies were highlighted as "Particularly effective" by the *Financial Times*. But development activities are not limited to graduate scheme entrants. The Group offers opportunities for personal and professional development at all levels. Its young managers and specialists are working to individually tailored development plans.

In 1990, GKN set up its own International College of Engineering based in Germany to develop the key competencies of technical staff and managers. More than 500 employees a year take part in its programmes. Developing people in their working lives and encouraging them to play a full part in their Group companies are at the heart of GKN's business strategy.

GKN is also committed to a highly qualified workforce. It encourages and supports its engineers in acquired chartered status, while finance graduates specialising in accountancy also receive training and support towards acquiring the Chartered Institute of Management Accountants (CIMA) professional qualification.

Pay and Benefits

GKN pays competitive salaries, a stance that it needs to take in order to attract and retain the best people. Pay increases are largely determined by individual performance.

The company offers UK employees the opportunity to join an SAYE share-option scheme. More than 50% of eligible employees hold share options. There is also an excellent pension scheme and lively sports and social events in many locations.

The Future

The Group's strong international market positions have been built up over the long term through hard work, carefully applied strategy and excellent products.

To maintain and improve on these positions will require a continual flow of good employees and managers creating new leading-edge products. The key to this challenge is to invest in research and development as well as in training to ensure the continued provision of customer satisfaction.

GlaxoWellcome

Glaxo Wellcome

Glaxo Wellcome is the world's largest pharmaceutical company, formed by the merger of Glaxo and Wellcome in March 1995, with a 5% share of the world prescription market. With global headquarters in Britain, the Group had annual sales of around £8 billion and trading profits of £2,581 million in 1995, operating companies in 83 countries, supplies over 150 markets and employs approximately 60,000 people (13,000 in the UK).

The company's mission statement is concise: 'Glaxo Wellcome is a research-based company whose people are committed to fighting disease by bringing innovative medicines and services to patients throughout the world and to the healthcare providers who serve them.'

Biggest Plus: A great achiever in a rewarding industry

Biggest Minus: The pace of change is frenetic

Glaxo Wellcome plc
Lansdowne House
Berkeley Square
London W1X 6BQ
Tel: 0171-493 4060
Fax: 0171-408 0228

The Business

The pharmaceutical industry is particularly exciting and very challenging at the moment. Companies are consolidating, amalgamating, and adapting. The profile of the customer is also changing, as is the diversity of markets and the areas of technology. Glaxo Wellcome is at the forefront of these changes.

Glaxo needed to leverage its size as a global player, concentrating at the same time on the subtleties of local markets. At the time of the merger with Wellcome, chief executive Sir Richard Sykes said: "Glaxo resolved to be at the head of the process, not be dragged along by it. We recognised that the successful pharmaceutical company of the future must have scale and strength in research and development, sales, product range and services. Wellcome was a good fit for us, with a similar culture based on science, sound research, a complementary range of products, and high quality staff."

Glaxo catapulted itself to prominence in the early 1980s through the phenomenal success of its anti-ulcer drug, Zantac—the world's first $1 billion drug. A dedicated commitment to developing new products, accelerated by the Wellcome merger, has reduced the new Group's dependence on Zantac from 43% (as Glaxo only) to 28% of sales.

"Disease has no greater enemy than Glaxo Wellcome" is the message in the first ever TV advertisements run by the company. Glaxo Wellcome is indeed a research-based company with a keen eye for commercial opportunity. The company concentrates its scientific, technological and marketing skills on the creation of new medicines in disease areas where there is a balance of unmet medical need and commercial opportunity. Glaxo Wellcome has an excellent spread of products and therapeutic areas of research, but is particularly strong in gastro-intestinal, anti viral and respiratory.

With rapidly changing technologies, particularly in biotechnology, genetics, and combinatorial chemistry, the whole industry is metamorphosing at a breathtaking rate. This provides both opportunities and challenges, for the work force. The acquisition of Affymax N.V. in 1995 highlights Glaxo Wellcome's intention to stay at the forefront of innovative research and development.

Company Culture and Style

Glaxo's corporate culture was a strong one, as was Wellcome's. Time will tell how quickly any new hybrid culture emerges. The new organisation is intended to empower and release the energy of its people, recognising that Glaxo Welcome is nothing but 'a collection of intellectual capital'. It has to be a learning organisation.

Glaxo Wellcome is shifting from a 'cradle to grave' work culture to a more flexible way of working—the company does not assume that its staff will necessarily remain with it for their entire working lives, and nor do they. This implies a renegotiation of the psychological contract between employer and employee, and the fusion of two of the UK's leading pharmaceutical companies provided a helpful catalyst to this process.

Individuals who flourish in the company tend to be energetic, commercial, communicative, enthusiastic, able to respond to challenges, and to take 'risks' in certain areas to maximise research and commercial opportunities. The company seeks to encourage a non-hierarchical organisation, rewarding individuals' contributions to the whole.

There is probably no superior corporate citizen than Glaxo Wellcome. The company is dedicated to the highest environmental standards, and is also one of the largest 'corporate givers'. Glaxo Wellcome contributes approximately 3% of UK pre-tax profits in a wide-ranging programme to charitable and community causes, particularly in healthcare support.

Human Resource Priorities

The board regards HR as an integral part of business strategy. HR priorities include supporting the organisation through change; maximising the personal effectiveness of its staff in an ever-changing market; and helping the business achieve its short-term goals while developing sustainable long-term growth.

"We are committed to harnessing the potential of all our staff, be they in the research, development, manufacturing or commercial areas of the business," says Tim Miller, director of human resources and UK coordination. "In return, the company provides excellent remuneration and benefits, high quality working environments, and great opportunities for personal growth and development."

Glaxo Wellcome is a leader in many HR best practices. For example, there is a range of programmes to support women in the work place, including child care facilities, enhanced maternity leave, and 'phase back' arrangements. Glaxo Wellcome is also proud of its record in diversity, in terms of employment of cultural, ethnic or disability groups. Glaxo Wellcome believes strongly in the Investors in People standard in the UK; its site at Speke has attained recognition already, and other sites are in the process of doing so.

The successful integration of Glaxo and Wellcome is now largely complete and HR played a critical role in this complex process. Some job losses were inevitable as operations were streamlined, but excellent, comprehensive severance and support programmes were provided for those leaving the company, as well as making major efforts to refocus and support staff working for the new organisation.

Glaxo Wellcome is now evolving and moving forward and recruiting the best people. Around 100 graduates are taken on each year and, due to the nature of its business, the company hires many postgraduates and direct entry professionals.

Career Opportunity and Development

There are excellent opportunities for stimulating, rewarding careers throughout the company. While the resulting 'flatter' structure might mean fewer vertical career moves, there is an increased emphasis on enhancing skills to the highest standards.

Individuals are increasingly responsible for their own careers, and development programmes, organisational models and principles are there to assist. In the UK and elsewhere, competency-based performance and reward processes have been developed and implemented.

With increasing talk of 'a team-based culture', development programmes are built around teams as much as the individual. Networking between businesses is encouraged in order to share and transfer beneficial experiences and practices.

All this makes for a more versatile, flexible organisation, where the company benefits from the excellent skills of its staff, who in turn enhance their own market-ability. Tim Miller agrees that there is a shift towards employees recognising themselves as a marketable resource in their function or discipline, appreciating that they may not work with the company forever. This is openly accepted, with the company aiming to maximise their contributions while people are there.

Pay and Benefits

Glaxo Wellcome recognises that to attract the best people, highly competitive salary and benefits packages must be offered.

The merger brought together a myriad of inconsistencies in the area of pay, benefits, holidays, shifts and so on. Harmonising them into a single system has been an important focus and an integral part of forming the new culture. Glaxo Wellcome has recently introduced a new company pension scheme, which it describes as 'leading edge' due to its flexibility and portability.

There are many schemes, including a Share Save scheme and facilitating financial vehicles, to encourage staff to become shareholders in the company.

The Future

Glaxo's 'wonder drug' Zantac is nearing the end of its patent life, as are certain others, presenting the company with the opportunity to seek ways of extending the life of key products, while bringing new compounds successfully through the research stage into the company's product portfolio.

The toughest 'people' challenge facing Glaxo Wellcome, and the most important one, is to maintain the commitment of all its employees as the pharmaceutical industry undergoes rapid, sometimes bewildering, change. Not that this commitment is in question, but putting motivation at the top of the agenda seems a sensible move.

Having led from the front of the industry, and with a strong corporate awareness, purpose, and set of values, Glaxo Wellcome intends to create more self-reliant, as opposed to patriarchal, structures within the business.

Within the human resources function, the company is looking at specific areas including team-based pay and competency pay, creating more flexible ways of working, and maintaining a continuous commitment to improving performance.

Glaxo Wellcome is a much-admired company, showing great vitality and business focus for such a large organisation. While Glaxo Wellcome is a global business, it must remain focused on its customers and the local market place. 'Think global, act regionally, think locally' sums up the company's approach.

With frontier areas of technology revolutionising the industry, Glaxo Wellcome finds itself at the centre of a demanding, but exciting business. The constant theme is the task of fighting diseases, which adds a rewarding dimension to work and achievement in a company that has a superb track record of research and commercial success.

Goldman Sachs

Goldman Sachs International

Goldman, Sachs & Co. is a 127-year-old investment banking and securities firm serving corporations, governments, institutions and individuals in markets around the world. The partnership is guided by its Business Principles emphasising commitment to clients, excellence in service, teamwork, integrity and creativity.

World-wide, Goldman Sachs employs approximately 9,000 people, of which 2,000 are in Europe, 1,700 in the UK. Goldman Sachs has gross revenues of $15 billion and total assets in excess of $125 billion. A quarter of the firm's assets and its people are outside the USA, a trend likely to increase.

Biggest Plus: The premier investment bank with an open, friendly culture

Biggest Minus: Inevitable long hours and pressure of work

Goldman Sachs International
Peterborough Court
133 Fleet Street
London EC4A 2BB
Tel: 0171-774 1000
Fax: 0171-774 4477

The Business

Goldman Sachs has few peers in investment banking, and consistently receives high ratings in the business media for its management style, and in surveys on advisory and execution services. From the inside, employees believe that its premier reputation is based on several key points—a flat structure, a distinct Goldman Sachs culture, a heavy emphasis on teamwork, a proud history as a firm, and offices in 18 countries.

"We are not a US firm operating overseas," says Peter Sutherland, chairman of Goldman Sachs International in London. "We are a global investment bank."

Goldman Sachs Business Principle No. 5: "We make an unusual effort to identify and recruit the very best person for every job. Although our activities are measured in billions of dollars, we select our people one by one. In a service business, we know that without the best people, we cannot be the best firm."

Goldman Sachs is a premier provider of high value-added, integrated services to large multinational corporations as well as to high growth emerging companies. Goldman Sachs favours applying its skills to complex, challenging and demanding situations where there is the opportunity to provide high value-added services rather than 'commodity' like business.

The firm focuses on the major European corporations, institutional investors and high net worth individuals, providing advisory services, financing, and sales and trading. In addition, Goldman Sachs is very active in the principal investments area. There is a balance between issuing and investing clients, as well as agency and principal transactions.

Company Culture and Style

Goldman Sachs is guided by its Business Principles—of which it articulates 14— and it only does business consistent with these principles. That means clients' interests always come first, the foundation of relationship banking.

Skills valued at Goldman Sachs include integrity, high motivation, intelligence, creativity, and commercial sensitivity, with an emphasis on long-term relationships as opposed to immediate transactions. Goldman Sachs executives must feel comfortable relating to and counselling clients; they must establish credibility, honesty and trust, and sometimes disagree. "Often the best advice is just don't do the deal," says MD and co-head of the investment banking division in Europe, Richard Hayden.

Goldman Sachs is a flat organisation—the firm has very little in the way of hierarchy. Team building is fundamental across all of the businesses. This is *one* firm. Goldman Sachs emphasises an open environment, where it can encourage people not to be afraid to make 'the right kind of mistakes'.

Goldman Sachs is a meritocracy, a collaborative firm where camaraderie is spontaneous and genuine, and where people think of each other as friends as much as business colleagues. There is also a strong sense of justice in the firm; if people ever feel they have not been dealt with fairly, the chairman's door is open.

Indeed, all partners' offices are open, and they never ask beforehand why you want to see them.

Richard Hayden believes that, "You are either going to love or hate this business. The work is hard and intense, often involving long hours; and you must feel comfortable with the people around you, because you spend so much time with them."

Human Resource Priorities

Goldman Sachs realised that as it became global, excellent HR policies in recruiting, developing and motivating people would be essential to establish points of difference and to build a group capable of delivering its services at international levels for the next five, ten, and fifteen years.

In recruitment, Goldman Sachs goes to considerable lengths to ensure that a candidate will fit in. Some say that people get too involved in the process, but this is just indicative of the care taken in securing the success of the firm. It's a two-way street, and at the core of the interview process is the wish for the firm to get to know the individual, and the individual to get to know the firm.

Goldman Sachs has done relatively well in retaining its people, made easier by the success of the firm and the industry in recent years. Goldman Sachs' people will always be attractive to poachers, but the firm avoids competing in the 'spot market', preferring instead to emphasise the tremendous long-term career opportunities available. "The better you do, the further you go" is one of the biggest attractions of the firm to individuals.

A European-wide staff survey was designed to improve understanding employees' thinking, priorities, issues, and what the firm could do better. The feedback was constructive, and is helping the firm to maintain its focus on employees' priorities as it continues to grow. One of the key issues for HR is to communicate effectively to everyone as Goldman Sachs grows bigger and extends globally.

Career Opportunity and Development

'An exceptional place to pursue a career' is how Goldman Sachs has been described. Careers are highly mobile, across functions and between locations. Too often there is an external perception that people go into one type of career or business, and then stay there. At Goldman Sachs there are many types of functions, providing fascinating opportunities to re-start careers on a regular basis. This is one way in which the firm keeps people with considerable experience in the business—the 'culture carriers'.

Goldman Sachs also encourages global mobility. Head of personnel, David Duffy, suggests that, "There are many pretenders to being a global firm, but only if you have people with international experience and a global mindset are you really able to make that claim." Goldman Sachs believes that it is important to maintain the cultural glue by sending staff abroad. In doing so, the values of Goldman Sachs are exported.

Everyone is reviewed by 360 degree career performance management. This is time-consuming when a significant number of people can be giving opinions on an individual, but it enables people to get honest, objective feedback, which in turn makes career planning more effective. Themes from 360 degree feedback are not forgotten until next year—they percolate directly into compensation. Individuals never leave their review without taking away between five to eight key things to concentrate on *and* they must come back with a personal development plan incorporating these issues.

Pay and Benefits

Pay is essentially performance-based. Goldman Sachs pays very well, starting at graduate level. The firm wants the best people, and pays at the top level, but where there are 'spikes' in the competitive market, Goldman Sachs tries not to get drawn into these situations. It prefers instead to emphasise the substantial benefits of long-term career ambition. If people are successful in the firm they will find themselves at or near the top of any pay scale offered by competitors.

The Future

Goldman Sachs of course cannot ignore its core client relationships, which historically have been the source of its profitability. At the same time, the firm must continue to look for new areas of opportunity, where complexity and risk create a need for high value-added services. For example, Goldman Sachs has been spending a great deal of time implementing an emerging markets strategy.

Recognising that rapid change will be continuous, and being first or second in virtually everything it does, Goldman Sachs is only too aware of the dangers of complacency. The firm must make sure that it avoids any 'institutionalisation of success'. Communication is fundamental to the firm's success. There is a genuine, open dialogue to ensure that everyone is fully aware of the firm's strategy, so that people and capital resources are always allocated consistent with these objectives.

Goldman Sachs aggressive recruitment has produced a very young professional group. The firm believes that as it expands, it needs to strengthen lines of communication between 'seniors' who lead the firm and formulate strategy, and the young professionals who are inevitably closer to the markets and are the sensors of the firm.

This will become vital as the firm extends its global reach. It knows that markets, business practices and cultures are different, and hiring new people who are sensitive to local conditions will be very important. In attracting the best people, Goldman Sachs is likely to continue to stress the long-term opportunities in the firm.

Goldman Sachs people regard the firm as being 'something special', and want to work hard to leave behind something better. With this in-built commitment to the highest standards, and a culture that values everyone in the firm as being important, people are rightly proud to say that they are a professional at Goldman Sachs.

GUINNESS PLC

Guinness PLC

Guinness is an international company producing, distributing and marketing branded consumer products throughout the world. Its core business is premium quality alcoholic beverages, particularly spirits and beer. Guinness employs 21,500 people world-wide (around half in the UK, where its head office is found).

It is one of the major exporters from the UK, and is the largest exporter in the food and drinks sector. Export earnings in excess of £1,130 million represent 90% of the group's profits. The group has two principal operating companies—United Distillers (spirits) and Guinness Brewing World-wide (brewing).

Biggest Plus:	Exciting jobs working with some of the world's most famous drinks brands
Biggest Minus:	Career development in specialist functions seen as a greater priority than general management

Guinness PLC
39 Portman Square
London   W1H 0EE
Tel: 0171-486 0288
Fax: 0171-486 4968

The Business

If you are searching for the owner of premium drinks brands such as Johnnie Walker, Bell's and Gordons, the answer is Guinness. And it also produces Guinness stout itself. These are only a few of the famous names in the portfolio and, as a genuine brand-building company (of which there are not so many in the UK), Guinness is also a financially successful company.

The company's origins can be traced back to 1759 when Arthur Guinness bought the brewery at St. James's Gate in Dublin and one of the world's truly great beers was about to brewed for the first time. 'Ireland's dark secret' is hardly a secret anymore. Much of the production from Dublin is exported, and Guinness is also brewed at the slightly less romantic place of Park Royal in West London.

Spirits contribute more profit to the group today than beer. The contrasting statistics that half of the group's employees are in the British Isles, yet 90% of earnings come from overseas, offer useful clues as to where whisky is made and where it is consumed.

The Guinness Group is truly international in its operations and markets, and increasingly in its culture and management. Guinness owns brands and operations in the USA, South America, Australia, Germany, Spain, and many more countries.

Notable business achievements in the 1980s included buying-out third party distributors, and the strategic alliance forged with LVMH Moët Hennessy Louis Vuitton and bonded by cross-shareholdings (Guinness owns 34% of the Moët Hennessy drinks business; LVMH owns 21% of Guinness plc). The alliance has established 17 joint ventures world-wide distributing complementary drinks portfolios.

Company Culture and Style

Tony Greener, chairman: "We have to do better than our competitors in two key areas, in our depth of understanding of the consumer, and the efficiency of our total business system in servicing the consumer."

Guinness is building an international culture on top of the structure of a world-wide company. The executive committees of Guinness Brewing World-wide and United Distillers are at least 30% non-British, a management cocktail bringing different perspectives, debates and emotions to bear on business strategy.

The style is entrepreneurial, but the international culture has to be balanced by some recognition that the company's two major brands, Johnnie Walker and Guinness, have strong nationalistic or ethnic identities. Unlike global brands such as Coca-Cola or Nike, the way that Guinness' brands are exploited internationally requires a local approach, with the caveat that country managers cannot tamper with valuable brand images and values. But they have a portfolio of superb brands to play with, and crafting the right marketing mix and distribution choice creates plenty of opportunity.

People are increasingly attracted to this international environment at Guinness. The company has a richer international flavour today than it did five years ago, due to many cross-divisional and international appointments at all levels.

There are few apparent strains between structure and culture. There is an organisational framework of course, but there is also considerable freedom to express yourself at Guinness. The pendulum is still swinging towards 'what you do in the market place', with little interference in-between, in something resembling an 'hourglass' management structure.

People who flourish at Guinness are bright, do not suffer fools gladly, and know what they are doing, but have good inter-personal skills. The company likes drivers and achievers. It does not like politicians, or rather people who think that they will get along just by knowing the right people in the company.

In brand marketing, there might be a tendency for individuals to feel a little more related to their discipline than their operating company. Guinness increasingly emphasises that its people are a group resource, and do not belong solely to one company, division or brand. This loyalty might not happen automatically, with phenomenal brands such as Johnnie Walker having strong international identities of their own, but the Guinness Group is emphasised deliberately and increasingly. Wide ownership of Guinness stocks and shares helps in cultivating this affection.

Human Resource Priorities

HR has a genuine strategic agenda at Guinness. While HR director John de Leeuw has a seat on the main group board, key issues are not top-down missives, but rather the results of an iterative process. Good HR professionals throughout Guinness build the agenda for the group, its divisions, and the head office team.

Management of talent is crucial, as Guinness searches for ever-increasing quality of people. This involves striking the right balance between internal development and external hiring, succession planning for key positions, and the recruitment of young, talented people. While training used to be a needs-driven activity left to the divisions, a greater group emphasis has triggered increased management skills training.

Change management figures highly on the HR agenda, and while de Leeuw acknowledges that 'managing change' is hardly a new idea and is an obvious business dynamic, he is aware that the rate of change is accelerating.

When you have HR as a strategic agenda, you don't just use words and jargon. The fallout hits line management hard. Workshops, like those run by director of employment policy Mike Redhouse on how to reward *team* accomplishment of business goals, get very positive feedback. In this way, HR is helping line managers become more aware of behaviour and actions required, and how to reinforce them. Measurement and consistent judgement are vital, harnessing the processes of performance reviews and organisation/management reviews, where action plans are set, revisited and reviewed.

Career Opportunity and Development

The career playing field is the world-wide group, and is quite green. Guinness is not a company which says 'come on in, we'll take care of you'; instead, a two-way process is inherent; Guinness encourages good people because they will need them, but your career is also your responsibility and you must seize the opportunities. And there are many opportunities at Guinness to realise your ambitions.

The two executive committees at United Distillers and Guinness Brewing World-wide convene every month where career paths and planning has bubbled to the top of the agenda.

The individual is prompted to consider 'Is a step into general management possible, desirable or feasible?' or 'Why be a general manager when there is so much more to learn, aspire to and achieve within the specialist functions?' "The easiest thing to say is 'I want to be in general management'," according to de Leeuw, "and they need to get this into perspective."

There is an increasing emphasis on recruiting young talented people—new graduates of course, but increasingly people in the 25–30 years' bracket. Guinness claims that with 21,500 staff it is still a 'small' company, and can also offer tremendous opportunities to assistant brand managers with that essential first few years of experience under their belts.

Pay and Benefits

Remuneration packages are good. Guinness pays upper-quartile salaries for good people—in the brand marketing industry, you must be competitive.

Guinness is becoming strategic and innovative in its reward systems, identifying individual behaviours, including teamwork and performance, needed to meet business objectives and then match instruments of reward to encourage and instil such behaviour. Reward is also being geared towards building relationships and business partnerships with customers. This is engendering an entrepreneurial spirit among country managers, releasing energies where managers may have part of their reward at risk.

This approach is also revealed in a highly geared employee share ownership plan. All group employees can buy shares at a discount, and all UK and Irish employees become shareholders through profit sharing arrangements. The SAYE scheme operates in no fewer than 27 countries, ensuring a large global audience for what has generally been a strong Guinness share price.

The Future

"Building Guinness into a world-leading consumer-brand marketing company is a major challenge in the very different business environment of the mid-1990s," according to Tony Greener.

John de Leeuw's HR professionals need to ensure that their high profile, high-powered strategy agenda has buy-in from line management, which is charged to implement it in full. HR's challenge is to become business partners in a commercial team. Only if HR lives up to the expectations and standards of its peers can it succeed in changing its perspective from an HR function into a business function.

From an organisational standpoint, Guinness must supply excellent management succession over the long term. It must also ensure that Guinness remains an interesting place to work and join.

Brand marketing jobs will always be attractive, but in changing to a more delayered structure, the implicit contract between company and employees has changed. There is a more intrinsic basis of working together in what for both sides is a marriage of reason. The evidence suggests this is a working environment in which people can perform to their fullest potential.

G W R group plc

GWR

GWR is one of the fastest-growing local radio groups in the UK. Since its formation in 1985 in Swindon, Wiltshire, it has increased revenues considerably, to approximately £50 million. The GWR broadcasting group now has 32 local radio licences, broadcasting to a potential audience of 11 million listeners across a wide area of Southern England, the Midlands and East Anglia.

In 1995 GWR acquired Chiltern Radio, and is also a shareholder in London News Radio Limited, the re-launched LBC. In 1996 GWR bought Classic FM, opening up a national audience. In addition to Classic FM's operations in Holland, Finland and Sweden, GWR has interests in Radio FM Plus in Sofia, Bulgaria, Radio Edelweiss in Austria, and Prospect, New Zealand's second largest radio group. GWR has around 650 full-time employees, plus another 150 freelance employees, including presenters.

Biggest Plus: Fast-growing, exciting and fun media business

Biggest Minus: Some processes and systems lag behind, still in a melting pot

GWR Group plc
PO Box 2345
3B2 Westlea
Swindon SN5 7HF
Tel: 01793-422700
Fax: 01793-422772

The Business

Group chief executive Ralph Bernard's strategy has been to grow GWR quickly through acquisition, to get the necessary critical mass to have clout. This it now has. Because of restrictions on ownership imposed by the radio authorities in the UK, GWR is concentrating on the quality of its portfolio of licences and the performance of individual stations.

Radio remains the fastest-growing sector of the UK media, having grown from 45 stations a decade ago to nearer 180 today. Commercial radio's share of the listening population has increased at the expense of the BBC. Commercial radio's share of total display advertising has risen from 3.6% in 1994 to 4.5% in 1996.

While there is a finite number of people in the country, the proportion of younger listeners in the 18–24 age group listening to commercial radio has risen—a disaster for the BBC. The young adult group is the predominant one of interest to advertisers. GWR has around four million adult listeners each week.

GWR has successfully harnessed these market dynamics, and aims to become the premier radio group in the UK.

Company Culture and Style

The radio business is characterised by youthfulness, fun, and immediacy. At GWR, all three pervade throughout the whole organisation.

A young people's business, the average age of GWR staff is around 30 years. It has to be fun if radio is to attract advertisers. Many different people like being associated with their local radio station because it is 'fun'. This is evidenced by the number of people asking to gain work experience at local stations and indeed, the flood of job applications received for full-time positions.

Radio is in operation every minute, 24 hours a day, and therefore immediacy is inbuilt. Unlike TV, radio is not about pre-planning months or even years in advance; it is about what is happening in the local community today. Sensitivity to very local factors—sports, traffic, even the weather—makes for a different kind of culture. Ralph Bernard identifies "Local commercial radio's key strength is its freedom to respond to local concerns."

Structure is important to a growing radio group like GWR, with 20 different stations, and this has an impact on the company's culture. To some extent, any company bought by GWR will be subsumed into the culture of the group, but GWR recognises the important interaction of individual stations with their local communities and is working hard to bolster local cultures, within the overall environment of the group's culture.

One of GWR's core values is a caring attitude to its various stakeholders—staff, listeners, advertisers, and shareholders. Deputy chief executive Patrick Taylor suggests, "We regard staff as the first stakeholder, but the shareholders as the ultimate stakeholder. Any media business is best served by first getting the motivation of its employees right." Without motivated people releasing their creativity, there are no listeners, hence no advertisers, and no financial returns for shareholders. The virtual circle is a reality.

GWR is a highly professional business and pursues efficiency, requiring highly competitive systems to support finance, broadcasting and sales operations. GWR admits that it is not there yet, symptomatic of an acquisitive business that inherits diverse systems, but is beginning to introduce standard company-wide systems to achieve a common platform of performance across the group.

GWR is a research-based business. Stations such as Capital Radio might have intuitive, self-styled programming directors who feel the pace and pulse of the local environment and the people in it. GWR instead favours doing a lot of research to find out exactly what its (diverse) local audiences are interested in and the music policy they like. A template of research and subsequent programming formats is best suited to GWR's network of stations.

Human Resource Priorities

Taylor argues it is particularly important in the radio business to excite and motivate staff by demonstrating a caring attitude. This includes pay, but also providing other valued factors such as decent working conditions, team spirit, managing well, and informing employees how well they and the business is doing.

GWR's HR function is conducted principally through the management structure. Cultural direction comes from GWR's central management team, while regional managing directors, regional sales directors, and station managing directors meet regularly to generate ideas, information and communication.

Patrick Taylor believes strongly in harnessing the creativity and ideas of all people in the organisation, and is looking at ways in which employees and management can communicate together effectively to build a mutual interest of staff and company well-being.

GWR's HR department has been under-resourced, and lagged behind the company's dramatic business growth, but an HR director has been appointed. GWR aims to standardise across the group the ingredients of a good employer—appraisal forms, employment contracts, pension schemes, exit interviews, bonus and incentive schemes, and training. At present, these aspects apply at different levels across the group.

Career Opportunity and Development

There are any number of career functions within GWR, but the two core competencies are in programming and advertising sales. Career paths through programming include presenting, planning and production; the sales route begins at sales assistant, through executive, manager, and director, to regional sales director. There are the usual array of specialists in finance, IT, engineering, HR and administration.

One enlightening aspect of GWR is succession management. The 'old' GWR companies in particular try to identify immediately a successor to a manager put in place—one of the reasons GWR has been able to fuel its expansion plans. When Chiltern Radio was acquired in 1995, GWR was able to implant some of its key managers without exposing the stations they were taken from.

You do not have to be a programmer or sales executive to get into general management. Many station managing directors have come from a news environment (rare) and even from accountancy (almost unheard of). This is all part of GWR's culture—the company can train talented people with intrinsic qualities to become general managers. Group chief executive Ralph Bernard himself comes from a journalistic background.

GWR has three divisions: UK National Radio, UK Local Radio, and Overseas. People do move a lot between local stations (not yet overseas), and all vacancies are advertised internally.

The sales force receive much specific training on 'the product' and courses deliver spin-off benefits in the guise of revitalising people's efforts and building team spirit. As GWR grows, it is increasing the emphasis on more general skills training. Communication skills are regarded as important as any.

Extending the belief in harnessing the ideas and creativity of its people, GWR is also looking to train its managers to help people convert ideas within the corporate environment and develop the business. GWR recognises that for this to work, there has to be a culture in the company of trying things out, without fear of failure. A blame culture is rarely an innovative one.

Pay and Benefits

Basic pay at GWR is generally quite good—maybe even slightly above market rates—but remuneration has not taken into account other factors, such as the business outlook and general demeanour of the work place.

Again, pay policies and benefits, including profit-related pay, pensions and company cars, differ between stations in the group, and GWR intends to seek some conformity in this area.

The Future

With the acquisition of Classic FM, GWR is at the limit of the number of allowable listening population 'points'. Under current regulation, the company must concentrate on improving the quality of its licences, which might involve trading its portfolio. "Playing a game of monopoly," as Patrick Taylor puts it. The group is likely to stay on the look-out for more overseas radio opportunities.

Within the UK, GWR will be looking for novel ways to build new enterprises from its relationships with listeners, going beyond straightforward broadcasting. Other radio stations have developed restaurants, web sites on the Internet (with subsequent new advertising opportunities), and even newspapers. GWR will be assessing its best options, exploring the dynamics of the wider relationship with the listener, deeper involvement with local communities, and the leveraging of the brand name across different products and services.

GWR's cross-media ownership will offer advertisers a broader media portfolio in an excellent heartland covering the Midlands, the South and East Anglia. With Classic FM, it not only has national coverage, but arguably the single best-known flagship in radio in terms of reaching decision makers.

The shareholder structure and director profile of GWR is rather exciting. GWR shares are quoted on the London Stock Exchange, but half are in non-institutional hands. The Classic FM deal brought-in EMI and entrepreneur Sir Peter Michael as shareholders. With a highly entrepreneurial bunch of people managing the business, backed by experienced shareholders including the Daily Mail Trust, GWR is likely to remain a growing company doing exciting things.

Halifax Building Society

Halifax is the UK's largest housing finance lender with a mission to become the biggest and best personal financial services business in the UK. In 1995 Halifax merged with the Leeds Permanent Building Society, extending its customer base and widening its product range. Halifax Direct, the telephone banking service, was introduced in October 1995 offering an additional and efficient way of doing business. A further development, the take-over of Clerical Medical Investment Group, is expected to be completed in 1996. This will strengthen Halifax's position in the long-term savings and life assurance product areas. Halifax now offers current accounts, credit cards, telephone banking, mortgages, insurance and many other products.

In 1995/96 Halifax recorded pre-tax profits of £1.1 billion with total assets of £100 billion. With over 1,000 branch offices and 700 estate agency offices, Halifax employs about 34,000 staff, around one quarter on a part-time basis.

Biggest Plus: Exciting prospects in a brave new world

Biggest Minus: Review process of organisational structures will be ongoing

Halifax Building Society
Trinity Road
Halifax
West Yorkshire HX1 2RG
Tel: 01422-333333
Fax: 01422-333000

The Business

The merger of Halifax and the Leeds Permanent Building Society on YorkshireDay, 1 August 1995, took Halifax substantially towards the goal of becoming the UK's leading provider of personal financial services.

After almost 150 years as a mutual building society, Halifax plans to become a public limited company in June 1997, when its shares will be listed on the London Stock Exchange. Jon Foulds, chairman of Halifax says, "Our principal objective is for Halifax to become market leader in UK retail financial services. We are committed to maintaining our leading position in our traditional business areas while growing the newer areas of business."

"Conversion," adds chief executive Mike Blackburn, "will create the UK's largest ever shareholder base."

Company Culture and Style

Working in a heavily regulated environment, where consistency of service across a national network is a key factor, Halifax needs to have an effectively structured organisation. Accountabilities are defined, and there are very well-developed management control mechanisms.

That said, setting the target of flotation triggered the need for some changes to its corporate culture. With the pace of change ever-increasing, a more flexible 'psychological contract' is in place between company and employees. The traditional 'cradle to grave' long-term basis of employment has given way to a more flexible agreement based on competitive remuneration and the chance for genuine self-development and skills enhancement. Change has also brought the possibility of rapid promotion in some of the new business areas that are opening up.

Staff are encouraged to take an active role in the business. The Staff Suggestion Scheme was dramatically revamped in 1995 to stimulate the inflow of ideas from all parts and levels of the organisation. That 37,000 suggestions have been received in 12 months since September 1995 suggests in itself that staff are passionately involved in the business, and some 10% of their ideas have been implemented, leading to significant improvements in the business.

Halifax is keen to improve communication lines within the organisation. This starts at the top, with the senior management committed to communicating with, and listening to, staff in an honest, open and planned way. Halifax rightly believes that good internal communications can help processes operate more smoothly.

Halifax runs an annual competition between teams working with local charities in Community Development Circles. The climax to this is finals night, involving a stage presentation with members of the executive and directors in the audience. The event is inevitably amusing and entertaining, but is also worthwhile and educational, and helps cement the culture of the company. Halifax Direct also encourages 'fun' at work—not a trivial aside, but an enlightened approach which recognises that happy staff tend to be productive and motivated.

Human Resource Priorities

Human resources management is viewed as a key determinant of corporate success. The overall HR strategy is to recruit, develop, motivate and retain staff to support the achievement of Halifax's business objectives. HR is represented at board level, and its role is that of a business partner, helping to link corporate plans, business strategy and financial targets, HR's objectives include seeking maximum value from current and future staff by continuous assessment, objective selection and effective placement. This is supported by cost-effective training and personal development programmes to enhance personal, technical and managerial skills.

Pay and benefits packages are designed to encourage and reward specified levels of performance. HR must also ensure that Halifax is seen as a high quality employer and that working practices fully support operational requirements.

Halifax is dedicated to managing internal communications within its multi-site organisation. Management of communication is handled skilfully and professionally, employing a mix of appropriate media including live television to all sites, a regular staff newspaper *The Fax*, the Staff Suggestion Scheme, and team meetings.

Halifax is totally committed to equal opportunities for all. Its policy is to link equal opportunity initiatives to the company's mission and values, so that staff are quite clear about what they are trying to achieve. This emphasis placed on diversity extends beyond Halifax seeking a wide representation in its work force of ethnic groups, disabled people and the male/female split, taking into account the diverse needs of its customers as well. Halifax compares well to industry averages—for example on the number of women managers—and is a member of Opportunity 2000. Equality is a fundamental business issue at Halifax, which permeates all parts of the business and is an integral part of the company's culture.

Career Opportunity and Development

Halifax has tended to prefer a good blend of external specialists, as well as entry level recruits, and many of its senior managers and executives have risen through the ranks. This reflects the desire to offer long-term career planning for talented people, and the need for succession planning, which Halifax takes very seriously.

Career development is a shared responsibility between the individual and the company, but there is a lot of support provided. Training programmes are in place to help staff acquire the necessary competencies and personal skills which will enable them to progress through the organisation, and into management levels. Development reviews and assessment centres, which use a Halifax competency framework, help the company to assess individuals and put round pegs in round holes.

A range of management development programmes is also in place, including the graduate fast track development programme and a similar scheme for existing staff, ensuring that Halifax taps into its talent bank to the full, whatever their educational background. At middle and senior management level, very successful modular programmes have been developed jointly with leading business schools to develop high potential staff.

Halifax is fully committed to providing training for all staff. The company has played an active part in developing NVQs for building societies and estate agencies. Other specific training courses are delivered within the head office complexes or through training centres. Open learning and a network of computer-based training also feature, and there is a training channel on Halifax's internal television network.

Pay and Benefits

Halifax pays competitive rates in the financial services sector for staff within the graded salary structure. The salary bands are set so that outstanding performers can move to maximum salaries within given bands at a rapid rate. In 1996 junior managerial salaries were in the range £16,400–27,500, middle managerial grades between £31,600–50,500, and senior salaries started around £60,000. Graduate entrants started at around £14,000. Pay is reviewed through a quarterly review and annual appraisal system, where individual performance is linked directly to pay increases.

Graded staff participate in an annual bonus arrangement, an element of which is paid under the profit-related pay scheme. Private medical insurance is available at all managerial levels, and there are full-time occupational health advisers and nurses at the head office in Halifax. The vast majority of staff are eligible for the company pension, there is also a concessionary staff mortgage scheme, where the maximum loan at the concessionary limit is in the range of £30,000–55,000. Most managers get company cars, as do others where the job requires. As part of its flotation arrangements, Halifax intends to give free shares to all qualifying employees.

The Future

The next few years to the new millennium will be simultaneously interesting and challenging for everyone at Halifax. First there is the immense task of the flotation in the summer of 1997, which will be the largest stock exchange listing outside the UK privatisation issues.

More importantly, Halifax has challenged itself to become the biggest and best provider of financial services in the UK. The rest of the sector will not be standing still, and Halifax will look to its excellent reputation for integrity, competitive pricing and customer service to help it achieve its objectives.

The pace of change has accelerated—from the 1980s to the 1990s, and in Halifax's own transition to a bank. So far the company has coped well, due in no small way to it being extremely diligent in its task, resourcing wherever and whenever the needs occur. Technology has played a major part, and Halifax has been quick to harness its benefits in business.

HR has played, and will continue to play, a central role in this process of change. It will have to ensure that new business areas are resourced with staff with the right skills, adapt reward systems to meet individual business requirements, and coach staff constantly to improve their own skills to help ensure the success of the organisation.

HAYMARKET PUBLISHING GROUP LIMITED

Haymarket Publishing Group

Haymarket is the UK's largest privately owned magazine publisher with around 50 titles in the UK, and others in the USA. The company launched an exhibitions division in 1990 and has significantly expanded its involvement in events and conference organisation. The group employs over 700 staff and has turnover in excess of £80 million.

Biggest Plus: Excellent training commitment in the fast-moving business of publishing

Biggest Minus: An introduction to the world of deadlines from day one

Haymarket Publishing Group
12-14 Ansdell Street
London W8 5TR
Tel: 0181-943 5000
Fax: 0171-413 4051

The Business

Haymarket Publishing Group is a major force in periodical publishing, a market which generates an estimated £1.2 billion a year in the UK. Around 8,000 titles are in circulation and over 30,000 people are directly employed by magazine publishers. Many thousands more depend on the magazine publishing industry for their livelihoods in printing, typesetting and distribution.

Haymarket's success has been achieved in a remarkably short period. In 1964, when the company was founded, it owned one magazine and had a turnover of just £50,000. Ten years later the portfolio had risen to 28 magazines and turnover approached £8 million; today it is over £80 million.

This rapid growth has been sustained through innovative launches, the purchase and revitalisation of existing magazines, and continued development of its titles. Haymarket is one of Britain's largest publishers of business and consumer magazines, leading the market in many sectors including motoring, marketing, medicine, public relations, advertising, printing and commercial horticulture.

Company Culture and Style

Haymarket could be described as having a young and enterprising culture, and it needs to be this way—the publishing business is very competitive. Haymarket is populated by young, intelligent and dynamic people. Those who enjoy the challenge of working to strict deadlines will thrive in this environment—working on weekly and monthly magazines demands high energy levels and a determination to succeed.

Being client-sensitive is fundamental. Media sales specialists need professionalism in building good relationships with clients, whether they be advertising agencies or marketing managers at product companies. Getting on the same wave-length can count for a lot when it comes to achieving a sale.

"They are professional, efficient and do the job very well. It's not all smart suits and slick presentations. They are very knowledgeable," says one client. "The people I deal with have an ability to listen to the client's requirements and interpret them, rather than the typical media sales person who is just trying to flog space," adds another.

Maintaining the high standards of the group's magazines requires a high calibre of creative talent, and selling them to advertising agencies and their clients calls for incisive, analytical and intellectual minds.

Haymarket is an innovative and responsive publishing company, where fresh ideas can find a happy home. A frustrated soccer fan was so fed up with the puerile style of football magazines, she decided to do something about it. Haymarket listened to her ideas and a new publishing sector—adult soccer—was born. Haymarket's FourFourTwo now leads the market with a circulation of 80,000. Initiatives like this are essential to foster a pioneering spirit, and to provide attractive career development opportunities.

Human Resource Priorities

Haymarket aims to recruit and develop the right calibre of staff to grow the business and grow with the business. Recruitment is often the responsibility of managers and editors, as is development, to help individuals reach their own goals.

Haymarket, as policy, promotes equal opportunity in all aspects of employment, from recruitment and training to promotion opportunities to conditions of employment.

Haymarket is committed to providing the most comprehensive training and career deployment programmes available in the industry. This ensures that every individual achieves the maximum rate and level of career development and advancement possible.

Johnny Morris, of training company Pragmatica, regularly runs courses at Haymarket. "We often use Haymarket as an example of a company committed to training and development, a commitment that never faltered even during the recession from which we are slowly emerging," he says. "Training has been a cornerstone of Haymarket strategy. The company recognises that people skills give it an edge in competitive markets."

Career Opportunity and Development

Employees joining Haymarket are ensured of a working environment that is both stimulating and rewarding. To achieve its ideals, the company has a policy of employing only the best graduates who are able to combine creativity with commercial awareness. There is enormous competition for graduate entry positions. Every year Haymarket receives thousands of job applications—a fortunate few will be offered positions based at the company's offices in London and Middlesex.

A career at Haymarket has some distinct advantages for graduates. From the first day, everyone has a real contribution to make to their magazine. The responsibility grows, along with a career, as fast as each individual's skills and ability allow.

Haymarket employs over 200 journalists on some of the UK's top magazines, including household names such as *Autocar*, *What Hi-Fi?* and market-leading titles for professionals in business, including *Management Today*, *Marketing* and *Campaign*. Opportunities in editorial require a combination of high journalistic ability and considerable knowledge of the specialist sectors covered by the magazines. Recruitment opportunities are generally restricted to people with this experience, although some fiercely contested graduate entry routes are available.

Managers of advertising departments, with as little as two or three years' experience, can be responsible for multi-million pound sales budgets on leading magazines. This brings responsibility for tracking major markets, and the big advertisers within them; responsibility for analysing trends, planning sales strategy and campaigns; and identifying key targets and bringing in the revenue.

Haymarket Publishing Group has a high reputation for top media sales executives. Those who stay the course are likely to become senior managers within the company. They benefit from a comprehensive grounding in all aspects of modern magazine publishing, sales and management techniques.

company. They benefit from a comprehensive grounding in all aspects of modern magazine publishing, sales and management techniques.

These are not careers for people lacking self-motivation. Sales executives are given virtually free rein in what is a very competitive external environment. Training comprises both on-the-job training from manager and team, one-to-one training by manager/training manager, team training, central and external courses. Team training focuses on magazine competitors, the marketplace and selling skills.

Promotion can be rapid for fast learners with real ability. The sales route is probably the best one to becoming manager of a £1 million magazine. Haymarket provides an excellent environment for graduates and direct entry professionals to pursue a long-term, highly motivated and rewarding career.

Pay and Benefits

To attract and retain the best staff, Haymarket aims to make all pay rates competitive with market rates in comparable publishing houses. All staff are entitled to have their pay reviewed upwards annually, and the policy is to at least match increases in the RPI.

Staff over 25-years-old may, if they contribute 5% or more of their basic salary, take out a personal contributory pension plan to which Haymarket will add a contribution. Participants in the plan also receive free private health insurance. All employees receive free life assurance cover at three times their salary.

The Future

Haymarket is an ambitious company and its commitment to further expansion is backed up by one of the largest research and development units in the industry. This unit will have to pay as much attention to the host of new electronic media that are flirting with the publishing industry as to the latest vogue or interest areas for conventional magazines to exploit.

The foray into events and exhibitions suggests exciting opportunities. This relatively new venture is fast-growing, and at its core is a number of ventures with the BBC, based around popular programmes. The division has now expanded into trade and business exhibitions. This business area is a logical one for Haymarket to extend into, and it will be interesting to see if it needs to grow by acquisition.

Hewlett Packard

Hewlett Packard is among the global leaders in the manufacture of printers, computing, communications and measurement products. It began as a maker of scientific and technical measuring instruments, but entered the personal computer market in the early 1980s. It is now market leader in printers, and a growing proportion of turnover comes from PCs, servers and workstations. It employed 102,300 people at the end of 1995, including 5,000 in the UK.

Biggest Plus: The HP way pays and rewards better than most

Biggest Minus: The HP way can demand even more

Hewlett Packard
Cain Road
Bracknell
Berks RG12 1HN
Tel: 01344-360000
Fax: 01344-363344

The Business

Once dismissed as a test-equipment company that dabbled in PCs, Hewlett-Packard (HP) is on course for entering the top three of the world's PC makers in 1997. It has more than doubled its revenue in the past five years, with strong earnings growth balanced across its businesses and around the world. Ask any company in the industry and its top people will tell you how much they respect HP. This is a business that changes lives—and creates the future.

Founded in 1938 by two engineers in Palo Alto, California, HP produced the world's first desktop scientific computer in 1968 and the first scientific pocket calculator in 1972. But until the late 1980s, its growth was solid and unspectacular and it was described by the *Wall Street Journal* in 1990 as "a torpid dinosaur among fleet-footed little predators".

In 1992 HP closed 10 out of 12 PC factories, moved more quickly than its rivals into client-server networks, and consolidated its lead in ink-jet printers so that by 1995 it had one-third of the market. This helped the company build a strong position in distribution and marketing, essential for success with its mid-1990s' range of products such as a low-priced multimedia PC.

Hewlett Packard's net revenues grew by 26% in 1995 to $32 billion, its net earnings by 52%, and net earnings per share by 51%. Printers account for around 40% of global revenues. Employee numbers, which had not grown in three years, went up by 4,000 to 102,300. "Our ability to innovate and adapt has fuelled these results during a time of real industry upheaval," the company said.

Senior vice-president of research & development Joel Birnbaum says: "HP's success will depend more and more on newly emerging technologies." Spending on basic 'blue sky' research, as well as applied research, is being stepped-up.

In the PC business, the company has been critically successful in reducing not only costs, but also cycle time—how long it takes from the customer placing an order to switching on.

Company Culture and Style

If any company can claim to have invented the term 'corporate culture' it is Hewlett-Packard, known as much for its management philosophy and style as for its technology. The 'HP way' was described by co-founder Bill Hewlett. "It is policies and actions that flow from the belief that men and women want to do a good job, a creative job, and if provided with the proper environment, they will do so. Closely coupled with this is the HP tradition of treating each individual with consideration and respect, and recognising individual achievements."

There is emphasis on an inner core of shared values: trust, total integrity, teamwork in achieving common objectives, flexibility and innovation in responding to challenges. HP introduced 'management-by-objective' 40 years ago, working on the principle that day-to-day work decisions are best made by those closest to the action—a management discovery made relatively recently, if at all, by many big corporations.

At the same time it formalised the corporate objectives which outlined goals in terms not simply of profit but of customers, fields of interest, growth, people, management and citizenship...a bit like stakeholders?

In the 1980s in a joint venture in Japan the group introduced Total Quality Control, which led to a dramatic turnaround and spread what was then a new concept across the company. The HP tradition of first-name informality was built in at the outset, as was the production bonus which in 1962 became a company-wide profit-sharing plan.

Grass-roots creativity is encouraged at HP Labs, the central research organisation, where selected engineers are now provided with funds to investigate their own ideas.

Human Resource Priorities

In the earliest days, the company decided not to take on large contracts which could lead to 'hire and fire' employment instability. And in 1970, when the economy and orders fell sharply, HP introduced a nine-day fortnight, with a 10% cut in work and pay for all management people, to avoid the need for forced redundancies. The founders rejected offers for the company because they didn't want employees exposed to unknown motives and decisions of new employers.

HP pioneered the concept of flexible working hours. When times have been hard management has always chosen to reduce costs in as many ways as possible, but to accelerate training and development, in anticipation of the upturn.

The 1995 rise in net earnings of over 50% was achieved with an increase in employment of only 4%. "That's a real tribute to HP's people, who continued to show tremendous skill, energy and resourcefulness in anticipating and responding to customer needs," said chief executive Lew Platt.

But it also raises issues of productivity, fairness and reward. "Productivity in the 1990s requires more than laptop computers and voice mail," says the company. "It means enabling employees to stay creative and motivated by providing support and tools that help people balance the demands of work, family and other commitments."

In 1995, after analysing the results of 14 trials involving more than 500 employees, HP implemented variable work schedules as an option available at all US sites. The number of staff using existing options such as job sharing, part-time work and telecommuting also grew in 1995 to more than 15% of the total work-force.

HP also joined the American Business Collaboration for Quality Dependent Care, a group which sponsors projects aimed at improving facilities for children and senior citizens in the communities where the group operates.

The company is a great believer in workforce diversity. In 1995 it set up a Diversity Leadership Council, a team of high-level managers from all business sectors, to strengthen its commitment to "benefit from the ideas of women and people of all nationalities, races and lifestyles".

Career Opportunity and Development

Europe's business graduates voted Hewlett Packard number one in the league of ideal employers in a 1995 survey. In 1996, HP was still in the top 10—but IBM had slipped from 4th to 13th, and Apple dropped out of the top 20.

"At HP, we're determined not to let our recent strong results lull us into complacency," said the group in 1996. "We're obsoleting our own products by replacing them with better ones before competitors can, and we're asking basic questions about priorities and processes throughout the company. We know that the formula for success in the future will be different from what it is today." But the HP way ensures that personal evolution, through continual training and development, is the engine of company growth.

At South Queensferry near Edinburgh, a site established in 1965, the group runs telecoms, microwave and telecom systems divisions, which serve the test equipment and systems needs of telecommunications and microwave communications customers. Queensferry also houses the UK transaction processing centre, and a software productivity centre which is a joint venture with Scottish Enterprise.

HP has also announced a £19 million expansion plan for its leading-edge research laboratory at its main Bristol site, which accounts for around one-third of its global research effort, including the longer range and higher risk projects.

The company recruits graduates for both of its UK sites, and the Scottish businesses looked in 1994 and 1995 to hire 100 people a year. Turnover in the three businesses was 38% ahead at the end of 1995, and HP said it was having to import telecoms and software graduates from England because demand was outstripping supply.

There are also career opportunities in the network of more than 4,000 consultants world-wide, who help large enterprises implement open-systems IT projects.

Pay and Benefits

The unchanged single status approach ensures that all employees receive the same proportional production bonus, from janitor to senior manager. In 1995, at the height of the group's growth, a record £135 million was paid out on profit-related bonuses to staff world-wide. HP's 5,000 UK employees shared around £6 million, and an employee with at least six months' service earning £20,000 received £1,100 or 11% of the previous six months' pay. The scheme pays out twice a year, and since it began in 1962, workers with six months' service have received an average 6.75% of earnings through the bonus.

The Future

Chief executive Lou Platt told a meeting of international managers in 1995: "What makes us highly successful this year could be our downfall next year."

HP has global strength but small company speed and intelligence. It recognises that it will prosper only by creating the future. It must prize above all its hothouse of individual and team creativity, orchestrate HR policies to support people under pressure of non-stop change, and so continue to demonstrate that it is not a product or a technology but a management culture—and one built to last.

Hydro-Electric

Hydro-Electric is an electricity utility based north of the Border, which unlike the English regional utilities, generates power as well as distributing it. It employs 3,380 people in three divisions: generation, power systems, and commercial. One-third of its electricity is now sold in England, where it sells to business customers and is involved in joint ventures for combined heat and power, and gas-fired electricity.

Biggest Plus: Everything is geared to individual performance

Biggest Minus: Everything is geared to individual performance!

Scottish Hydro-Electric plc
10 Dunkeld Road
Perth PH1 5WA
Tel: 01738-455040
Fax: 01738-455045

The Business

Hydro-Electric (HE) has transformed itself from a public sector institution serving the north of Scotland into a hard-nosed commercial company. An advertising campaign showing how HE Energy has won new customers such as Harvey Nichols, Thermos, and Triumph Motorcycles, has highlighted the Perth-based group's success in the first wave of UK-wide competition for business and industrial users.

But HE's corporate mission statement stresses a commitment to all its stakeholders. The Scottish utilities were privatised later, and on much tougher financial and regulatory terms, than those in England, and they have avoided 'fat cat' boardroom excesses. HE has led the industry in the efficient production of electricity, in its environmental policies, and in a complete reshaping of its industrial relations.

Its accident and safety record is far better than it was pre-privatisation, and failings on customer service have fallen from several thousand a month to fewer than 20 a month.

In 1996 in association with its trade unions it developed a new company-wide agreement, including a single grading and salary structure, one of the first of its kind in the industry. It also introduced flexible benefits, and became one of the first companies to extend its executive share option scheme to every member of staff.

Company Culture and Style

Chief executive Roger Young says: "Before 1990, electricity companies were an instrument of government policy. Their most important function was not to embarrass ministers. They were hidden tax collectors and also instruments of social policy, seen as providers of employment and used to prop-up manufacturing industry. Customers were low down on their list of priorities."

Under a new management team, put in place before flotation, HE embarked on reinventing itself well before any of the other utilities. Onto a culture of extreme loyalty and pride at HE's place in the north of Scotland community has been grafted the new virtues of performance and customer orientation. In 1990 a Customer Focus programme began with a full-time team of 20 people training every member of staff in new skills, new methods, and new attitudes.

At the same time, 370 Performance Circles were set up to debate team and company performance. In 1991, when numbers had already been reduced by 13%, some staff were invited to participate in restructuring their own jobs. "People came up with more daring solutions than their managers expected or probably would have done," Roger Young says. Out went layers of management, in came teamwork and more accountability.

By 1998, every employee will be producing four-and-a-half times more electricity than he or she was ten years earlier. While unable to maintain its policy of no compulsory redundancy, HE looks to avoid it wherever possible and emphasises employability. Alan Scott, director of human resources, sees the move away from national negotiations as a major change. "What used to be an entitlement culture, where you were entitled to salary progression and a job for life, has become a performance culture." Breaking down barriers has been a strong theme.

Teamworking is already firmly in place in many parts of the company, where managers have been replaced by team leaders. An annual survey, sent to the home of every employee, is dissected to produce action plans which each director brings to the management board. Nine key values of HE have emerged, and been tested in management and staff conferences, before being launched across the company alongside the strategic HE objectives. Scott says strong leadership at the top has set the tone. "We are all trying to get the best out of people and we know there is much more to give."

Human Resource Priorities

The three HE businesses have set up their own joint arrangements (with the trade unions) for negotiating business agreements. That has meant drafting in new HR managers with modern skills, part of a 22-strong team. Over 70% of staff belongs to trade unions, and while avoiding the over-used word 'partnership', the company has invited the unions to participate in a new approach to negotiations involving shared information and full consultation.

One of the first key tasks was a comprehensive job evaluation exercise. Staff have been placed into ten grades (previously there were 31), and they will progress through these grades according to performance, and each will have a personal development plan.

HE takes measurement seriously. A survey goes out to key internal customers on a quarterly basis. The HR team not only regards itself as an internal consultancy, but also ensures that its members have been trained in consultancy skills.

Equal opportunity is given a high priority, and in 1995, HE received an award from the European Commission for gender equality.

Career Opportunity and Development

The company has an educational opportunities scheme available to all staff, enabling study for further qualifications. The performance management process emphasises the development aspect, and a key output of this is an individual training and development plan for the coming year. In a further initiative two groups have been identified: 'developers' and 'feeders'.

"They are the people of potential," says Alan Scott. "The developers are the senior group, they are between 35 and 45, the feeders are between 25 and 40." A process called 'Potential' is used with the feeders to assess individual strengths and implement a learning contract between the employee and his or her manager.

Pay and Benefits

The move away from nationally-negotiated pay to local bargaining enabled HE to conduct a survey of large Scottish companies, and it promises that its pay will be competitive (above the median) against them.

Staff covered by agreements, and those on personal contracts, all have the opportunity to move through the 'performance zone' of their grade salary on the basis of regular reviews. All managers have been through training modules on setting and reviewing objectives in a coaching-based system.

The company has a profit-related pay scheme, which in 1996–97 is estimated to be likely to pay out an extra 5% on salary for most staff, in addition to the 3.3% pay award.

A SAYE share scheme has always had a high uptake, and the company has added a third element by granting 500 share options to every member of staff working 20 hours or more —a move almost unprecedented among UK companies. HE sees the three measures together as "increasing involvement and interest."

Flexible benefits were introduced in 1996 for the 500 personal contract staff, with plans to extend it across the whole company as part of the removal of status and barriers. The menu includes critical illness cover, dental insurance, financial counselling, private medical cover, holiday, and personal accident cover.

The Future

HE has been highly active in managing a very marked culture change. It now needs to let the first and second wave of its initiatives bed in and yield more value. But it also intends to keep scanning the market, notably the USA, for examples of best practice elsewhere.

All of its programmes have been aimed at achieving personal accountability, and leadership, at all levels of the organisation. In continuing to seek new ideas and to benchmark itself against good practice in the UK and USA, management recognises that it still has a distance to travel.

Its continuing business challenge is to accommodate the commercial, political and regulatory pressures to drive costs down, while finding growth from new markets. It will want to retain its position in industry polls as the company that best satisfies its customers. So it needs to take its staff, and their trade unions, on board as it enters the next wave of competition, when two-thirds of its own output to domestic customers is opened up to outside suppliers in 1998.

Alan Scott admits: "The greatest concern for our staff is uncertainty, and by that they mainly mean their own jobs. It can get translated into morale." Added to that is the fact that the job evaluation exercise established that around half of HE's staff are already substantially better-paid than their counterparts in similar-sized companies in Scotland. Their pay is protected for at least the duration of the current agreement, but it is clearly a situation that will need careful handling.

So while the new values, the mission statement, the performance system, the personal development plans, and communication initiatives, will take the company a long way down its ambitious track, staff will want to know that it also means what it says about employability.

Roger Young is a firm believer in motivating people by getting them to do the job better, and giving them the means to do it. He says: "A company becomes most efficient and most agile in responding to its stakeholders' needs if the power is next to the job." If the indicators of the company's success in the first half of the 1990s are accurate, Hydro-Electric is already ahead of most of its competitors and has put a solid foundation in place for the future.

Iceland Group

Iceland is Britain's leading specialist food retailer. Iceland operates a nationwide chain of over 750 stores offering the widest possible choice in frozen foods, principally under the Iceland brand, as well as selected grocery, chilled and fresh products. Iceland's aim is to meet all the needs of the everyday food shopper in convenient and attractive stores, with a reputation for good value and service.

Iceland has an enviable record of having achieved increases in turnover and profit in each of its 25 years since the company's launch in 1970. By 1995, turnover had risen to £1,375 million, and net profits to £72.6 million.Towards the end of 1996, around 17,000 people were employed in the group.

Biggest Plus: An impressive growth story, the atmosphere is still that of a young, dynamic company

Biggest Minus: Increasingly tough market place, nothing guaranteed

Iceland Group plc
Second Avenue
Deeside Industrial Park
Deeside
Flintshire CH5 2NW
Tel: 01244-830100
Fax: 01244-814531

The Business

Unlike the vast majority of the food retailing sector, Iceland is in vigorous expansion mode. Some 50–60 new stores have opened each year to date. Research suggests that there is ample room in the high streets and shopping centres throughout the UK and Ireland for Iceland to double its store total from 750 to 1500. The company also runs the food halls at Littlewoods—'Iceland at Littlewoods' it is called—and described by Iceland as 'The affordable Marks & Spencer'.

Under chairman and chief executive Malcolm Walker—also the company's founder—Iceland has enjoyed tremendous success. It's proposition, an emphasis on frozen food rather than general grocery retailing, has enabled it to grow. Walker says: "The UK food retailing market has undergone revolutionary change in the 1990s, resulting in a significant increase in competitive pressures. In this new environment, we have undertaken a comprehensive review of our strategy, positioning management and systems, and implemented a real step change in the way we view and run the business."

Iceland's point of difference is being *the* frozen food specialist. "If you want it fresh, buy it frozen" is a crusading rally cry, which seems to have an increasingly large following. A *Money Observer* survey found that only 14 UK quoted companies, including Iceland, had managed to increase annual earnings in each of the last ten years.

Iceland's strategy aims to strengthen its management and enhance its focus on its traditional strengths, frozen food. Increasing store profitability per square foot and attacking the cost base go hand-in-hand, but this will not hold back the company's continued expansion plans.

Company Culture and Style

As the company refocused its business strategy, it also started to reconsider its corporate culture, and ensure that one enabled the other. There were many good parts that the company was determined to keep: the fun, friendly and informal environment; the ability to move quickly; and a tenacity to make things happen and get the job done.

Standing still is not an option at Iceland, which makes the business quite exciting. The atmosphere is very much 'can do' and everyone is given full rein to use their initiative. The style is not to stand on ceremony, and you are more likely to see the directors out in the general office areas, the stores or the depots, than in their head office suite.

Iceland recognised, however, that it had grown into a large company, and had to evolve its style in certain respects. In particular, it needed to enable and encourage decision making at a lower level, become customer-focused in *every* part of the company, and become better in helping all staff achieve their full potential.

People work in teams in an aggressive and fast-moving marketplace so there is a strong sense of camaraderie. Open communication lines upwards are manifest. The majority of the management team has been working together for years and it is their belief in the teams that propels much of the company ethos.

Product innovation is second nature to Iceland. It is constantly developing new and exciting food ideas, launching some 200 new products every year. The company claims "it can take us just six weeks to get a product from brainwave to freezer."

This is a genuinely concerned company. Iceland contributed over £400,000 to charities in 1995. And over five years, Iceland staff have raised and donated over £1 million to Petö UK, enabling the construction in Birmingham of the first phase of the National Institute of Conductive Education for disabled children.

As a long-time member of Greenpeace, Malcolm Walker has ensured that Iceland is Green with a capital G. Iceland was the first to remove CFC gases from redundant freezers, developed the first CFC-free freezer, and opened a state-of-the-art cold store warehouse and distribution centre using ammonia as the refrigerant.

While Iceland has achieved much in its 25 years, it has managed to preserve the atmosphere of a small, lively company. The staff canteen—known as Roxy's Diner—would do any West End theme restaurant proud, complete with its centrepiece Harley Davidson motorbike. Personnel director Janet Marsden says: "Our visitors reckon we put something in the coffee machine. The atmosphere definitely is different. It is bound to have something to do with the way our small organisation has grown very big, very quickly."

Malcolm Walker sums it up: "Working at Iceland is demanding, never anything less than hard work, challenging at the very least, sometimes frustrating, occasionally annoying, incredibly satisfying. But above all else its fun. And that's the way it should be."

Human Resource Priorities

HR has a strategic role at Iceland, to ensure that the company has the people, the skills and the culture it needs to achieve its business objectives.

The company is rigorous in its recruitment, using a combination of interviews and psychometric assessment to identify individuals who will flourish in the Iceland environment. Iceland prefers to combine home-grown talent with people with experience gained elsewhere, which can allow a cross-fertilisation of ideas.

As a result of reconsidering its corporate culture, Iceland has redefined its company values and translated them into Leadership Practices, or management style. Every manager in the business is being put through a development programme, to help drive the culture in a direction that will make the company more customer-focused and make better use of its people.

Stores director David Brown believes that "The most important person in our company is the store manager." Iceland's retail operations have been restructured to widen the scope of area managers and empower managers with the independence to make a range of decisions for themselves. Certainly imbued in the Iceland philosophy is the need to make decisions quickly.

Iceland employees are kept informed of the group's performance and activities through regular briefings and staff newspapers. Directors and senior executives visit stores frequently to brief staff and discuss matters of concern or interest.

Career Opportunity and Development

Iceland makes it perfectly clear that it is not offering anyone a job—it is offering an opportunity; an opportunity for individuals to develop a career that matches their needs with those of the company. There are careers in general management, retail, marketing, buying, supply chain, accountancy and IT. Promotion can come very quickly.

Iceland has a long-standing commitment to staff training and development, recognising that in the fast-moving food retailing industry, it must be in a constant state of change to maintain competitive position in the market place. For example, Iceland moved into supplier partnering three years ago, which involved developing a different skill set for its buyers and technologists.

Initiatives range from a well-established graduate recruitment and training scheme to its Retail Development Programme for area and store managers. Staff at all levels have undergone training in customer service as part of the company's 'Serious About Service' campaign, and Iceland continues to provide opportunities for some employees to train for NVQs. The system of annual appraisals gives all staff the opportunity to make a real career at Iceland, progressing through supervisory grades and into management. Iceland's commitment to training and development was recognised early in 1996 when it became one of the few retailers to attain recognition as an Investor in People.

Pay and Benefits

Iceland's rates of pay are comparable to other major retailers. A profit-related pay scheme was introduced for all staff in 1996. The company pension scheme is among the best in the industry, and Iceland encourages all full- and part-time staff to join as soon as they become eligible.

Iceland operates an SAYE share option scheme, for which all employees with more than 12 months' service are eligible. In addition, there is an executive share option scheme for senior managers. All managers are covered by private health care insurance and enhanced maternity benefits are provided for staff who meet service criteria.

The Future

Iceland's strategic vision is based on a detailed understanding of what its existing and potential customers want. The company has re-thought its product range and its marketing strategy accordingly.

Clearly Iceland faces a business challenge to persuade regular shoppers to spend more and infrequent customers to shop more often. It will have to be careful about sticking to its proposition and making it clear where the company is coming from. The onus is firmly on the frozen side of the business.

Within the company, there is the continuous challenge to maintain the resourcing of Iceland's outstanding growth, which in turn involves the extension of its culture into one that suits the needs of a larger organisation. Adding the new without losing the old is never a task to be underestimated, but Iceland has already come a long way while preserving an open friendly style, and sees no reason for this to change as its growth story enters another chapter.

ICI Group

The ICI Group is one of the largest chemical companies in the world, with international strengths in the areas of paints, materials, explosives and industrial chemicals. ICI operates its main businesses on an international basis. The ICI Group has 65,000 employees world-wide (15,000 in the UK), more than 8,000 products, and manufacturing sites at over 200 locations in more than 30 countries.

ICI describes itself as "a science-based chemicals company which produces consistently outstanding performance through market leadership, technological edge and a world competitive cost base." In 1995, it reported trading profits of £994 million on turnover of £10,269 million, an improvement of 69% over the previous year.

Biggest Plus: A proud company with a clear vision of its future

Biggest Minus: Further to go, a lot of hard work lies ahead

ICI Group PLC
Imperial Chemicals House
9 Millbank
London   SW1P 3JF
Tel: 0171-834 4444
Fax: 0171-834 2042

The Business

ICI is one of *the* names in British industry. Even following a major reshaping of its operations in the last five years, which included a reduction in the number of people working for ICI and the demerging of its bioscience businesses into a separate company Zeneca plc in 1993, ICI still stands as a tower of strength across the world.

Chairman Sir Ronald Hampel: "Reshaping will of course have to continue as markets change, but we believe we now have a portfolio of winners and we will be driving them hard."

The modern ICI is an international organisation—global businesses multicultural in make-up. ICI is still founded on a strong scientific and technological base. In all of its operating businesses, it is a significant player in its markets—for example in paints, acrylics and polyurethanes, it is number one or two.

Company Culture and Style

In 1995, Charles Miller Smith became chief executive, and Sir Ronald Hampel acknowledged that "...his personal style has already made its mark in accelerating the culture change of recent years and in further liberating the talents of our staff."

He is referring to the development (by Miller Smith and the executive) of 'ICI's Vision'—in the broadest terms, to be the industry leader in creating value for customers and shareholders.

Its first tenet is market-driven innovation in products and services. Each business is responsible for implementing the technology strategy for its own market, with the centre facilitating the sharing of ideas and expertise between businesses. The second value is winning in quality growth markets world-wide—ones in which ICI has a strong position.

The third value is ICI's belief that the inspiration and reward of talented people lies at the heart of the company's future success. If the quest is productivity improvements, the drive is to create a company where everyone knows what is expected of them, but in turn, where people have the freedom to take initiatives and show creativity. Accountability for the result is matched with appropriate reward for achievement.

ICI also seeks an exemplary performance in safety and health, and responsible care for the environment. Finally, ICI is committed to the relentless pursuit of operational excellence, embodied in a drive for 'best in class', excelling in everything it does. In 1995, ICI launched the 'Value Gap' initiative, a major programme to seek a further £400 million improved value from existing businesses.

Miller Smith's vision and values have cascaded down the organisation at rapid speed, through various processes including a live Q&A satellite hook-up of 24 ICI sites around the world. John Watt, general manager personnel, admitted to being 'amazed' how far the message had been disseminated, with employees identifying with 'what it means to me and my business unit', bringing the 'ICI Vision' alive.

Leadership is an important concept at ICI—not just in its operations, but in other values. The statement has real depth. Charles Miller Smith's ideas have been bought into, but with 65,000 people in the organisation, the ability of leaders to span across cultures and issues, and explain what values and ideas mean to the individual, is a vital task—and skill. The ability for a leader to articulate where each business unit is going after 'the broad ICI bit' is very important.

ICI leaders need to be knowledgeable and skilled, flexible, personally motivated, and able to inspire others. Simple 'control merchants' cannot work in the delayered, product/tube environment which is ICI today.

Human Resource Priorities

HR's broad remit is to support the values of the company. John Watt suggests that meeting the organisation's requirements is about getting "the right people, the right place, the right time, the right motivation."

If perhaps ICI took its eye off the ball post-demerger, it has now created a clear role for HR and beefed the function up considerably. HR occupies a lot of air time at senior management meetings, driven by the company's need to address human resources, rather than the other way around.

Geoff Tudhope, group HR development manager, believes that you should not articulate on vision and values unless you back it up and share this with the public. ICI's next (1996) annual report will have measurements associated with HR's delivery against the company's values, such as training days, employee survey findings, and feedback through the consultation process.

Extraordinarily, ICI has managed a downsizing of its UK operations between 1989–1996 from 60,000 employees to just 15,000 with minimum industrial disruption. This is testimony to the caring attitude ICI adopts to all its employees.

There is greater awareness in the company of the need to communicate effectively. Employee survey issues are picked up specifically, and responses are quick. The cascade process involves the usual range of newsletters, noticeboards, corporate briefings and email and electronic communication to share information. 'The Way Forward' global satellite link-up has become an annual event, but ICI stresses that there is no substitute for the face-to-face meeting of a work group with the leader playing a critical part in the process.

Career Opportunity and Development

The requirement to move across territories, functions and product lines for those with higher potential is almost a given. ICI is determined to utilise the best people right across the organisation and career development groups are geared to work across country, business and functional boundaries.

If ICI has been accused in the past of rotating jobs too quickly, it now seeks bigger jumps, but for longer durations. This demands clear, long-term development plans for the individual in making this jump.

ICI needs people who are internationally sensitive and adaptable. Gaining this experience might involve secondments, short-term assignments and projects, allied to the fact that ICI's business is international anyway. At present, the global business community often takes its cue from the West, particularly the USA and UK. ICI is asking, conversely, what it can learn from countries like China and play back into the West, and increasingly tries to benchmark with Asian companies.

Recruitment is both internal and external. Internal promotion is the norm, but ICI increasingly defines what it wants, and refuses to compromise standards. ICI also has greater cultural diversity at the top of the company, with talent being promoted as opposed to 'safe options'.

A core training and development programme is based around helping people improve basic work practices and professional skills. ICI warms to the concept of 'learning for life', renaming its training and development department 'ICI Learning'.

ICI recruits around 120 high calibre graduates in the UK, as well as many more overseas, particularly from Asia. The intake number is usually pre-set, recognising the need to sustain a middle/senior management group in future years. Graduate retention rate is pretty good, for ICI offers graduates good career opportunities, a proactively managed succession, international exposure, and an opportunity to grow and develop in terms of skills and experience.

Pay and Benefits

ICI benchmarks pay against other major industrial companies—blue chips generally, not just chemical and oil companies. The company has moved along the road towards performance-related pay, and is also examining various new schemes, including team-based pay.

The company provides most of the 'usual' benefits, including a SAYE share scheme. ICI has always been a supportive employer, and regards its company pension scheme as being 'top quartile'.

The Future

Delivering international growth is ICI's greatest business challenge. The changes in size and scope of opportunities—particularly in the Asia/Pacific region—are considerable, and ICI needs to deliver higher financial performance in an increasingly competitive market by getting more out of what it has got.

HR's role will be to resource this growth, which gets back to the company's values. If it succeeds in creating a culture where the work force is motivated, creative, challenged and innovative, it will give itself every chance. This will entail developing and retaining leaders, achieving a full deployment of business excellence processes, with the ability to manoeuvre into a place while retaining stability of purpose.

If ICI has any weaknesses, some of its products and businesses are cyclical. And the company will have to get even quicker in making good, swift decisions, putting an onus on its marketing skills and the supply chain and logistical areas.

There have been changes in the relationship employees have with their company. There is greater sharpness in team accountability and, as the company has delayered, the focus has been on products and streams. Information technology makes this process easier, but there is nowhere to hide—in itself a step change from the ICI of ten years ago. Many people excel in this environment, while others might feel more uncomfortable.

If the business world has got tougher, ICI has not lost sight of the people dimension and that its employees work hard to help each other. These factors add up to make ICI an attractive company, in terms of broad opportunities, challenging careers and real jobs.

JOHN LEWIS PARTNERSHIP

The John Lewis Partnership

The John Lewis Partnership is one of the largest retail groups in the UK, operating 23 department stores and over 100 Waitrose supermarkets. In addition, the company maintains three textile production units, a furniture and bedding factory, plus extensive farming and fruit-growing interests in Hampshire. John Lewis employs 41,100 members of staff (16,300 part time).

Biggest Plus: Unique co-ownership philosophy. Profits earned are shared among staff

Biggest Minus: Heavily structured organisation can tend to stifle initiative

The John Lewis Partnership
171 Victoria Street
London SW1E 5NN
Tel: 0171-828 1000
Fax: 0171-834 5491

The Business

In 1864, The John Lewis Partnership (John Lewis) began trading from a small draper's shop in Oxford Street, London. At the heart of John Lewis's success is a partnership ethos. All permanent employees are effectively co-owners of the business, receiving a share of the profits and uniquely motivated to improve the company's performance.

John Lewis is 'Never knowingly undersold', meaning that its prices cannot be beaten by a competitor. That necessarily has a ripple effect upon other areas of the business: advertising campaigns might be forsaken to preserve margins; word-of-mouth among customers could be relied upon instead of self-promotion.

The Partnership's commitment to employees is exemplary, providing a rare measure of job security. Hard-hit by the recession and the advent of Sunday trading, John Lewis kept the faith and refused to lay-off members of staff, relocating employees elsewhere in the group. Now as consumer confidence seems to be returning, John Lewis appears set to prosper. Having seen profits decline to £71.4 million in 1993, John Lewis recovered to post a pre-tax profit record of £150 million in the year-ending January 1996.

Company Culture and Style

Contemporary personnel and human resources gurus may advocate the merits of staff mobility, but John Lewis anticipates that many employees joining the Partnership will stay there throughout their working lives. Statistics support this claim. Several hundred employees every year take advantage of the six-month sabbatical offered to staff with 25 years' service.

John Lewis is owned and run by its employees, which creates a tangible bond and a friendly environment confirmed by a managerial open door policy.

"It all boils down to people," says Charity Leonard, manageress of the haberdashery department in Bristol. "There's an atmosphere of trust and honesty that I thought had gone out of fashion in today's society. Everyone is given a say in what goes on and receives plenty of information about how the business is doing."

All staff participate in the business through a variety of committees. The Central Council is not only an elected body, representing all ranks and occupations within the Partnership, but could even bring about the chairman's resignation if a two-thirds' majority judged that person as unfit to hold office.

Any employee dissatisfied with treatment by a superior has direct access to a second manager. Knowing that members of staff can circumvent direct authority does help to focus the minds of managers onto the importance of creating quality inter-personal relationships.

Every branch has a registrar, who is not accountable to line management, and can assist staff with all manner of personal and work-related problems. Registrars may provide help at times of bereavement, offer advice on legal matters and even channel requests for financial assistance to a peer-group committee.

Human Resource Priorities

All companies seek to recruit the best people. At John Lewis, however, the aim is to look beyond personal qualifications and take into account the aptitude of potential employees to fit into a collectivist culture.

"We have a moral obligation when we take people on," stresses head of management development, Sally Carruthers, "not to turn around six months later and say 'tough, it didn't work out'. You must be careful when you're dealing with people's lives."

Sally Carruthers is attached to the personnel function for department stores, distribution and production units. Although personnel policy is established at the centre, every branch has its own HR specialist. At John Lewis, Brent Cross in North London for example, Andy Collins is supported by three assistants plus a team of secretarial staff.

HR is viewed as pivotal to John Lewis's success. Over 240 members of staff are devoted to the function, while a further 150 focus on training priorities.

"We know," continues Sally Carruthers, "the only way we can make money is by having the right people—not by making acquisitions or opening-up overseas. Along with selecting the right merchandise for our stores, HR is one of two fundamentals driving the company."

Career Opportunity and Development

Energy, purpose, initiative, enthusiasm—these are the qualities that set apart future leaders of the John Lewis Partnership. In order to cultivate these qualities, training is deliberately wide-ranging. Retail management trainees are exposed to every aspect of store life—merchandising and display techniques, product knowledge, pricing and buying policies—combining on-the-job experience with seminars and external residential courses.

John Lewis's emphasis on personal development is underlined by the fact that programmes are also tailored to match individual aspirations. Each recruit is assigned a management trainer, charged with setting and reviewing objectives in tandem with the trainee's line manager.

John Lewis's HR specialists maintain 5, 10 and 15 year succession plans, projecting the source of probable vacancies and planning career strategies for every member of staff.

A comprehensive graduate recruitment programme is also maintained: 25 graduates are recruited each year into the central graduate scheme, a further 60 join local branch schemes, 20 more enter the information technology scheme, while Waitrose takes on 15.

Three of the last four head of branch appointments have been filled by ex-members of the graduate training scheme, and with two major branches opening in 1999 (Blue Water, Dartford and Glasgow), vacancies are set to appear for 150 new managers.

Staff are quick to pay tribute to the impact of John Lewis's training schemes. "At the end of the day," says Waitrose pork buyer David Jones, "it's all about cooperation and sharing a common goal—not just with the branches but with the suppliers. Meat production can be technical and I have to make sure that suppliers follow our stringent standards, even if it means going right back to the farmers."

"The trainer at my first branch," recalls store managing director Simon Fowler, "suggested I write an action plan. I still have that piece of paper. I kept it...both as a commitment to myself and a guide as to how I was progressing. Now as managing director of my own branch, responsible for 500 staff and a multi-million pound branch, I've reached that goal—three years ahead of my original schedule."

Pay and Benefits

Rates of pay for all John Lewis employees are calculated on an individual basis. Topping-up annual increases broadly in line with department store rivals, John Lewis provides merit awards based on performance over the previous 12 months.

All members of staff are subject to an upper pay limit including the chairman. The maximum salary ceiling is determined by a complex formula based on the hypothetical earnings of a man with four dependent children on the equivalent of £5,000 in 1900 (approximately £500,000 in 1996!) Such restrictions may appear idiosyncratic, but reveal John Lewis's democratic philosophies—the rewards of success are not kept for the board and shareholders, but shared at all levels.

After deductions have been made for pensions, tax and future expansion plans of the business, profit is split among permanent employees as a percentage of salary. Over the last 10 years, bonuses have averaged 15%. John Lewis operates a noncontributory pension scheme.

John Lewis offers a broad range of benefits. Medical insurance is provided for executives, while chiropodists and physiotherapists soothe aching feet and backs in the branches. Five weeks' holiday is standard after three years' service, and all partners enjoy substantial discounts on Waitrose and department store lines.

The Future

John Lewis maintains a delicate balancing act. While striving to retain a refreshing degree of corporate intimacy, only by pursing a policy of innovation combined with value, choice and service can the company compete effectively in an overcrowded market.

"Merchandise, price, location and people—we must strive to improve on all fronts," concludes Sally Carruthers. "Meeting employee aspirations is also essential. So is giving people control over their own careers and the feedback they need in order to assess their next career move."

John Lewis remains unique. Controlled by those who serve in the stores, an unparalleled structure might be regarded with alarm by outsiders but it continues to generate a singular degree of loyalty and motivation among committed members of staff:

"Our unusual structure," notes chairman Stuart Hampson, "establishes a unity of purpose to focus on doing things better. It enables us, particularly, to do *difficult* things better. For example, running a haberdashery department...meeting the exacting requirements of the customer's eye or the environmental health officer's swab. Moreover, it enables us to prove that a full-assortment department store is not an historical aberration but can outperform the toughest competition."

Johnson Matthey

Johnson Matthey

Johnson Matthey is a world leader in advanced materials technology, applying the latest technology to add value to precious metals and other specialised materials. The group's principal activities are in the manufacture of electronic materials; plastic laminate packages for semiconductors; catalysts and pollution control systems and pharmaceutical compounds; the refining, fabrication and marketing of precious metals; and the manufacture of decorative and specialised materials for the ceramics industry.

With British origins, Johnson Matthey is extremely multinational. Of its 7,500 employees world-wide (10,300 including Cookson Matthey Ceramics, its joint venture with Cookson), around 2,500 are in the UK. Johnson Matthey has operations in 37 countries, and sells its products around the world. In 1995 its operating profits were £100.4 million on turnover of £2,261 million.

Biggest Plus: A friendly company—multinational, but with room for that personal touch

Biggest Minus: Some traditional values still remain

Johnson Matthey PLC
2–4 Cockspur Street
London SW1Y 5BQ
Tel: 0171-269 8400
Fax: 0171-269 8477

The Business

Johnson Matthey's corporate strategy has involved a deliberate shift away from a dependence on its traditional precious metals businesses towards a wider range of advanced materials products. In 1995 it concluded two significant acquisitions in its electronic materials division and another in its ceramics materials joint venture. While Johnson Matthey's precious metals and catalytic systems businesses are important ones, with medium-term growth potential of their own, the company is expecting engine room growth to come from its ceramics and electronic materials businesses.

Chairman and chief executive David Davies has a well-thought through strategy aimed at delivering profitable growth for the benefit of shareholders. For example, he demands a 20% return on assets in all businesses.

Johnson Matthey (JM) is a multinational business, but is small enough to retain that personal touch. The company is very communicative—to both external and internal audiences—and the directors of the company go to great lengths to know people in the organisation. Employees say 'it is easy to get noticed'.

The complement at the company's head office overlooking Trafalgar Square is lean—some 70 people—reflecting a hands-off approach to day-to-day operations. Each of JM's four divisions is fairly autonomous, reporting to chief operating officer Chris Clark. The four divisions are globally managed, reflecting the fact that JM's customers are too.

Company Culture and Style

It was not always thus. Johnson Matthey's precious metals business conjures up images of a traditional company with a fundamental history and a reputation for integrity. The latter value still remains, but the Johnson Matthey of today is much less bureaucratic, and a lot slicker and faster in its dealings.

The old conservative business was first swept aside by former chief executive Eugene Anderson in the late 1980s, and in the last few years, chairman David Davies has stamped his own mark on the company and built a modern business for the future. His vision has been clearly communicated and subscribed to by employees—perhaps because many of the values were latent in the company, and just needed articulating. Many JM people—starting at the top—are almost indoctrinated with values of 'quality' and 'customer focus'.

Today, JM is characterised by individual leadership, fast decision making, getting things done and local responsibility. There is a heavy emphasis on innovation these days—necessary for an advanced technology company, but people really feel it. The type of person who flourishes at JM is bright, sparkly, quick-thinking and action-oriented. JM employs people with character—not clones. The company's directors have their own individual characters and there might be a suspicion that they recruit and promote others of the same ilk.

Human Resource Priorities

There is an enormous amount of emphasis placed on people in Johnson Matthey, which begins with the board and the Management Development & Remuneration

Committee (MDRC). The board has a *major* interest in graduate recruitment, believing strongly that far too much talent from UK plc is diverted into the City or the Civil Service instead of British industry, where it is needed most. JM has therefore established very close and personal links with the top universities in the UK in its quest to attract the cream of British graduates. Peter Garfield, group personnel controller, has to present to the board twice-yearly on progress and success in recruitment, an event for which he hauls in the various HR directors from around the world.

There is also a monthly meeting of all directors at the Executive Development Committee, the prime purpose of which is to encourage and facilitate cross-divisional moves, assess vacancies across the group, the talent available, and development and training programmes.

Each division has its own management development processes, culminating in each one having to make an annual presentation at Trafalgar Square to all group executive directors. Peter Garfield follows this up by summarising for the board the group's succession plans.

Because of this strong emphasis given by the directors, HR policies are linked closely to business goals. HR is also strong in running and leading strategy seminars—for example setting the programme for the Annual Group Conference—leading to a lot of 'people stuff' on the agenda.

JM cannot guarantee jobs for life any more, but it can give people enhanced skills and greater employability.

Garfield suspects that 'teamwork' is probably all the rage at present, but recalls that JM was one of the earliest companies to introduce it. In 1991 at its Royston chemicals facility, it introduced teamwork and invited *everyone* to apply for the team leader roles, using psychometric tests in the assessment process. Some shop floor people suddenly found themselves team leaders, while former supervisors found themselves concentrating instead on training and problem solving. Garfield noted that there were some 'difficulties' at the time, but believes that the approach works well. Pay systems reflect this team-based way of working.

JM expects to attain IiP recognition early in 1997. In terms of internal communications, while using the usual range of techniques and media, JM contends that team briefings lie at the heart of the process.

Career Opportunity and Development

The current, long-serving board members all reach retirement age at about the same time, at the turn of the millennium. David Davies jokingly asked when three of his directors were due to celebrate their centennial combined years of service! So JM needs to plan for a new generation to come through, and in planning succession, the impact flows right down the organisation.

JM regards its development planning as being excellent. Graduates and other 'bright' employees go through an annual business training course. Fast-track middle managers join the management development programme, which is mirrored in the UK and USA. Senior managers may find themselves on courses at INSEAD, Wharton and Harvard. High potential people have personal development interviews at appropriate intervals.

There is maybe more emphasis on bringing in people from outside than before, but JM retains a strong tradition of developing from within. When Peter Garfield adds that "even if it involves an expatriate, it's better the devil you know," you believe that he may be serious. All vacancies are advertised internally.

In an international group with divisions organised globally, there are frequent overseas and cross-divisional opportunities. JM doesn't expatriate people for the sake of it—the driver is 'who's the best man for the job?', underlining the importance of acquiring portable skills.

JM is a very technology/science-driven company, but would like to recruit more non-specialists, for example with business or language skills. 15–25 graduates are recruited annually from 'the best' UK universities, while the number recruited in the USA has risen to around 50.

Pay and Benefits

JM aims to be competitive on pay and benefits, and the MDRC receives regular advice from consultants on the pay and incentive arrangements prevailing in comparably sized industrial companies in each country in which JM has operations.

On top of pay, an annual bonus is paid (at the most senior levels, this might amount to 40% of salary). The top 50 executives also get a term plan bonus, which is related to the earnings per share performance of the company. A share option scheme, also with performance criteria that trigger their exercise only if the company is on an upward path, is open to JM's top 150 managers. Below manager level, each business is encouraged to have some sort of incentive scheme in place. JM operates a highly rated upper quartile pension scheme.

There is a 1:1 matched share participation for everybody (up to 5% of salary each month can be contributed). Over the last ten years, this has proved to be a very good deal. And it enjoys a good take-up. Employees studying a sheet of paper outside the company restaurant in head office are not pondering the delights on the day's menu, just checking on JM's latest share price.

The Future

In business terms, JM faces the challenge of managing the faster growth expected in its electronic materials and ceramics businesses, while still extracting something from its other activities. Maintaining world-leading positions is often harder than getting there, and JM is competing, increasingly, on a global stage.

This creates a real need for people who can deal with these pressures and be better than the competition. Of course, everyone wants these people, and JM recognises that recruitment, training and development are fundamental to having the right people for the right jobs.

JM employees probably do feel more in control of their own destiny today. The changes from the 1970s, which included JM de-recognising the unions and substituting instead a real commitment to open communications, teamworking and individual development, have left employees in no doubt that they must be able to look after themselves. It seems to be working.

John Laing plc

John Laing is a major force in the construction, housing and mechanical engineering markets in the UK, with operations in a growing number of overseas markets and increasing involvement in investment-led projects.

Employing up to 12,000 full- and part-time employees at any time, the company has a distinguished history of staff welfare initiatives and has emerged revitalised from a period of retrenchment brought on by the recession.

Biggest Plus: Paternalistic attitudes generate significant levels of staff loyalty

Biggest Minus: Lack of open communication channels

John Laing plc
Page Street
Mill Hill
London NW7 2ER
Tel: 0181-959 3636
Fax: 0181-906 5297

The Business

The first Laing house still stands. Built in the Cumbrian village of Sebergham in 1848, the house is now used by the Salvation Army as a rest and holiday centre. In a 19th century business environment that paid scant attention to staff safety, Laing introduced a range of visionary schemes. Not only were pension and health programmes implemented internally, but Laing promoted such schemes across the industry as a whole.

Developing rapidly during the early part of the 20th century, the company rose to national prominence during the 1950s and 1960s, securing contracts to build sections of the M1 and to resurrect Coventry Cathedral.

Now firmly established in the top five UK construction companies, Laing continues to focus on its core construction and homes businesses, developing ancillary skills and activities to reinforce those strengths.

In recent years, the work of the group has included such diverse projects as the completion of several sections of the M25, the continued restoration of the Bank Of England, Sizewell B, airport terminals at Stansted, Birmingham and Luton and the Millennium Stadium at Cardiff Arms Park.

No industry is more exposed to the effects of a downtown and Laing was hit hard by the recession. However, group turnover of £1,206 million for 1995 (gross profits £20.1 million) indicates firm evidence of recovery, and the impact of PFI (the Private Finance Initiative) suggests that a period of prosperity lies ahead.

Company Culture and Style

"For many years, the company has maintained a tradition of caring about the people it employs." (Kathie Jones, group publications manager.)

John Laing plc is a solid, stable, traditional organisation, a company driven forward by a hard-working ethos. Although always keen to import fresh ideas, the values propounded by its founder, James Laing, are still firmly in place—an enduring focus on quality, reliability and craftsmanship.

Long service is the norm, nurturing an atmosphere of stability for employees who tend to be industrious, family-oriented and non-controversial. Apart from the Laings, many other family names span the history of the group and staff address each other on first-name terms regardless of seniority.

Some old habits die hard, however. Management still has a tendency to disseminate information on a 'need to know' basis, but that approach is changing. Significant efforts have been made to improve team briefing and cascade processes, and for over 150 years, all employees have received a copy of the house newspaper *Team Spirit*.

Laing operates a wide-ranging charitable trust. Although rarely publicising its activities, the Trust helps those who have fallen on hard times (for example meeting the heating bills of pensioners). The Trust also contributes generously to worthwhile causes, supporting up to 500 charity publications each year.

For many years, Laing has been in the vanguard of environmental campaigns. Among the tenets of Laing's own environmental policy are pledges to use recyclable materials, safeguard against pollutant emissions, and reduce noise at every opportunity. A senior manager in each division is responsible for ensuring comprehensive implementation of these objectives.

Human Resource Priorities

Group personnel policy is set out in a staff handbook given to each employee upon joining the company. Policies are designed to ensure that consistent treatment is provided to members of staff while affording sufficient flexibility to accommodate the traditions and business requirements of all activities within the company.

HR policies are also designed to train employees for senior positions, bringing through the next generation of potential executives.

A leading light in the provision of apprenticeships during the 1960s, Laing now takes a proactive role in YTS schemes, offering teenagers a vocational grounding and jobs on site when contracts permit.

Maintaining an illustrious welfare tradition, HR concerns continue to occupy senior minds. Continually updating and reinforcing health, pensions and welfare programmes, Laing's commitment at boardroom level is reflected by the fact that only asset management, marketing concerns and work-in-progress occupy more time on the management agenda.

Personnel managers are assigned to each division. Training, payroll, welfare, industrial relations are all covered by a team of over 140 professionals.

Staff attitude surveys are conducted on an anonymous basis. Results are published to members of staff and comments are passed down to the relevant departments to be actioned.

Career Opportunity and Development

John Laing aims to provide all staff with the opportunity to develop their full capabilities and a range of facilities exist in support of this goal.

Recruitment of school leavers and graduates into company training schemes leading to technical and professional qualifications is a well-established Laing tradition. In addition, the training department offers a range of internal courses covering technical, personal and management skills.

The director of career development takes note of those moving up the corporate hierarchy. For those identified as having the potential for senior roles, individual development packages provide selective use of courses offered by the major business schools. Laing maintains strong links with Loughborough University, tailoring a postgraduate diploma in Business Management to suit the needs of the company.

Although officially it does not operate a 'fast track' programme, Laing has historically provided high-fliers with a two-week residential course. An intensive programme incorporating a variety of role-play exercises, the course is attended by members of the board who pass on the fruits of their wisdom to leaders of the future.

99% of promotion is internal. Laing is a staunch believer in promoting from within and actively encourages secondments abroad. Overseas affiliates may offer postings in Europe, the Far East, Middle East, India and South Africa; a Learning Resource Centre equips self-starters with the tools to learn a foreign language.

Pay and Benefits

Pay increases have averaged 2% over the last couple of years. Discussions between members of the executive and the personnel director continue over a period of months, with the salary process being kick-started by line managers recommending rises for each member of their team.

Staff appraisals are held every two years, where individual goals are set, training requirements pinpointed, and long-term career paths highlighted. A stretching mechanism structured to encourage achievement, targets are agreed during the course of appraisals, forming the basis for salary reviews.

Laing has just announced details of its third share option scheme. The first two schemes were heavily oversubscribed and staff now hold 15–20% of shares in the company (the Laing family retains 61%).

The company maintains a voluntary private medical scheme, and all management are eligible to join. Employees with over five years' service are covered by a non-contributory pension scheme and Laing also maintains a permanent health scheme for seriously ill members of staff, with employees remaining on the payroll although no longer able to work.

"I cannot thank the company enough," recalls employee Charlie Hicks, "for the support I received when I suffered a kidney failure. I subsequently had to undergo a transplant, and Laing's support allowed me to triumph over a series of health problems."

Laing's philanthropic credo is epitomised by a Corporate Welfare System. All 3,000 ex-employee pensioners are visited every six months by welfare officers to identify their needs and act accordingly.

Other perks include 25 days' annual leave, staff discounts on Laing homes, membership of a sports club and a maternity scheme in line with statutory entitlements.

The Future

The changing face of the construction industry is presenting many new challenges to John Laing. In recent times, the Private Finance Initiative has been introduced by the government to develop a fresh partnership between the public and private sectors.

Laing has played a leading role in this initiative. The company has experience of operating private motorways in Spain and recently completed the second Severn crossing, linking England and Wales. Laing construction managers now take a broader view of industry and employ new disciplines previously divorced from their world.

PFI is just one of a number of changes taking the construction industry into the new millennium. Laing is set to remain at the forefront of developments, promoting fresh client relationships without sacrificing its impressive commitment to staff welfare.

"Whenever I have the opportunity to go round the country," concludes chairman JMK Laing, "I cannot be but impressed with the enthusiasm and dedication that our staff bring to the business. Despite some of the difficult times we have had to go through, those efforts are a source of immense pride."

LASMO plc

LASMO is one of the UK's leading independent oil and gas exploration and production companies. The UK Continental Shelf and Indonesia are LASMO's principal areas of activity, but the company has exploration and development interests in 14 countries, in eight of which it acts as operator. In 1995, LASMO made pre-exceptional operating profits of £142 million on turnover of £637 million. Its total oil and gas reserves stood at 724 million barrels of oil equivalent at the end of 1995. LASMO employs around 750 staff world-wide, with 300 based in the UK.

Biggest Plus: Staff innovation actively encouraged

Biggest Minus: Business prone to oil price fluctuations

LASMO plc
100 Liverpool Street
London EC2M 2BB
Tel: 0171-945 4545
Fax: 0171-606 2893

The Business

Founded in 1971, LASMO quickly established a dynamic reputation in the petroleum industry. Actively pursuing a policy of growth by acquisition—of oil assets, licences and companies—the company has built an international portfolio of high-quality assets across Europe, south-east Asia, South America and the African continent.

Once regarded as the high-flying 'kids on the block', LASMO acquired Thompson North Sea and Ultramar during the late 1980s/early 1990s. Some adverse City reaction was followed by a boardroom reshuffle, and a restructured management team committed to strengthening the balance sheet and redefining corporate culture took the helm.

Having fought-off an unwanted take-over bid from its main rival Enterprise Oil in 1994, LASMO is back on an upward trend of financial performance, and has built a solid platform for further growth.

Corporate Culture and Style

There is nothing like a take-over bid to focus the mind and spur a company on to greater efforts, and that is what LASMO has done successfully. The company has recently completed a year-long programme, 'LASMO 2000', aimed at further improving efficiency and cost-effectiveness in the company, and at redefining its corporate culture. With the help of external consultants Hay Management Group and Ernst & Young the programme, which is ongoing, has banished old department-focused structures, and moved towards creating multi-disciplinary teams that can take a broader view of the business as a whole, while maintaining strong management of specific assets and defining accountabilities.

Emphasis is placed on providing shareholder value and developing 'stretch' corporate objectives. Each employee is made aware of these objectives through cascade processes, with appraisals and reward systems geared towards measuring performance.

Management attitudes highlight the new approach. LASMO strives to respond to individual needs while maintaining consistent company-wide policies. When necessary, LASMO takes a compassionate option that may not be available to larger companies concerned about setting a precedent.

Human Resource Priorities

An attitude survey carried out towards the end of 1995 revealed a need to improve internal communication and a desire for information to be fed down—as well as up—the organisation. LASMO 2000 re-emphasised the vital importance of good internal communications. HR is now recognised as a key department in LASMO's change process, with a focus to help the business units succeed.

Human resources strategy and policies cover recruitment, employment, compensation, training and development. Barry Page, human resources supervisor, summarises three main tasks for the HR department: Trying to foresee where problems might arise and 'heading them off at the pass'; importing the right quality of staff at the right price, maintaining attractive levels of remuneration, and achieving consistency across the group; and offering development opportunities throughout people's careers.

With employees spread across the globe, LASMO's team of HR specialists has a daunting range of responsibilities. On a day-to-day level, the department actively supports all the business units, but it could also be called upon in a variety of emergency situations. Arranging support for a medical emergency in Indonesia, helping staff deal with an outbreak of civil war in Yemen, recruiting geologists urgently needed in Libya—all fall within the ambit of HR.

Career Opportunity and Development

LASMO's business change process also re-emphasised the whole area of career development. The HR function is charged with initiating the effective management of career planning processes, to produce appropriately trained and experienced personnel to meet the company's future needs.

The annual process of appraisal begins with each employee assessing their own performance as a forerunner to discussions with a supervisor. Such dialogue encompasses the setting and achievement of objectives, career planning and training. Remuneration strategy is linked directly to performance.

Ongoing dialogue is provided through monthly HR/function meetings and discussions between HR and line management. As a result of these meetings, decisions are reached about training needs, succession plans and means of stretching individuals by moving them around the world. With the number of global positions everchanging, outstanding candidates earmarked for possible advancement have ample opportunity to demonstrate and realise their potential. This includes working overseas—more than half of LASMO's staff are outside the UK at any time.

LASMO's overall approach to training and development is geared towards helping employees at all levels improve performance and develop skill portfolios, achieve specific objectives based on job descriptions and performance standards, and provide a continuous and integral part of the management process.

In 1995, LASMO introduced an upgraded management development programme. Customised to meet the needs of the company and run in conjunction with educational bodies including Cranfield and the London Business School, the programme covers such issues as presentation skills, techniques for negotiation, crisis management, staff development and leadership programmes.

The training calendar is impressive. LASMO runs 10 major management development courses each year plus a host of technical programmes covering every discipline from geology to law. A substantial sum is set aside each year for external courses and a number of UK employees are currently studying for MBAs.

Pay and Benefits

LASMO recognises the need to offer highly attractive benefit packages, and compares favourably against direct competitors. Managerial base salaries range from

£30–70,000, administrative staff between £15–25,000, and graduates joining LASMO in 1996 started on a base salary of £19,500. Among the factors that enter the pay equation are salaries offered by competitors, the performance of the company as a whole and personal levels of achievement and experience.

LASMO operates SAYE and profit-share schemes. Roughly 80% of UK employees are now shareholders in LASMO and an executive share option scheme is also in place. No formal arrangements exist for profit-related bonuses, but ad hoc awards may be given at the discretion of the chief executive.

Benefits include generous relocation packages and expatriation allowances for staff moving abroad, a non-contributory pension scheme for all UK employees, and a heavily subsidised private medical scheme. People eligible for a company car may opt instead for a monthly allowance; LASMO tends to offer this benefit at lower grades of job than many companies in other industrial sectors.

Esprit de corps is actively encouraged, at work and at play. UK staff have their own sports teams, organise quiz nights and enjoy corporate membership at the Broadgate Sports Club in the City, the Hogarth Club in Chiswick and the Credo Fitness Centre in Aberdeen.

The Future

LASMO has now entered a period of growth, and significant progress has been made pursuing fresh business opportunities. LASMO recently announced the award of new exploration licences in Egypt, Italy, and the Falkland Islands, and the company has also established a joint venture based in Kuwait to pursue new business opportunities in the Middle East.

Chief executive Joe Darby is confident about the company's outlook. "LASMO is well-positioned to pursue opportunities in countries where it is already established and in several new countries which offer potential access to sizeable, low cost reserves. Our efforts will continue to focus primarily on exploration and development, but we shall also look to invest in related business opportunities, including projects in the integrated gas chain through to power generation."

As exploration efforts continue in order to sustain growth, HR challenges will naturally cascade from such ventures. Barry Page is encouraged by the change in the HR environment, allowing LASMO to meet its business objectives while taking care of individual needs. "We can draw real satisfaction," he suggests, "from the changes produced by LASMO 2000. We're not only a company which is highly activity-driven with specific technical objectives, but also one that is placing considerable emphasis on good people management."

The petroleum industry will always be at the mercy of oil price fluctuations. However, LASMO's return to profitability represents a significant upturn in fortune for a company that is currently marking its 25th anniversary, celebrating maturity with a fresh philosophy towards staff and an enlightened attitude to HR issues.

LEHMAN BROTHERS

Lehman Brothers

Lehman Brothers is the world's second largest underwriter of equities and bonds and probably the world's fifth most active adviser in mergers and acquisitions. A global investment bank, Lehman serves the needs of individual, institutional, corporate, and government clients. One of the oldest Wall Street houses, the official company headquarters is in New York, with major offices in Asia and Europe. London is the major European focus and about 1,300 staff work in the City.

The average age of staff is 32 years, and more than half are between 25–35. The average length of service is four years; more than 40 different nationalities can be counted in the ranks and 26% of staff have been with Lehman for more than five years.

Biggest Plus: Exciting position at the forefront of a global industry

Biggest Minus: Tough and demanding work in a very competitive sector

Lehman Brothers
One Broadgate
London EC2M 7HA
Tel: 0171-601 0011
Fax: 0171-260 2999

The Business

Lehman Brothers' goal, to quote from the firm's own induction handbook, is 'to maximise profitability and optimise market share by integrating the Lehman organisation with the organisations of its investment customers and banking clients.' When those clients are investing hundreds of millions and billions of pounds Sterling, they want, demand, and deserve sterling service.

Lehman believes that its 'one firm' philosophy keeps it special. This integrated approach means that no matter where in the world the client is, regardless of time, there is always a Lehman person close at hand to provide service and up-to-date information. The quality of the service is the same across the firm and across the world.

Business units are managed globally and strategic plans are formulated by the global business heads and executed regionally. The firm's 15-member Operating Committee, which sets business policy, comprises the senior managers from every major area of the organisation. This structure provides all parts of the organisation with an equal voice in managing the firm, enabling Lehman to identify rapidly and address opportunities and issues on a global, firm-wide level.

This one firm focus is a recent development. In the 1980s, Lehman went through a series of changes in ownership: Shearson, Hutton and American Express all took their turns at the helm. Since 1994 Lehman has been a publicly traded company, and in a sense, staff agree it is almost as if it has started anew. "We take tremendous pride in the corporation and are very excited about being independent again, in charge of our own destiny," says John Godfrey, director of corporate communications for Europe.

"We focus very much on international and cross-border business, and having the 'one firm' philosophy makes us unique," continues Godfrey. There is one profit and loss account right across the firm that eliminates squabbles between different profit centres. Teamwork is therefore of the utmost importance and trust is both earned and rewarded. From a culture that was deal-oriented, Lehman is now equally focused on strong management.

Company Culture and Style

The culture instils that the firm's whole is greater than any one part. The Lehman crowd accept that what they do reflects on the company as a whole, not just on them as individuals. There is a set of values that employees seem to internalise and practice.

The first is a bias for action. A lot of emphasis is put on the close relationship with customers and providing for their needs. The work is hands-on and value-driven and as a result, staff across the different sectors tend to and are expected to pile-in and help. As a client-driven business, Lehman believes that repeat business comes from satisfied customers and in a sector not renowned for its loyalty, Lehman has a good record.

The idea of a 'head office' is one that seems to be outdated at Lehman. Although the firm has headquarters in New York, because of the one firm mentality,

London-based employees feel just as much a part of the firm as those in the Big Apple. The global chief economist is based in London.

According to staff, Lehman people are easy to spot. They are that much hungrier, talk and walk that much faster. The Lehman Europeans are also easy to distinguish. While the British banker is always immaculate in a stiff blue business suit, the Italians, the French and the Spanish rarely wear ties, often sport green jackets and ooze casual, continental style and sophistication. To understand how integrated foreign staff feel, Americans at Lehman's prefer to drink tea.

Money has to be a motivating factor in this highly rewarded business, but a highly skilled and intellectual workforce has made the industry more efficient, professional and difficult to get into. Intellectual curiosity seems to be de rigeur. People attracted to this industry will be intrigued by working across several time zones, functioning in various languages, in different cultures, in a truly international business. Sealing a multi-million pound deal also tends to send the adrenaline rushing.

In the early 1980s, banking appeared to be the yuppies' game. It is now highly professional. Whereas ten years ago there was little need for a degree, presently Lehman could not imagine hiring a senior executive without one good degree, if not two. The firm is virtually littered with academics, several with doctorates in esoteric subjects such as physics and mathematics.

Human Resource Priorities

Human resources works with line managers from all divisions, and the effective management of all employees is considered to be of the utmost importance. The employee relations manager or specialist is usually the first point of personnel contact for any employee when they join the firm.

You can be the perfect candidate in every respect, but if you are a prima donna, you won't fit in. If you are not a team player there is no way you will forge a career at Lehman, a firm that puts openness and communication at the top of its list of priorities. If someone cannot communicate properly, the business does not work, and every year the ability to communicate with colleagues is something on which each employee is assessed. Managers are expected to lead by example. Even the chairman, who in this flat organisation is accessible, zaps 'desk drops' to staff who have been outstanding. Little gestures that increase loyalty.

Career Opportunity and Development

Candidates applying to join Lehman tend to be academically very gifted, a large number coming from Oxford, Cambridge, INSEAD, Harvard and Yale. These days, languages are a must and secretaries are often trilingual. Bankers must be able to understand how business is done in each country, predict trends, and be at ease working with clients and colleagues from around the world. Long working hours are not stipulated in the contract but anyone who wants to get ahead will know that the days start early and finish late.

New graduates are rotated around different parts of the organisation. This gives them the sense of being part of a larger entity. Most graduates will spend between six to eighteen months in New York. Besides ensuring that all employees have common training, it offers a great opportunity to build a network of contacts from the beginning.

Lehman offers three distinct training programmes for graduates in Europe: the investment banking analyst programme; the sales, trading and research programme; and the systems development programme.

Pay and Benefits

Lehman has categorically stated that it does not pay anyone in gold bullion, port or vintage wine! It does, however, reward its staff generously and accepts the fact that it has to be 'creative' in how it manages remuneration. There is no company car scheme, but it does give people car allowances because it is tax advantageous.

A share plan was introduced globally which ran into problems when it proved to be a tax hazard in the UK, and totally illegal in Belgium. At the time of flotation in 1994, only 3–4% of staff were shareholders; this figure is now around 21–22%, and rising. For everyone, a proportion of their compensation is made up of equity in the firm—as a result, staff act sometimes like proprietors.

Lehman generally transfers people to work as 'locals' in foreign countries, meaning that the air fare is paid for, but without the traditional expatriate 'package'.

The Future

In the USA, Lehman is an established investment bank with a track record that attracts repeat business. The real business challenge lies in foreign domains such as Europe and Asia, where it comes head-to-head with local and other international firms. The only way to beat the competition is by doing a better job in this very tough, unsentimental market.

Levi Strauss (UK)

Levi Strauss is the leading brand name in the sale and manufacture of denim jeans and other clothing. Levi Strauss UK is an affiliate of this privately owned US firm, which operates in 42 countries with 56 owned and operated plants (in addition to numerous contractor arrangements), selling products in 900 Original Levi's Stores world-wide, as well as through franchise, third party jeans and multiple retailers. Levi Strauss has 37,000 employees world-wide.

1,700 employees are found in the UK, 200 at the head office, administration and distribution centre in Northampton, and 1,500 at three manufacturing sites in Scotland, which report to a regional HQ in Brussels. The UK affiliate handles marketing, sales and distribution. Of the 34 Levi's Stores in the UK, all but one are franchised, the exception being the London flagship store in Regent Street, which is as much a 'retail theatre' as a place for Londoners to buy trousers.

Biggest Plus: A family company with real values in people and business

Biggest Minus: Subsidiary of US firm sometimes limits opportunities

Levi Strauss UK Ltd
Moulton Park
Northampton NN3 6QG
Tel: 01604-790436
Fax: 01604-790400

The Business

Levi Strauss is one of the world's largest private companies, ownership having returned to the descendants of Levi Strauss in 1985 in one of the biggest leveraged buyouts in the USA at the time. Being privately owned allows Levi's to do things in its own style.

The family history is salient in the minds of staff, who can still relate to the company's founder. Chief executive Bob Haas is the great-great grand nephew of the original Levi Strauss and this mental link to the founder and his values still pervades through the organisation. It has helped make Levi's a value-driven business.

Levi's also benefits from the favourability of its brand name, indeed, it has uniqueness. Levi Strauss invented jeans in 1853, which enables product values and strengths to be claimed with some justification. Levi's certainly produces memorable and stylish TV, cinema and print advertisements, particularly for its legendary 501 jeans.

Company Culture and Style

When Levi Strauss claims that it is a values-driven business, these are not idle words—they do underpin everything that the company does, and are integrated into the way in which the company does business. 'The mission of Levi Strauss & Co. is to sustain responsible commercial success as a global marketing company of branded apparel' is the opening gambit to the company's mission statement. Not far behind are people. "The thing that gives us our strength is our people...our challenge is to put people at the centre of our business," are the words of chief executive Bob Haas.

Commercial success comes first, otherwise there is no business at all. But Levi Strauss does believe strongly that how you do business is important. Values such as teamwork, diversity, recognition, ethical management practices, communications and empowerment may be found elsewhere. But Levi's believes in them so firmly, that the performance management system actually rewards people for success and achievement against these values, and not just against financial results.

Educational programmes make employees aware of what these values are, and what is expected of them in their day-to-day work. It would appear to succeed—these values are held spontaneously, are not imposed, and employees themselves prove to be the greatest ambassadors of what the company stands for. Non-believers would probably leave. Donna Goya, senior vice president, HR, Levi Strauss & Co. says, "We believe that the quality of our employees' lives is just as important as the quality of our pants". This value is just as true in the UK as in the USA, although Donna would probably translate it to 'trousers'.

Teamwork is high on the list, and performance assessment also attempts to measure the efforts and achievements of cross-functional teams. The environment at Levi Strauss is one of openness, bordering sometimes on vocal. People are willing to state their views and challenge situations and ideas.

Levi's staff have tremendous loyalty to the company, which has not gone unnoticed or unrewarded. In June 1996, Levi Strauss announced its much publicised 'Global Success Sharing Plan'. All employees, whatever their position or role, are to receive one year's salary as a recognition payment (on top of salary and bonus) in 2002, coincided to mark the new millennium.

While this generous act diverts funds away from shareholders to employees, it has the former's full support, and goes a long way to recognising that people are global employees in a global company. The Industrial Society complemented the 'cleanness' of this reward scheme. There are no differences for different business performance across the world, and the Plan does require what the *Financial Times* described as 'eminently achievable cash flow targets' to be met, but final amounts will be pro rata above as well as below these levels.

The informal air at the company means that if you expect to find people wearing suits, you will probably be disappointed. In its Aspirations Statement, Levi Strauss invites staff 'to have fun in our endeavours'. While many companies may hope for this, few put pen to paper. 'Summer hours' is a popular arrangement. Closing at 1pm on Fridays is not a facet of flexible hours, but a real wish for people to enjoy the British summer (and now the other three seasons)—sometimes via a barbecue on the lawn outside the office. Interestingly, when 'summer hours' was introduced, the reaction of many staff was "but we need to be here to look after our retailers".

Human Resource Priorities

HR places a major emphasis on guiding employees through the ongoing process of change, and in turn ensuring that the organisation has the skills and expertise available to manage itself through change. Responsibility is devolved to line managers rather than have initiatives seen as 'another HR policy thing'. Internal communication and follow-up is handled in a personal fashion.

The requirements of the business are tracked closely, and Levi Strauss has undertaken surveys among its retailers to identify how it could perform better. Their suggestions, often relating to distribution and lead times, inevitably implied better use of systems. The apparel industry is hardly noted for its front-running in the use of information technology, but Levi Strauss considers itself to be quicker on the uptake here than its rivals.

The pending move to a new distribution site gave Levi's the chance to involve 'the people who wear the building'. A randomly selected group of employees were charged with producing ideas on the building's layout, specification, needs, and improvements on the existing work place.

Diversity in the work place has always figured prominently on the company's agenda. Gillian Rutherford, HR director, observes that this includes obvious and non-obvious diversity, requires employing people from different groups and backgrounds, and creating an environment where all ideas and perspectives are valued and respected. The need to reflect customer diversity is also apparent, but is relevant to many other audiences. Levi's does not see the drive towards diversity as being the sole responsibility of managers, but of all employees.

Career Opportunity and Development

The UK affiliate is small in the context of the Levi's world-wide empire, and low staff turnover hardly helps to create vacancies, but events in the last 12–18 months have spawned new opportunities. Levi's first aim is to recruit internally (to a certain level) where possible. Jobs are posted, and advertised on 'Eureka' (Levi's worldwide information sharing network, or Intranet).

In terms of marketing and customer service, the UK is a very sophisticated market with a highly developed multiple retailing network, compared to continental Europe. Consequently, UK staff are in demand by Levi's affiliates across Europe, on a permanent, project or task force basis. This has given the company the chance to develop people with potential, although by and large, the onus is on individuals to say what their skills needs are, and express their ideas and personal aspirations for now and the future. Levi's will listen.

Levi's doesn't engage in graduate recruitment. Like many lean US organisations, Levi Strauss is 'hung up on headcount', recruiting only when it has a vacancy. But it is very strong in the area of student placements. 2–3% of the work force might be undergraduates performing real jobs and controlling real resources. CVs are genuinely enhanced, and some students do return after graduation.

Pay and Benefits

Levi's aims to be market competitive. Pay comprises three elements: base pay, an annual bonus (all employees are eligible) and a long-term component, measured as contribution to the long-term success of the business. Pay increases are based 100% on performance. A package of benefits is offered, but being a private company, there are no employee share schemes.

The Global Success Sharing Plan is a one-off recognition payment outside pay policy, and is something which senior management had probably wanted to do and had been planning for some time. If its announcement was timed to mark the new millennium, it has also raised awareness of the company judging by the flood of job applications it received soon afterwards.

The Future

Levi's major challenge is to remain competitive in a tough market, dictating the need to continually motivate employees so that they are prepared and equipped to meet these challenges. Levi's regards this as doing more of what it does already—reinforcing values, and keeping telling people that change is normal.

Management is conscious that change should not be viewed as a number of 'steps', interspersed with gaps, but is continuous, and essential for a healthy business. Communication plays an important part, informing staff why change is necessary, how it is achieved, and what it might mean at the individual level.

People are also encouraged to take charge of their own development, rather than the company taking responsibility. This is never really an issue at Levi's, and again the emphasis is more upon continual communications and perceptions. Employees of the company have long since learned to involve themselves in the business openly and directly, and a more loyal work force may be hard to find.

THE

Littlewoods
ORGANISATION PLC

The Littlewoods Organisation

The Littlewoods Organisation is one of the UK's largest privately owned groups. It was founded by Sir John Moores in 1923 and remains wholly owned by members of the Moores family. It operates primarily in two key business sectors: retail and leisure. The retail business includes Littlewoods Stores, with over 130 stores nationwide; Littlewoods Home Shopping, the UK's second largest home shopping business; Index, the catalogue shop with over 130 UK stores; and Littlewoods International, responsible for international sourcing and trailing retail concepts. The leisure business includes Littlewoods Pools, the world's largest treble chance football pool; Littlewoods Lotteries, which sells charity scratchcards; and Spot the Ball. Group turnover in 1995 was £2.6 billion and pre-tax profits £97 million. The Littlewoods Organisation employs 30,000 people.

Biggest Plus: Determined company, sweeping with a new broom

Biggest Minus: Competitive environment, new journey only just begun

The Littlewoods Organisation plc
100 Old Hall Street
Liverpool L70 1AB
Tel: 0151-235 2222
Fax: 0151-235 2981

The Business

Over the past few years, the Littlewoods Organisation, like many other retail and leisure companies, has been affected by the slow economic recovery from recession, and by intense competition in retailing. The National Lottery has also had a significant impact on the Pools business.

To meet these challenges, each of the group's operating divisions has focused on implementing strategic plans designed to improve the performance and profitability for the benefit of all stakeholders. The Littlewoods Organisation remains one of the most financially strong companies in the retail and leisure sectors, with negligible borrowings and a strong balance sheet. This has enabled it to invest substantially in each of its businesses, both to ensure greater focus on meeting the needs of customers and to equip employees with the technology and resources to work effectively and efficiently.

The group is moving forward strongly and the businesses are well placed to take advantage of the growing economic recovery. Littlewoods Home Shopping continues to be a leader in the fast-changing home shopping market. The division's latest innovation is the launch of Index Extra, a new direct-to-high street customer catalogue that aims to deliver greater value and choice to consumers. The business has also been investing heavily to improve its customer service and national distribution systems, with the recent introduction of a 48-hour delivery service.

Littlewoods Stores is focused on improving its offer to customers with the introduction of the Berkertex brand throughout the product range, combining quality with the Littlewoods reputation for value. The Stores division is also investing substantially in store refurbishment to introduce a more contemporary retail environment.

Index, the catalogue shop, is in the process of renewing its outlets and is putting considerable resources into improving catalogue range, design and customer service—which also includes a 48-hour guaranteed delivery system.

Internationally, Littlewoods is actively trialling retail concepts in Russia and India.

On the leisure side of the business, Littlewoods is fighting back against the National Lottery with exciting new soft gambling initiatives. These include a high profile relaunch of the Pools offer with an aggressive and high-profile marketing programme, as well as diversifying into other related leisure propositions, such as scratchcards.

The Littlewoods Organisation has undertaken a review of its corporate governance arrangements, which has led to greater clarity between the roles of the owners and the management of the group. James Ross, the former chief executive of Cable and Wireless, has recently been appointed chairman of the Littlewoods Organisation and, in conjunction with revitalised management teams, has focused on bringing every aspect of the business up to best practice methods and performance.

Company Culture and Style

The Littlewoods Organisation has a distinct company culture based on strong values and a deep commitment to employees and the communities in which it operates. As a result, Littlewoods is now one of the country's leading employers in promoting equal opportunities and is one of the 'champion' companies in the 'Race for Opportunity' campaign. Littlewoods is a founder member of the Employers Forum on Age and is one of the 12 core members of the 'Employers for Childcare', ensuring that maternity, paternity and adoption leave are available to all employees.

Littlewoods continues to play a significant role in the community at large and partners with and contributes to many good causes to improve the quality of life in the north west and across the UK. Following in the footsteps of Sir John Moores, the group and the Moores family continue to support youth opportunities, education, sport and the arts.

These strong values will remain at the heart of the company, but at the same time a new spirit of professionalism and dynamism is being introduced by management teams. According to Ford Graham, group human resources manager, "We are successfully creating a strong and positive team culture among our employees, focused on providing a quality service to the customer that will result in customer satisfaction, repeat business, increased profits and greater job security."

Human Resource Priorities

There is a heightened level of commitment to the role of the human resources function from the very top of the company. The drive for efficiency and improved performance is balanced by an understanding of the need to have effective two-way communication, and to fully enrol the interest and loyalty of employees.

The group has worked hard to reinforce the sense of mutual trust and understanding built up with the work force on a direct basis and through the unions. Ford Graham: "The consultation process at Littlewoods has been recognised by the Trades Unions as the professional and most effective method of 'doing business'. It enables the businesses to take their employees with them during times of major change."

This strong contact has enabled the unions and work force to understand the company's commitment to them, and also to recognise the fierce challenges it faces. That relationship has endured the acid test of significant staff reductions over the past few years, which was achieved on a joint basis.

Communication is a central avenue for publicising the new policies, initiatives and opportunities. This is achieved through team briefings, group newspapers and employee reports, with a new magazine dealing with issues of equal opportunity.

Career Opportunity and Development

As part of the Littlewoods Organisation's revitalisation programme, greater resources have gone into training and career development, including the appointment of a group career development manager, Hilary Farrar. She comments: "Investment in these areas, both in time and cost, has increased significantly in the past two years. All businesses run appraisal schemes which include training plans, and employees can apply for help with college-based courses to back up their current or next roles." Studies range from BTec to MBA and include professional exams.

Around 40 graduates join each year. Many will have relevant degrees for the specialism they choose to pursue, such as buying, store management, finance and general management, and particularly information technology.

The general management stream will often be selected from individuals without any particular specialism who are seen as having high performance potential. Littlewoods has long had a high reputation for its management training.

The quickening pace of the group's development, and its need to be on the cutting edge of innovation, means that talent is being capitalised on at every opportunity. Employment in a group with diverse businesses enables employees to enjoy a wider career experience with differing business challenges.

Multi-disciplinary teamwork is playing an increasing part in Littlewoods' fast-moving business. This, together with a greater share in the responsibility for the success of the group, makes for good career opportunities for involved and committed employees.

Pay and Benefits

The above change programme with its associated objectives and values are being supported and underpinned by a remuneration policy that will attract, retain and motivate high calibre employees. In addition, the levels of remuneration are continually benchmarked against the market place to ensure the company remains highly competitive.

The Future

The drive to improve performance and revitalise its businesses has restored a real momentum and direction to the Littlewoods Organisation. There is a growing emphasis on quality, value and customer focus; and Littlewoods has strong ambitions to be among the best of the UK's retail and leisure companies.

Both the UK retailing and leisure sectors are undergoing rapid transformation, and Littlewoods is determined to be one of the winners. While the group continues to operate in highly competitive markets and faces significant challenges, the ongoing transformation across the retail and leisure businesses has ensured that Littlewoods is increasingly well placed to take advantage of the improving economic environment.

The barometer of success will be improved financial performance across the group. Challenging everyone in the company, James Ross believes that "If this group is not capable of doubling its profits over five years, it is not living up to its potential."

MARKS & SPENCER

Marks and Spencer

Marks & Spencer is one of the leading high street retailers in the UK, with 646 locations world-wide, an annual turnover exceeding £7.2 million, and over 65,000 employees. Its stores sell high quality goods made to its own specifications under the St Michael name. Marks & Spencer boasts the highest profit of any retailer in Europe. As well as its own-name stores, it sells through franchises and through Brooks Brothers (in the USA and Japan) and Kings Super Markets in the USA. It has many financial activities, including Marks & Spencer Financial Services Ltd.

Biggest Plus: A company that lives up to its high reputation

Biggest Minus: Hard work, long hours

Marks and Spencer plc
Michael House
37–67 Baker Street
London W1A 1DN
Tel: 0171-935 4422
Fax: 0171-487 2679

The Business

Marks & Spencer (M&S) is so well known as to hardly need any introduction. Since its beginnings in 1884 with a Penny Bazaar in Leeds, it has been a tremendous success story. Every week, millions of people around the world shop in its stores or franchise shops, buying goods from an extensive range of products which includes food, clothes, household goods, decorating materials, everything in fact from a 39 pence loaf of bread to a £1,000 sofa.

It is the only retailer in the world to have an AAA credit rating. As well as its stores, M&S has other activities, of which the most important is financial services, providing Chargecard accounts, unit trusts, loans, life assurance and pensions.

The foremost commitment of Marks & Spencer is to the customer. Its mission is to sell high quality merchandise at outstanding value, offering the highest standards of customer care in an attractive shopping environment.

M&S is also committed to developing long-term partnerships with its suppliers and to expanding its overseas business. It already has stores or franchise shops in Hong Kong, Hungary, France, Belgium, Spain, Holland and Germany, and many other countries.

Company Culture and Style

Quality is the key word in describing the culture and style of Marks & Spencer. The company insists on high quality in its products, its stores, its customer service and its staff.

In the words of John Stanley, divisional director, "Quality is a corner stone of the company. Quality is an attitude of mind. It starts with the quality of people. The importance of quality must be understood right through the business, from the directors to the part-time sales assistants filling up the counters on a Saturday. This sort of quality culture can only be achieved if we treat people in a quality way."

Last year 1,500 extra staff were recruited to enhance customer service. Everyone in the company is asked to identify his or her customers, both internal and external, then to examine the service they provide and ask their customers how this could be improved. In return, the company aims to give staff progressive personnel policies and good remuneration packages.

As in other retailing operations, unpredictability, juggling many tasks at once, and physically and mentally challenging work is a fact of life.

Company philosophy is to 'challenge relentlessly'; that is never to be satisfied with the present way of doing things, always to explore different better ways of staying ahead.

Retailing is an extremely competitive sector and even a company so well placed as Marks & Spencer is fully aware that it can never rest on its laurels. So it values individuality and creativity in its staff. Its managers come from a diverse range of backgrounds and educational achievements, but have in common the ability to plan and organise, assertiveness, leadership skills, job motivation, analytical consideration, awareness of others, teamworking skills, as well as the relevant functional and technical skills.

The company has a strong tradition in equal opportunities and community involvement. It has an Ethnic Focus Group, is a member of the Employers' Forum on Disability and belongs to Opportunity 2000. M&S contributes over £8.5 million to a range of community projects and organisations concerned with education and training, the arts and heritage, the environment, and health and care. The company seconds its own managers to other organisations such as Business in the Community and Young Enterprise.

Human Resource Priorities

The underlying principle of Marks & Spencer's HR policy is to match the highest standards of customer care with the highest standards of employee care. It is committed to the welfare and personal development of its people and is well known for the various benefits it provides to its employees.

The company's training and development policy is to provide appropriate and cost-effective training at the right time to ensure that staff are skilled and motivated, and are able to achieve personal and commercial objectives; at the same time, the company promotes self-development to help people maximise their full potential.

Every UK employee has an annual personal development review and a record of achievement.

The Management Development programme offers part time secondment to about 140 secondees each year; they work about one day a week with a charitable project, after careful choice to ensure that each individual can use his or her skills and have a targeted development opportunity and challenge.

There is a tradition of consulting and communicating directly to staff on operational issues as well as on benefits and conditions. As a result, more flexible working practices have been introduced to suit individual needs. There are now many different working patterns where flexibility is the watchword.

Career Opportunity and Development

Careers at M&S are wide-ranging, and include commercial, financial, personnel management, merchandising, selection, technology, information technology, buying and many others.

There is much competition to work for M&S. Annual labour turnover is lower than the rest of the UK retail industry. Each year, the management recruitment team handles 12,000 application forms, conducts 2,500 interviews and then makes 600 job offers.

Internal promotion is the norm and a programme publicising management opportunities exists throughout all company divisions. As well as progressing upwards through the company, there are five planned routes into management. The first is the Young Management Training scheme for school or college leavers. There is also a Gap scheme for people taking a year out and wanting to work for Marks & Spencer for at least six months with the possibility of then joining the Young Management scheme. The Graduate Entry programme recruits just under 200 people from the 7,500 applying to join it. Sandwich students can find work experience under the Business Placement scheme. Finally, people with at least two years' relevant line management experience in other companies can start a management career at an appropriate level.

Nigel Rea's first job with the company was as a Saturday assistant during his 'A' levels, then as a full-time trainee supervisor. After four years, he applied for a management position and got his first assistant manager job. Since then he has worked in various stores, had a spell at head office and is now managing the first M&S store in Germany. He says, "I came from a retail family and knew from the start that was where I wanted to make my career. I decided to join Marks & Spencer because I knew I wanted to work for the company. Heading the team to open the new store in Cologne was a fantastic opportunity and I'm open-minded about where my career could go from here."

Quality training is fundamental to the success of the company. Schemes include NVQs, professional qualifications, and extensive internal training. All stores are working to achieve Investors in People recognition by the year 2000, building on the success of a pilot programme.

Pay and Benefits

The company aims to give store staff the best remuneration package in the high street. Benefits include profit sharing, profit-related pay, staff discounts (20% after two years' service), a pension scheme, share option schemes, subsidised catering, relocation assistance, health education and screening programmes, and discounted private health schemes. Doctors, nurses and chiropodists' help is available and emphasis is put on health awareness and sickness prevention—for instance, all staff are offered flu vaccinations each autumn. The 1996 starting salary for graduates is £16,000 with a 14% increase likely in the first 18 months.

The Future

Over the last few years, low growth and low inflation have created a very competitive retail climate in the UK, with 'replacement expenditure' the order of the day. Future expectations are that customers will become even more skilled and demanding in their purchasing decisions. Other business challenges are posed by price discounting, out-of-town shopping malls, rising expectations of good service, technology, the global market place and other factors.

One of these is quality, which has always been part of the Marks & Spencer tradition and one which the company must preserve in order to survive in this challenging environment. Sir Richard Greenbury, chairman, says "We have always placed a high value on people and the strength of the team I am privileged to lead, and the training that we give them puts us in a strong position to succeed now and well into the new century."

Mars, Inc.

Mars, Incorporated, is a world-wide leader in its main markets with global sales of US $13 billion. Mars has factories and offices in more than 60 countries, and employs 28,500 associates. Mars UK is a major subsidiary of this privately owned US giant.

Famous for its confectionery brands such as Mars, Snickers, Galaxy and M&Ms, Mars contains some surprises. Its confectionery products are just part of a massive snack foods business; Mars brands are the outstanding market leaders in the important petcare market (for example Whiskas and Pedigree Chum); Master Foods business produces a range of leading main meal foods, including Uncle Ben's and Dolmio; its drinks group Four Square is at the forefront of drinks vending systems; Mars Electronics International and Information Service International complete Mars' portfolio of businesses.

Biggest Plus: A strong, unique culture that you might love

Biggest Minus: A strong, unique culture that you might hate

Mars UK
3D Dundee Road
Slough
Berkshire SL1 4LG
Tel: 01753-693000
Fax: 01753-533172

The Business

Mars is characterised by two things—its superb brands and its unique corporate philosophy. Mars is a global business and its markets are huge. In the UK alone, £4 billion is spent on confectionery each year—70% on chocolate (Mars holds 30% of this market segment). The canning factory at Melton Mowbray produces up to 500,000 tonnes of petfood per year. Every day, over 100 million people world-wide use MEI coin, note and card payment systems.

Mars is governed by 'The Five Principles' of quality, responsibility, mutuality, efficiency and freedom. In reality these are a practical and productive way of doing business, and also foster Mars' unique culture. Forrest Mars Senior instigated the notion of single status, an egalitarian attitude to the work place which is embodied in a flat corporate structure.

Egalitarianism does not come at the expense of profit—profit is seen as the catalyst that sets the company free. Mars' open, informal working environment makes for easy communication and a fast-moving, responsive organisation where decisions are made quickly. Above all, it is a meritocracy, where rewards are high and reflect individual levels of responsibility.

Company Culture and Style

People say that working for Mars is different, and it probably is. The ethos at Mars is apparent the moment you walk through the door—any door that is, because the basis on which the work place is laid out is almost identical at any of the company's sites—open, integrated, with a logical layout of different work functions. Managers sit among their colleagues in an open plan environment that might be an investment bank dealing room, but where the currency is brands and the emphasis on people.

The Five Principles demand that Mars' associates think and act differently towards other associates, brands and the business. The Five Principles are demanding, and Mars knows that it doesn't always achieve everything that they demand. They run deeply through the organisation and underpin everything that Mars does.

The Five Principles give way to a set of shared values, which Mars believes must be kept firmly in sight, lest they become subsumed under structure. Shared values may be between two individuals, a team, or a business unit. It requires a different emphasis, looking at what people want from their jobs and the interdependency of working. Mars believes that society in recent times has over-emphasised the 'I', with less on the 'we'. In its own backyard, it puts this right.

The resulting culture at Mars has many aspects. Mike Hutter, HR manager, mentions "restless dissatisfaction", which he explains as follows: "We're very hard on ourselves. Mars tends to attract people who are their own biggest critics, who set themselves almost unachievable targets."

Individuals have real freedom to make a difference—individuality is encouraged, as is the ability to think for yourself and challenge the status quo. Yet people are very supportive of one another. It is easy for any company to say that it does not want clones; Mars suggests that 'individual characteristics' might mean the type of person you would want as a dinner party guest, or someone who is passionate about their hobbies.

Flexibility in mind, not just work, is another important attribute. The 'helicopter mentality', or an ability to analyse and criticise from different positions and to know one's own subjectivity, is a characteristic that Mars particularly admires.

Not surprisingly, Mars believes that there is real strength in diversity and that to succeed in the future, it must harness all diversities—of culture, time and geography. Mars wants a work force that reflects all diversities: opinions in the communities in which it operates; consumers are very diverse and you must have the right mix to understand them; and people think very differently, within countries and internationally.

In the obvious area of ethnic diversity, Mars has a senior manager responsible for driving forward a multi-cultural business at all levels. Mars also advertises in *Kaleidoscope*, the magazine for racial equality in graduate employment. "If you believe in something, you must back it up and put resource behind it," says Colin Knight, associate relations manager.

As to any psychological contract, Mars sees no value in anyone joining under false pretences. Individuals offered positions are invited to spend a day in the work place to make sure that Mars is the right place for them before they say 'yes'. It gives the best chance of Mars' values being shared rather than imposed.

Human Resource Priorities

HR at Mars is known as 'P&O'—personnel & organisation. This should not suggest that Mars is wedded to organisational structure—its philosophy, values and culture make sure it isn't—but it perhaps recognises that the way people are organised in the work place has a direct influence on behaviours and performance.

P&O has its own role, mission and set of responsibilities—for example in pay and benefits. In other areas, managers are more responsible (especially in recruitment, where P&O plays a supporting role).

Mars recruits people for careers, and is looking for the best people. In the UK, it recruits 15–20 graduates who have the potential to become senior managers in the business, rather than 150 graduates for middle management.

The personnel liaison group, chaired by Mike Smith, UK personnel director, ensures that all UK-based businesses are operating consistently. Smith says, "Because the culture is so strong, you have to work quite hard to live up to it. If you have a principle of single status, it's quite hard to achieve so you spend time and effort maintaining it."

Effective internal communications include job involvement sessions, team briefings, and company newspapers and magazines. Line managers are used as conduits for two-way communication. Mars has a template of electronic communications, covering bulletin boards, email, and access to minutes of meetings any-where in the organisation. Other companies have web sites too, but Mars devotes an awful lot of time inputting the information to access in the first place. But face-to-face communication always comes first at Mars.

Career Opportunity and Development

There are marvellous career opportunities to be had at Mars. The much-vaunted Mars Management Training Programme will hold people in good stead for the rest of their careers. Its design gives trainees a variety of experiences and challenges across functional and national boundaries, equipping them with the commercial, market and cultural perspectives needed to become a successful manager. Once through the management training scheme, the typical job cycle is 2–3 years. If this sounds a long time, the 'job size' is large, and its scope can change considerably in this time. Jobs are not rigidly defined—it can be where you want to take it, within reason. 'Boredom' is a word seldom heard. "And promotion is not the solution to motivation," suggests Mike Hutter.

International opportunities are plentiful—you are an associate of Mars, Inc.—and almost all jobs are advertised internally. Mars is expanding heavily into Eastern Europe (it was particularly early into Russia). While it wants local management, many Mars Western European associates find themselves seconded to fascinating opportunities in these emerging markets.

Pay and Benefits

Pay policy subscribes to the view that high calibre people deliver high performance; needing fewer people means you can reward them with high pay. To attract, retain and motivate high calibre people, Mars pays at the 90th percentile of best-paying UK companies. Graduates started on £21,000 in 1996. All associates have parts of their pay linked into the overall performance of the business.

Mars offers a good range of benefits, and those which it has, it does well and aims for consistency across all levels. The pension scheme is non-contributory, and private health insurance was only introduced when the company could offer it to every associate. 'Extra curricular' benefits sometimes figure—Mars Confectionery once booked Thorpe Park exclusively for its UK associates.

The Future

The overriding business challenge is the brand perspective—Mars aims to put customers in a position "where they feel compelled to purchase Mars' products." The outside world thinks Mars isn't innovative in terms of new products, but it is—the company virtually invented the confectionery ice cream market.

Mars will need to keep it this way, and looks closely at the dynamics of its markets, the ingredients in its products and changes in eating habits (pets as well as people). The company's links with Waltham Pet Nutrition Centre—the leading European research organisation for pet nutrition—highlights this intention.

Within the cultural dimension, Mars wants to operate with the lowest possible business overheads. This means having the minimum number of managers for the business to be effective and breaking down any remaining divides between managers and non-managers. As a 'family-friendly employer', Mars will continually look for ways in which work can be designed to complement people's home lives. The reality of making this happen within the principles of the business is the biggest challenge.

McKinsey

McKinsey & Company

McKinsey & Company is, arguably, the leading firm of management consultants in the world. Founded in 1926, McKinsey has enjoyed continuous growth since that time and is now a truly international firm with about 4,000 consultants in 70 office locations around the world. McKinsey has world-wide revenues of around $18 billion and has over 550 partners.

In the London office there are around 300 consultants, including industry and functional specialists, and a further 200 staff who provide a support and information service.

Biggest Plus: McKinsey on your CV is a virtual passport to success

Biggest Minus: Heavily set culture, staffed with similar people—situation may have to change

McKinsey & Company
1 Jermyn Street
London SW1Y 4UH
Tel: 0171-839 8040
Fax: 0171-873 9777

The Business

McKinsey is the most powerful consulting firm in the world. McKinsey's pre-eminence stems from the reputation it has earned for objectivity and independence, and for bringing the highest intellectual and analytical skills to bear on the major challenges confronting the world's leading businesses and institutions. For this, McKinsey—or 'The Firm' as its members have long since called it—relies on the professionalism and dedication of its consultants.

Other firms may have the same brain power, but they lack the reputation. Quoted in *Fortune* magazine, Fred Gluck, McKinsey's managing director says simply, "All I know is that every consulting firm anybody talks to always says they're second to McKinsey."

McKinsey's client list is impressive—virtually a 'Who's Who' of the world's major corporations. Their clients are often leaders in their fields and look to McKinsey to address their most important business problems. This means working in the fields of corporate strategy, organisation, operations, and mergers and acquisitions. It also includes helping clients grow and increase productivity, and tackling issues in functional areas such as finance, marketing, research and development, manufacturing and distribution.

The reach is global. The Firm derives more than half of its revenue from outside the USA and expects future growth to be fuelled by such fledgling markets as Russia, Eastern Europe and China.

Company Culture and Style

There is a widespread view that McKinsey people really do think that they are better than anyone else. They certainly inspire awe in many, which could have some-thing to do with the premium placed within the McKinsey culture on being 'bright', often a word for clear thinking analytical ability.

McKinsey's offices share a common philosophy and adherence to the same high standards of client service. McKinsey views client concerns from the top management perspective, and only accepts assignments from clients where The Firm is confident it can bring about beneficial change.

Outsiders have never regarded McKinsey as an open organisation, and the company certainly shuns publicity. This all adds to its mystique. It tends to deal with things internally. McKinsey accommodates a broad diversity of opinions, fostering rigorous debate to get the right answer. Yet it tries to achieve things collectively. An alternative view on diversity is that the McKinsey culture functions so well because it hires the same people over and over.

Fundamental to McKinsey studies is teamwork. A team's success hinges on the ability of its members to work together to gather the information and do the analysis that will enable them to prove or disprove their hypotheses. The McKinsey environment is a mutually supportive one, where teams may be made up of people of different backgrounds, but with a similar intellect and level of commitment.

Human Resource Priorities

HR policies necessarily have a major priority in recruitment and, in particular, development.

McKinsey typically recruits around 20 people in the UK each year—graduates and postgraduates—to become business analysts. Analytical and communication skills are regarded as important, as is the aptitude to work effectively in a team. The recruitment process can be a gruelling one, but this makes sure that the candidate is right for the firm, and vice versa.

Training is an essential and continuous part of the development of consultants, and is one of the human resources priorities at McKinsey.

Career Opportunity and Development

Training is a critical element in McKinsey's development programme for business analysts. In addition to on-the-job coaching, which is fundamental to every study and where most learning at McKinsey is likely to occur, there are several formal training programmes.

A three-week Induction Programme aims at providing business consultants with the skills needed to get started. The Analyst Training Programme is a firm-wide programme to further develop consulting skills such as problem structuring and solving, analytical techniques, accounting and interviewing. Communication training and language training courses are also encouraged.

Consultants at McKinsey are responsible for managing their own careers within the Firm. There are development leaders to support individuals, however, who monitor their development based on appraisals received after each study, provide formal feedback twice a year, and advise on any career issues of concern.

After two years, there are options. Consultants may opt to take an MBA at business school, or pursue a career in business. Most McKinsey business analysts choose to attend business school and McKinsey offers financial help to analysts who have performed well and secured a place, individuals deciding that management consultancy is not for them will find that their time with McKinsey has opened doors to positions they could not otherwise have achieved.

Of course, many people return to McKinsey after business school and enjoy long and rewarding careers with the Firm. Career paths then tend to be more clearly defined and as consultants, will gradually undertake larger and more complex sections of work. Training continues as careers progress.

Working for a large management consultancy like McKinsey offers advantages. Consultants are likely to encounter a greater range of industries, clients and issues. Due to the multinational client list, many studies will have an international component, and foreign travel can be regular. The Firm's level of accumulated knowledge is deep, and there is a readily available network of experts to contact world-wide.

Opportunities for career progression are not confined to the Firm. McKinsey's reputation, and the work carried out by its consultants, make people attractive propositions to other employers. The McKinsey alumni is found all over the business world, many at the head of very large companies and corporations.

Pay and Benefits

Management consulting is a well-paid industry, reflecting the calibre, importance (and quantity) of work performed for clients. McKinsey certainly pays attractively and is at least competitive with other leading management consultancies. To get some indication of long-term perspective, in the USA a junior director earns around $800,000 a year, and a junior partner around half a million.

The Future

In a world seemingly overpopulated with consultants, the main question is whether McKinsey can endure as one of the ultimate world-wide brand names—the Rolls-Royce of its industry?

Other consultancies may claim that McKinsey's consultants are no brighter than their own, probably with some justification. But McKinsey has the reputation, aura and credibility that appears to be unquestionable and unstoppable. Whether it is on a perch from which it could fall is sometimes asked, but usually by competitors. But no chief executive ever lost his job by hiring McKinsey. The Firm just goes from strength to strength.

The nature of its clients' businesses is continually changing, however, and this raises a genuine debate whether McKinsey needs to shift with it. As a 'top management' strategy consultancy, McKinsey has eschewed areas such as implementation and information technology based consultancy, which it leaves to others. With the increasing importance of technology in just about every industry and business, this may have to change.

And there is the question as to whether management consultancy can and should be sold as 'products', something which Boston Consulting Group initiated years ago. McKinsey eschews 'flavour of the month' consulting ideas, preferring instead to market intelligent thinking to strategic issues. But the Firm may have to consider shifting this stance and try to sell the next big idea.

These may be distractions. McKinsey's core consulting service rests on deep relationships with senior managers in business, who return to the Firm time and time again. McKinsey remains the consulting firm others would like to emulate.

The Morgan Crucible Company

The Morgan Crucible Company plc, a global and diverse business, develops, manufactures and markets technologically advanced materials, chemicals and components. With over 150 businesses operating in 41 countries, and selling into over 120, Morgan Crucible focuses on four product divisions: carbon, technical ceramics, thermal ceramics and speciality materials. 3,000 employees work in the UK out of a world-wide total of 13,500.

Biggest Plus: A culture which truly incorporates and nourishes individuals of every type

Biggest Minus: Resilience, inner strength and self-esteem needed in a flatly structured organisation

The Morgan Crucible Company plc
Morgan House
Madeira Walk
Windsor
Berkshire SL4 1EP
Tel: 01753-837000
Fax: 01753-850872

The Business

The catch phrase at Morgan Crucible (Morgan) is 'think globally act locally'. Statistics illustrate the reason behind the company philosophy. Although a British plc and proud of it, only 12% of sales are now in the UK, with 88% coming from overseas. 40% of profits were made in the USA alone. On a 1995 turnover of around £900 million, profit before tax was up 17.1% to £85 million. Morgan attributes its significant growth to its ability to develop and market new products, estimating that 20% of sales during the last three years were produced by products not in existence three years ago.

The organisational structure is, by the company's own definition, flat, and the corporate HQ in Windsor is lean. 60 people deal with the central issues of global focus and strategy. Subsidiary companies operate autonomously, and have their own boards and external non-executives. They are responsible for their own marketing, sales, manufacturing and industrial relations. Each has a clearly defined strategy and budget and is accountable directly to head office for performance. As a result, Morgan believes that it is quick to respond, flexible by nature, with good corporate communications across the continents.

"There is a well-known saying that a company is only as good as the people it employs. In Morgan we can be justly proud. In addition, the proportion of long-serving employees continues to increase, reflecting the two-way loyalty that is a hallmark of the Group," says Dr Bruce Farmer, group managing director.

Recruitment philosophy is to hire high quality, highly motivated, well-trained local people to run national businesses with support, training and encouragement from the centre. This is local implementation of global outlook and strategy. Part of this entails temporarily bringing people to the UK base to get the feel of the British organisation. The practice has recently expanded into South East Asia and China to reflect Morgan's growth in this part of the world.

Company Culture and Style

When Andy McIntosh, director of group personnel, says: "Our employees are the greatest asset we have," you believe him. The company has a clear definition of who it wants to attract and why. "We naturally attract people who relate to Morgan and our structure," continues McIntosh. "We don't provide the vertical opportunities of a huge multinational, the chance here is to grow and expand laterally. We have a no boundaries, open style of management."

The type of person who will succeed at Morgan will be professional, high on work commitment and work ethic, flexible, with excellent interpersonal skills. They also need to be confident and self-assured and be able to assess their development and competence without the constant reassurance or feedback of management or colleagues.

The culture of Morgan provides the atmosphere in which individuals can take risks and honestly express themselves without penalty. Morgan is also one of the few companies to preach employee satisfaction—it has a 90% retention record of graduates after two years' employment, 85% after five—and monitors this through mentoring and regular reviews. 'Fun' is spontaneous rather than scheduled—a quickly organised cricket match, or a round of golf when travelling. The motto is: 'take the job seriously, take your responsibilities seriously'.

Morgan does, however, see its responsibility to the community as being important. The company has its own corporate management development programme from which a local school realised its staff would benefit. In typical Morgan style, a deal was done, and Morgan committed to providing teachers with places on their Interpersonal Skills Course over a three year period, with all costs being picked up by Morgan. The course teaches interpersonal relationship skills, problem solving and crisis management. Such gatherings also help to recharge batteries and renew enthusiasm.

Human Resource Priorities

Morgan has a well-established HR group around the world, although this does not mean that there is necessarily a full-time HR manager at every company. Where one does not exist, the general manager or MD will take active responsibility for this role.

Around the world a small, high quality group of HR people draws upon a spectrum of external specialists and consultants in niche subjects such as remuneration, development, training and incentive schemes.

Hiring policy is fairly traditional. Applications are studied, followed by an interview where the applicant's attitude towards work ethics, commitment and flexibility are explored. Candidates are also required to be able to handle extensive travel, and long periods of separation from their families, as well as dealing with numerous problems at once.

Restructuring, as McIntosh has admitted, has been an uncomfortable but inevitable part of recent years. The company thinks itself fortunate in that there has been no major downsizing, although individual businesses have had to implement some difficult decisions. Morgan attributes this to careful expansion during the last ten years focusing, during that time, on the cost base and maintaining a competitive cost position, even when things were good. Wherever possible, Morgan's policy has been to find displaced people positive alternative positions within the company. When this was not possible, Morgan employed outplacement consultants on an individual and group basis.

Career Opportunity and Development

Good people are what Morgan believes gives the company its competitive edge. It feels that the best way to maintain this tradition is to include high calibre graduates in the recruiting programmes. To maintain the best in the business, the company also provides good developmental opportunities through its network of programme modules. These include teaching negotiating skills, effective presentation skills, managing working capital, selling skills, creativity and problem solving, international executive development and an advanced management programme.

People are moved around the world for developmental purposes, for training, and to provide specialist technical support. Morgan encourages building on its strong, informal network. There are 20 separate corporate development programmes a year where up to 20 executives from different countries, different businesses and different functions are all brought together at any one time. They are all encouraged to keep in contact with each other once the course has finished, building a world-wide network of internal contacts.

McIntosh frowns on the term 'fast track'. "It sounds elitist. It applies to a certain type of individual, and we like to be aware of all the capabilities of everyone in the organisation. People should be able to move into a programme of accelerated growth at any stage in their career. Fast-tracking generally excludes late developers. We have to be as flexible as we can to cater for all types of individuals. We like them to be well-rounded, interested in sports or music and bright, but that does not necessarily mean academic."

About 80–85% of promotion is internal.

Pay and Benefits

60% of Morgan's employees are shareholders, and the company would like to see this become 100%. It is currently looking at ways of making increased share ownership a viable proposition. Due to the myriad of separate foreign tax restrictions and governmental regulations, this has been difficult. There is a pension plan, health care, life insurance, annual bonuses (of up to 30%), company cars, share options and share ownership schemes, statutory maternity leave and an informal paternity scheme. Pay is aimed at being above average.

The Future

"For us the challenges are very much related to our continuing growth as a global player. We have very exciting joint ventures in China, India and the Pacific Rim; Hong Kong, Taiwan, Thailand, Korea and Malaysia offer enormous opportunities. North and South America are both important to us, as is Europe," says McIntosh.

Morgan is taking a positive view about changes on the Continent regarding the Social Chapter. Unsure as to what the constraints will be, Morgan is determined to meet every potential hurdle as representing new opportunity. The company hopes the changes will have a beneficial outcome, adding the proviso that if Europe becomes too expensive, it will quickly become uncompetitive.

The 1990s have brought about a better understanding of the need for realistic employee demands. Regular work, recognition and the ability to grow with the company are key for both employee and employer at Morgan, and as a result, communication throughout the organisation has improved. Both parties look to the long, rather than the short term.

The major challenge will be meeting the needs of emerging markets, for example the former Soviet Union and the Far East, while at the same time strengthening the company's position in its established markets. Morgan estimates that many of its product groups will have tremendous growth opportunities as the company looks to continue its march towards the millennium and beyond as an ever more influential player in the field of technologically advanced industrial materials and components world-wide.

MORRISON

Morrison Construction Group

Morrison Construction Group is a broadly-based construction and development group, active throughout the UK and in selected overseas markets. The company was floated on the stock market in 1995 and employs 1,600 people.

Roughly half of the company's business is in Scotland and half in England. Morrison was the first and leading UK company involved in the rebuilding of Kuwait after the Gulf War, and it has continued its strong financial performance since its flotation.

Biggest Plus: A big premium on innovation means plenty of scope for
                  fulfilling jobs

Biggest Minus: Pay and benefits structure has not quite caught up with the big
                  ideas elsewhere

Morrison Construction Group
Morrison House
12 Atholl Crescent
Edinburgh EH3 8HA
Tel: 0131-228 4188
Fax: 0131-3371880

The Business

Morrison was a family-owned business which, unlike the rest of the construction industry, continued to thrive through the recession. It was this consistency which paved the way for the transition to becoming a publicly-listed company in late-1995, when an initially sceptical City was convinced by the Morrison story.

Its success stems from a bold strategy of being different, notably in the way that it tenders for a growing proportion of its business by treating the client as a partner, not an opponent. That philosophy is consciously mirrored in the way the company looks after its people. It has a mission to 'be the best in the business through the strongest commitment to quality and customer service' by the year 2000. And it intends to measure itself against the rest of the industry on criteria which include the amount of training it provides for each employee, its safety record, and how much waste is being eliminated through staff initiatives.

Company Culture and Style

Morrison is a leading proponent of change in the way the construction industry works. By 2000 it intends to win 80% of its business by offering value for money based on its own creative ideas rather than the lowest tender price to a client's design. These often provide a better building solution for a community, or the environment.

It means an end to the old 'antagonistic' culture where the client wants a job done quickly and cheaply, and the contractor turns problems into legal wrangles which squeeze more money out of the job. That in turn has helped create a climate of partnership inside the company too, rather than a 'blame culture' said to be all too common in the industry, where somebody has to pay for mistakes.

It means an atmosphere where ideas and innovation are key skills in the search for ways of improving the business. Chairman Fraser Morrison, whose father founded the original business in the north of Scotland in 1948, bought it back from a multinational company in 1989 and established his imprint. He, along with other members of senior management, visit offices and sites regularly, and first-name terms are the order of the day.

The company's central office in Edinburgh is 'group office', to emphasise the teamwork culture, and other moves to change the 'them and us' culture are underway. Regional directors, who run the individual businesses around the UK, have a high level of autonomy within their own budgets. They are encouraged to initiate their own ideas for local project solutions. On site, the Morrison tie is worn with pride, and though construction disciplines to some extent limit free expression, the ideal job candidate is imaginative and 'change-oriented'.

Human Resource Priorities

Morrison was one of the first UK-operating construction companies to be awarded group-wide Investors in People recognition in February 1995. It now hopes to be able to prove it is the best in the business by 2000, as much in quality of human resources as on a financial level.

It began with nine benchmarks for monitoring progress, and is doubling these to 18. There are 17 professionals in HR, training and safety across the group, and the group HR manager chairs a group training committee, and reports to the financial director on the main board.

As a growing company, redundancies have been relatively few and far between during the recession, with normal peaks and troughs in workload being handled through the use of sub-contractors.

A high priority has been put on internal communications, in recognition that previous efforts have not always penetrated to site level. Monthly team briefings are cascaded down from group office to regional offices, but there is now more emphasis on creating a focus of local interest for each site, with regular customised bulletins featuring site news first and group news second.

"Site staff, for instance, want to know why construction is to start at one end of a site rather than another, or why a particular sub-contractor is not arriving until next week," says group HR manager Peter Stroud. He says an open door policy is symbolised by the chairman's site and office visits, when a wide range of staff are encouraged to speak to him.

Career Opportunity and Development

Everyone in the company has an annual performance appraisal to review and set objectives, and identify training needs. Each operating unit has an annual plan setting out training and development policies and objectives, but fleshed out by a directory of the training needs and solutions of each member of staff. Through Investors in People, any training courses build-in pre-course and post-course briefings to measure their effectiveness.

Each employee has a personal training and development folder which is updated when new activity is undertaken, and receives an average five days' training a year, compared with a more typical industry figure of three days or fewer. Anyone who believes they can benefit from any training or qualification is encouraged to approach their manager.

The company acknowledges its past lack of focus on management development, having had to fill a number of key vacancies from outside, not always by choice. A Morrison management development programme launched in November 1996 for senior managers and directors is intended to address a wide range of needs, and create a pool of talent available to fill such jobs in the future.

The group's overseas interests, involving up to 50 employees, ensures a range of secondment opportunities. It is also responding to people who feel they need a career change.

The company selects about 10 graduates a year from 150 applicants, without advertising, and typically has retained over 90% after two years. Around 27% of the workforce are professionals, 21% are graduates, 23% of senior managers have more than 10 years' service, and the labour turnover rate in 1995–96 was 16%.

Pay and Benefits

There is very little published information about pay rates in the industry but Morrison is said to be highly competitive. In recent years the annual rise has been set at or above inflation despite rates in the industry falling behind. The annual appraisal is not connected to remuneration. Merit rises are negotiable and are awarded at regional directors' discretion. A performance and profit-related bonus scheme pays out up to one month's salary at lower grades, but up to four months' salary higher up the tree. Rises for weekly-paid staff are in accordance with industry-wide 'working rule agreements'.

When the company floated, there was a priority share allocation for staff and 10% bought shares immediately. Another 30% joined a Sharesave scheme which entitles them to buy shares at the flotation price after five years.

Benefits are offered strictly according to status band with, for instance private health benefits open to senior management, but no flexible benefits. All permanent staff, however, can join a pension scheme with a 10.9% employer's contribution (5% employee's) and enjoy discounts on home-buying and some services negotiated with external suppliers by the company.

The Future

Gordon Morrison, brother of Fraser and a director of the group, says: "Anyone can talk the talk, but if there's not a genuine and deeply-held commitment to fundamentally changing your thinking in the way required to make partnering work, then, frankly, you should forget it." He is talking about a model partnership with Thames Water whereby Morrison has helped Thames improve its service levels by 50% and reduce work backlogs by 70% and customer complaints by 80%—basically by digging-up the streets efficiently.

The same applies to Morrison's innovative approaches in road-building and property development. In getting its message accepted by clients, the company is pushing at an open door, because clients prefer partnership and problem-solving to confrontation and conflict.

The challenge for 2000 is to make sure that its people can enable the group to take advantage of the undoubted opportunities. Its Total Quality Morrison approach has in the past underplayed the importance of grooming its own managers, and the necessity of involving staff at site level in the process of communication, feedback and innovation.

Fraser Morrison says the group is committed to continuous quality improvement, to achieving an unequalled level of customer service, and to a team approach aimed at becoming the best in the business. "The result is an enviable reputation for early completions, award-winning quality and delighted clients."

But encouragingly for employees, he concludes: "Continuous improvement in job satisfaction and quality of life for our people is the end result for which we are all striving." If it can evolve and develop its human resources initiatives to fully harness the energies, morale, and pride in the group's achievements which give it a clear edge over its rivals, Morrison will continue to stand out as a different company offering a level of job security and satisfaction not easily found elsewhere in the industry.

Nationwide Building Society

Nationwide is the largest of the UK's mutual building societies and has declined the current trend of conversion to a bank. Nationwide offers its seven million customers a broad range of financial services beyond its traditional savings and mortgages business into areas such as life assurance, unit trusts, and personal pension plans. In 1995/96, Nationwide recorded pre-tax profits of £459.3 million and reserves stood at £2.2 billion. It has 10,724 employees in the UK; 1,850 are located at the Group's impressive head office in Swindon, and Nationwide has 689 branches.

Nationwide's mission statement is more of a customer proposition. 'Nationwide puts customers first by providing a full range of top value, quality financial services that are widely available and delivered with speed, courtesy and reliability backed by underlying policies of fairness, honesty, staff importance and corporate responsibility.'

Biggest Plus: Clear vision, linking interests of customers and employees

Biggest Minus: Beating the banks will require a big effort

Nationwide Building Society
Nationwide House
Pipers Way
Swindon SN38 1QQ
Tel: 01793-513513
Fax: 01604-498497

The Business

Nationwide's chief executive Brian Davis is truly a champion of mutuality. In deciding to remain a building society, Nationwide is putting its customers first. This is a genuine belief, and is really quite crucial. Mutuality is where the company's roots are, it is where they feel comfortable, and it is a position which Nationwide honestly believes will benefit its customers most. Brian Davis says "...but I am not a crusader for mutuality as a substitute for running a good business operation. Nobody owes us a living and they will certainly not provide it if we simply insist that they come to us because we are mutual. We have to deliver the best value and that means running an efficient and effective organisation."

Nationwide has managed to communicate what this means for customers and staff in a meaningful way. It has three memorable statements:
- to be first choice for customers
- have the best industry ratings
- to be a business where staff want to work

Nationwide contends that it is able to put customers first because it has no shareholders, while publicly-quoted companies have a primary need to deliver shareholder value, meaning that customers often come second. And Nationwide has a lot of customers—seven million of them in fact.

Brand awareness of Nationwide has been raised considerably by its sponsorship of the Football League, which has brought with it a host of local community initiatives and a real challenge for its marketeers to exploit a generic name that the Football League could not have improved on had they dreamt it up themselves.

Company Culture and Style

The customer service ethos is very much Nationwide's overall business culture, and one which Nationwide people respond well to, feeling a sense of participation in a customer-owned organisation. If this sounds like 'we're the good guys', it is important they feel it, because the business proposition of mutuality is actually quite tough and the road ahead potentially a rocky one.

In building its 'good business to work for' culture, Nationwide invests heavily in training and development, linking business planning with personal development. Investors in People accreditation, achieved three years ago, was seen as exactly the type of framework and independent recognition the company wanted. Nationwide believes that people need to feel fairly rewarded for what they do, and 'fairness' is one of the most frequently quoted words in the company.

A similar priority is put on honest, open communication. Nationwide for many years has canvassed employee opinions confidentially through its Group Attitude Survey 'Viewpoint'. Any unpalatable truths are listened to and acted upon.

Like the rest of the financial services industry, there used to be jobs for life. This knot, ultimately, has to be loose. The deal today is that you get a good learning opportunity and career development at Nationwide, and if you have to leave, you are very employable.

Jeremy del Strother, director of human resources, believes, however, that people still have a greater loyalty to their company than to their profession or discipline. If this refutes Charles Handy's idea of portfolio careers, it is because the man in the street doesn't believe it. Even when people start with a new firm, they set out again with the same values, one of which is loyalty.

'Extraordinarily nice' people work for Nationwide, and people who do well combine this characteristic with customer focus and shared values. Businesspeople are more likely to be balanced and flexible rather than extremely or overtly entrepreneurial, as skills need to be applied to diverse tasks and environments.

Nationwide also plays an active part in the community. In addition to its core community affairs programme, the Nationwide Macmillan Campaign (1994–96) has been very important to the organisation, helping to build team values. With Nationwide's support, employees from around the group have organised events that have raised over £1 million for the cancer charity.

Human Resource Priorities

At the highest level, HR must build a future view of corporate competencies, and an understanding of what this will mean in terms of numbers and types of people employed. Seeing the shape of future employment really sets the HR agenda.

One of the biggest areas is instilling the right competencies at the crucial customer/staff interface. Particularly in the branches, many managers have progressed quickly through excellent technical, product or process skills. HR wishes increasingly to blend in vital management skills of leadership and people management. Nationwide believes that it spends more on overall training than any of its peers.

Nationwide is heavily committed to demonstrating continuous improvement in Investors in People and disagrees with companies that don't pursue recognition 'because we're doing all the things anyway'. Del Strother believes that if you are confident about this, then let someone assess you.

In an industry that has experienced rapid change, particularly in the sales functions, HR takes on the key task of building a more flexible organisation. This has meant removing organisational blockages, bureaucracies and obstacles as a means of enabling people to absorb change.

Career Opportunity and Development

There is a wide range of jobs on offer at Nationwide. While there are always opportunities for people with specialisations, technical expertise and professions, Nationwide would like to see career development become more wide-ranging and give people experience across the business.

You can move quite quickly at Nationwide. There have been directors in their late 30s and Nationwide tries hard to promote from within. The company recruits management trainees (typically graduates) who have a rigorously defined training programme with specific goals in a two-year contract, but a real appointment waiting for those who succeed.

Everyone in the business has a performance agreement ('what should I contribute this year?') and their own development plan. There are no promises, but this does make for a better relationship between manager and employee as to what a person can achieve and how. Nationwide takes equal opportunity very seriously indeed—probably as much as any company. More than half of its managers are women and it seeks a fair representation among its employees of the diverse make-up of the UK population. Nationwide is an active member of Opportunity 2000 and the Employers Forum on Disability, and a founder member of the Employers Forum on Age. Not long ago, the company had only a few people over the age of 50. This figure is now 530. Nationwide was also a joint winner of the Newcomer category in the 1996 Parents at Work 'Employer of the Year Award'.

Jeremy del Strother says, "We do know that by denying yourself access to a sizeable chunk of the UK population, you are also denying yourself access to a bank of talent. These are not words, but a key business tenet that equal opportunities are important."

Pay and Benefits

You might not get rich working for Nationwide, but people do receive fair reward for their individual contribution, and are paid market rates.

In addition, the performance-related bonus scheme is calculated on a basis common to everyone, using a complicated formula involving surpassing minimum levels of profitability, efficiency gains, a 'customer satisfaction' index and individual performance.

A recent survey by Union Pension Services ranked the Nationwide group pension scheme third out of 200 schemes that it assessed.

The Future

Nationwide is growing into its role as the UK's leading mutual building society. The really big challenge is to demonstrate that there are real customer benefits from what it is doing. Much publicity surrounded Nationwide's £200 million special dividend 'returned' to customers in terms of better product pricing in February 1996. Nationwide said it could do this because it doesn't have shareholders to satisfy.

The company will only succeed eventually if it can demonstrate that it has more to offer than the banks. Technology has a vital role to play, and after introducing multimedia kiosks and innovative cash machines, Nationwide is at the leading edge.

Nationwide is not immune from the dynamics of the financial services industry, and continually improving efficiency, finding ways of doing more with less, and asking more and more of its employees will be difficult. In return, higher demands are matched by higher rewards, better opportunities, and substantial personal training and development.

Nationwide's spirit should give it every chance of success. The company describes itself as 'in tune with people' and this seems a plausible claim. Chief executive Brain Davis maintains Nationwide's football association by turning out regularly for a 'Nationwide Casuals' side. Most importantly, staff at all levels believe in what they are doing and pull together as a team.

Nestlé UK Ltd.

Nestlé is the largest food manufacturing company in the world. The Nestlé Group employs 220,000 people world-wide in more than 70 countries and sells over 15,000 products in almost every country in the world. In the UK, Nestlé has no fewer than 250 products including many household names such as Nescafé, Kit Kat, Findus, Crosse & Blackwell and Quality Street. In all, Nestlé UK has brand leaders in 36 sectors. It also has 23 factories, over 14,000 people and a turnover in 1995 of £1.74 billion.

Nestlé can trace its origins in the UK back to 1866. The present company, Nestlé UK, was formed following the acquisition of Rowntree Macintosh in 1988. Nestlé UK comprises: Nestlé Grocery Division, Nestlé Rowntree Division, Nestlé Food Division, including Nestlé Lyons Maid, and Nestlé Food Services Division and Fox Confectionery.

Biggest Plus: International careers working with some of the world's leading brands

Biggest Minus: UK food industry is highly competitive at present

Nestlé UK Ltd
St. George's House
Croydon
Surrey CR9 1NR
Tel: 0181-686 3333
Fax: 0181-667 607

The Business

You cannot really think of Nestlé as one company, or compare it to one other company. Nestlé is a very diffused business, operating in different markets with different competitors. Nestlé describes itself as 'The World Food Company' and believes that its success comes from combining autonomy for each individual Nestlé market with European and global strategies that encourage the exchange of ideas and people throughout the business. Many companies in the group were aggregated as a result of acquisition, and Nestlé is not only a Swiss-owned corporation, but a truly international business.

Nestlé is essentially a branded food manufacturer. While the company does supply own-label products to retailers, Nestlé is all about branding. Sometimes it is bewildering to appreciate the sheer diversity and number of brands that Nestlé owns, many of them lovingly preserved after acquisition.

Nestlé is as international as any company in the world. It takes a fundamentally long-term view of world markets and their development. This might mean establishing a base in a country where it may not make profits for a number of years, but will build a factory, employ local people and set about creating a solid, long-term business.

Company Culture and Style

Nestlé's fundamental business culture world-wide is based on quality. This means building good brands by keeping abreast of changes in public tastes, responding with innovative products, backed by the latest technology. £400 million is spent each year on research alone.

In the UK Nestlé puts considerable effort into articulating its values. 'Vision-Mission-Priorities-Values' is the result of many surveys, task forces and brainstorming sessions of Nestlé UK's 1,600 or so managers. The direct involvement of UK chairman and chief executive David Harris ensured that the Management Committee was fully involved and subscribed to the process.

"Cultural values previously existed in different forms, at different levels. We are now trying to establish one company, upon which we can build anything," says John Reid, personnel director. Being all about purpose, the company places much more emphasis on the 'Priorities-Values' part of the pyramid. Values have at their heart the need to set standards, meaning an ethical approach to doing business, respect for the individual, and managers needing to manage.

If there are differences in business style between the Swiss and British—in the UK things are probably more open and informal, and perhaps come to the point a bit faster—they do not pose any problem. Nestlé is a very international business, and the group has long since learned to allow individual country cultures to exist within an overall corporate framework.

Human Resource Priorities

The Nestlé UK Management Committee (on which John Reid sits) puts personnel issues high on the agenda. It realises the importance of discussing these issues clearly, agreeing what to do, and doing it together.

Personnel at Nestlé UK supplies, and therefore needs to mirror, the business structure. Divisions have their own heads of personnel, but there are also 'dotted lines' from managing directors to director of personnel. The function is resourced further at sites and head office by specialists covering remuneration and benefits, pensions, occupational health, training and development, and employee communications.

Quality personnel policies such as the pension scheme, training, recruitment, and expatriation all represent areas of heavy expense, which Nestlé has been more than happy to invest, believing it should be expected of a company of its stature.

Nestlé cares about hiring, caring and developing people. It would rather develop its own people, and grow them into whatever they can be. While it recognises that this doesn't always work, Nestlé always tries to replace internally first. Around 50 graduates are recruited each year. Chairman David Harris puts it: "..to drive our business forward we need more than just the best brands—we also need the best management."

Career Opportunity and Development

Careers at Nestlé can be anything you want them to be. Nestlé is very international, and the company believes that it is important to offer managers the chance to work abroad; but it is not compulsory—many people elect to stay in their own country or market—sometimes for life.

Nestlé is developing so rapidly in places like Eastern Europe and China, that demand for seasoned managers is high. Nestlé UK sent 50 managers abroad in 1995, and at any one time has 200 expatriates away. In the group, Nestlé has the ability to get and send anyone from just about every country.

Nestlé's career management system allows each functional group (for example technical, commercial, financial) to get together and perform continuous rolling assessments of vacancies, potential, and moves. At senior management level, this is backed up by succession management planning. HR aims to get as wide a range of people together as possible, to build quality across the company and encourage more moves between divisions and functions.

Opportunities sometimes present themselves through informal invitations, a phone call out of the blue. Increasingly, Nestlé is trying to make sure that these opportunities are channelled properly, and that individuals who want to work abroad, in another division or function, are identified through the performance management process.

There is a huge commitment to training. Nestlé runs the bulk of courses at its own residential training centre at Maidenhead, and at its York facility. It will go outside as well—for example Senior Management Development courses structured in conjunction with Warwick University.

Employees are encouraged to help develop themselves, backed by line management and personnel doing the right things. John Reid recently asked a graduate intake group whether they thought they could plan their career any more. The answer was 'No', which Reid said is how his career with Nestlé had evolved. "I suggested to them not to worry too much about planning each step. Develop yourself, enjoy it, work hard, don't stress yourself, and always keep your mind alive to opportunities. They will come naturally."

Pay and Benefits

Nestlé's pay scales are around the median/upper quartile level, more likely the latter for senior management, and there are good elements in the rest of the remuneration package. The pension, for example, is highly rated.

Nestlé as a business is very cautious about bonuses, but has implemented profit-related pay. If Nestlé UK meets its targets, employees could receive around 5–6% of their salary (capped at £1,600 in 1960).

The Future

Nestlé UK is very much concerned with growth, and realises that the market place is extremely competitive. Nestlé could just concentrate on its most established, very successful UK businesses, but this is not the company's way.

Consequently, Nestlé UK is trying to build one more big food business—'the third leg'—to balance its UK strengths in coffee and confectionery. Of course, this is eating up a lot of resource, but is in keeping with the company's long-term growth strategy. The company has bought Nestlé Lyons Maid, the ice cream business; has expanded its frozen food interests through Findus and chilled foods through a range of Nestlé chilled desserts. The Crosse & Blackwell business has been re-launched and the Buitoni pasta range is being extended.

This challenge to Nestlé to grow its brands in this market will be a hard one—some brands are presently only number three or four in their markets, with own-label products pushing at one end, and the number one and two brands applying pressure at the other.

Being the biggest food company in the world, having the best human resources functions in the UK is something the company believes it should not only aspire to, but deliver. Nestlé has made a lot of progress since the UK organisation was launched, and this will continue.

This will mean more working together, the further introduction of good policies, and good systems. New software systems are being introduced to give greater transparency of information and break down functional barriers. Personnel's main challenge will be to take advantage of the opportunity to build a system in pace with the rest of the company.

Nestlé has undergone change and consolidation in recent years, but the company's dedication to long-term growth, and excellent branded products, make it a company where opportunities are considerable.

Northern Foods

Northern Foods is one of the UK's leading food producers, focusing on two distinct areas in prepared foods and dairy. The prepared foods division is Britain's foremost supplier of high quality chilled foods. Providing own label products for several major retailers, the division also maintains a strong branded presence in biscuits, frozen food and savoury pastry products. The dairy division is the UK's largest supplier of liquid milk to retail customers and doorstop end-users.

Northern Foods operates over 50 manufacturing sites throughout the UK and Ireland, employing 24,000 members of staff. Turnover was £2 billion in 1996, and profits stood at £124.2 million (up 4.1%).

Biggest Plus: Freedom of action encourages initiative

Biggest Minus: Manufacturing products with limited shelf-life tends to produce short-term decision making

Northern Foods plc
Beverley House
St. Stephen's Square
Hull HU1 3XG
Tel: 01482-325432
Fax: 01482-226136

The Business

The prepared foods business concentrates on serving major multiple retail chains. Two- thirds of sales derive from own-label products for retailers including Marks & Spencer, J. Sainsbury, Tesco, Safeway and Asda. Northern Foods' own 'in-house' brands include Fox's Biscuits, Ski Yogurts and Goodfella's Pizzas.

The dairy division accounts for 22% of the entire milk market in England and Wales. As the UK's leading liquid milk organisation, Northern Foods provides fresh milk to customers under the Dale Farm, Express and Northern Dairies brands.

The business is emerging from a painful period of restructuring. Having reduced the workforce by 3,300, the trauma of redundancy has been mitigated by Northern Foods' extensive programme of consultation, compensation and assistance in retraining and job placement.

Company Culture and Style

Fast-moving but friendly, hard-working but non-bureaucratic, Northern Foods is committed to stretching employees in a supportive atmosphere. All members of staff address each other on first-name terms, an open door policy typified by the accessibility to chairman Chris Haskins to all employees.

"Whenever I describe the company to outsiders," says group personnel executive, Phil Ward, "I'm always struck by the extent to which culture starts from the top. The company reflects Chris's own style. He's a pragmatic, down-to-earth individual, calls a spade a spade, and loathes pomposity. It's an attitude that percolates downwards."

Employees flourishing at Northern Foods tend to embrace responsibility. The company seeks out managers who are able to influence others by force of argument rather than by directive, pay attention to detail without losing sight of the big picture, and put into practice highly developed personal skills.

Fun at work is actively encouraged in a non-hierarchical structure. Reporting lines are decidedly short but support is always at hand.

The company is committed to operating sound environmental practices. Environmental issues are considered at all stages of production; milk is delivered in reusable glass bottles, and energy consumption is carefully monitored.

Northern Foods has a long tradition of supporting charities and voluntary associations. Setting aside 0.5% of pre-tax profits for charitable gifts (£702,000 in 1996), Barnardos, The Samaritans, Oxfam, The National Association For One-Parent Families and The Runnymede Trust all received generous donations.

Human Resource Priorities

Northern Foods' commitment to HR has been manifest since the earliest days of the company. Not only has the personnel function enjoyed board representation for almost 50 years, but Northern Foods' first personnel director was a woman—virtually unique during the 1950s.

The group personnel director still sits on a board devoting significant time and energy to HR issues—notably over the last couple of years, as the delayering process rolled out and structures changed to suit modified circumstances.

Considerable resources are devoted to a function charged with realising the maximum potential of all the company's employees. Ten specialists work from the centre, with each plant benefiting from a personnel presence. 100 HR specialists are found in various parts of the group in total, and the annual HR budget comfortably exceeds seven figures.

Northern Foods has a long-standing commitment to providing equal opportunities. Recruitment, pay, training and career development issues are all judged solely on individual ability, without regard to gender, race, age, disability, marital status or religion. Underlining this commitment, the company has staged over 120 workshops for directors and managers on equal opportunity issues.

Career Opportunity and Development

Training and development form an integral part of the planning process at Northern Foods. Helping people make the most of their talents while fulfilling the commercial needs of the business, employee development is currently addressed through a combination of group initiatives and specific activities within operating companies.

At shop floor level, safety within the business has always been a priority. The company's Food Safety Programme is widely regarded as leading-edge, and completion of this programme is mandatory for all employees. Supported by tutorial-based open learning programmes and senior management seminars, a similar programme entitled 'Help Stop Accidents At Work' is also compulsory. Both utilise computer-based learning techniques.

For graduate trainees and potential managers, Northern Foods offers comprehensive training, both on and off-the-job. Programmes are structured to develop a range of core competencies including Leadership, Commercial Awareness, Change Orientation, People Development, Practical Thinking, Quality Focus and Planning.

In addition to functionally specific training, which may include studying for relevant professional qualifications, for example IPD and CIMA, trainees take part in four off-the-job modules: Induction, focusing on basic management skills; Manufacturing Management, outlining the principles of management and how to run production lines; Commercial Awareness, highlighting the commercial aspects of modern business and including a simulated exercise in which trainees run their own companies; and a Self Development Course, augmenting overall management competencies.

All trainees are encouraged to use their skills for the benefit of the local community during two-week secondments.

"Just lately," recounts process technologist Lorraine Palmer, "I've been involved with a class of nine-year-olds, demonstrating the safety rules needed in food production (you should have seen the mess!). I've also helped a group of people with learning difficulties to make weekly meals for themselves. With so much going for you, it's nice to put something back."

Trainees usually spend an initial period gaining a broad range of experiences in one of the operating companies. Support on site is provided by senior line managers and personnel staff, and head office monitors developments on a regular basis.

"The training is superb," enthuses assistant management accountant, Perven Maan. "It's totally geared to meeting individual needs and interests and I'm currently studying for my Stage 3 CAA."

"I'd already experienced two years in public sector recruitment before I studied for my degree," confirms personnel officer, Jill Anderson, "so I was impatient to start putting my training into practice. I didn't have to wait long. After just four months at head office in Hull, I was given the chance to become personnel officer at Colwyn Bay—a brilliant if somewhat nerve-racking opportunity."

Pay and Benefits

Northern Foods does not believe in issuing edicts about pay (or anything else) from the centre. Each company acts as an autonomous entity, enjoying considerable discretion to determine pay levels.

Unions are recognised on many sites, where pay increases are negotiated by collective bargaining. A range of factors tend to enter the pay equation, including inflationary pressures, union demands, increased/decreased hours of working, and holiday allowances. Pay rises across the group averaged 3.5% during 1995/96.

Northern Foods maintains a fleet of 1,000 cars, allocating vehicles according to job demands. A contributory pension scheme is open to all employees, and those with over four years' service are also eligible to take part in an annual profit share scheme. Around 13,500 currently do so.

Other benefits include 20–25 days' holiday, an enhanced maternity scheme (six months at full pay for senior managers), subsidised canteens, and a range of sports and social activities at generously discounted rates.

The Future

As one of the UK's leading food producers, Northern Foods is focusing on growth markets and servicing the major multiple retail chains. The power and influence of those chains over food manufacturers continues to escalate.

The challenge for Northern Foods is to continue delivering services and products superior to those of the opposition, looking beyond price to factors that include quality, distribution, convenience and innovation.

Customers also present a significant challenge. Northern Foods is constantly seeking to identify trends, interpret demographic changes, develop products to fill gaps in the supermarket shelves, and meet the expectations of customers demanding an ever-expanding diversity of choice. All this in a market that is static in terms of total population.

Northern Foods is also seeking to expand beyond its traditional UK base. Undisputed leaders in the field of chilled foods, the company is enjoying rapid sales growth across continental Europe. Capitalising on this considerable opportunity seems likely to focus senior management minds in the short-to-medium term.

ORACLE®

Enabling the Information Age

Oracle

Oracle Corporation is the world's second largest software company and the largest supplier of software for information management. The company offers its database, tools and applications products—along with related consulting, education and support services—in more than 90 countries across the world.

Of the 22,000 people employed at Oracle, more than 3,000 work for Oracle Corporation UK Limited, the group's largest subsidiary outside of the USA. A powerful combination of business expertise and technical innovation continues to deliver phenomenal growth across Oracle's global operations. With annual revenues of more than $4.2 billion, in 1995 alone world-wide revenues soared by 50% and profits reached nearly $450 million.

Biggest Plus: Phenomenal growth, loads of exciting opportunity

Biggest Minus: Internal structures are not there to organise you

Oracle Corporation UK Limited
Oracle Parkway
Thames Valley Park
Reading
Berkshire RG6 1RA
Tel: 0118-924 0000
Fax: 0118-924 3000

The Business

Oracle is a growing company that has doubled in size almost every year since 1984. By anticipating and responding to increasing globalisation, business complexity, and technological developments, Oracle has probably become the most important company in the IT industry, behind Microsoft and IBM—a gap that it intends to close. The battleground will be the Microsoft-dominated PC market, with Oracle championing the coming of the network PC. Chairman and chief executive Larry Ellison believes: "With continued good fortune, we could end up the most successful firm in the software business."

Oracle has always championed the importance and versatility of the database, and its central product, the Oracle 7™ multimedia database, has emerged as the key building block of the data highway. Oracle has built an enviable track record by providing innovative, flexible, high quality software solutions and 24-hour technical support to thousands of organisations in the public and private sectors.

Oracle does have a certain reputation for being an aggressive company. But as Vance Kearney, vice president human resources, EMEA, puts it "Oracle has not grown from nothing into a $4 billion company by being shy and retiring. If our sales effort is forceful, we are still delivering outstanding value and outstanding products to our customers."

Company Culture and Style

Oracle has a real purpose and ambition about it, and its results-driven culture is one that calls for a particular blend of personal and professional skills. It is an extremely demanding environment—not because of any corporate decision, but because of the high standards and expectations of the thousands of intelligent people working within the company. People may work long hours, but they do so in the knowledge that they are achieving real success. Those who are not succeeding tend to move on to other companies. It's as simple as that.

Above all, Oracle is driven by a passion for innovation. Larry Ellison rejects the current vogue of 'being market-led', arguing that we didn't find out that people wanted TV by doing market research. He regards it as part of Oracle's role to define and lead the market through continuous innovation. The radical effects of that innovation will become apparent over the next few years as Oracle challenges the conventional wisdom on personal computers, and predicts an alternative world of main server networks accessed via mobile data network devices.

There is nothing stereotypical about the people charged with delivering Oracle's future vision. They are original thinkers, individuals who look beyond conventional ways of doing things in pursuit of creative solutions. But they do have common traits. They are all self-motivated, in charge of their own careers and lives, with strong self-belief backed by energy and enthusiasm. They welcome ambitious targets and take full responsibility for meeting them. They thrive on constant challenge and expect their achievements to be acknowledged and rewarded.

For the right people, Oracle offers an environment of enormous stimulation and potential. But it doesn't suit everyone. People are expected to deliver results, and while Oracle will support people with the resources and incentives to excel, it will not tolerate sub-standard performance. This has given Oracle a reputation for being a very demanding company.

Oracle is very outward-focused (around 80% of jobs are client-facing) and people need more than just technical expertise to make their mark as part of the Oracle team. Strong interpersonal skills, self-confidence and the maturity to manage and develop high-level client relationships are also needed.

The word 'dynamic' is much over-used in corporate circles. But you only need to look at the revenue growth and number of people employed at Oracle—both have trebled over the last three years—to understand what dynamic really means.

Human Resource Priorities

With its external focus on the evolving needs of its customers, Oracle appears to have little need for formal policies, rules and frameworks. The HR team seeks instead to support and nourish an environment in which Oracle people can succeed.

Vance Kearney suggests that there is no place for loners in the company. The interaction with and support from your work colleagues is vital. Although you will need to work out some complex problems for yourself, you will be encouraged to share experiences and aspirations with your colleagues—around 800 of whom will have joined the company only the year before you. HR instils and encourages teamworking, ensuring that people talk and communicate in teams, in pursuit of common business objectives.

With the hectic pace of technological and organisational change, the ability to constantly acquire new skills is a top priority at Oracle. Kearney points out that to create a true Learning Organisation, Oracle needs people who can accept change, embrace ambiguity and respond flexibly to new challenges and opportunities.

Perhaps 95% of what newcomers need to know will come from practice, experimenting, and tapping the knowledge of colleagues. Oracle also goes to great lengths to promote learning and development. Its own web site is used as an interactive tool for identifying key training needs and options available; it is also used as a medium for employees' opinions. And HR often runs 'interventions' and workshops with a heavy focus on business needs, action learning and working in groups. The company also sponsors MBAs and diplomas, and offers a range of behavioural and technical programmes.

Allan Miller, employee development manager, suggests that people perhaps have two levels of required development. "Just dealing and coping with Oracle is the first stage. When they are able to move on, real personal development can begin, given the scope that Oracle can offer."

The task of recruiting high calibre staff is, of course, a huge responsibility for the HR team, and there is currently a full-time team of ten people dedicated to recruitment alone.

Career Opportunity and Development

When it comes to providing a continuous flow of great career opportunities, nothing compares to a rapidly growing company. Oracle expects to recruit an incredible 1,000 extra people in the UK in 1997, including 150 new graduates.

With the right skills and approach, you can achieve pretty much what you want to at Oracle. Who knows what the next ten years will bring in the computer industry? The only certainty is that it will be very different—and it's a fairly good bet that Oracle will be leading the way.

People can move internationally if they want to, and many hundreds of Oracle's UK staff have worked in the USA and other important countries. Oracle, as a global organisation, requires the same skills wherever its products and services are used. And the continuous growth of its subsidiaries is creating even more opportunities for overseas travel and experience.

Oracle has a large educational business selling skills enhancement and training software to customers, and the company leverages its expertise in all these training areas by training its own staff. If you join Oracle's applications business, for example, you will find yourself on an eight-week training programme before you actually start work—even if you are highly experienced. What's more, technical training will be constant throughout your career.

Pay and Benefits

Oracle aims to be competitive on pay at the upper quartile of the computer industry. The package of benefits is equally competitive, with an emphasis on flexibility and innovation, aimed at maximising each employee's personal satisfaction.

The Future

Oracle looks set to sustain its tremendous rate of growth. That in itself presents a challenge in recruiting the right people—people who can learn quickly and match the rate of change in the business. Like all evolving organisations the company's infrastructure is likely to alter in line with emerging needs and opportunities.

New joiners have much to offer and Oracle will need to maintain a creative balance between doing things its own way and incorporating the ideas and approaches of new people. When once it recruited mostly hunters—the more aggressive, sales-driven individuals capable of delivering results in the face of enormous competition—the company is also recruiting farmers, the individuals with the strategic vision to consolidate its achievements and maximise the performance of its existing client portfolio.

The company is also beginning to get a feel for what an Oracle manager looks like—someone who believes in empowering others rather than simply exercising power, who creates opportunities with both clients and staff, and who combines leadership skills with a determination to ensure that work always retains an element of fun.

The result is an organisation with a depth of technical, commercial and intellectual resources that will keep it at the forefront of developments in the IT industry of the future.

Perhaps the single most important feature is the sheer scale of Oracle's ambitions. Oracle has positioned itself in direct competition with Microsoft, which dominates the world's IT software market, and tackling that domination by backing the future of network computers. Interesting times lie ahead.

ARUP

Ove Arup & Partners

Ove Arup & Partners is an international firm of consulting engineers providing design, planning and project management services for civil, industrial and building developments.

Employing over 4,000 members of staff in more than 40 countries across the globe, all Ove Arup employees are members of the partnership and receive a share of corporate profits.

Biggest Plus: Extensive opportunities for secondments overseas

Biggest Minus: Collectivist philosophies may not suit all

Ove Arup & Partners
13 Fitzroy Street
London W1P 6BQ
Tel: 0171-636 1531
Fax: 0171-465 3716

The Business

Founded in 1946 by a Danish engineer, Ove Arup & Partners has just celebrated its 50th anniversary. Propounding the merits of 'total architecture', Arup took a holistic view of his speciality, humanist values still practised by the company bearing his name.

In addition to core engineering skills, services offered by Ove Arup cover every stage of projects from inception to completion, incorporating consultancies in such wide-ranging fields as economics, acoustics, fire safety design and risk analysis.

Projects in which the company has latterly been involved include motorway widening schemes (M1, M6, M25), the Channel Tunnel Rail Link, Manchester's NYNEX Arena and Cape Town's bid to host the 2004 Olympic Games.

When the company was last reshaped in 1977, the founding partners vested their interest in a trust for the benefit of all employees. Earnings are now shared among members of staff. In 1995, Arup reported pre-tax profits of £2.8 million, of which £1.7 million was distributed to employees.

The balance of fee-earning projects has shifted dramatically since the start of the decade. In 1991, 80% of Arup's fees emanated from the UK. By 1995, that figure had declined to 51%, as subsidiaries in Asia, the Americas and continental Europe came to the fore.

Company Culture and Style

In 1970, Ove Arup delivered an address to partners known as 'The Key Speech'. During the course of that address, Arup delivered a statement of corporate aims and credos that continue to drive the company forward.

Those principles include a humanitarian attitude, creating a philanthropic and friendly organisation; rejecting discrimination on grounds of sex, race, creed or religion—the company strives to engender prosperity for all its members; and that work should be excellent, interesting, rewarding and benefit society at large.

Ove Arup focuses on quality engineering. Profitability, although essential, has never been the prime motivation of an organisation genuinely concerned for the welfare of its staff. Even so, Arup is no place for the passive, and a challenging environment encourages employees to take a certain responsibility. Staff who tend to fall by the wayside are those who need to be told what to do.

Everyone works as a member of a project team, which can range in size from one to 400. Project engineers and group leaders play a pastoral as well as a technical role, acting as mentors, reviewing performance and encouraging competencies. Enjoyment at work is regarded as essential, not least to keep standards high: "It is very important," indicates associate director Patrick Morreau, "that people enjoy what they do, otherwise they are unlikely to perform as well as we would want. If people say 'it's just a job', then we have failed."

"Large does not mean impersonal," agrees Anita Bramfitt of Arup's industrial engineering division. "On the contrary, the atmosphere at Arup is relaxed and friendly, yet professional. This really is an organisation in which people are valued, treated as individuals and encouraged to develop their full potential."

Human Resource Priorities

Arup's HR function operates under the title of 'Staff Office'. Aiming to recruit high-calibre engineers with a wide variety of skills, Staff Office specialists endeavour to seek out individuals in tune with corporate thinking. Arup tends to attract staff with a strong social conscience unafraid of challenging established behaviours.

HR issues are firmly at the forefront of managerial minds. Over £1 million per annum is currently devoted to the function (excluding training), and concern for personnel matters filters down to all levels of the company.

Due to the high level of ongoing, informal consultation, Arup feels no need to conduct formal staff surveys. However, a close eye is kept on key indicators such as staff turnover and the contribution of the department is closely monitored by a Staff Policy Committee (SPC). The SPC assembles every second month to reflect on the performance of the Staff Office and sets targets for the forthcoming year. The Staff Policy Committee is itself subject to assessment, reflecting Ove Arup's commitment to an open flow of communication across the organisation.

Career Opportunity and Development

Supporting engineering staff attempting to gain professional qualifications, Arup provides not only on-site experience but also off-the-job training. All candidates receive personal guidance with access to a supervising engineer. Arup even provides courses in essay writing and presentation skills for those sitting exams.

The company aims to provide several days off-site training for all employees each year. A far-reaching choice of modules includes interviewing skills, motivating project teams, highways and bridge design, emergency first aid, MS Windows 95 and client care. Training funds are controlled from the centre and are strongly influenced by the ongoing priorities identified by group leaders. Arup's current annual budget stands at approximately £2.5 million.

Arup does not have a formal fast track of management development. The appraisal system identifies those individuals with the ability to move forward to leadership positions, a process that brings them to the attention of senior leaders.

Abundant opportunities exist for secondment. In fact opportunities are so plentiful that Arup can hardly find enough employees to fill them. At any given time, approximately 10% of the UK office will be working overseas, amounting to 300 members of staff.

Numerous examples may be found of employees rising through the ranks. Ove Arup's chairman Duncan Michael, and joint deputy chairmen Bob Emerson and Mike Shears, all joined as graduate engineers. Virtually all promotion is internal. Ove Arup is committed to developing its own management team, although external recruitment has been stepped up in recent years as the company embarked on a diversification programme.

While it does sponsor staff to take postgraduate degrees, Arup rarely encourages MBAs. History has suggested to them that MBA students rarely return, instead changing direction as their studies unfold.

The company maintains an active graduate recruitment scheme, taking on 80–120 applicants each year. Approximately 50% of these recruits emerge from the university 'Milk Round', with the balance applying directly to the company.

Pay and Benefits

Ove Arup policy dictates paying the highest wages that the business can afford. Aiming to feature in the upper quartile of the engineering industry pay league, increases that are marginally ahead of the rate of inflation are boosted by profit shares, to which every member of staff is entitled.

The pay process is complex. A Salary Review Committee takes marketplace research into account before considering budgetary constraints and allocating funds to group leaders. Merit awards may also be given in recognition of outstanding performance, with interim increases occasionally redressing shortfalls.

Senior staff (associates and above) receive company cars. 24 days' holiday is standard after two years' service, and Arup's final salary pension scheme is open to all employees over the age of 21. Arup also provides life insurance (four times salary), accident cover (five times salary), all employees over 40 are entitled to a biannual check-up from a Harley Street GP, and 'well-woman' screenings are arranged at similar intervals. The firm also sponsors a wide range of sports activities including golf, sailing and cricket clubs.

The Future

Leaving aside the obvious challenge of gaining fresh contracts in a highly competitive market (and doing so profitably), Ove Arup's chairman, Duncan Michael, identifies at least six critical issues.

First, he aspires Ove Arup to become a truly transnational organisation, not merely international. At the same time, it must remain close to the prime centres of capital spending. Thirdly, the business should endeavour to balance size, success and financial security with staying 'quick on its feet'.

In so doing, the firm needs to express Ove Arup's beliefs and attitudes across cultural and language barriers, and to spread appreciation—internally and externally—about the value of Arup's endeavours. Finally, Duncan Michael insists that at all times, the firm should stay young in attitude, facing outwards and avoiding self-absorption. "None of these challenges," Duncan Michael admits, "has an easy solution. All require continuous effort and can only be met by working hard."

In the sphere of human resources, the main challenges facing Arup are the recruitment, training and retention of high quality graduates capable of becoming world class engineering specialists.

Overcoming such significant hurdles demands appropriate training, helping female members of staff achieve their potential, recruiting employees who share Arup's belief in corporate profit share, and keeping at bay predatory firms who prefer to recruit talent trained by others.

Above and beyond all those challenges, Arup remains guided by one overriding principle—to maintain the highest standards of professional integrity in an increasingly competitive and money-minded world.

Pearl Assurance

Pearl Assurance is a wholly owned subsidiary of AMP (Australian Mutual Provident) following its acquisition in 1989. In a market transformed by regulation, Pearl remains one of the financially strongest life offices. The company warrants a triple 'A' rating from Standard & Poors and is committed to being a first choice employer for insurance high fliers. Pearl currently employs 8,700 members of staff in the UK.

Today, Pearl has total assets in excess of £13.5 billion. In a recent survey, Pearl's free asset ratio (assets left once all liabilities are subtracted) was rated highest of the top 10 life and pension insurers. The company has more than 2.5 million customers. Pearl's holding of stocks and shares is worth more than £7 billion.

Biggest Plus: Good, open communication in a period of change

Biggest Minus: Sector-wide uncertainty. The financial services industry rule
                  book has been totally rewritten during the 1990s

Pearl Assurance plc
Lynch Wood
Peterborough PE2 6FY
Tel: 01733-470470
Fax: 01733-472300

The Business

Pearl's core business focuses on providing middle and low income families with a range of financial products and services. Pearl is a traditional player in a rapidly changing industry, Valuing home service as fundamental and placing great emphasis on providing a relationship-based service to its customers. Pearl has also widened its business scope, including the development of telephone call centres, database marketing methods, and the automation of sales forces.

In 1995, Pearl unveiled a new strategy called 'New Pearl'. Effectively a major rebuilding programme aimed at customers, regulation and jobs, it included a simplification of Pearl's entire product range.

Demutualisation was one important prompt to this process of change. Mergers and take-overs among banks and building societies have demolished traditional boundaries in the financial services industry, bringing a flood of new competitors to the established order. Other pressures have forced Pearl's hand. Increasingly sophisticated consumers are now more prepared to shop around, while important regulatory changes have demanded higher educational and compliance levels among salespeople and agents.

Pearl is responding to the fresh environment. With the 'cradle to grave' career pattern now pretty much dead and buried throughout the industry, Pearl is encouraging its staff to recognise, accept and adapt to change, and to drive the company forward by sharpening its market competitiveness.

Company Culture and Style

Changing times prompted a re-think on cultural values. Decades of industry inertia—traditional names with stable market shares adopting paternalistic attitudes towards staff—have been swept aside at Pearl, and displaced by a market-driven culture which offers 'employability' instead of jobs for life. The 'New Pearl' programme introduced a fresh way of doing business that brings to bear new ethical standards and upgraded professional qualifications.

Pearl is also encouraging staff to acquire a basket of new skills (for example in sales, computing, NVQs), which dovetails with the company's own development ambitions and simultaneously improves the marketability of staff. Staunch advocates of continuous learning, Pearl views the relationship with staff as a pact.

"We aim to be the employers of choice," says human resources general manager Gareth Trevor. "What we are trying to do is align corporate values with individual needs, such as appropriate rewards, personal development, providing a good place to work, and engendering excellent team spirit."

Pearl is a friendly organisation and a palpable sense of camaraderie is evident at its breathtaking, award-winning offices in Peterborough. Although many members of staff failed to make the trip up the A1 when the company moved out of London over 1988/89, the average length of service is still in excess of eight years.

Open communication is practised and preached. The management team regularly holds informal lunches with groups of employees to gather feedback. Key messages, such as the new Pearl initiatives, are communicated face-to-face throughout the company in a series of meetings, starting with Richard Surface, managing director, briefing his management team and lay opinion formers.

A particularly striking example of Pearl's open communication was a live forum hosted by BBC presenter Nick Ross. A private fax and phone line were installed, allowing Ross to take comments and questions from staff anonymously, and in turn grill Richard Surface for two hours on any matter of concern.

"I have never known anything like it," commented Ross. "It is hard to imagine any other company, or managing director, putting themselves though such an extraordinary ordeal—inviting anyone in the business to come and throw the toughest questions in person or anonymously. And, if that was not enough, to hire an external moderator with a specific brief to select the most penetrating—even intimate—criticisms and complaints."

Human Resource Priorities

HR's days as an administrative function are over. Instead, it has become the lynchpin of Pearl's drive towards delivering key objectives of high performance, continuous learning and cost effectiveness. The head of HR sits on the key Management Committee and the skills of HR professionals are no less valued in the company than those of colleagues in finance or marketing. No fewer than 140 people (including 35 specialists) are assigned to the function.

HR is responsible for bringing intellectual rigour to all aspects of Pearl's change initiative. This is a proactive role. HR's brief is to anticipate ideas, development and benefits that staff will need to equip them to meet the competitive challenges facing Pearl.

Staff in turn are regularly invited to give their views on the HR function, on the basis that 'you're only as good as the respect your customers give you'. Pearl has undertaken various surveys on cultural issues covering empowerment, employee contribution, paternalistic attitudes and creative styles. Pearl also sends out questionnaires to customers, inviting their comments on the quality of service provided by its sales force. And each manager must spend two days a year dealing with telephone complaints in the Customer Centre—an enlightening experience for most.

Career Opportunity and Development

Recognising that organisations are getting flatter, limiting opportunities for vertical career advancement, staff are encouraged to manage their own careers via individual development plans. Training programmes heighten technical and managerial skill development of all employees, while leadership programmes are aimed at senior managers. Employees are encouraged to study for professional qualifications and Pearl sponsors a number of MBA programmes each year.

Pearl keeps a close eye on individuals identified as having the greatest ability to shape the future of the business. A structured development process, controlled eventually by the managing director, identifies Pearl's future senior management, and plans their development and succession. Fast-track mechanisms are in place at all levels, to develop high potential employees by placing them in a wide range of business situations and in contact with different managers. In 1996 the company took on 20 graduates. All positions up to management level are advertised internally, and Pearl employees are at least considered before external candidates. Many senior managers have risen through the ranks

Being owned by an Australian mutual insurer, most secondment opportunities are 'Down Under', notably to Australia and New Zealand, but also in the wider Pacific region where AMP is represented, including Indonesia and Hong Kong.

Pay and Benefits

The overall remuneration package offered by Pearl is widely recognised as one of the best in the industry. Salaries are determined by a mix of factors including benchmarking with competitors, the level of inflation, overall business profitability and—above all else—individual and team performance. Objectives are agreed between employees and their managers and progress is reviewed regularly.

In 1996, managers' salaries ranged from £46–85,000, with executive directors in the £100–125,000 bracket. Professional staff salaries varied between £21–35,000, and administration staff between £11–25,000. Graduate starters launched their careers on £17,000. Profit-related bonus schemes and long-term incentives kick in at senior management level, while all employees can reap the benefits of Pearl's profit-related pay scheme.

As always, the sales force (around 4,000) has the opportunity for greater variance in pay based on commission levels and minimum targets. Pearl has encouraged its salespeople to identify more closely with the overall performance of the business by introducing various long-term incentives.

All permanent employees are eligible to join a non-contributory pension scheme. Pearl has its own Sports & Social Centre in Peterborough, which includes crèche facilities.

The Future

The rapid pace of change in the financial services industry is only likely to accelerate. Further mergers and sharper competition will become business reality, a reality Pearl must address by continuously seeking to streamline operations and make them more cost-effective.

Gareth Trevor believes that, "our biggest challenge will be to retain the loyalty of our people through a period of change more extensive than anything we've ever seen. Only through their efforts will we emerge stronger and better equipped."

Pearl is realistic enough to appreciate that putting in place policies and structures will mean very little unless employees can relate to them, and are able to identify just what is required of them in their day-to-day work and in the context of the company's longer term aspirations. Fundamentally, they must trust the organisation that they work for. The message appears to be getting across. Staff at Pearl are learning to take change in their stride, adapting to a new era by adding new skills and, more importantly, putting them into practice.

Managing director Richard Surface backs his colleagues unreservedly. "The changes make it exciting to work at Pearl right now. We are taking the first steps towards the rebirth of one of the UK's most important companies. The result will be that Pearl reclaims its birthright as a major provider of essential retirement and savings needs in this country."

 **Pitney Bowes**

Pitney Bowes

Principally engaged in the manufacture, supply and service of mailing machines and office equipment, Pitney Bowes Ltd. is a wholly owned subsidiary of US conglomerate Pitney Bowes Inc.

Having introduced the first postal franking machine to Great Britain in 1922, Pitney Bowes Ltd. now enjoys a dominant position in the UK market. With 1,600 employees in Great Britain (1,200 at its HQ in Harlow), Pitney Bowes reported pre-tax profits of £11.4 million in 1995 on turnover of £135 million.

Biggest Plus: Progressive organisation with a highly developed HR environment.

Biggest Minus: Lack of credible competition doesn't force the pace of change

Pitney Bowes Ltd.
The Pinnacles
Elizabeth Way
Harlow
Essex CM19 5BD
Tel: 01279-426731
Fax: 01279-449175

The Business

Poised at the intersection of digital and paper-based communication, Pitney Bowes Ltd. (PB) is the UK's principal supplier of mailing and office equipment. Serving 220,000 customers throughout Europe, the company pursues a philosophy of customer-led innovation, reacting and responding to their needs.

Central or local government agencies and multiple-site corporations are principal customers for a variety of products which includes mailing systems, fax machines, photocopiers, supported by a broad range of financial services.

Company Culture and Style

People matter at Pitney Bowes. The flesh on the bones of a corporate philosophy stressing 'the five Fs'—fun, flexibility, focus, friendship and feeling—is provided by a nourishing atmosphere that is simultaneously professional and relaxed.

New recruits are welcomed and supported in a non-hierarchical, non-competitive environment which anchors and measures 14 key management competencies (including leadership, customer awareness, problem solving, accountability, mentoring, openness and coaching).

This focus on people applies both internally and externally. Pitney Bowes has twice received the British Safety Council's Sword of Honour. Dubbed the 'Oscar of the Safety World', and awarded for outstanding commitment to accident prevention, the Sword of Honour underlines PB's continuing efforts to protect personnel from injury.

Externally, Pitney Bowes is very much customer-driven. Dedicated to improving client satisfaction, PB invites its customers to complete a Satisfaction Survey, allowing the company to assess how customer needs are being met in terms of sales and service. Over the past few years, the survey has produced several major developments in customer relations including a computerised hotline service, providing customers with online assistance and a guaranteed response time to enquiries. Delivering quality service is such a high priority at PB, that measurements of customer satisfaction are built into staff compensation plans.

Apart from a wide assortment of sports and social activities, PB's communal atmosphere leads to informal events such as 'Family Fundays', barbecues, five-a-side tournaments, and kids' Christmas parties, preserving an environment in which members of staff feel genuinely valued.

Human Resource Priorities

Committed to building a flexible organisation with flexible employees possessing flexible skills, Pitney Bowes HR mission statement aims 'To deliver an appropriate range of HR services in support of European strategic business needs: by facilitating organisational development to create the culture needed to meet business objectives'. Major resources are allocated to HR and the European HR director occupies a seat on the main UK board.

Pitney Bowes has embraced the concept of a stakeholder society, recognising that competitive advantage depends on heightened contributions from every employee. Attaining Investors in People recognition focused employees on the important challenge of linking business vision with people performance.

At the heart of Pitney Bowes's HR credo is the desire to create a Continuous Learning Organisation, fulfilling the potential of every member of staff from boardroom to shop floor. PB is moving away from tight job descriptions and clearly defined roles towards proactive functions for each member of staff, providing skills that are transferable across internal and external job markets.

Pitney Bowes ensures that HR policies amount to more than superficial initiatives. In 1995, the company commissioned a MORI survey to examine employee opinions. Earnings, training, career paths, job satisfaction were all covered in an exhaustive questionnaire, and real action was taken. For example, responding to complaints about the lack of a pan-corporate incentive scheme, Pitney Bowes introduced profit-related pay; comments about lack of information on earnings were addressed by the introduction of Total Pay Statements.

Career Opportunity and Development

In January, Pitney Bowes prepares a schedule of training for all sales, service and management staff. As the year progresses, schedules are updated at quarterly meetings of managers and directors. Advisers responsible for specific business areas review training programmes on an ongoing basis, adding courses where needs or gaps are identified.

At the heart of Pitney Bowes' commitment to personal development is a programme called 'Genesis'. Designed to identify needs on an individual, operational and organisational basis, Genesis determines key competencies required for each role. Managers are assessed against these competencies, encouraging the development of essential skills, which in turn builds a reservoir of executive talent.

Psychometric assessments provide another invaluable source of data. PB's 'Manspec' programme comprises a battery of tests evaluating human potential, measuring individuals against profiles for each job.

The company has recently invested in a state-of-the-art Open Learning Centre, providing a development focus for employees who wish to acquire fresh skills (often unrelated to their jobs), and forming part of a broader policy to encourage employees to take responsibility for their own training.

All jobs are advertised and filled internally where possible. In an era of flattening organisational structures, however, PB encourages staff to develop broader skills in existing roles. Occasional secondments to Hong Kong, USA, France and Australia provide international opportunities for UK staff.

External qualifications are actively encouraged (e.g. NVQ, MBA, Open University degrees). 71 employees are currently engaged in external study, and career breaks and study leave are provided where appropriate.

Pay and Benefits

Pitney Bowes aims to provide a package of benefits above and beyond the median level in the marketplace. Emphasis is placed on *total* reward. PB's pay levels are market average, but when the range of benefits are aggregated (e.g. 25–30 days' holiday, 12.9% non-contributory pension), packages are in the upper quartile.

The popularity of the profit-related pay scheme introduced in 1996 was endorsed by a 98% take-up by staff, who are currently enjoying a monthly boost of £20–70 in their pay packets.

On average, pay increases combined with productivity improvements have improved Pitney Bowes' competitive market pay position during the 1990s. Managerial salaries range from £30–60,000 a year, administration staff £11–14,000, graduates start between £12–18,000. PB's sales force can aim for high rewards for outstanding performance. Pay increases for all staff, ultimately, rest on individual performance.

Pitney Bowes has just launched its eleventh annual Share Option scheme. Operated in conjunction with Halifax Building Society, over 50% of staff have taken up options to date, reaping significant financial rewards. Those opting into the 1990–95 Plan, buying shares at £10.39 and selling five years later at £28.44, realised a tax-free profit of 173.6%.

PB's menu of flexible benefits is currently being expanded. All grades of management receive medical insurance with the ability to up or downgrade, while staff receiving company cars can take cash allowances as an alternative. Pitney Bowes offers a range of health facilities, including an in-house company doctor, on-site reflexology, stress counselling, and health awareness checks.

The Future

Despite an upward profit trend and impressive record of HR innovation, Pitney Bowes resists all thoughts of complacency. Standing at the forefront of technological change, the company faces a constant challenge to keep pace in the communications market place. Globalisation is an increasing fact of business life, and as products span geographical boundaries, HR initiatives also need to extend beyond parochial boundaries.

"All business challenges," suggests European HR director Gerry Duffy, "spinoff into HR. Take mobility of labour for example—we need to know how to move people around and reward them for doing so. Composition of the work force has never been more important. Getting the right male/female split and providing equal opportunities for all is vital when you are trying to gather a diverse range of skills and experiences. Our aim is simple. We want the best people at Pitney Bowes, a stream of talent ready to move into executive roles, a highly skilled work force able to meet the needs of today and tomorrow."

Pitney Bowes avoids the tired cliché of proclaiming 'our employees are our biggest asset', preferring instead to demonstrate an ongoing commitment to employee welfare and a genuine concern for personal development—traditional values cherished by CEO George Harvey in Pitney Bowes' annual report: "I would like to think that no matter how much the world changes...Pitney Bowes stands for values that do not get pushed aside for the expedient. Respect for the individual, trust, integrity, fairness and personal responsibility date back to the earliest days of our company, and give our employees the power to realise their hopes and achieve their dreams."

Price Waterhouse

Price Waterhouse

Price Waterhouse provides a wide range of professional services, including advice for improving business performance and enhancing shareholder value, effecting organisational and strategic change, using information technology for competitive advantage, and meeting audit and tax requirements. As well as being part of a world-wide organisation with 53,000 professionals in 119 countries and territories, the firm has 19 offices throughout the UK, staffed by over 6,000 people.

Price Waterhouse's ambition is to be the leading global consultant to top-tier companies, committed to solving their complex business problems. In 1995, Price Waterhouse audited 82 of the top European companies in the FT Euro 500 listing, and 13% of Fortune 500 companies.

Biggest Plus: Opportunity for real empowerment in a progressive professional services firm

Biggest Minus: Changing from a directive style will take a little more time

Price Waterhouse
Southwark Towers
32 London Bridge Street
London SE1 9SY
Tel: 0171-939 3000
Fax: 0171-378 0647

The Business

With 434 offices in 199 countries, by anyone's standards Price Waterhouse is a major global player. The firm is committed to long-term relationships with clients, offering specialist, innovative services that are managed in a truly integrated way across international boundaries. Price Waterhouse focuses on successful large or growing companies within carefully defined market sectors, including banking and financial services, media and telecommunications, energy and utilities, retailing and entertainment.

"Our strategy for growth is closely aligned to the fundamental changes taking place in the global business market place," says Ian Brindle, chairman of Price Waterhouse UK. "We bring to our clients a reputation, built up over 150 years, as a leading professional services firm with strong values, the highest standards and a determination to be at the leading edge of innovation."

Price Waterhouse's UK operation is an important part of the business, but the same high standards, business approach, culture and opportunities apply through-out the global organisation.

In 1993 Price Waterhouse Europe launched the 'Best and Brightest' initiative, a plan to ensure that the firm achieved its vision of being seen as the best provider of professional services. To achieve that ambitious goal, Price Waterhouse realised that it had to make people issues a major strategic priority. Although the market focus has changed—the firm increasingly operates globally—the commitment to its people remains a critical part of Price Waterhouse's strategy.

Company Culture and Style

The cultural transformation is not yet complete but concepts and practices such as coaching, mentoring and upward appraisals are now generally accepted. Jeremy Franks, the head of UK human resources, admits: "You cannot change things overnight but we are getting there—the management style in the 1980s was very directive. That is not a way to treat highly intelligent, highly motivated and very committed people."

Client service remains absolutely fundamental to everything which Price Waterhouse does. Clients quite rightly expect much from the firm and the demands placed on the organisation can be great. While this makes the cliché 'work hard, play hard' appropriate, Price Waterhouse motivates its people by creating an environment of openness, opportunity and, if needed, support. Price Waterhouse's strong internal culture is based on respect for colleagues and clients, and the firm's Quaker origins are still seen in a tolerant organisation where different types of people and behaviour are welcomed.

Price Waterhouse's drive towards a coaching-based rather than a hierarchical culture is designed to ensure that all of its employees feel they have a sense of ownership and responsibility for every task they perform.

With responsibility comes obligation and Price Waterhouse expects its employees to show real commitment to the company and to its success. Franks, insists, however, that "Price Waterhouse does not always come first," and the firm definitely has a sensitive, human touch.

Human Resource Priorities

In aligning the firm's human resources with its business objectives, the HR team is charged with recruiting, retaining and motivating high calibre people. The motivation for this is partly in response to changing market needs.

Jeremy Franks notes: "The job market for our people is good and it is of crucial importance to our success that we retain our top talent." It is also based on feedback from major clients who demand a service based on teamwork, where every single Price Waterhouse employee working on a project, however junior, felt responsible for that project and for their colleagues.

The coaching culture encourages employees to make suggestions on how to improve the quality of service to clients. An upward feedback mechanism is designed to achieve just this. Staff complete a questionnaire after every work project, with suggestions as to how the job could have been better completed. If the feedback produces valid ideas for organisational or procedural changes, those ideas will be implemented.

Day-to-day responsibility for human resources management is shared between the HR team, managers and partners. It is hoped that as the coaching culture becomes more all-embracing, the need for paper-based appraisals will diminish as managers and the managed communicate more freely and openly. Price Waterhouse says this is already starting to happen.

Internal communication is central. The 'matrix management' structure ensures that employees are never too far away from somebody that can influence the decision-making processes within the firm. Price Waterhouse staff are also kept informed of developments via the monthly *Price Waterhouse Reporter*, the bi-monthly *Euronews* publication, and *The Globe*, a world newsletter. Partners also communicate with departmental staff via email briefings and periodical management meetings, and at occasional 'away days' and conferences.

Career Opportunity and Development

The range of work experience and the global market place offer great opportunities at Price Waterhouse for people of all types and at all levels. Career development is underpinned by an extensive commitment to training and development, irrespective of role and position.

Graduates now join Price Waterhouse in a wide variety of roles: accountancy, actuarial, consultancy, corporate recovery and tax. Graduate recruits undertake their professional training within the firm and, for those taking accountancy exams, there is the backing of an in-house exam support unit.

With Price Waterhouse operating increasingly as a global organisation, the opportunities for anyone to work overseas are extensive. This is often on assignments where a client demands certain skills and expertise, but the firm uses secondment and exchange opportunities overseas to develop individuals and also to benefit the firm in the longer term.

Price Waterhouse provides extensive training and development programmes for all staff, an important activity that continues throughout your career, including at partner level. Typically, employees spend 12 training days per year on job-specific and personal skills training. The firm organises many courses and programmes in-house, or it will encourage people to take external qualifications.

Career development is planned involving appraisals, counselling and mentoring and individual objectives and development plans are set and monitored. The emphasis is on employees taking greater responsibility for their own development in the light of the firm's ambition, activities and competencies.

Long, successful careers are still pursued at Price Waterhouse, although recent years have seen a shift in perception away from guaranteed careers for life with large employers. After two years, 90% of graduates are still with Price Waterhouse and after five years, only around one-third have left the firm. The majority of promotions are internal—many of the firm's partners joined as trainees.

Driven by the need to provide the highest level of professional service, Price Waterhouse necessarily hires experts and specialists from the market, particularly into key consulting roles. The firm is perhaps recruiting as many experienced people as it does graduates. With increasing numbers of specialist recruits joining, the firm's profile may well change over time.

Pay and Benefits

Price Waterhouse's salary levels are highly competitive and generally above industry norms, around the upper quartile. The company also runs a profit-related bonus scheme, which replaces up to 20% of pay with profit-related pay. Graduate trainees started on £16,500 plus a £1,000 'settling-in' package in 1996.

The firm offers a progressive 'flex' benefits package, with employees able to tailor their package, allocating credits to more holiday, grocery vouchers, dental insurance, greater life insurance, etc. Funding for cars is provided for managers and above but any member of staff may use their flex fund for a car if they so wish.

Price Waterhouse also offers enhanced maternity pay and arrangements and, unusually for a British employer, has also introduced two days' paternity leave. The firm won The Parents at Work 1996 Employer of the Year Award (large employer category). Price Waterhouse is also at the forefront of flexible ways of working.

For those who want a social life through the firm, there are plenty of activities to choose from. In London, there is an on-site swimming pool and gym. In other locations, membership of local sports and social facilities is available.

The Future

The biggest challenge facing the firm at the moment comes from the market place. The need to provide expertise in a wide range of products and market sectors, and to mobilise people from anywhere in the world to offer a full service to clients quickly, is demanding.

As a multi-disciplinary professional services firm, Price Waterhouse is looking to match the increasing sophistication, complexity and internationalisation of its client base. The success of the integrated services offer against highly specialised service providers will be interesting to watch.

For Price Waterhouse, the move to an open coaching culture is far from complete and it recognises that there are still hearts and minds to be won over. The tide appears to be running strongly in the right direction.

Procter&Gamble

Procter & Gamble

Procter & Gamble Limited is a wholly owned UK subsidiary of The Procter & Gamble Company and has been in business in Britain since 1930. Employing around 5,000 people, five diverse businesses cover consumer products, health and beauty care, cosmetics and fragrances, pharmaceuticals, and food service and industrial products. At the year-ended 30 June 1996, turnover stood at £1,504.3 million.

Biggest Plus: Integrity, ethics, consistent treatment of all employees

Biggest Minus: Possible over-emphasis on promotion from within

Procter & Gamble Limited
PO Box 1EE
St. Nicholas Avenue
Gosforth
Newcastle upon Tyne NE99 1EE
Tel: 0191-279 2226
Fax: 0191-279 2849

The Business

Listing among its famous brand names Ariel, Fairy Liquid, Max Factor, Pampers and Vidal Sassoon, Procter & Gamble (P&G) represents an integral part of modern British life. P&G makes and markets a wide range of products for both consumer and institutional use and the company has on-the-ground operations in 57 countries, conducting business in more than 140 countries.

With 96,500 employees world-wide, P&G has operations in all the European Community countries plus technical centres in the UK at Egham, Newcastle and Staines, plus Brussels and Schwalbach in Germany.

Paul Polman, UK chief executive and vice president and general manager, laundry and cleaning, beverages and paper, said that in Britain, P&G's seven manufacturing distribution units and three research centres cover the length and breadth of the country.

P&G also has three administrative headquarters, at Brooklands in Weybridge, Newcastle-upon-Tyne and Staines. The Procter & Gamble Company has its headquarters in Cincinnati, Ohio, USA, and has been in business since 1837. P&G was recently ranked No. 2 on the *Fortune List*, as America's second most admired corporation, according to the magazine's annual survey of corporate reputations. This was five places higher than the company's 1995 ranking.

P&G was ranked near the top in three of the eight categories covered by the survey: Quality of Management; Ability to Attract, Develop and Keep Talented People; and Value as a Long-Term Investment.

Company Culture and Style

Each of P&G's five businesses has its own culture but all are strongly influenced by the parent company. What comes across very strongly is a belief in promotion from within, based on ability. A great deal of time is spent on developing individual expertise.

Doug Elliott, associate manager human resources, said: "Everybody who gets to the top has been with P&G for most of their working life. This corporation is like Brighton rock. It has Procter & Gamble running all the way through it." He added: "We act with integrity at all times. There is no tolerance for unethical behaviour."

"The 'bosses' are accessible to staff, always, and everyone is on first-name terms. This includes vice presidents. The company is very strong on celebrating service anniversaries, birthdays and retirements.

P&G claims that most people enjoy their work. Humour is encouraged at meetings and individuals must be very fair and scrupulously honest. If an individual cannot accept the way in which their workplace operates, they will not survive because the culture is actually everybody else around them. This integrity is carried over into business ethics, where every P&G customer gets the same price list.

There is no one type of person who flourishes within P&G. Yet the company sees similar skills in individuals who 'get on': very bright, assertive and knowing what they want to do. And good listeners. A 'new start' undergoes a total-immersion course and he or she gets to know thoroughly the multifarious P&G products.

Draw Doug Elliott back to culture and he once again talks about P&G people. At management level, only graduates are hired. However, administration and technical (A&T) staff can, and are, promoted into the managerial ranks.

Marion Dalziel, senior secretary, commented: "I have worked with other companies and P&G is best because it is the one which makes me feel appreciated."

Human Resource Priorities

P&G has around 40 HR specialists in its UK operation plus personnel groups at the five major plants. There is an HR board member as director and HR is a full partner in business planning.

Line managers are described as partners. One way P&G measures the effectiveness of HR policy is by the number of managers it retains. The company lays great store by recruitment of women and their subsequent career development.

Paul Polman said: "You can have all the products and brands you like, but at the end of the day, nothing happens unless you have in place the right people to drive the business forward."

P&G believes in listening to its employees. "We then try to match individual career ambition to a business need," he explained.

One example of theory in action: P&G was told by two female sales staff that they wished to develop their career overseas. Doug Elliott said: "Mexico was top of their list and we discovered there was a requirement for two salespeople out there. So off they went." There have been other similar successful transfers to Australia and China.

Elliott added: "If a person has a particular ambition and does not tell us, how are we supposed to know! We encourage staff not to hide their light under a bushel.

"The transfer idea doesn't always occur of course," he said. "There may not be an opening or the person concerned may not be the right person for that particular move. But we try our best to accommodate wishes."

Career Opportunity and Development

P&G is a big exporter of management talent. "We send a lot of people abroad," Doug Elliott explained. "China, Russia, Hungary, South Africa, you name it." It reflects a long-standing policy of choosing who should run the business overseas.

A new staff member has an individual development plan worked out initially in his/her function. Training is 'on-the-job' topped up with some corporate skills training. P&G only promotes from within and employees have regular career discussions. Promotion is a daily occurrence.

An example of an employee rising through the ranks is that the current chief operations officer of P&G World-wide started as a brand assistant in Holland 20 years ago. Also, a recently retired senior HR manager started 44 years ago in the London factory.

Amanda Raby, marketing services group manager, said: "I joined P&G as a secretary seven years ago and I'm overjoyed at the commitment of senior managers to the development of their people. "For myself, I was promoted to management four years ago and have just been made a group manager with responsibility for other managers," she added. "Now I must help them develop."

A series of corporate training courses is staged constantly, open to all staff, whether management or A&T. Staff are encouraged to learn how to write recommendations and reports. An employee will have on average 25 days' training in year one.

Courses range from general management training to finance and technical. P&G discourages acquisition of qualifications for qualifications sake. Except in finance, where a CIMA certificate would be needed. P&G believes an employee can learn—and earn more—in two years running the business than in a similar time span acquiring an MBA.

Between 100–150 graduates and postgraduates are recruited each year within UK operations. Numbers have increased since 1986. Retention rates are healthy, standing at 85–95% after two years and between 60–75% after five years. Graduates in 1996 started on a salary of £19,020, more for a PhD.

Pay and Benefits

P&G pays in-line with other leading national companies where similar kinds of work are performed. A national salary structure is operated for management grades, but at local level for A&T and hourly-paid employees. All salaries are determined individually, based on performance. Average pay increases since 1990 run at about 20%. Regularly, individuals will have received more due to merit. Each individual salary is planned and reviewed at least annually but an increase can be granted at any time.

Each group function has a pay structure with normally four pay ranges, below director level. Individuals are paid in range band based on performance and experience.

As with other big companies, there are policies for a share purchase scheme, where four out of five P&G employees are members; P&G does not operate a profit-related bonus scheme. A family medical insurance plan and private health checks and private life assurance for employees are promoted. Average non-contributory company pension scheme and maternity leave conditions apply.

The Future

P&G would be the first to describe itself as a complex group and a priority now is to succeed in integrating its diverse businesses into a European organisation. The company is well down this road, with many of its brands already managed on a European basis.

It realises it has to be quicker in its delivery of products to market because the competition is getting better. The group is actively ensuring that any competitive advantages it had in years gone by are not eroded, wherever possible. The situation is not made any simpler in that some of P&G's major customers are competitors!

P&G has in the past been viewed as somewhat bureaucratic and perhaps slow to act or innovate until such action is needed. Staff are currently being urged to become more focused in their respective areas of business. In HR terms, the challenges are to increase but at the same time manage diversity within the group where work processes have to be constantly simplified. P&G's clear objective remains 'let's get the business done'.

The Rank Group

Rank Group has staged a remarkable comeback. Written-off by City oracles just a decade ago, a multinational with interests spanning the breadth of the leisure industry has defied the prophets of doom, posting pre-tax profits in 1995 of £407 million.

40,000 staff are employed in various divisions which include video and film (Pinewood Studios), Holidays (Butlins, Warner, Oasis), Recreation (Mecca and Top Rank Bingo, Grosvenor Clubs, Odeon Cinemas) and Restaurants (Hard Rock Cafe).

Biggest Plus: Strong sense of employee ownership. Staff live, eat and breathe the businesses

Biggest Minus: Individual strengths of subsidiaries greater than the sum of the whole

The Rank Group
6 Connaught Place
London W2 2ER
Tel: 0171-872 6763
Fax: 0171-872 6842

The Business

British wrestlers rarely achieve world-wide fame. However, after winning a bronze medal at the 1952 Olympic Games in Helsinki, Kenneth Richmond gave up the noble art of grappling to bang the gong for J. Arthur Rank. Today, Richmond's torso (with the gong) remains the enduring symbol of a corporation with diverse interests spanning the leisure industry.

Employing 40,000 members of staff in directly-managed businesses, the group also has a major investment in the Rank Xerox operations outside the USA (contributing £187 million to the profit in 1996) and an ongoing partnership with MCA in Universal Studios.

Rank's recent corporate renaissance was kick-started by decentralisation, giving each business control over its own destiny with minimal interference from the centre.

Profit-driven philosophies may have reaped business dividends but created HR problems that are being addressed by a reshaped board. Having staged a comeback worthy of Lazarus, Rank appears poised for a period of growth and stability.

Company Culture and Style

The turnaround at Rank began with Mike Gifford taking the helm as managing director. Bringing hard-nosed, financial measures to all aspects of the business, Gifford devolved responsibility to the line, focusing on short-term survival rather than long-term issues such as management development.

That task completed, Gifford stepped down and was succeeded by Andrew Teare in April 1996. The new MD has brought a fresh atmosphere to the business—a willingness to facilitate the exchange of best practice information, a commitment to employee communication, and putting quality of replacements at senior management level at the top of Rank's list of priorities.

Further down the organisational ladder, personal contact with the customer has always been central to success. Divisional MDs regularly visit Rank's night-clubs, cinemas and bingo halls, while inductions, rewards and recognition mechanisms have played a central role in the rise and rise of the Hard Rock Cafe.

Fun is essential in a customer-contact industry. Discos, restaurants and bingo halls regularly stage pre-opening sessions, getting staff warmed-up before the patrons arrive. Staff tend to fall in love with the business, exhibiting a rare dedication. One bingo manager even embarked on a busman's holiday, spending his annual break going round other halls talking to customers.

Although operating in a sector with a high degree of staff turnover, jobs at Rank have been comparatively secure. One-third of all staff have been with the company for over 20 years, while those who leave tend to do so out of choice. Rank understands that even the most committed night-club manager or barman may not want to fulfil that role for the rest of their lives.

Rank is a committed equal opportunity employer. 80% of bingo hall staff are female and part-time employees, comprising two-thirds of the work force, and are sufficiently valued to merit inclusion in profit share schemes.

Human Resource Priorities

With the arrival of Andrew Teare, human resources issues have assumed a greater importance within the company, each subsidiary being encouraged to develop policies reflecting its individual business requirements.

At the corporate level, HR does have a significant influence in Rank's corridors of power, and the function is represented on the Executive Committee alongside finance and operations. This commitment to HR is further demonstrated by the financial resources dedicated to the function at group and subsidiary level.

Specific goals that have been targeted for HR include taking on staff who will have fun at work and pass on that enthusiasm to customers; building a flexible and progressive career structure, offering a broad range of experience for staff of similar grades; and developing career progression at senior level. Andrew Teare has not only identified management development as one of his top priorities, but he also will be looking to broaden and develop further the senior executive population so that it will be able to deliver the stretching long-term objectives of the business.

As HR increasingly assumes centre stage, measuring the effectiveness of new policies is far from straightforward, but these policies are designed to have a major effect on the bottom line.

Career Opportunity and Development

Formal training and development processes are in place for all levels of management within subsidiary companies. While a framework for developing the senior executive body has been lacking in the past, some general management programmes are run throughout the year by Sundridge Park and Duke University, covering such areas as finance, marketing, IT, strategy formulation and implementation.

The new broom is sweeping away career cobwebs. Structured management development processes are now in the advanced stages of planning, ready for implementation early in 1997. Development centres will identify strengths and weaknesses, taking the best people and practices to where they are needed.

Further down the organisation, comprehensive training programmes are already in place, from junior management up to executive level. External qualifications are strongly encouraged with internal programmes tied into business schools and academic bodies to produce formal recognition. Moreover, several managers are currently undertaking MBAs.

Lack of formal qualifications is no bar to reaching the very top of the organisation. Indeed, one of Rank's youngest managing directors joined the company as a school-leaver and has worked his way up through the business.

Rank operates an informal secondment scheme—staff expressing a desire to transfer across subsidiaries are accommodated wherever possible—and the company recruits both graduates and non-graduates.

Potential managers need enthusiasm and a flair for customer service. Putting a bingo card in the hands of prospective employees and seeing who gets a buzz from the game has proved far more productive than taking on students with first class degrees.

Pay and Benefits

While salaries at Rank are attractive by leisure industry standards, bonus incentives provide the opportunity for upper quartile rewards. Each subsidiary determines its own level of remuneration. Collective bargaining arrangements characterise the film and TV divisions, but rises elsewhere are determined according to individual merit. Three factors are taken into account— market rate for the job, inflation and performance.

Bonus payments can amount to 5–25% of basic salaries. Three-quarters of managers and virtually all staff enjoy a myriad of bonus schemes. Targets are set by divisional MDs, and bonuses paid if individuals meet between 95–120% of their pre-determined objectives. Two-thirds of all businesses have achieved 105% of performance targets over the last three years, leading to a 15% bonus pay-out.

Rank's top 400 managers benefit from executive share option schemes. All other permanent employees, full and part time, can join the company's SAYE share option scheme.

Senior executives earning typically in excess of £30,000 are also offered their choice of company car or a cash alternative. Other managers are given cars where either the job or where market-place pressures make it desirable to do so.

A private medical scheme covers senior managers, along with their families. Two types of pension arrangement are available—a final salary scheme and a money purchase scheme—while all permanent staff on the payroll are covered by life assurance. Other perks include relocation packages incorporating interest-free bridging loans and staff discounts on a range of Rank products (up to 50% off selected holidays, 40% off entrance tickets to Universal Studios in Florida).

The Future

Times are changing at Rank, an evolving business demanding a nimble HR function. Building on the firm foundations that have been laid, development programmes and customer care initiatives in the subsidiaries demonstrate a real commitment to developing the business through people.

The development of Rank's people resources to provide strong successors to pivotal positions has in the past been limited by a failure to encourage cross-fertilisation of ideas and developmental moves across subsidiary businesses. The company has also historically been a risk-averse organisation, too slow to react in a fast-moving business environment.

Determined to resolve those issues, two key areas of corporate challenge stand out—maintaining levels of customer service, and making sure that corporate development adds value at all levels of management.

Rank is also wary about the ageing profile of its senior management. Another major challenge is to produce more home-grown executives of the future, bringing through the next generation without disrupting the business. It's a challenge that Rank looks forward to meeting, taking the company forward with confidence into the 21st century.

Reckitt & Colman

Reckitt & Colman is a global company with a tradition in a wide variety of leading household brands that dates back to 1819. Its leading UK brands include Disprin, Lemsip, Brasso, Haze, Deltox, Dettol, Harpic and Mr Sheen. It now operates in two core sectors: household products, and over-the-counter (OTC) pharmaceuticals. It has manufacturing sites in 35 countries and markets its products in over 120. 1995 sales exceeded £2.3 billion, and the majority of its brands hold number one or two position. The corporate headquarters is in London and the UK operational sites are in Hull and Derby.

Biggest Plus: A wide range of career opportunity, including overseas employment and working internationally

Biggest Minus: The UK is a relatively small market for household products, limiting opportunities for expansion

Reckitt & Colman plc
1 Burlington Lane
London W4 2RW
Tel: 0181-994 6464
Fax: 0181-994 8920

The Business

Reckitt & Colman used to be best-known for its Colmans mustard and Robinsons fruit drinks. With its food businesses sold off in 1995, Reckitt & Colman's key strategic aim is to be the world's leading household products company. Its secondary aim is to be market leader in OTC pharmaceuticals in its present categories and countries and to enhance category and geographical growth through alliances. The two core product groups now represent over 90% of group turnover.

Reckitt & Colman (R&C) has bought and integrated a major US household cleaning products company, Lehn & Fink, but now intends to concentrate mainly on organic growth. In 1995 it underlined its aim of being a truly global company by setting up global management teams in six key areas: supply, research and development, human resources, finance and planning, information systems, and global management of key product categories. This is intended to create real advantage from global scale, by sharing best practice and learning throughout the world-wide business.

Investment in research and development, which plays a critical role in product innovation, has been increased, and a separate research and development director appointed at board level.

Chief executive Vernon Sankey says: "Our brands across the world enjoy very high levels of consumer loyalty and are the prime drivers of our growth. At the same time, the rationalisation of manufacturing and distribution and the strengthening of our business processes will progressively improve efficiency and productivity, and keep costs down."

Company Culture and Style

The R&C culture is an informal one, with colleagues on first-name terms throughout the company. It is consciously open and participative, helping employees to feel that the organisation is genuinely caring without being overly paternalistic. But while the environment is supportive of staff, there is a strong expectation of performance and delivery.

"Compared to the mass market household giants, we are a David against Goliaths, and this has a lot to be said for it," R&C says. "In marketing terms the company has never been afraid to go into battle and win, on the basis of playing to its strengths. Smaller means more agile, quicker to manoeuvre, prepared to upset perceived wisdom when it comes to innovative advertising, more than happy to try new approaches. It doesn't stand on its dignity, it stands on its results."

A team approach, with a minimum of hierarchical barriers, is important. "People are encouraged to express their views and there is a high degree of autonomy," the group says in relation to its crucial marketing function. There aren't many companies of this status where personalities really shine through, and as for friendliness, few compare.

Human Resource Priorities

The cornerstone of the human resources strategy is to create a positive climate where people feel committed and motivated, and hence make a significant contribution to the company's ability to meet its business objectives. Reward, career development and training are all designed to promote a climate of excellence and achievement. There is a strong emphasis on living the values of the organisation and promoting key behaviours which will help R&C to achieve its mission of becoming an outstanding global company.

Like its competitors, R&C cannot offer a job for life. Employees in companies with even the finest traditions have to adapt to the modern realities of global business. "Even in lean times we would not have a policy of mass exiting," says group organisation and development manager Paul Allen. "But people understand the risk and reward associated with working in a large multinational. Where people do leave the organisation, support and counselling are given. We are certainly not a short-term hire and fire organisation."

Career Opportunity and Development

There is a structured approach to management training, with an active development policy from senior executives down. The emphasis is on developing the leadership behaviours and professional skills required to meet the needs of the business and the career aspirations of the individual. R&C has links with a number of business schools and is strengthening these partnerships as part of its career development strategy.

Career progression is based on merit; there are excellent opportunities for good graduates to gain experience in a number of functional areas, including international assignments.

General training is provided in a variety of formats according to individual needs, including support towards achieving professional qualifications.

In sales, where the emphasis is on establishing and maintaining close customer partnerships, potential managers are given opportunities to work in a variety of roles. "We are great believers in people understanding the broad picture, while having the opportunity to create a lasting impression," the group says.

In marketing, where the priorities are strong long-term brand management and bringing to market innovative products which delight customers, the high degree of autonomy encourages rapid personal development. Research and development offers 'experience across all scientific areas of the work as well as exposure to essential commercial aspects of the business'. The other main opportunities are in pharmaceuticals manufacturing, including production management, engineering, procurement, quality assurance and finance.

R&C is certainly among an elite group of UK companies that are small enough to value the individual, but globally ambitious enough to be able to offer new recruits an international career after only a few years.

Pay and Benefits

R&C aims to be competitive in overall pay and benefits packages. Salaries are in broad band ranges, acknowledging the fact that a flat structure no longer provides obvious promotion routes. A whole series of performance-linked pay frameworks has been introduced, linked to the performance development review system.

The R&C pension scheme was rated among the top three company schemes in the country in a 1996 survey by Union Pension Services. A standard profit-related pay scheme is due to come into force on 1 January 1997, and an SAYE sharesave scheme has long been in place at the company.

The Future

Reckitt & Colman is putting in place new programmes to align business strategy with both operational and human resource programmes, enabling the company to resource appropriately and to attract and retain exceptional employees. To this end the company is implementing a major change programme that is affecting every area of the Reckitt & Colman world—its people, its structure and its processes. It is an ambitious programme aimed at meeting customer and consumer needs more effectively than its competitors and at achieving the company's vision to be 'an outstanding global company with leading brands and exceptional people that together really make a difference'.

Transformation (as it is known) marks a profound change in the way the company thinks, works, organises, and manages the business. Massive commitment, energy and enthusiasm are now focused on this global opportunity for the company. It is up against stiff competition in world markets, which is where future growth opportunities lie, but a clear focus and the harnessing of new energies make the company's prospects good.

Rentokil Initial

Rentokil Initial plc

Rentokil Initial is the world's largest business services company capitalised at approximately £6 billion. Its services include pest control, office cleaning, healthcare, security, hygiene services, tropical plant maintenance, office machine maintenance, property care, catering, textiles services and much more. Towards the end of 1996, Rentokil Initial was approximately the 36th largest quoted company in Britain, and it employs 150,000 people world-wide, 85,000 in the UK (including part-time equivalents where several part-time workers equate to one full-timer).

Biggest Plus: Impressive growth and equally impressive career opportunities

Biggest Minus: Many people still don't realise the diversity of its operations

Rentokil Initial plc
Felcourt
East Grinstead
West Sussex RH19 2JY
Tel: 01342-833022
Fax: 01342-326229

The Business

Founded over 60 years ago, Rentokil was by the early 1980s essentially a UK property care and pest control business worth just £100 million. Its transformation to its current eminence may seem extraordinary; yet its growth has been due to a clear objective and an equally clear strategy. The objective is to increase profits and earnings per share by at least 20% every year as long as this is not at the expense of long-term growth. This objective has clarity and measurability. The strategy is to develop a range of value-added services that can be marketed in the world's developed economies using brand strength. This is achieved through the successful management of well-recruited, well-trained and well-motivated staff who work primarily in other people's premises without direct supervision.

This objective and strategy have been followed unchanged since adoption in the early 1980s. As a direct result, the group has expanded enormously through acquisition: over 200 companies have been acquired over the last ten years. This policy reached its most important milestone to date in April 1996 when Rentokil acquired BET for £2.2 billion—one of the largest acquisitions in British corporate history. This brought together two great companies that had previously operated as competitors, giving many benefits of management and economies of scale. Particularly important was the fact that BET included Initial's Clive Thompson, group chief executive: "Initial is one of the great brand names and is as synonymous with textile services as Rentokil is for pest control and property care." It was therefore decided to combine Rentokil and BET under the dual brand names of Rentokil and Initial, giving the group a wider product and service ambit.

Company Culture and Style

Rentokil has a distinctive and possibly unique style—which has been recognised by numerous awards. For example, a *Management Today* survey in 1994 voted Rentokil Britain's most admired company. This style will increasingly be introduced into the BET parts of the business to give a group approach. This will be a gradual introduction and will also include two-way movement; Rentokil acknowledges that some BET systems and procedures will be taken up and introduced as group policy. In short, the best of both companies will form the style of the group as a whole.

One important aspect of the Rentokil style is the avoidance of traditional specialist functions such as marketing, sales, production, personnel, finance and so on. Rentokil has minimum reporting lines and devolved profit responsibility as far as possible down the organisation. There are virtually no marketing departments or personnel staff, and no sales staff above branch level. Instead, there is a uniform management and financial structure across the businesses that are then run geographically rather than by international business stream.

It may seem especially surprising that a group of this size can survive without traditional marketing departments. Group corporate affairs director Charles Grimaldi: "This is possible because we have embedded marketing deeply into the culture of the company; it has become an indivisible component in the everyday decision-making process within our businesses all around the world. All decision making is influenced by the reality that customer focusing and a true 'customer needs first' orientation is the only effective way forward in today's business environment."

The culture of the company is founded on two elements: a deep commitment to meritocracy (*Acquisitions Monthly* called Rentokil, "A 1990s meritocracy par excellence") and the desire to constantly improve service and customer attitudes. Promotions and even pay rises are very much about personal performance.

The 'Be Proud' initiative recognises anyone who has served his or her customers well—and because 'customers' are the people served directly, this can include typists and wages clerks as well as technicians and joiners. On the basis of customer endorsement, three or four people are nominated each month and twice a year, and they and their partners are whisked off to a European weekend break. A similar scheme honours top sales performers. The chief executive's award goes to those who perform well against their own previous sales levels. And there are numerous divisional incentive programmes operating in the different businesses around the world.

Internal communications are served by a group-wide magazine twice a year covering results and top-level promotions; individual country magazines for staff and customers which report on wider job movements, new developments, services and environmental initiatives; and the usual range of traditional means.

Human Resource Priorities

People are fundamental to the core of the corporate strategy. Rentokil Initial believes that personnel issues are best handled at the branch level. Branch managers within the group are effectively running their own businesses while enjoying the support of a much larger organisation. As a result, they are trained to be responsible for many areas, including personnel—they are taught employment legislation and handle all HR issues except payroll and pensions. This means that these subjects can be handled flexibly and with an eye to local conditions.

There is a management development director responsible for tracking management to identify successful managers as candidates for movement and/or promotion.

Career Opportunity and Development

There is enormous scope for movement within Rentokil Initial for anyone with talent and the appetite for hard work—both between the 20 or so divisions and geographically. The group operates in over 40 countries, including every major economy of Europe, North America, Asia Pacific and Africa. And because all businesses are about people management, all are structured on exactly the same lines. A manager can move from Toronto to Sydney and find the same structures in place. This is course is good news for the customer too, since the company style will not change with that appointment. Indeed, there is a parallel between Rentokil Initial and a company such as MacDonalds, which offers essentially the same products and a consistent service anywhere in the world in which it operates.

As to starting a career with Rentokil Initial, this again goes back to the company's commitment to meritocracy. It is said that there are only two ways to join the group: at the bottom or through acquisition. Graduates joining Rentokil start at the grass roots like everyone else—but many prefer this to being expected to manage from day one and feeling threatened by often unrealistic expectations. As a result, they learn the business inside out, and by the time they become branch managers they have plenty of confidence. Good graduates are fast-tracked and can be branch managers by the age of 30.

Training receives high priority and considerable resources at Rentokil Initial, the aim being to develop skills and adopt better working methods and habits on an evolutionary and ongoing basis. Division-specific training is offered for technical, sales, computer and administration matters, while management development is all done on a cross-divisional basis. This has the added merit of bringing people together from different aspects of the business. All development programmes are held at the Group Training HQ at Yew Lodge, East Grinstead, apart from the International Senior Managers' programme, which is held at Sundridge Park, Kent.

Pay and Benefits

The Group regards itself as being in the upper quartile for pay, and remuneration is broadly according to local market sectors. It rewards success; there is no ceiling on commissions, and sales people can enjoy high earnings. Managers also benefit from bonuses when above their targets. Managers have scope to reward individuals according to performance when pay reviews are decided.

Benefits include a UK profit-share scheme (after a two-year qualifying period) which offers cash, shares or a combination; not surprisingly, the proportion opting for shares has risen from 30% to 69% over the last five years! There is also a good pension scheme, healthcare provision for all graded managers, cars for managers and sales people (who get a new car every year), and numerous sports and social events which reflect the vibrant team spirit found throughout the group.

The Future

With such an ambitious growth rate built into the company's objective, the HR policy must be at the heart of the company's future challenges. As Charles Grimaldi says, "We must find and train enough talented people to manage our future growth. Acquisitions have and will continue to help here; we have a thirst for people with talent and ability because of our ever-expanding opportunities."

This approach gives the group a constant feed of talent, aided by its policy of promoting from within wherever possible.

The strong objective, strategy and distinctive style of Rentokil Initial look to stand it in very good stead as it approaches the new millennium.

RMC Group plc

The RMC Group is the UK market leader in the extraction of aggregates and the production and supply of ready mixed concrete, and the largest building materials supplier in Europe. It is also a growing force in a number of related fields. Operating within 18 countries, RMC's total sales in 1995 exceeded £4.6 billion. The group employs 26,000 people world-wide, 13,000 of whom work in the UK.

Biggest Plus: Superb training and the chance to achieve tangible results

Biggest Minus: Extraordinary hours are sometimes required!

RMC Group plc
RMC House
Coldharbour Lane
Thorpe
Egham
Surrey TW20 8TD
Tel: 01932-568833
Fax: 01932-568933

The Business

RMC's origins go back to 1931, when the UK's first ready mixed concrete plant was built. This material was ahead of its time, only becoming widely used many years later; but this early start has helped the group become the world leader in the supply of ready mixed concrete, as well as a leader in the development of concrete technology. The forward-looking, innovative approach of RMC continues to this day.

The core businesses of the group remain based on the extraction and supply of quarried materials and the production and supply of ready mixed concrete. In the UK, the group has also built strong and successful operations in the related fields of road surfacing, concrete products manufacture, waste control, builders' merchants and DIY retailing. Hall and Co., Hales Waste Control and Great Mills are among the many well-known companies making up the group.

RMC is noted for responsible land management. The group has transformed many former sand and gravel pits into agricultural land, wildlife reserves and leisure facilities. These include Thorpe Park, the Surrey theme park owned by the group which attracts over a million visitors annually to its 500 acres of lakes, rides and attractions.

Company Culture and Style

Perhaps the first thing to note when it comes to culture is the diversity of the group. In the UK alone, the group operates from 1,000 different locations and in many different fields of business. Yet paradoxically there is a huge sense of pride in RMC. Personnel department's Chris Gay explains it this way: "Everyone speaks the same language; we all tend to be down to earth and direct. The group knows its business very well and excels at meeting customer needs. That engenders a strong feeling of community, even with such a widespread operation."

People who do well at RMC tend to be outgoing decision makers who like to see the results of what they do. They enjoy taking responsibility, solving problems, working as part of a team. They can handle the pressure of very rapid developments, but also put in the effort when it's needed. As Gay says: "RMC people are full of commitment, truly dedicated to their job. It's not unusual to see people working extraordinary hours to get the job done right. This spirit produces a kind of fellowship; it's like belonging to a family."

It has been suggested that, in the past, RMC did not have an especially open culture. Now there is a perception that things are changing. The culture is becoming more open and also more sophisticated where necessary. Driving this change are both the external environment and also sound business reasons. Many of the group's UK markets have reached a plateau, meaning that future growth can be helped by unlocking the potential of its employees and focusing on providing customers with outstanding service. RMC's quality, service and technical standards give it an in-built advantage here.

In the field of communications, the diversity of the group is perhaps a disadvantage. For the UK, there is a quarterly full-colour newsletter that is edited and printed in-house to a high standard; and many subsidiary companies produce their own communications vehicles. The group has recently appointed a head of corporate communications to develop world-wide communications.

Recently, a number of companies within the group have conducted attitude surveys and discussions. This process has produced an interesting debate, but it is acknowledged that it must go further and create changes where the employees' views do not match those of their managers. Again, increased openness must be the goal.

Human Resource Priorities

RMC regards human resources policy as important, as underlined by its goals in this area: to attract good people and develop them; to give them as much responsibility as they can handle and to prepare them for that responsibility; and to foster learning and the self-development process.

There's a strong feeling that complacency must be avoided at all costs. Chris Gay: "We're the market leader—but that's not enough in itself. We need to *stay* the market leader. One of the ways to maintain our competitive advantage is through HR policy: to promote openness, fairness and fitting rewards for work done. We're currently examining management styles where necessary, so as to ensure that people have the opportunity to make real contributions to the group's future."

At RMC, the attitude to HR is that the managers are there to manage people: and HR policy is to provide help through specialist advice in creating a climate which fosters that process. Although not board-represented, personnel people have all the access they need to ensure their concerns are discussed at the highest group level.

Career Opportunity and Development

Among other training schemes, RMC operates two schemes designed to attract graduates and holders of good HNDs: the Technical Management Development Scheme (for those holding civil engineering or science-based qualifications) and the Management Trainee Programme (for those holding engineering or business qualifications). Between 10 and 20 people join RMC through these schemes each year, often with work experience as well as academic qualifications.

The Technical Management Development Scheme is positioned as enabling the right candidates to move on to their first technical management roles within the group. A structured programme, the scheme combines planned work experience at different locations with formal technology and supervisory skills training. Chris Davies, who graduated in 1995 with a degree in Material Sciences from Oxford: "The training was well-structured and involved all aspects of the business. My work experience covered concrete companies in Wales, South West and East of England." After eight months he took up the post of technical training supervisor while continuing to receive further training.

The Management Trainee Programme prepares high calibre young people to take on management responsibility in a production or commercial role. Kirsty Coutts graduated in 1993 with a degree in Environmental Engineering. She commented: "I was attracted to RMC by the career opportunities and the comprehensive management training programme. The training lived up to my expectations and I had complete access to information and was encouraged to ask questions. In March 1996 I become an area operations manager responsible for nine concrete plants."

All RMC jobs for supervisor or above are advertised internally, and the group prefers to promote internally unless the required skills are not available. Most divisions have a system of identifying those with special potential, aided by annual assessment programmes. Limited job opportunities already exist in the group's overseas operations, a trend which is likely to increase in the future. Senior managers will almost certainly have gained experience in several UK operations.

The group is hugely committed to training. This is largely internal, aided by a superb training complex at its head office site in Surrey. There is also a team of regional training managers providing internal training within the regions. External training covers such schemes as NEBS and DMS, as well as some specialist courses.

There are many instances of people moving up through the ranks at RMC. The managing director of the Readymix Sand and Gravel Division was originally a sales representative, while the previous chairman joined as a field technician. A large number of employees have worked for the group for over 10 years, while periods of service of up to 40 years are not uncommon. The group continues to offer a strong career path.

Pay and Benefits

Pay within the construction materials sector is perhaps not as high as in some other sectors. However, RMC believes its levels are median or above for most grades. Pay rises are a function of affordability coupled with the person's knowledge, overall value and job responsibility.

Certain roles have pay bandings. Progress to the mid-point is planned, while further progress is slower but very much due to the sustained contribution made by the individual.

Benefits include an SAYE share-options scheme and an annual Christmas bonus. Every employee can join an occupational pension scheme.

The Future

RMC acknowledges that it needs to maintain its edge in the market place; this cannot be taken for granted. Creativity and innovation have taken the group to its present eminence, and these traits must continue to be found at all levels if it is to retain its market leadership.

Another challenge is to weld the group into a more cohesive whole. Each company has its own way of doing things in certain areas, and these approaches often contain innovations that can benefit the group as a whole. This is true both across the UK and world-wide, and RMC needs to make more of this potential and thereby reap more rewards from its international nature.

On the HR side, Chris Gay is convinced that people are the key to the group's future success. "We must take our people with us as we develop and ensure a flow of ideas and initiatives throughout the group. Drive and energy have brought us to where we are today, and they can help us become even more successful tomorrow."

Roche Products Ltd.

The main activities of Roche Products are the manufacture and sale of pharmaceutical specialities and fine chemicals in the fields of human health care and animal nutrition. The Roche Group is divided into four discrete business divisions: pharmaceuticals, vitamins and fine chemicals, diagnostics, and fragrances and flavours. The Swiss-based Roche Group is a truly international organisation, employing 55,000 people world-wide in operating affiliates in over 200 territories.

Roche Products UK Ltd. is one of eight major subsidiaries, with a turnover of £350 million in 1995; prescription pharmaceuticals accounted for 60% of sales. Roche Products UK Ltd. employs 2,400 staff at eight sites around the country.

Biggest Plus: An ambitious company in a challenging industry

Biggest Minus: In transition, within markets and within the organisation

Roche Products UK Ltd.
PO Box 8
Welwyn Garden City
Hertfordshire AL7 3AY
Tel: 01707-366000
Fax: 01707-338297

The Business

Roche has always been a leader in pioneering science. Creativity, professionalism and sophisticated automated systems are key productivity factors that help keep Roche at the cutting edge of pharmaceuticals research and development. Roche is committed to the discovery and development of novel pharmaceutical compounds and diagnostic systems directed at the underlying causes of diseases, and the company has played a leading role in efforts to combat AIDS-related conditions, as well as many others.

Across the Roche Group, pharmaceuticals is by far the largest business area. With the integration of Syntex in 1995, which enhanced Roche's position in world pharmaceutical markets particularly the USA, pharmaceuticals accounted for 63% of group sales in 1995.

Roche's vitamins and fine chemicals business represented 21% of sales, and is the world's largest supplier of vitamins. Diagnostics at 6% of sales, and fragrances and flavours at 10%, are both world leaders in their fields. In all of its activities, Roche has earned an international reputation for innovation and excellence.

In 1996 Roche celebrated its centenary and 100 years of considerable achievement. The company is looking forward to the next century with confidence.

Company Culture and Style

The world markets in which Roche operates are highly competitive, and are also experiencing radical change. The pace of development in bioscience is breathtaking, and customers are becoming increasingly complex in profile, and more cost-conscious in habit. Roche has been at the forefront of change, adapting quickly to stay ahead.

In the Roche Group's 1995 annual report, chairman Fritz Gerber noted: "They [the group's employees] have shown their willingness to take up the challenge posed by radical market change and their ability to constructively support the necessary internal structural adjustments, difficult as some of these have been."

In the UK, under the guidance of new managing director Nic Holladay, Roche Products UK Ltd. (Roche) is going through a period of significant cultural change. To meet the needs of a flatter, leaner organisation, bureaucratic attitudes have been swept away. A new environment fosters employee involvement and responsibility, an open culture, and an open management style.

At the forefront of change is 'Roche Leads', a programme for cultural and behavioural transformation designed to ensure that the company's considerable achievements will continue into the future.

Having conducted employee surveys, Roche identified six areas that it wanted to improve—performance management, internal communication, people development, customer commitment, values and behaviours, and human resources policies. Each area became a separate project under the 'Roche Leads' initiative.

The aim of 'Roche Leads' is simple—to create a high-performance environment that is rewarding for employees, encouraging everyone to play an active role in the company's continued success. And the philosophy underlying the programme is 'Roche leads by inspiring its people to win through innovation'.

Several initiatives are already in place and are having a positive impact. "Our main concern, however, is to build on the many fundamental strengths which Roche has always had, rather than force through any wholesale change. We do not want to throw the baby out with the bath water," says 'Roche Leads' project manager, Matthew Dyal.

Human Resource Priorities

Roche's UK divisions operate in increasingly competitive and demanding market sectors, and the human resources contribution must be fully integrated at each local business level to ensure alignment with business goals.

"The real challenge," observes Chris Bennett, human resources director of Roche UK, "is for the function to be less administrative and more business-oriented. HR must continue to make a genuine value-added contribution as an integral business partner in the management team."

Human resources priorities are based around six principal themes. Roche wants to attract and retain the highest calibre staff, and then encourage high performance, including measurement and recognition practices. This entails maintaining a competitive reward and remuneration strategy.

Sustaining a continuous programme of employee training and development is held to be crucial, something which Roche has a long-standing commitment to.

HR is playing a central role in the process of change, promoting, facilitating and encouraging the behavioural and organisational changes being implemented under the 'Roche Leads' programme. This also includes major efforts to support a high performance, open communication culture.

Career Opportunity and Development

There are exciting and rewarding careers to be had at Roche in many disciplines. Necessarily there are many opportunities in scientific research and development, but also in a range of commercial functions.

Joining Roche means joining a very international company. The UK operations all have strong ties with the corporate head office, and with other Roche companies around the world. Career opportunities are not confined to the UK, and may well include secondments to Switzerland, the USA, and other countries, as well as working in cross-functional project teams with colleagues from around the globe.

The company encourages training and development of staff appropriate to function. At the core of Roche's commitment is the concept of employability, recognising that employees at all levels require a basket of skills—for the benefit of the company, but also for the long-term benefit of the individual, whether they pursue a long-term career at Roche or elsewhere.

Roche has strengthened its training and development infrastructure. There are now around a dozen full-time training staff, of whom half are field-based, emphasising Roche's belief that on-the-job training is a vital part of its development portfolio and at least equal in effectiveness to traditional courses.

Staff are encouraged to take some responsibility for their own career development, with the company careful not to abdicate its responsibility for providing advice and training where needed.

"At the same time," says Chris Bennett, "the company must be open and honest since unrealistic expectations do no one any good; frank discussions and honest commitment are essential."

In the group context, Roche's UK HR development function is designing a range of development programmes to ensure the high quality development of its senior managers, to dovetail with head office Basel's top level programmes.

Graduate recruitment at both first degree and postgraduate level is vital to Roche's aim to recruit the best employees. Individuals joining Roche can look forward to high quality development that not only encourages the acquisition of skills, but also higher qualifications in business-related areas. A number of staff undertake PhDs and MBAs, while many others are pursuing other academic or vocational qualifications
.

Pay and Benefits

Roche maintains market competitive remuneration and benefit packages as an integral part of attracting and retaining high calibre employees. Increasingly, rewards recognise high individual and team performances.

Benefits include a final salary pension scheme rated in the upper quartile of industry schemes, free private healthcare insurance, progressive maternity (and paternity) arrangements, and an Employee Assistance Programme offering 24-hour professional advice and counselling. Each Roche site provides a variety of subsidised sports and social activities, restaurants and shops, and at the head office in Welwyn Garden City, a fully staffed occupational health centre.

The Future

Roche is facing up to market change by grasping opportunity. Nic Holladay, managing director of Roche UK, says "Roche has a very strong ambition to become a top five UK company by the year 2000, which is a big challenge because we're currently sixteenth. We're very strong in the hospital market where we're number four, but less strong in the retail sector, where we're number eighteen, and that's an area we need to expand urgently."

Roche has recently implemented a regionalisation process, aimed at bringing the company closer to its customers and getting more in tune with their objectives. Regionalisation has created five regions which mirror NHS boundaries. Changing from a product culture to a customer culture is not always an easy task, and there are dangers of getting too far ahead of the customer, but the response and feedback from Roche's field force has been encouraging.

Roche will need to continuously produce innovative products from its R&D pipeline, and continuing investment in new technology and processes will enhance Roche's ability to compete from its strong manufacturing base.

The future will undoubtedly hold further change for company and employee alike. This includes a shift from 'time-secured' to performance-led' employment, establishing a new contract between company and employee; in return for high performance and innovation from employees, the company will provide support and commitment to training and development to enhance all employees' future employability.

Rothmans International

Rothmans International

The fourth largest international tobacco company in the world, Rothmans operates in 160 territories across the globe, running 33 manufacturing plants and employing 20,800 staff. Rothmans also retains one of the largest trademark portfolios in the UK, encompassing over 50,000 marks.

Biggest Plus: Staunch believers in promotion from within

Biggest Minus: Staff may be posted to 'interesting' or remote countries

Rothmans International Services Ltd.
Denham Place
Village Road
Denham
Uxbridge
Middlesex UB9 5BL
Tel: 01895-834949
Fax: 01895-834757

The Business

Founded by South African entrepreneur Dr Anton Rupert, Rothmans is a truly global corporation. Having emerged from a period of reorganisation across Western Europe and North America, Rothmans is currently undergoing a period of rapid expansion throughout East and South Asia and Central and Eastern Europe. Only 10% of employees are based in the UK, including 200 staff at the corporate HQ in Denham. HQ's role is strategic—to create the policy framework within which regions and business units have licence to operate.

Company Culture and Style

Despite Rothmans' geographical diversity, the corporation retains a familial air. Emphasis is placed on relationships and mutual respect for colleagues. Rothmans strives to retain a human face, paying considerable attention to the needs of staff often seconded to remote parts of the globe.

The 'work hard, play hard' ethic flourishes at Rothmans, where stringent demands on lifestyle (e.g. anti-social hours, extensive travel, etc.) are balanced by appropriately generous rewards and opportunities to relax and have fun.

Rothmans thrives on diversity. While each business is managed locally, no one ever feels isolated This gives managers the scope for self-expression and creativity, allowing them to put their stamp on the business within the overall structure of the group.

"The way we manage our business," asserts HR director Alan Popham, "is appropriate to each local setting. There is no one way of doing things—our rule book is one of the thinnest I've ever come across. Underlying principles do shape people's behaviour, but they are adapted to suit local conditions.

"It also helps for people to know that we're in tobacco, and we're in it for the long haul. Rothmans is not seeking to diversify. Anyone joining our profitable and growing business must realise that we intend to keep it this way."

Rothmans firmly upholds the principle of equal opportunity, and is something of a melting pot of cultures and nationalities—18 are represented in one Swiss plant, and no less than 27 at another factory in the North East of England.

Displaying a similar tolerance towards staff encouraged to make their own choices, many Rothmans employees are non-smokers. That approach has paid handsome dividends, Rothmans' ongoing success being driven by pride of performance among a loyal and committed work force.

Human Resource Priorities

Rothmans' central HR team is charged with developing an enabling framework of forward-thinking policy and practice. Complex policy manuals are eschewed. The framework has clearly articulated principles which management on the ground can readily comprehend, interpret and adapt to local circumstances.

150 HR professionals are employed throughout the group and significant resources are devoted to the function. Dr Rupert established long ago that two key dynamics of the business were trademarks and people. HR is considered so vital at board level that only the marketing function is allocated more time on the management agenda.

Employee attitudes are canvassed on a regular basis although consistent measurement is complicated by geographical difficulties. What is appropriate and relevant in Great Britain may not apply in Vietnam. Rothmans has just completed an executive opinion survey across the top 300 managers in the group. Managers spanning five continents were invited to fill out questionnaires covering a range of corporate issues including business strategy and the effectiveness of decision-making processes, pay and benefits and career development prospects.

Career Opportunity and Development

Rothmans encourages staff to take responsibility for their own career planning. Career development workshops provide the requisite focus, identifying strengths and development needs, building personal plans of action in each case.

"There is no one route that takes you to where you want to be," observes Alan Popham. "We prefer to think in terms of a 'career lattice', painting pictures of the options available, allowing people to exercise choice."

Without subscribing to a philosophy of 'cradle to grave', Rothmans vigorously defends the principle of promotion from within. Rothmans' emphasis remains firmly on promoting from within, but occasionally, outside expertise is needed in particular skills or technical areas. International secondments are an integral part of the development process. Staff are expected to move across territories, meeting fresh challenges and migrating expertise.

To provide a comprehensive analysis of in-house capabilities, Management Development Reviews are held annually, to help put in place succession plans for the top 400 positions in the organisation. The chief executive takes a direct and personal interest in this process, which reviews management development programmes, cements succession plans and measures achievement against agreed goals.

This review process is based on management competence profiles. Built up over three years, the competencies pinpoint the attributes of successful managers, providing an objective basis for assessing future management talent.

"Our business," explains chief executive Bill Ryan, "has gone and will continue to go through a period of dramatic change, to the extent that management styles based around rigid central controls and hierarchies can no longer meet our needs. What we need for the future is a more dynamic, less bureaucratic empowering style of leadership.

"It is clearly not sufficient to develop your own leadership style in isolation. Managers must also strive to develop people below them as well, so that they also adopt this style and acquire the skills to meet future needs."

Such development programmes put high fliers on a fast-track to the top. Joining the company as a trainee accountant, Pieter Keijzer worked his way through the sales and marketing functions in the Netherlands, Switzerland and the UK before being appointed European chief executive at just 43 years of age.

Rothmans recruits 20 graduates in the UK each year on starting salaries ranging from £15–20,000. External qualifications (e.g. MBAs) are actively encouraged, usually through supported study rather than sabbaticals.

Pay and Benefits

Rothmans has a clear remuneration policy. Highly competitive in all pay-related matters, Rothmans has historically offered benefit packages in the upper quartile of the corporate sector. Reviewed on an annual basis, awards are governed by three prime determinants—market-place standards, individual performance, and overall business performance.

In years of business prosperity, staff share the fruits of their labour. Even when overall results fall short of expectations, however, individual achievement is recognised through pay. During the 1990s, pay increases have significantly outstripped inflation. Collective agreements are in place for the unionised work force, which are negotiated on a local basis.

As Rothmans is privately owned, there is no scope for employee share options. However, SAYE schemes are offered in line with local market practice, and incentive arrangements are also available to sales-oriented categories of staff. All such schemes tend to be volume rather than profit-driven rewards determined by hitting pre-set targets. No more than 15–20% of salary is usually 'at risk' in such cases.

Rothmans operates a flexible company car scheme. Upper limits exist for each level of management, but those eligible can either opt out altogether (taking a cash alternative) or contribute towards a superior model.

All UK employees are covered by private medical insurance, an area of special focus at Rothmans. The company's own doctors scrutinise medical facilities in every corner of the globe, safeguarding the welfare of employees by placing rescue and emergency services on stand-by where necessary.

Pension scheme arrangements also extend to all employees, while maternity leave is consistent across the group. Paternity leave arrangements continue to evolve, varying in line with local practice.

The Future

Rothmans has reached a crossroads. North American and European markets are now mature and staying competitive demands leaner organisational structures. The downsizing and delayering process in these mature markets is almost complete, but opportunities for promotion have diminished as a result. Staff are encouraged to move across functions and territories, especially into rapidly expanding markets, broadening their canvas of skills before taking the next step upwards.

Moving towards a new millennium, the HR challenge at Rothmans is two-fold: to continuously upgrade management skill levels to handle fresh international challenges; and to create an environment that will harness the creativity and innovative abilities of all staff. If it succeeds, Rothmans will continue to be an exciting company to work for.

Ryder

Ryder plc is Britain's leading highway transportation services supplier. Its parent company, Ryder System, Inc. of Miami, USA, is one of the world's largest providers of road-based transportation, has operating revenues of $5 billion, employs over 44,000 people, and maintains a fleet of over 200,000 vehicles. Ryder plc's turnover in 1995 was £182 million, and the company employs some 3,100 people in the UK.

Biggest Plus: A strong sense of job security

Biggest Minus: You can't always ask your boss for the answer!

Ryder PLC
Ryder House
16 Bath Road
Slough   SL1 3SA
Tel: 01753-735000
Fax: 01753-735499

The Business

Ryder was founded in 1933 in the USA, when citrus fruit shipper Jim Ryder found himself with excess transportation capacity. He decided to hire his idle trucks to his neighbours—and in so doing quickly created a profitable business. The organisation began to expand geographically in 1971 when it created Ryder plc in the UK. The corporation now has operations in Poland, Germany, Canada and South America. Meanwhile, in less than 30 years, Ryder plc has come to dominate the UK road transportation services industry.

Many people think of truck rental when they think of Ryder plc: not surprisingly given the familiarity of the yellow rental trucks on Britain's roads. The company has over 50 rental outlets, over 2,500 rental vehicles and 24-hour roadside assistance. But this is just part of Ryder's operations. The company also provides global freight management, defence contracts, nationwide home delivery and vehicle insurance services, and is a major player in the fast-growing field of integrated logistics.

In the last six years, while some companies in the sector have stagnated or apparently lost direction, Ryder has had a clear vision that has helped its revenues triple. Small wonder that journalists regularly look to Ryder for leadership comments when it comes to industry matters.

Company Culture and Style

Ryder plc's impressive growth throughout its 25-year history has made it that rare thing: a company with a strong sense of job security. From drivers to executives, anyone willing to work hard and build a career can do so at Ryder; indeed, opportunities are probably outstripping work-force size. This culture of security, growth and strong direction permeates the company. Employees and outsiders alike see it as a company that is going places.

It's also a very open company. Rather than having hordes of secretaries and support staff, people tend to do things for themselves. Staff are on first-name terms, and the bosses take a hands-on approach. Flexibility is the watchword of the operation; employees see their role as providing solutions to transportation challenges. As a result, people willingly take ownership of problems, even where they fall outside their job descriptions. Empowerment is high and the company has a devolved structure.

Managing director John Hodges sums up the culture: "We expect people to work hard, but also to find the work interesting and stimulating. We try to watch the market and develop with it, so we ask our people to think. You can't always ask your boss for the answer here! That's because we try to find solutions to customers' problems—and find them at the front line."

Culture and style come together in the company's communications programme. This includes *Ryder Viewpoint,* a friendly quarterly newsletter for staff, and a glossy production, *Ryder Solutions,* for customers as well as employees. There is also a video four times a year, team briefings cascaded downwards, bulletins, press cuttings and annual conferences: one company-wide event and smaller gatherings for the various groupings within the company.

To help promote excellence, the group has an incentive scheme known as the

Ryder Roundtable. This scheme, for contract hire sales, rental sales and (new in 1996) maintenance, recognises the best of the best who can meet stringent and long-term superlative standards. Selected by their peers, the top people are then inducted into an elite club that carries with it a coveted yellow jacket. There are 200 Roundtable members, including nine from the UK. As demonstration of their excellence, those nine have generated revenues in excess of £250 million.

Human Resource Priorities

The company's stated HR aims are to attract, retain and develop high calibre staff; treat all staff with dignity and respect; and encourage empowerment through involvement and devolution. A personnel director at board level helps ensure these aims are met, while close liaison with line management and joint reviews of policy underline their implementation on the ground.

For Hodges, HR is much more than simply filling in forms. "In practice, we want our HR department to be proactive. I believe that HR should give management the tools to manage, such as competitive remuneration and benefits packages, and innovative policies and procedures. If the company looks after the employees they will look after the customer, and this is essential in a service organisation like Ryder where the customer is king."

The effectiveness of this policy can be seen at all levels of the organisation and ultimately in the high standards of customer care Ryder achieves. Despite a turnover that approaches £200 million, Hodges received only ten complaints in 1996.

Career Opportunity and Development

Although most of Ryder's top jobs are already held by graduates, a formal graduate recruitment programme was started only this year. The scheme is set to expand in the future. The ideal graduate trainee is said to possess motivation, innovation, planning and action skills, commercial awareness, and both teamwork and leadership potential.

Other recruitment schemes are important at Ryder, including a well-established apprenticeship programme. The company speaks to schools and colleges to overturn negative perceptions, including a widespread belief that jobs in road transportation are unpleasant and lacking in career direction. John Hodges cites as typical of Ryder's career development programme's possibilities an employee who started as a mechanic and now manages 20 garages.

But whether school leaver or graduate, the people most likely to succeed at Ryder are intelligent, flexible, and practical: they have a 'can do' attitude. For those in this mould, career development can be swift. The current personnel manager was once Hodges's secretary; the director of rental started as a rental rep; and Hodges himself is the first Briton to be MD of Ryder UK.

Career development is aided by succession planning to evaluate people in terms of competencies rather than by job title, experience or other criteria. Development to the next level requires certain competencies, added to by training, new responsibilities or other routes. There are also several opportunities each year to develop a career by working abroad, particularly in the USA.

Training is taken seriously at Ryder, with total training spend doubled over the last year. The UK operation benefits from the huge training facility in place in Miami. UK staff often evaluate US training programmes in terms of their suitability for the UK. There is also a wide range of in-house training, from management skills to special projects. The company sponsors MBA study and currently has four MBAs on the payroll.

Redundancies are rare: only 1% of the work force has been made redundant since 1990. Nevertheless, contracts come and go and job losses are occasionally inevitable—although the company always tries to redeploy people if possible. Where this cannot be done, compensation is paid and outplacement counselling is offered to senior managers.

Pay and Benefits

Out of the entire UK work force, 1,800 are drivers, mechanics, maintenance engineers and warehouse staff, traditionally not highly paid roles. Yet Ryder is competitive throughout its industry—and at the very top in terms of rewards to its sales people. Managers' pay can range from £15,000 to £47,000, while executive director salaries average £55,000.

Pay increases are decided through an appraisal system, which evaluates many aspects of performance against set targets and produces a grading of 0–5. A grading of 3 would result in a pay increase in line with inflation, with 4 or 5 producing a pay rise in real terms, perhaps as high as 10%. The system is one of self-appraisal that is then discussed and agreed by the boss or manager.

Benefits at Ryder include a share option scheme for all staff, an executive share option scheme, an incentive share plan for senior management based on profitability, a profit-related pay scheme (unusual for this industry), private medical insurance for middle and senior management, a company doctor for private consultation, an excellent final salary pension scheme whereby if the employee contributes 2–4% of salary the company will contribute 10% of salary, a relocation package, and company cars for managers and on an 'as-needed' basis.

The Future

On the business front, an important challenge is cost. As Hodges puts it, "How do you cope with that pressure while still remaining a human company which looks after its employees?"

Perhaps the biggest challenge for Ryder plc, though, is to continue to grow the company. John Hodges: "We want to remain a leading contract hire, integrated logistics and rental company. We believe we provide a better service, and we must continue to do so."

This requires a supply of future managers, but these cannot be simply acquired. Rather, they have to be recruited, retained and developed. The supply of new managers can ultimately put a brake on the company's growth rate; however, it is doing its part to develop this flow through its apprentice, graduate and other recruitment schemes. If the company continues to treat its work force as it has done in the past, its future, even in the competitive market place of the next century, looks assured.

SAINSBURY'S

J Sainsbury plc

J Sainsbury plc is one of the world's leading retailers, operating four separate store chains in the UK and USA, which together serve more than 12 million customers a week. In the year to 9 March 1996, group sales were £13.5 billion and group pre-tax operating profits £854 million. The group employs 160,000 full-time and part-time staff, most of whom work in the UK.

Biggest Plus: Great training, diverse opportunities

Biggest Minus: Intense pressures in UK food retailing

J Sainsbury plc
Stamford House
Stamford Street
London SE1 9LL
Tel: 0171-921 6000
Fax: 0171-921 6496

The Business

Founded in London in 1869, Sainsbury's was privately owned until 1973, when the company was floated on the London Stock Exchange. Sainsbury's supermarkets remain the largest part of the group, accounting for 87% of pre-tax profit. The aim for the supermarkets is to be the first choice of the British consumer for food shopping: it is Britain's most profitable retailer, and the largest of the 365 stores stock over 20,000 product lines.

In the UK, the group also owns Savacentre, the country's only specialist hypermarket company, and Homebase, a chain of home improvement and garden centres. Homebase recently acquired Texas Homecare, which it is currently integrating with its own operations.

The group's US holdings comprise Shaw's Supermarkets, Inc., a chain of 101 New England stores. It also has a 20% interest in Giant Food, Inc., a supermarket group that is the market leader in Washington, DC and in Baltimore.

Company Culture and Style

The various operations of the group have their separate cultures, but overall is dominated by Sainsbury's supermarkets, which employ 115,000 people in the UK: two-thirds of the total are women and the same proportion work part-time. A real sense of pride in the Sainsbury's identity is to be found both in the supermarkets and in the other parts of the group—as evidenced by a recent staff survey.

Underlying that sense of pride are the principles which Sainsbury's embodies: quality and value run through everything. Both staff and customers receive the highest standards. Customers depend on the company for efficiency, convenience and service, while staff have outstanding opportunities in terms of both personal career development and reward relative to the rest of the sector.

So, what type of person flourishes at Sainsbury's? Food retailing is a fast-changing and often unpredictable world, and Sainsbury's is able to react to those changes through its dynamism, flexibility and innovative approach. Men and women with these qualities are likely to progress rapidly; other useful attributes would include good people focus, the ability to work as part of a team, a desire to take responsibility at an early stage, creativity, assertiveness and flair.

These broad aspects of the culture have been in place for many years, but the overall style has changed somewhat in recent years. A major restructuring process began in 1994 has helped to reduce the levels of hierarchy and make the company a more open and empowered place. However, hard work and pressure are as evident as ever.

A group-wide JS Journal is produced. This is a large, full-colour 24-page monthly packed with interesting information about product and personnel initiatives, and staff news. The June 1996 issue covered among other things the 'Talk-back' employee attitude survey, in which staff were encouraged to give their opinions about the company in a questionnaire—and an impressive 83% of staff responded. Other communications initiatives include a growing use of email, meetings, noticeboards and conferences.

Human Resource Priorities

At Sainsbury's, HR is a board-level issue, and the values of the company are constantly aired and discussed at this level. The company is committed to the welfare and development of its staff—although it acknowledges that it could do even more in this area. Nevertheless, much has already been done.

Personnel director John Adshead: "One of our corporate objectives at Sainsbury's is to offer all our staff outstanding opportunities in terms of their own personal career development. In support of this commitment we spent £30 million on training and development last year." The 'Choices' programme offers staff career guidance and helps them to identify ways of achieving their potential.

Career Opportunities and Development

Sainsbury's has both a school leaver's recruitment and a graduate recruitment scheme. The latter has taken graduate intakes for over 20 years. As such, it understands the needs and aspirations of graduates better than many employers. Of 750 management trainees, including business placements and vacation training, around 550 will be graduates. Graham Jolly recalled his time on the business placement scheme: "On a day-to-day basis we were assigned to departments on two- or four-weekly periods, shadow managers, or cover for them if they're away from the store. You learn about the way things operate very quickly. You're also paid between £11,000 and £14,000 for your placement year, so if you're trying to save for your final year, it's a real bonus."

Rebecca Liebling joined Homebase following graduation with a Design and Media Management degree. "I was looking for a challenging retail environment where I could develop my skills. Homebase painted the best picture. After completing the Management Training Scheme with placements across the business—Warehouse, Garden Centre and DIY—I'm now deputy DIY manager at Croydon."

Whether school leaver, graduate or other recruit, promotion can be rapid for talented, hard-working individuals who are prepared to commit to the business and its future. A significant number of high-ranking people started at the bottom and worked their way up. John Adshead: "In one district alone, three managers started in the company as a warehouseman, a checkout operator and a replenishment assistant. All had moved through the training and development programmes to run stores employing 700 staff and with a multi-million pound turnover." David Bremner recently rejoined the company at board level having originally entered as a graduate trainee, and a number of board directors have risen through the ranks.

The group takes training very seriously. The nature of this is changing to make it more effective. In the past, there was a tendency to assume that employees needed to be trained in everything. The trend now is to tailor training to individual needs, experience and skills to produce good, well-rounded people able to progress more rapidly.

Following intense training at entry levels, it continues in a more flexible way through a blend of internal and external workshops. Self-help packages in learning centres and elsewhere assist with development; and self-managed learning is actively encouraged. The stores themselves also have a significant commitment to training, both within the stores and at district training centres.

Pay and Benefits

The company believes itself to be competitive in its industry sectors. Remuneration is increasingly about merit, aided by introducing in-store incentives for those who meet both their profitability and sales targets. An annual performance review helps work out each individual's competency on a 1–7 scale, and hence the pay increase due.

Graduates expected to start on £14,600 in 1996, rising to £17,000 or so if they have relevant work experience. Senior middle managers would be looking at £25,000 to £35,000 depending on the location and their experience.

Benefits include a profit-share scheme that can be taken in shares or cash, a staff discount scheme, an SAYE share option scheme, and a contributory final salary scheme that includes life cover. At certain levels, private health insurance and cars are provided. Holiday entitlement ranges from 22 days to 27 days at senior levels. Subsidised meals are provided, and the Sainsbury's Staff Association subsidises all kinds of activities from sport to theatre.

The Future

The UK food retailing sector is particularly competitive and cut-throat at present, with discounting having an adverse effect on profitability. Increasingly, supermarkets are looking for additional revenue streams, and Sainsbury's has been slower than others in exploiting the sale of petrol at its sites. The announcement of a deal with the Bank of Scotland to offer banking facilities in its supermarkets, and experiments with home delivery of telephone-ordered groceries shows that the company is nimble and innovative enough to rise to the challenge.

It is its core business that the company will want to address most, however, with Sainsbury's still smarting from having been overtaken by Tesco as the number one food retailer in the UK.

John Adshead: "Change has been the most consistent theme of the century and the pace of change has been accelerating. This has meant that it has become increasingly difficult to keep up with and to meet the challenges that the rapidly developing living and working environment demands of us all." The way to meet that challenge is to remain flexible: to meet the challenge of change and to never stop learning. Certainly, Sainsbury's flexibility, its ability to broaden its appeal through acquisition, and its determination to restructure itself for the future augur well in these areas.

Scottish Equitable

Scottish Equitable

Scottish Equitable is a life insurer headquartered in Edinburgh that has established itself as one of the top pension providers in the UK. It has 2,200 staff, 650 of them in 32 branches across the country, and is part of the international Aegon group based in the Netherlands.

Biggest Plus: Company knows where it is going and is trusted to provide job security

Biggest Minus: In a rapidly changing industry margins could be squeezed and so could pay

Scottish Equitable plc
Edinburgh Park
Edinburgh EH12 9SE
Tel: 0131-339 9191
Fax: 0131-549 4242

The Business

In the early 1990s, Scottish Equitable made a series of highly successful and well-timed executive decisions. It opted to turn itself from a mutually owned organisation into an arm of a financially strong continental insurance group, before the pressures on small mutual insurers began to bite. It also decided to concentrate on its core pension business, at a time of growing opportunities for well-focused providers with good products and performance.

It made one of the few serious attempts by a UK company to establish a European presence, which is now bearing fruit as the market opens up. Most importantly, it began to align its business strategy with its human resources perspective, in a series of initiatives designed to link performance with reward.

Its new business has increased in the past three years by over 20% at a time when many rivals have been pedalling hard just to stand still.

Company Culture and Style

In many organisations, a change of ownership can generate uncertainty, turbulence in staff morale, and a climate where individual performance may go off the boil. Not so in the marriage of Scottish Equitable with Aegon of Holland, which was formalised on 1 January 1994. Any loss of identity as an independent Scottish institution, founded in 1831, has been more than outweighed by the awareness of a financially strong parent who has taken a healthy interest without interference. Staff know Aegon wants a good return from its protégé, is getting it, and is prepared to back success with reward. The cultures of the two organisations were a close fit.

Group personnel director Gareth Humphreys describes the tone as relaxed but professional. "It is an unusual and difficult combination, and it comes from quite a protracted period of business success, which makes it a lot easier to set the right kind of tone for the organisation."

A recent staff association survey found that job security was the most important issue, and that staff by and large trusted the company to provide it. Branches have been increased from 30 to 32, at a time when many companies have been losing branches as the market squeezes weaker players out of it, which demonstrates the company's confidence in the future.

Although the company's structure is flatter, there has not been dramatic change. Rather, the style has been to harness systems, processes, staff and management to a customer focus, to enable a quick and flexible response to a changing market.

That means people must be asked to contribute internally, and be willing to listen externally. Gareth Humphreys: "And it is fun, to be around people who are committed and professional; there is a buzz about the place."

Human Resource Priorities

The group sees its three key achievements in recent years as the introduction of performance management, performance-related pay, and enhanced flexible benefits. This demonstrates the priority for human resources, served by 16 HR professionals in a 70-strong personnel and training department.

The company is participating in 1996 in a benchmarking exercise involving a number of major financial services companies. It holds focus groups of staff to discuss HR performance, and attaining Investors in People is now under way.

The company has used its success to cushion the impact of necessary restructuring that has swept through the banking and insurance industry. Although staff are switching from an administrative 'back office' role to an active role in supporting the independent financial advisers (IFAs) who are the company's principal distribution channel, the exercise begun in mid-1996 does not have to be completed until the end of 1997.

The company is self-critical about its internal communications, reflecting its view of their importance. Media and methods include the company magazine *Equinox*, a management publication *Prismatic*, team briefings that have been relaunched to ensure a more interactive two-way format, and chief executive's briefings for the 100-strong management group. The new open plan HQ, where only the executive have cellular offices, helps to ensure that an open door communications policy is a reality.

Career Opportunity and Development

"Retention and development of quality staff has remained a key policy," says marketing director Graham Dumble. "A changing, enhanced staff benefit programme and a move to new purpose-built premises, which form a superb working environment, are evidence of this ongoing commitment."

Scottish Equitable runs an in-house structured training programme for staff up to middle management. It acknowledges that less attention has in the past been paid to senior management needs and is developing a new training and development programme to enable middle managers to move up, and top management to develop further. The company has a good record in training and promoting its own managers.

The Aegon connection is now bringing some opportunities for secondment to Holland and other countries including USA and Spain, while the steady growth of Scottish Equitable International based in Luxembourg offers another avenue for learning new skills.

Open learning, as an extension of computer-based training, has been developed to a relatively high level, and is used increasingly on skills training and some aspects of management training. A Scottish Equitable health and safety learning package, on display screen equipment, has been adopted by the Scottish Office. There is a regular intake of graduates as actuarial, investment and IT trainees, and the investment and IT staff are largely former graduate trainees.

Pay and Benefits

Edinburgh's financial companies are in a centre of professional excellence in actuarial and investment skills. That means a core of well-paid specialist jobs, as well as diverse professional opportunities in the departments of sales, marketing, customer services and finance.

The company sees itself as striving for value—for the individual, and for the company. Performance-related pay was introduced at a time of low inflation, which created some negative impressions among staff of the new system. But surveys have found them to be generally satisfied on how it works. Appraisal is twice a year, related either to competencies or objectives, and each employee is rated on a 0–4 scale.

The increase available for salaries across the group in 1996 was 4%, which was then split between divisions, and finally between individuals, whose rises ranged from 0 to 8–9% and in a few cases 11%. The company aims to be competitive on basic pay, rather than market leaders. But it may be adding significant value with its benefits package.

The most radical and intriguing initiative has been Equiflex, the comprehensive flexible benefits package introduced in 1996. 42% of staff, a high take-up, have opted to flex their benefits in the first year, with 20% opting for shopping vouchers, 18% for dental insurance, and a small number for child care vouchers. The take-up has been impressive, given the already strong benefits package which includes subsidised mortgages. Two days' holiday have been added to Equiflex menu already, and mortgage and pension benefits may be added in the next stage of the programme.

New owner Aegon has introduced share options for all staff, and the first tranche of 50 shares given to all staff in 1994 is already showing a profit of over £2,000. Judging by the number of staff who daily use their screens to check the Aegon share price, the share option scheme is working.

The Future

In an industry where poor training, miss-selling and high charging have made the news in the 1990s, Scottish Equitable has maintained its reputation and brand image as reliable, trustworthy, and Scottish.

It has led to the company becoming the leading pension provider through IFAs. That means its staff can continue to be winners in the pensions revolution that will ensure rising demand for the group's core products. But only the consistent performers will prosper, so key investment professionals will have to be retained and developed.

There will also be opportunities in Europe and beyond, as the market opens up, and management will have to continue to show the patience of the early 1990s when they persevered in Italy in spite of slow progress. Looking ahead to the millennium, Scottish Equitable has to continue to deliver high levels of profitable new business, and it has acknowledged that its people are a key aspect of delivering that. Quality, innovation, and quick response to the market will be critical.

But for that business to be profitable, costs have to be contained. There will be a growing emphasis on productivity, and flexibility in working patterns—using the impressive new facilities to full advantage rather than as Monday to Friday nine to five offices. Graham Dumble said: "Scottish Equitable has a strong capital position, a strong market position, and a low level of expenses by current industry standards. It is this combination that enables us to take full advantage of the opportunities available by offering competitive product terms while retaining the margins necessary for growth. Staff will be a fundamental feature of this growth."

SCOTTISH & NEWCASTLE plc

Scottish & Newcastle

Scottish & Newcastle is a fast-growing business with interests in three major sectors—brewing, licensed retailing and leisure. The company is focused clearly on branded consumer goods. Scottish & Newcastle plc is an FTSE-100 company, with turnover for the year to April 1996 of £2,969 million. Scottish & Newcastle (S&N) employs 48,000 people world-wide, 41,000 in the UK.

In S&N's beer portfolio are well-known brand names such as Foster's, John Smith's, Theakston, Courage, Newcastle Brown Ale, McEwan's, Millers, Holsten, Coors and Beck's. In licensed retailing, branded pubs targeted at defined customer groups include Chef & Brewer, Barras & Co., T&J Bernard, Rat & Parrot, Homespreads and Old Orleans. In leisure, Center Parcs has led the sector for 30 years and the name Pontin's is synonymous with holiday clubs in the UK.

Biggest Plus: Fast-growing business, into many areas outside its traditional brewing interests

Biggest Minus: Individual subsidiaries are different and independent; little integration

Scottish & Newcastle plc
Abbey Brewery
Holyrood Road
Edinburgh EH8 8YS
Tel: 0131-556 2591
Fax: 0131-557 2178

The Business

While Scottish & Newcastle's historical roots are in brewing, the company has witnessed spectacular growth in recent years, extending its interests into retail and leisure, as well as expanding its brewing interests. The different businesses in the group operate fairly autonomously, and necessarily are at different stages of their evolution.

In 1995, the company achieved its long-term strategic objective of becoming a truly national UK beer business with the £425 million acquisition of Courage. The newly merged company—Scottish Courage—has a powerful brand portfolio, national strength and market share of approximately 30%.

In 1993, the company acquired the Chef & Brewer pub group from Grand Metropolitan in a £700 million deal. Scottish & Newcastle Retail now owns 2,600 pubs spread across the UK, with a strong concentration in London.

The company's leisure interests were formed in 1989 with the purchase of the majority shareholding in Center Parcs from its Dutch founder. Center Parcs revolutionised the short break holiday market in Holland three decades ago, and repeated this in the UK when the first holiday village was opened at Sherwood Forest in 1987.

Today, Center Parcs operates 13 holiday villages in Holland, Belgium, France, Germany and the UK, while Pontin's has 18 holiday centres in the UK, Jersey and Ireland. Superchoice, first to build a dedicated American-style summer camp in the UK, offers American-style holidays and educational courses for British youngsters from two sites in Dorset and the Isle of Wight.

Commenting on the company's dynamic business development, chairman Sir Alick Rankin said in the 1996 Annual Report: "Our group strategy today is little changed from a year ago. The focus rests on retailing, brewing and short break leisure. Each has almost unlimited potential, each has scope for organic growth both at home and overseas. Our forward view can now encompass a truly international perspective..."

Company Culture and Style

While each division of the company is largely autonomous, Scottish & Newcastle's clear focus is on the provision of quality branded consumer goods and services. In recent years, the company's competitive position in this regard has been enhanced through investment, commercial initiatives and employee training and development.

The growth of the company to its present day size, along with its divisional format, has resulted in a diversity of related cultures suited to individual business environments. These cultures are all underpinned by a number of key values as expressed by Henry Fairweather, group personnel and services director. "We seek to be a sharp performance-oriented business and to encourage people at all levels in the group to contribute to our performance. We aim to be a responsible company, to establish good relationships with our employees, our shareholders, our customers, our suppliers and the community at large."

Communication is another cornerstone as evidenced by S&N's recent decision to develop its long-standing Chairman's Forum into a European Works Council, giving a wider platform for employees from every part of the company to express their views. There are also well-established vehicles for communication, discussion and negotiation in each of the businesses.

Human Resource Priorities

Throughout Scottish & Newcastle, human resources policy is linked to business strategy, with all divisions having a personnel influence at board level. Since Center Parcs (UK) gained accreditation three years ago, Investors in People is being successfully pursued by the company at business unit level and this is an indication of the importance placed on people in achieving business success.

Within Scottish Courage, the recent focus has been on the successful integration of the two companies, with consolidated terms and conditions being achieved for some 2,000 managers in little over a year. Communication played a vital role in ensuring the integration went smoothly, with regular briefings, newsletters and conferences keeping all employees fully informed.

To support business objectives, Scottish & Newcastle Retail offers the largest National Vocational Qualification (NVQ) programme in the industry and since being established in 1991, Scottish & Newcastle Retail has won many national awards for training and development.

In the UK, Center Parcs has embarked on a fundamental review of its human resources strategy to develop new ways of promoting stable employment opportunities with a strong guest-oriented and continuous improvement culture—an approach mirrored in the European Center Parcs philosophy.

Career Opportunity and Development

The diversity of S&N's businesses offers a wealth of fascinating career opportunities, both within each division and across the company. Employees can pursue general managerial careers, but there is also considerable scope for specialists. S&N makes a considerable investment in new product development, for example, which presents many opportunities for innovative marketeers.

Individual career reviews, focusing on training and development needs as well as aspirations for the future, form the basis of subsequent employee development activity. S&N plays a supportive and encouraging role in career development, but increasingly, individuals are asked to share the responsibility for their own careers.

Recent acquisitions have created many career opportunities and internal promotion features strongly in all parts of the company, with more formal career paths mapped out in many cases. Movement across the company is encouraged and increasingly this has an international perspective, both for secondments and permanent moves. In this way, employees enhance their knowledge and skills, to the benefit of both individual and the company.

Given Scottish & Newcastle's dynamic and continuing growth, external recruitment at all levels will continue, adding to the pool of internal talent.

Pay and Benefits

S&N's approach to pay and benefits is to offer attractive packages, which also recognise individual contribution. Incentive schemes are also an important element in its pay and benefits strategy and are determined at business unit level to ensure a close link to business objectives.

Some 19,000 employees are shareholders, as a result of an employee profit-sharing scheme that ploughs back up to 5% of company profits into buying shares for employees. In addition, a savings-related share option scheme offers employees the chance to buy shares in the company at a 20% discount to the market price.

Flexible benefits packages are now available to senior managers, increasing the scope for individual choice in pay and benefits.

"Our aim is to maintain competitive pay and benefit levels which enable Scottish & Newcastle to attract and retain top calibre people. Our policies are also designed to encourage a high level of individual performance," says Henry Fairweather.

The Future

The fundamental challenge across the group is to tune its people into ever-changing and evolving consumer markets. "While consumers throughout Europe are becoming more fickle, more demanding and better informed, they are also showing a willingness to spend on superior products which offer quality and value," says chief executive, Brian Stewart. "The challenge in all of our businesses is to understand and track this discriminating consumer, to recognise the opportunities and to move quickly to capitalise on them."

The company is also re-examining the values that remain core to the whole S&N business. While it will continue to encourage and nurture the individual identities and cultures of the individual businesses, S&N believes that certain core values are important, and to which all divisions should adhere.

Scottish & Newcastle now has a pre-eminent position in UK brewing and licensed retailing and plans to build on this strength. Its international business is expanding rapidly with Newcastle Brown Ale enjoying cult status in the USA and opportunities are being pursued in places as far apart as China, South Africa and Australia. Scottish & Newcastle has firm plans to expand all three of its core businesses in beer, licensed retailing and leisure over the coming years and this successful growth story look set to continue.

Severn Trent Water

Severn Trent Water

Severn Trent Water forms the major part of Severn Trent plc, one of the world's leading water and waste companies, and is listed among the top 100 UK companies by turnover, which stood at over £1 billion in 1996. The Water company, employing around 5,800 people, provides water to more than 8 million people in an area of the Midlands stretching from Gloucester to Mansfield and Shrewsbury to Leicester; it also takes dirty water away, treats it and returns it to the rivers. This task has far-reaching consequences for health and the environment, and the utmost importance is attached to high standards. This has resulted in the highest quality of water and treated sewage in Britain.

Biggest Plus: An ambitious water company which has shed the bureaucracy of the old utilities

Biggest Minus: Bad image of water companies generally—fat cats, leaks and hose-pipe bans

Severn Trent Water Ltd.
2297 Coventry Road
Birmingham B26 3PU
Tel: 0121-722 4000
Fax: 0121-722 4800

The Business

Since the UK privatisation of water authorities in 1979, Severn Trent Water has gone through dramatic change. The work force has been reduced from 11,000 to around 5,800 and the ethos has changed from that of a public authority to "A lean, highly profitable business delivering a cost-effective service to the increasingly high level demanded by customers," as Austin Todd, human resources and logistics director, explains.

The word 'customer' is significant, as previously the focus was on 'supplying consumers', while now it is about 'satisfying customers'. This underlying cultural shift has come about through less bureaucracy and a more streamlined management, using new technology and working to develop its employees. Staff have accepted these changes, overcome the upheavals, and now feel they have clearer objectives with better focus and fewer hierarchies.

Supplying over 2,000 million litres of water every day and treating 2,740 million litres of sewage demands an efficient infrastructure, and plants are being upgraded continuously. Cleaning rivers, conserving water, promoting environmental awareness among customers and the community, even caring for nature reserves and woodlands, are all part of Severn Trent's work.

Company Culture and Style

The changes have led to a flatter management structure with more emphasis on teamwork. Severn Trent has adopted a set of seven 'company values' which permeate its culture. These are teamwork, integrity, care, competence, openness, respect and drive. Austin Todd describes openness as the key driving force within the company—key to both culture and communications, with a wide range of initiatives designed to achieve this. Among these are local improvement groups; a scheme called 'Brainwaves', which rewards employees for good ideas; *Newstream*, an in-house publication sent each month to employees' home addresses, and 'Hot News', ad hoc bulletins cascaded throughout the entire work force within a working day when the need arises.

Another feature is an annual questionnaire called 'Quest' that gives all employees the chance to feed back anonymously their views on job satisfaction, their manager and other aspects of their work. This is externally assessed and managers are then expected to react positively to the views of their staff.

Staff who go the extra mile are rewarded through another scheme called 'Saying Thanks', which provides gift vouchers for extra good work. An explicit company aim is that people should enjoy their work and increasing levels of job satisfaction show that this is indeed the case.

Competence is also key to delivering high quality services, and the company's commitment to training and NVQs illustrates this. Vic Cocker, chief executive of Severn Trent plc, emphasises the need for continuous improvement, saying "I am convinced that the provision of consistently high levels of quality and consumer service is the key to our development as a water utility. Inevitably, this means that we will have to review constantly the way we approach the delivery of our services

332

in order to find new and better ways of working. The staff of Severn Trent Water have helped to develop the culture of quality and service excellence which I believe lies at the heart of our business and our continued success."

Human Resource Priorities

The human resources and logistics director sits on the board, ensuring that HR has a key strategic input to the company. The aim of the HR department as described by Austin Todd is "To provide a cost-effective, high quality HR service to its internal customers, ensuring a continual supply of good quality employees who are well taken care of, feel valued, and are trained with the appropriate skills."

The seven company values shape HR policies, with particular emphasis on open communications and competence. The appraisal scheme brings together competence and company values and gives people the opportunity to identify their plans for career development and training. It also links into pay and bonus schemes.

There is a clear board directive that the dramatic slimming of the work force must enable people to leave the company with dignity; both internal and external outplacement services have been used, combined with good severance terms and an early retirement scheme. The reduction in staff numbers has been achieved through voluntary redundancy and natural wastage, with no industrial relations disputes since privatisation.

The Worcester Operational District is piloting Investors in People and there is commitment to build on this first trial.

Career Opportunity and Development

A formal career management system is being introduced, expanding on the new assessment centre format used previously. The Performance Review and Development (PRD) appraisal scheme identifies individuals with management potential. Candidates go through a management development programme and come out wiser for the experience and with the possibility of promotion.

A company target is that 85% of vacancies should be filled internally. Many directors have risen through the company, including Austin Todd, the managing director, and the customer services director, who joined as a manager of a small sewage works.

There are opportunities to work abroad in the USA, Belgium and Trinidad, and overseas secondments can be for weeks or years.

The training department provides and oversees training at all levels—nearly 3,000 craft and industrial staff have achieved NVQs and 750 customer service staff will go through the NVQ scheme. There is a YTS scheme linking with BTec. Management training takes place at Warwick University, with a small number of people sponsored on its MBA course.

The graduate recruitment scheme takes up to 30 people each year, mainly in operations, finance, engineering and purchasing. Most graduates stay with the company and can advance from a starting salary of around £14,000 (in 1996) to £18,000 after three years, with further possibilities of promotion after that. Shelley Whitworth joined the company six years ago with a degree in Microbiology, and is now manager of a water treatment plant near Nottingham. She says, "Severn Trent expects a lot from its graduate trainees—there is a high level of responsibility and commitment required from day one. In return, you are given a unique opportunity to experience a wide range of jobs and to meet a rich mix of people. I feel privileged to have been part of the training scheme which gave me the skills and confidence to progress to my current job."

So what type of person will thrive with Severn Trent? Austin Todd's answer is that "people with initiative, leadership and drive who acquire the right skills and deliver agreed objectives can go far."

Pay and Benefits

Taking the total package into account, Severn Trent is in the upper quartile and follows industry best practice on occupational pensions, holidays, maternity and paternity leave. It is the only water company to have a reward scheme for its 2,500 craft employees; £34 per week is available in child care vouchers and many people work flexible hours.

Severn Trent was the first water company to implement an Inland Revenue approved scheme linking 10–20% of pay to profits—this has now been adopted by other utilities. Other schemes encourage employees to hold shares in the company and 97.5% of employees have chosen to do so.

The Future

The HR team identifies four main challenges for the company. The first is the expectation that the director general of water services will continue to exert pressure on water companies to be more efficient. Customers' increasing expectations of ever-improving service and value for money create the second challenge. The third is at the mercy of the weather, with recent changes producing less rain and more demand for water, increasing the technical problems faced by the business. A final challenge comes from employees, whose expectations on pay, benefits, training and career developments rise continually.

Severn Trent has survived the change of privatisation with pride in its achievements so far. It still has to work on its public image—water companies have had much negative publicity in recent times, and Severn Trent has borne its share of bad press. If this were to continue, it could have repercussions for its staff in terms of morale and pride in the company.

There is some understandable concern about job security in view of the big staff cuts, but such concern is part of everyday life for most employees nowadays. Severn Trent employees have demonstrably come through pain of change to enjoy the benefits of being and owning part of a successful and profitable business.

Shell

The Royal Dutch/Shell Group of Companies (Shell) is a major player in the international energy business. With an Anglo-Dutch holding company structure, its operating companies are decentralised and focused on the key business areas of exploration and production, oil products, chemicals, and gas and coal. Shell has global turnover in excess of $150 billion from operations in more than 125 countries. Of 104,000 employees world-wide, over 10,000 work in the UK at any one time.

Biggest Plus: Almost any career aim can be fulfilled, around the world

Biggest Minus: Don't expect your hand to be held all the way

Shell International Limited
Shell Centre
London   SE1 7NA
Tel: 0171-934 3630
Fax: 0171-934 7606
http://www.shell.com.recruitment.html

The Business

By many parameters the largest company in the world, Shell is almost synonymous with unlimited career opportunity. This Anglo-Dutch giant is probably the most international of all companies, with an inherited culture and successful track record of working with many different nationalities and cultures. Shell has many upstream and downstream operations in Europe, particularly in the areas of exploration and production on the UK Continental Shelf.

People joining the company will usually come into immediate contact with other nationalities and will probably work abroad early on in their career. They also have the advantage of fast development opportunities. What they make of it is up to them, but a career intertwined between operating companies overseas and stints at Shell's central offices in London and the Hague compares favourably with others to be found in the industry.

Shell takes a long-term viewpoint in business, and with $10 billion of its own cash at its disposal at any time, it has the financial muscle to do so and invest in countries or risk scenarios that would be untenable, unpalatable, or impossible to most companies. Clear thinking, analysis, and scenario planning are vital in managing this risk.

Not that Shell is afraid to get involved in difficult business situations. In South Africa, Shell remained while others left under pressure from members of the international community; today, the company enjoys tributes from Nelson Mandela acknowledging that staying in was the best thing that Shell did for his country.

Anyone after a career that avoids risk, complex business situations, and significant contact with governments, would be best advised not to join Shell. If instead this sounds exciting, then Shell probably has no peer.

Company Culture and Style

A changing corporate culture is carrying traditional Shell values of integrity and professionalism into a new era where Shell is adding an emphasis on external focus. On customers; on looking outside the organisation for flexibility; valuing diversity and welcoming different lifestyles; working in teams and communicating with each other, maintaining the sense of 'fun' that is vital in teamwork.

Pursuing diversity means recruiting more women in technical functions (now at 30% in the UK), and encouraging people from a variety of different nationalities, cultures and lifestyles. And while one-third of Shell's high level graduate intake is from the UK, increasingly this pool is drawn from many more countries.

Creativity is valued highly, and not just in a marketing context. The aim is to have creativity in all areas—lightness of touch and flair in engineering, innovation in partnerships and joint ventures, and flexibility during inter-governmental negotiations.

Shell people can expect to spend a significant part of their career abroad. Expatriate packages are attractive—tax-free salaries, paid accommodation, business class fares home, school fees paid, sports facilities, and often a more recreational climate than the UK's weather systems permit. Even after the number of Shell employees in the group was reduced substantially to today's total of nearer 100,000, the level of expatriates, now at 5,500, has actually increased.

Human Resource Priorities

Human resources management in Shell is going through a transition. While there is still an HR manager facilitating the development of, on average, 300–400 staff, the planned approach to career development has shifted increasingly to getting individuals to take responsibility for their own development. Getting the balance between planned and self-managed career development is an HR priority where releasing the reins to let the horse go faster seems to be the guiding principle.

Another key role of HR is to give the organisation the right resources at the right time. Change happens quickly in the energy industry and sometimes this means moving people quickly too. One Shell company once had to withdraw and replace 100 people from a particular location at 48 hours' notice—a mission impossible, but one that Shell's system and its planners were able to accomplish.

Employee surveys are more relevant at the individual country or business, as opposed to group level, but one survey among 5,000 expatriates to assess their partners' needs was the biggest survey of its kind. Issues covered ranged from partner employment to provision of information and the results were fairly positive, identified the areas for improvement, and were acted upon. Other management consultants are still using the results.

Shell believes that it is 'not bad' at communication. With the drive for diversity increasingly important, the greatest challenges in communication are between countries and cultures. Andy Gibb, recruitment manager, human resources, believes that informal contact through people and software networks are important. "Part of teamwork is talking to others. You don't necessarily need to know, but you need to know someone who does, or someone who can get you the information you need."

Career Development and Opportunity

Being a huge company with operations in 125 countries generates an abundance of career opportunity for talented people, with a large number of international, responsible positions. Individuals can become general manager for a smaller country at a relatively early age, providing a self-managed business opportunity with bottom-line responsibility, but backed by Shell resources.

New recruits in exploration and production may start in the Netherlands followed by a second job in Aberdeen; after that they can expect to spend about half their career abroad. In other areas of the business, for example marketing, the choice may be yours whether your first job is at home or abroad.

Shell does not have a dedicated graduate training course. You do the job from day one, driven by the need to gain real experience. From there, individuals work out with their bosses what their own training and development needs are.

There are enough opportunities for good individuals to achieve their goals, including moving across companies and business functions. Until recently, Shell did not often buy in new, specialist skills, but it is now prepared to do so when it moves into different business areas. This deliberate attempt to refresh management and introduce new expertise does not have an adverse effect on incumbents' career opportunity—if anything it enhances it.

Pay and Benefits

Shell pays well and compares to other blue-chip multinationals when it comes to basic salary at executive and manager levels. There is also a significant variable pay element at senior levels. Variable pay, including bonuses, reflects company performance as well as individual contribution.

Benefits are good and cover the usual packages. Shell offers particularly attractive benefits in the area of equal opportunity. The company offers career breaks, and maternity arrangements are seen as among the very best.

The Future

Shell still believes that it must demonstrate to people that being a professional in the oil and gas industry is not just about engineering—it's about big business, people, fun and excitement. Having to shift perceptions might seem unusual for such a successful company that clearly has fascinating jobs to offer, but Shell believes that it must 'walk the talk' and demonstrate and communicate this, rather than just sell the words.

Employees recognised that recent downsizing and corporate changes were essential for the long-term success of the company as a whole, and that the challenges faced by company and individual alike to be up-to-date and competent were mutual challenges that were likely to continue.

Shell is still recruiting people for jobs in 30 years' time. The minimum requirement of a high level graduate or direct entry professional is the potential ability to manage a major business. The company recognises that this will require investment in people, and training and development budgets have increased. Jobs for life have never been guaranteed, but long-term careers are still highly valued, and are probably more rewarding than they have ever been.

SiliconGraphics
Computer Systems

Silicon Graphics

Silicon Graphics, Inc. (SGI) is one of the world's leading and most revolutionary computer technology companies started by a band of disgruntled American visionaries in 1982. By June 1996 the company had grown out of all proportion and turned over a staggering $2.9 billion. The headquarters is in Mountain View, California and SGI employs 10,000 people world-wide. The UK company, which now employs close to 300 people, has almost doubled in size in the last year with the acquisition of Cray Research and through organic growth.

Biggest Plus: An exciting, new wave company with vision, seriously committed to letting the individual flourish

Biggest Minus: A youth-based culture that is tough, no-nonsense, fast-moving, and unwilling to wait

Silicon Graphics, Inc.
1530 Arlington Business Park
Theale
Reading RG7 4SB
Tel: 01734-257500
Fax: 01734-257505

The Business

Silicon Graphics is a technology-focused company, spending between 11–13% of total revenue on research and development. That technology is used for real-world applications, enabling its customers to get a competitive edge. Indicative of those miracles of modern technology was the development of the Boeing 777 that, due to SGI technology, chopped tens of millions off the development cost and brought the project forward by several months. Silicon Graphics also provided the graphics technology for *Jurassic Park* and *Toy Story*.

Company Culture and Style

Besides its phenomenal technology, the company culture has to be the other most distinguishing characteristic of SGI and brings it under a heading of a new breed of business. There is a strong open door policy with Ed McCracken, the chief executive, sitting with the rest of his colleagues, sending out the corporate signal of openness and flat structure. People wear smiles as well as badges and SGI seems to have eliminated the politicking that so often hinders both personal advancement and corporate success.

It puts this down to its 'VIP' style: vision-innovation-passion. "People have a vision of what we are trying to grow in the UK. As a result they need to be prepared to innovate, to live with change, because the technology is changing and the way the company works is changing," says Nick Foster, human resources director. Work hard, play hard, serious fun, serious technology is the company philosophy and you are there to make a difference, not in six months but in two. "That's what I was told," says the youthful UK managing director (the average age of the work force is 33), Tim Robinson. "You have to get in there, get cracking, get connected and make a difference...fast."

When it comes to competition, SGI wants to be the best and implicit in that, although they themselves don't articulate this as such, you have to 'chew-up' the competition. The sharp end of computers is not for pussycats. The individual who will flourish here is a self-motivated team player addicted to technology.

"Space and freedom for the individual is the way we will get quantum performance. We breed a certain type of camaraderie because it is individuals all working together rather than individuals against the system. We almost deliberately deny the system and focus on the person," says Robinson.

Fun is a key word here. A month does not go by without employees getting together on a Friday afternoon for what is affectionately known as a 'Beerbust', where Robinson will talk informally about business priorities for the following month or two.

As a 'thank you' to the world-wide contribution of its people, Ed McCracken and his senior management took a full page in the *San Jose Mercury News*, read by most of Silicon Valley (proving that the printed word still has some currency left), and bought 7,000 Tag Heuer watches.

'Spirit' awards are given to those who most embody the culture. Winners last year were taken to Maui for four days to interact with the management. As a result

McCracken organised off-site symposia to deal with employees' suggestions. Employees are kept up to date through internal communication on the web site known as Silicon Junction which is one of the largest Intranet sites in the world.

Human Resource Priorities

With a company that considers people as one of its greatest assets, it is hardly surprising that its attrition rate is low—about 8%. SGI has a structured HR policy department which covers all the normal areas you would expect to find. The difference is that they became bored with the usual approach to an employee handbook and are currently using a journalist to redraft it into a 'magazine style' format. It includes 'dress down Fridays'. Equality and opportunity are enshrined in the ethos of the company, stressing its American parenthood, where any form of discrimination is frowned upon.

According to Foster, when circumstances dictate that SGI must lose people, the bottom line is to treat people honestly and decently, fairly and with dignity. It is essential to recognise the contribution that they have made to the company. It is also essential that they walk away from the company with their heads held high.

"One employee who left wanted to start her own business," said Foster, "so we provided her with certain SGI kit that we had basically depreciated which gave her a head start.

"No one is ever walked-off the premises and we notify people as quickly as possible about the situation. Some of them are still working with us three or four months later as part of a transition before ultimately leaving the company."

SGI sees itself as a learning organisation. McCracken summed up this period as, "Adolescence...you get tested. You learn that there's a lot left to learn." MD Robinson adds, "We do some stuff that's pretty good but we are miles away from where we want to be. If you stop listening and learning you become arrogant, hardwired and inflexible. To keep learning, that's the most important thing we can do."

Career Opportunity and Development

Joanne De Nobriga is the 1995 'Spirit' winner. "In terms of job development, and I have been here for seven years, sometimes I have moved to jobs I have sought out myself, sometimes they've been a natural progression, but they have been there and by going and talking to people and saying I need a new challenge or I'd like to try this, if people have confidence in you they will give you whatever support you need."

Training fuels growth and it is an area of increased investment. SGI has brought trainers over from the USA to ensure that all employees get the same programmes. Keen to keep the organisation flat, they have begun to introduce team leadership roles which will also come with training. Technical engineers often go to the USA for training, seminars and trade shows and a separate budget has been established for pre-sales and sales staff to benefit from 10 days of further training.

International secondment is an area of great excitement with the opportunity to travel within Europe or the USA for a week, a month, three months.

The duration of the stay is often left to the individual who can decide what is suitable for their family as well as their job. "It all comes back to respect for the individual, making them the arbiter of what the right thing to do is," says Robinson.

"Moving people internationally is important because there is a cross fertilisation of culture," says Robinson. "Many people go to HQ and get a feel for what the corporation is like. It's a great morale booster. It's a different environment where networks are built and you come back to the UK and find the whole communication tool has been strengthened. You get a much more international perspective and you start seeing things differently."

Pay and Benefits

SGI aims to pay among the leaders; it surveys the competitors and pitches salary levels at the 75th percentile of the market place. It achieves high margins and aims high in order to attract the best people. Salary increases are related to performance.

As for benefits, as far as possible SGI does not differentiate between hierarchical levels, so the pension plan is exactly the same whether it is the receptionist's or the MD's. There is an attractive employee stock purchase plan where stock is discounted for two years; this has a high take-up rate.

The Future

Long-term planning would be counter-effective in this business and SGI's talent is to be able to turn on a sixpence and embrace the new in this rapidly changing environment. It anticipates doubling in size over the next two years and 'will consciously recruit people who have the skills and competencies in areas like 3D graphics, digital media, supercomputing', and who bring vision, innovation and passion to what they do.

McCracken continues: "The only way we can make the right decisions quickly is to have a management team in place that is technically competent. That's the difference between how we've structured our company versus many of our competitors."

Foster feels that training and development are areas that need more emphasis. Due to mergers and acquisitions, the vision that has so defined Silicon Graphics has been diluted in part. Clarification of where the company is going needs to be looked at further to keep a firm hold on the buzz and excitement that make SGI the leader in this cutting-edge field.

SB
SmithKline Beecham

SmithKline Beecham

SmithKline Beecham is an international leader in the research, development, manufacture and marketing of healthcare products with global annual sales in excess of £7 billion. The company has three major business sectors: pharmaceuticals, consumer healthcare and healthcare services. Its common purpose is healthcare—prevention, diagnosis, treatment and cure. SmithKline Beecham employs approximately 52,000 people world-wide, 8,500 in the UK.

SmithKline Beecham possesses genuine global scale, both in terms of sales and the amount spent annually in the search for innovative medicines. Its global sales force numbers 5,000 and is active in all major markets. Over £650 million was spent in 1995 on research and development, the lion's share in pharmaceuticals, where more than 4,500 people world-wide focus their efforts in four therapeutic areas: neuroscience, inflammation and tissue repair, anti-infectives/biologicals (vaccines) and cardiopulmonary.

Biggest Plus: Working for a truly global organisation

Biggest Minus: Must be able to adapt to an environment that is continually
                  changing

SmithKline Beecham
1 New Horizons Court
Brentford
Middlesex TW8 9EP
Tel: 0181-975 2230
Fax: 0181-975 2774

The Business

When US SmithKline Beckman merged with UK Beecham in 1989, the company looked to a future of continual change. Today, having acquired Sterling Health in 1994, SmithKline Beecham (SB) is now the world's third largest company in the sale of over-the-counter medicines and the UK's second largest pharmaceuticals company. It has divested its animal health business, but moved into managed care. In collaboration with Human Genome Sciences, SB has established itself as a world leader in DNA research. And the company expects to make over 50 filings with regulatory agencies for new products or indications over the next three years.

Which is just as well, because the healthcare industry is changing fast. Frontier technology in bioscience is opening up the possibilities as never before. Meanwhile, the customer has metamorphosed from the healthcare provider to the one who pays the bills. Chief executive Jan Leschly, known for his 'if you're not keeping score, you're just practising' view, says "SB intends to continue to generate pioneering drugs which make the difference, but are cost-effective and value-added."

Company Culture and Style

SmithKline Beecham has self-styled the 'Simply Better' way, a cultural initiative dedicated to continuous improvement and the way business is done at SB. It is the framework that defines the systems and process by which all work is organised, and the methods and tools which are used to consistently achieve excellence.

'Simply Better' means building a working environment that motivates and then provides the means for personal and professional growth. It requires a process of continuous improvement, grounded in strongly supported company beliefs. The company's 'leadership practices'—nine habits that SB leaders are expected to cultivate—go the extra step to ensure that its core values of customers, innovation, integrity, people and performance are translated into everyday behaviour.

As a multinational, SB has to be sensitive to global cultural differences. Having already addressed subtle differences in business cultures of the USA and UK, SB is focusing on divergent cultural factors in Europe. 'Simply Better' puts great store by teamworking as a way of making better use of people from diverse locations and functions, saving time and resource as a result.

SB continues to dismantle bureaucracy and obstacles and, having delayered and empowered a lot, SB ensures that it gives employees a framework and terms of reference. SB seeks actively to reward risk (and discuss failure) and believes that if it doesn't give people a remit, they will be less inclined to take chances; to instil courage requires trust.

Leschly suggests that there are five personal characteristics that SB should seek in hiring people: smart (street, not dress), good judgement, energy, sense of humour, and care for people. More specific qualities for success might include the need to interrelate with others in a company driven by teamwork, and the ability to prioritise and take an overview.

Human Resource Priorities

In the UK, the shifting psychological contract has lessened expectations of spending working life with only one or two employers, but loyalty is still important. Salaries need to be fair; job satisfaction must be deliverable; people must be able to improve their own personal saleability and acquire new skills. As old structures disappear, HR on behalf of the company has to trade in certain reassurances, and it does. SB is very up front in saying, "we provide this... you get that."

HR is an integral part of the business—it has to be because of the premium placed on 'people values' in the organisation. Group HR director Dan Phelan is a member of the Corporate Management Team, effectively the senior operating committee of the company. "The end product of the HR process is that we have people organised in the right numbers, with the right skills, in the right place, at the right time, to achieve our goals."

The HR function is internal customer focused, and seeks to add real value offering a range of support mechanisms and services. It has service levels and partnership agreements, forged by sitting down with its 'customers', setting out their requirements, and then measuring against them to make sure they are met. There are generalist and specialist teams, in areas such as pay, benefits and recruitment.

SB is totally committed to diversity. For SB, diversity is about "creating an environment where the potential of the skills and expertise of all our employees is realised through individual people differences being recognised and valued," according to Sheila Boughton, manager, UK relations and diversity.

Career Opportunity and Development

Healthcare is a global business, and career opportunities at SB are global too. SB doesn't actually need to create opportunities; for a company changing so fast, there is a continual need for people to be flexible and move around. Vacancies are advertised company-wide in the UK, with plans afoot to widen this to the USA and Europe, and SB operates a global, comparable job evaluation scheme. There are many transfers around the business, particularly between the UK and USA, but cost implications dictate an evaluation of the cost and benefits to both company and individual.

SB gives individuals the scope to state their ideas and goals, encourages self-managed careers, and provides access to the necessary skills. Training is often job-related, but other skills can be acquired which have a wider or more saleable value outside if the individual leaves the company.

In a recent *Harvard Business Review*, a feature on cartoons by 4–5 year olds included a caption 'if you follow me, I am the leader'. Anyone can and should become leaders at SB, but some are more leaders than others—the company still has managers. But cross-functional Process Improvement Teams have leaders from anywhere in the organisation.

The sharpest training focus has been on self-development of leaders (sometimes using the 'SB University' or online training on PC), but the company has its Training Partnership which it offers to all employees. The number of programmes available are expected to double to 24 in 1997. One recently introduced was the Business Skills Diploma aimed at administrative staff. Apart from having external value, these programmes help SB assess levels of competency when looking at promotions.

Pay and Benefits

SB does a lot of benchmarking on pay, and has a global job grading scheme, but pay structures are essentially local-driven. All employees receive an annual bonus based on their business area achieving profit targets and individuals can also opt to participate in the profit-related pay scheme. Further up the responsibility line, SB is seeking 'enhancements' in performance-related pay, coupling incentives with the achievement of objectives and performance levels.

SB offers a generous total pay and benefits package, including a very good (and well-explained) company pension plan. SB has a 1-1 Share Matching Plan, a good way for employees to identify with the overall fortunes of the business. Non-cash benefits include an employee assistance programme, child care schemes, and a link line for carers. SB was singled out in a recent Mintel survey for its excellent communication with employees explaining financial benefits.

The Future

Delegates at the 1996 'Not Just Business as Usual' conference in Orlando learned of Leschly's high expectations for future company performance, admitting that stretch objectives would not be easy to reach. "By the year 2005, I challenge SB to increase sales to $25 billion and market value to $75 billion. Unless your reach exceeds your grasp, you'll never know how far you can go."

Therefore the priority, and continual challenge is to maintain SB's focus as a customer-driven, world class company. It must continue to develop pioneering products and services, and the pipeline does look very promising. But pioneering also means all employees constantly looking for and finding new and better ways of doing their jobs. And cost structures must be adapted all the time to the competitive environment—World-wide Supply Operations was created to deliver just this, by managing more effectively SB's global supply and manufacturing structure.

Balanced against these business needs, SB must also meet employee expectations. If it gets this wrong SB, like any other company, could ask too much of its employees. SB is intelligently aware, however, of the need for employees to prioritise and work smarter, and the company understands the danger of a macho culture of long hours and the 'jacket on the back of the chair'. It recognises that there is a finite limit, that life and work must co-exist in balance, and it helps and encourages its people to decide on priorities and achieve more efficient ways of working, driven as always by the need to meet customer requirements. SB places a premium on awareness of changes in technology and the major impact it is having on the way we work.

Employees seem to be genuinely motivated in this relatively young company, and aligned with its business objectives. This year, a record 231 teams submitted entries for the Continuous Improvement Awards, and their total ideas saved the business a staggering $451 million. 'Simply Better' is delivering real value.

WH Smith Group

WH Smith Group is Britain's leading retailer of books, videos, stationery and re-corded music, and the leading distributor of books and magazines. It is also strongly represented in the USA. Turnover exceeds £2 billion. The group employs 27,000 people in the UK and 8,000 in the USA.

Biggest Plus: A group with three diverse cultures—something for everyone

Biggest Minus: Having to decide which of the three to focus on!

WH Smith Group plc
Greenbridge Road
Swindon
Wiltshire SN3 3LD
Tel: 01793-616161
Fax: 01793-562560

The Business

WH Smith is without doubt one of the most familiar names on the British high street, where it has been represented for 203 years. There are over 420 WH Smith outlets across the UK, with another 80 at airports, stations and hospitals. Yet impressive though this network is, it's just one part of the group as a whole. Today, the group has broad interests across retailing, distribution and a US operation.

Retailing includes three highly distinct and well-known entities: WH Smith Retail; Virgin/Our Price (a 75% joint venture), the UK's leading specialist retailer of recorded music; and Waterstone's, the market leader in specialist bookselling.

In distribution, the group supplies newspapers and magazines to retailers through WH Smith News.

Finally, the strong US presence includes WH Smith outlets in hotels and airports, Waterstone's stores and "The Wall", a specialist retailer of recorded music in the north-eastern states with 167 stores.

Company Culture and Style

For any group as diverse as WH Smith, it is pointless to speak of a single culture or style. Instead, there is a set of very individual cultures. Taking just the retail side alone, it would be hard to imagine three more diverse companies. WH Smith caters for the whole family, Virgin/Our Price for the youth market, and Waterstone's for the serious bookbuyer.

This set of cultures, however, is seen as a plus point. Keith Broughton, compensation and benefits manager: "Our cultural differences add to our strength. The whole is greater than the sum of our parts." Furthermore, different though these retail outlets are, they share important similarities. As John Ainley, group human resources director, puts it: "Customer service excellence across the range of our operations is vital to our future. We want to be one of the best companies in the world." Group chief executive Bill Cockburn concurs: "We aim to please our customers by providing a standard of service that is consistently better than our competitors. We try to anticipate what our customers want, and to give them more than they expect." The group also has a youthful workforce profile, with an average age of just 31.

Given the diversity, let's take the individual cultures one by one. WH Smith itself is characterised by an open, honest and direct style. This is fostered by the growing trend towards accountability, trust and the removal of unnecessary bureaucratic rules. For instance, staff can now give refunds and change till-rolls without needing to call a supervisor—good news for both them and their customers. Waterstone's is known for personal service and knowledgeable guidance; staff here are often passionate about books, intellectually vigorous and individualistic—yet also commercially aware and customer-oriented. Virgin/Our Price staff tend to be enthusiastic and enjoy working with people, both fellow team members and customers. And the distribution and US operations also have cultures of their own.

Human Resource Priorities

Ainley: "Our people are very much a part of the mission of the company; our human resources policy is not separate from our business philosophy as a whole. The reason is simple. There's a clear link between satisfied staff and satisfied customers. We want our people to feel that their jobs are interesting and rewarding, and thereby build up mature, long-term relationships with them. Working for WH Smith plc should give people real satisfaction, wherever they work and whatever they do within the group."

Practices are tested against this philosophy, using an array of benchmarks. Employee satisfaction surveys are taken on an ongoing basis to ensure that the whole process is moving in the right direction. At the same time, those 'hidden' indicators of staff satisfaction—staff turnover, sickness and absence from work—are also continually monitored.

When it comes to internal communications, the group's employees are well looked after. A monthly newsletter, *Newslink,* goes to all group employees. Clean, fresh and stimulating, this focuses primarily on business news but also finds space to present some 'people' issues. Of special interest is a feature called 'Platform', which allows group employees to ask often searching questions of management with a guaranteed, often in-depth reply.

Each group also has its individual newsletter. In WH Smith Retail, a video is sent to all branches with news and updates roughly every six weeks. Branches hold regular staff briefings where product information, management changes and strategic changes are cascaded down. The openness of the group's communication is certainly a great strength; a recent far-reaching five month strategic review of the group's future direction perhaps inevitably led to fears and rumours of redundancy, but the uncertainty was greatly reduced due to regular information dissemination, including honest answers to tough questions.

Staff turnover currently runs at around 30%, but this of course includes part-time and counter staff where turnover is traditionally high. At the other end of the continuity scale, 40% of managers have been with the group for ten years or more.

Career Opportunity and Development

The group has a long tradition of graduate recruitment; as Keith Broughton says, "It's essential to take on new blood to continue to compete in the market place: these people are the seedcorn of the future." In 1995, WH Smith took on 12 new graduates, an average figure for the group. Of senior management functions such as buying, IT and marketing, 60% are held by graduates.

Joanne Tunnicliffe read Geography at Lancaster University and joined WH Smith News as a logistics trainee in 1991. "Logistics is another name for distribution and I look on it as the sharp end of the supply chain." Her graduate training scheme lasted two years and covered transport, the warehouse, systems, industrial engineering and planning.

Tim Batten read Drama and English at the University of London and ultimately joined Waterstone's. He rose rapidly to assistant manager level and then assisted with the opening of the company's first US store. Now a manager in Glasgow, Tim says: "I still love books, but they're no longer the prime mover for me. What I'm interested in now is management experience and challenges, and what I can bring to a situation."

But the group has many types of people, from those wanting to carve a management position to flexible work employees and part-timers, some working as little as four hours a week. For everyone, the group offers extensive training and development programmes. As Broughton points out, WH Smith was the first retailer to get the Investors in People category. Each business takes responsibility for its own training, but this is generally regarded even by outsiders as first class: everything from basic till training to courses at INSEAD! At higher management levels, leadership training is also available.

Across the group, there is a desire to help people progress to higher levels if they want to do so. This can include moving between the different operations. Richard Handover started his career in the WH Smith Retail branches and is now the MD of WH Smith News. There are limited opportunities to work abroad: these include some US assignments, as well as Irish postings for Waterstone's staff.

Pay and Benefits

For shop staff, the group aims to be in the top quartile on pay. For management, the group offers competitive salaries that reflect both business and individual performance targets. Pay reviews are largely performance-related, with the level of pay increase available decided either by negotiation (where formal trade union recognition exists) or by consultation. The WH Smith Retail and Waterstone's branches also have bonus arrangements based on their own performances.

Compared to other retailers, the group has a competitive benefits package, including a contributory money purchase pension scheme whereby the company matches the individual contribution up to 5% of pay; a group-wide profit sharing scheme for part-time as well as full-time staff; an SAYE scheme; and a staff discount of 25% that can be used throughout the group's businesses. Executive benefits can include a company car/cash scheme and private medical insurance.

Where redundancies are unavoidable, everyone is offered counselling with an outplacement company as well as individual consultation with an internal department. There is also an internal and external job-finder service, plus a workshop on setting up in self-employment.

The Future

Keith Broughton: "Retailing is vastly more competitive than even before. You could never have bought books at the supermarket or newspapers from your petrol station at one time, but these things and many others are commonplace today.

"Our challenge is to refine our understanding of the skills and competencies we need to respond to this fast-changing environment. That means repositioning ourselves to focus on what we do best, and of course acquiring and keeping the best people.

"Further down the road, electronic shopping and other trends will take more of our attention. Suffice it to say that the changing high street is affecting us enormously. We intend to remain on top of these changes and retain our leadership position."

Standard Chartered Bank

Standard Chartered is an international banking group with its headquarters in London. Operating over 600 offices in more than 40 countries and employing 25,000 members of staff, Standard Chartered specialises in the fields of personal banking, corporate banking, foreign exchange, money market operations and international trade finance.

Biggest Plus: Significant opportunities for international experience

Biggest Minus: Going through an unsettling period of corporate evolution

Standard Chartered Bank plc
1 Aldermanbury Square
London EC2V 7SB
Tel: 0171-280 6301
Fax: 0171-280 7705

The Business

Incorporated by Royal Charter in 1853, Standard Chartered spans the developed and emerging economies of the world.   Having fought-off a take-over bid during the 1980s from Lloyds Bank, Standard Chartered entered a period of dramatic transformation. A change in the board at the onset of the current decade kick-started a massive programme of cultural change, with each division being provided with greater autonomy to manage its own affairs.

Although operating in over 40 countries, Standard Chartered's activities concentrate on 10 main territories. 90% of its employees—from Botswana to China, Gambia to Singapore—do not have English as their first language. One-third of corporate profits stem from Hong Kong, one-third from the rest of Asia and the remaining third from the other four continents.

The change programme has already reaped spectacular benefits. Pre-tax profits for 1995 soared from £510 million to £661 million. Nearly 40% of all turnover is now represented by personal banking, credit card and mortgage transactions—a segment of the business that only started in earnest in 1990.

Company Culture and Style

By definition, Standard Chartered is a melting pot of cultural influences. A challenging, dynamic, demanding environment sets high standards of individual and corporate excellence, and staff versatility is essential to move with changing times. Open-mindedness is essential. Many best practice ideas are currently coming out of Asia and staff must be prepared to learn from all quarters.

Having driven the business forward by devolving power from the centre, Standard Chartered now encourages all facets of its organisation to think as one. The company has even adopted a pan-corporate blue and green livery, reaffirming a collective world-wide identity.

The pace of change cannot be over-estimated. Of the top 500 executives within the organisation, 350 have joined in the last five years. The 'old school' mentality has gone, and now meritocracy is the order of the day.

A friendly atmosphere pervades Standard Chartered. Everyone calls each other by their first names, colleagues settling disputes over a drink after work. Friday is a dress-down day, and even the chief executive can be found wearing casual trousers and an open-necked shirt.

Standard Chartered's reputation was seriously damaged by its involvement in several high-profile business failures (for example, Brent Walker). Determined to shake-off its chequered past, Standard Chartered has adopted a rigorous code of ethics employing the highest standards of professional conduct. Standard Chartered's Group Code of Conduct always takes precedence over less demanding practices. No breaches can be justified on the grounds of ignorance, poor judgement or pursuit of profit.

Human Resource Priorities

Supporting the development of an international business has fundamental implications for HR specialists at Standard Chartered, both in terms of the competencies required and in terms of helping the organisation to perform in an integrated fashion. HR strategy is global, focusing on developing cross-border businesses. Although the techniques employed are broadly similar to other leading-edge corporations, the bank's considerable geographical diversity renders the logistical exercise necessarily more complicated.

There are 485 HR professionals across the organisation (excluding training but including management development specialists). Particular emphasis is placed on information systems and the technology base—two of four priorities identified at board level.

Policy issues at Standard Chartered are largely determined by an extended management team that assembles four times a year. At the last two meetings of that management team, *half* of the agenda was taken up with HR issues.

Corporate attitudes were assessed by a staff opinion survey conducted in mid-1995. As a result of the findings, Standard Chartered set up London Forum, a working group dedicated to tracking measurable improvements. A team listening process has also recently been introduced, providing an upward-oriented form of team briefing.

Career Opportunity and Development

Standard Chartered considers training programmes as central to building people effectiveness. Chief executive Malcolm Williamson expects every member of staff to spend at least 10 days each year reinforcing their skills. Standard Chartered maintains a core curriculum of skills training at three levels: first line programmes, middle management programmes and senior executive programmes.

The Learning Resource Centre provides an impressive array of self-development tools. Materials relate directly to the bank's competency framework, including computer skills, presentation techniques, and product knowledge.

The bank also sponsors an MBA programme structured in tandem with Henley Management College. And 65 members of staff are currently enrolled on a course that includes five weeks of residential training. In total, Standard Chartered runs seven major programmes on a globally-integrated basis, supplemented by five modules in specific locations. These include a 10-day residential Business Goal Management Programme for rising executives. 200 high potential (HIPO) managers benefit from fast-track development.

Standard Chartered maintains an international recruitment and development programme. Targeting students from (inter alia) Imperial College, Oxford, Cambridge and the University of Southern California, the bank places 60 graduates each year on a six-month development programme that includes a 12-week assignment overseas.

Permanent members of staff are actively encouraged to seek out secondments. Postings can last anything from one month to three years and at any time, 5–600 managers will be assigned internationally across the group.

Most jobs are advertised internally by email. 60% of positions are currently filled in-house against a medium-term target of 80%.

Pay and Benefits

Benchmarking rates of pay against organisations in similar sectors (the likes of Citibank and NatWest Markets), Standard Chartered compares favourably against industry peers. The pay process begins with surveys commissioned from leading consultants, and business heads are advised on the overall level of provision they need to consider. Pay increases averaged 5.5% in 1996 (5% in 1995). Once the appraisal process is complete, line managers are invited to suggest increases for individuals based upon market indicators, internal relativity to colleagues in similar roles, and personal performance.

All staff participate in a bonus scheme, with pay-outs determined by group performance, specific team or business unit performance, and individual contribution. Incentive plans still function in selected areas (for example treasury dealing). The inclination at Standard Chartered is to move away from sales-related incentives, however, towards bonus plans that reflect group achievement.

Over 60% of UK staff have taken up options in Standard Chartered's Share Save scheme. As the share price has risen from 52p to £7 during the life of the scheme, several employees are sitting on useful profits.

All staff are covered by private medical insurance (an umbrella policy including spouses and dependants) and a defined benefit pension scheme. Company cars are offered at middle management level and above, while Standard Chartered's maternity scheme offers benefits significantly above the statutory minimum. Other perks include season ticket loans, subsidised mortgages up to £50,000, life insurance at four times salary, a subsidised staff restaurant and relocation packages for those undertaking international assignments.

The Future

The bank's aim in each territory is to have operations run by local managers. Indigenous managing directors must meet exacting standards laid down in the UK, however, placing stringent demands on training regimes.

Standard Chartered enjoys a privileged position in many territories, and is one of very few banks to hold an operating licence in countries such as Laos or Cambodia. As international markets increasingly open up to competitors with little or no experience of local conditions, Standard Chartered executives are bound to attract attention from head-hunters.

"The biggest challenge," declares Tim Halford, director of corporate affairs, "will be hanging on to the people we've got. We have to keep them motivated and committed. It's quite a compliment in a way. In order to remain a world class organisation, we provide people with excellent training, which inevitably makes them highly marketable. We therefore have to establish a culture which people aspire to belong to. This is the key."

Tim Halford estimates that in view of the rapid growth of Standard Chartered and the upgrading of many positions, the next five years will present outstanding opportunities at the bank. The scope for ambitious, talented, hard-working employees is obvious—taking centre stage in an organisation that not only boasts an illustrious history, but appears set for a productive future.

SUN LIFE

Sun Life Assurance Society

Sun Life is one of the UK's leading financial services providers. Its total new premium income of £1.2 billion in 1995 made it the fourth-ranked UK Life Company. Sun Life is now part of the UAP Group that employs 48,000 people world-wide; and Sun Life itself employs over 3,300 people in the UK.

Biggest Plus: Working in different departments is positively encouraged

Biggest Minus: If you're inflexible and afraid of change, look elsewhere!

Sun Life Assurance Society plc
Sun Life Centre
Brierly Furlong
Stoke Gifford
Bristol BS12 6SW
Tel: 0117-989 9000
Fax: 0117-989 1810

The Business

Sun Life was established in 1810. For much of its history, the company enjoyed moderate if unspectacular success and appeared traditional and paternalistic. In the 1990s, however, the position has changed radically. Faced with massive competition, deregulation and a widespread shake-up of the insurance industry, the company has transformed itself into a dynamic customer-oriented organisation.

The impetus for the changes came from John Reeve, the company's managing director who took office in 1990. After examining the company's changing market place, he commissioned a major market research programme. This led in turn to a substantive review of customer services, with a view to introducing much speedier and team-based work. The result has been a dramatic improvement in service delivery and considerable expansion for the company; in 1989 it was ranked only eleventh largest of the UK Life Companies.

Ownership of the company has also changed. In 1995 the French insurance giant UAP took control, providing even greater financial stability and growth potential. The popularity of the company's new look was demonstrated in 1996 when 40% of Sun Life shares were floated; the issue was 2.7 times oversubscribed. Today, Sun Life manages funds in excess of £19 billion and has received numerous awards for customer service, including PIMS Company of the Year 1993, 1994 and 1995.

Company Culture and Style

The culture of the company is unrecognisable from just a decade ago—despite the fact that many of the same people work for the organisation! Michael Baker, general manager (human resources and office services), describes the culture now as "Open, honest and performance-driven. It's a culture which seeks to give people more opportunity to develop and grow. At the same time, the jobs are far more interesting. Whereas once they were narrow in scope and functionally organised, they are now team-based and have broader responsibilities."

The approach now is to train people in terms of knowledge, skills and competencies and test them against those criteria—and then empower them. However, there is always support from a team leader or other supervisor if needed. The philosophy is to bring decision making as close to the customer as possible.

The structure of the company has also changed. In the past, Sun Life had a multi-level hierarchy. As a result, promotions were more frequent but often of little importance. The structure now is flatter; promotions are fewer but far more significant.

All this means that the profile of the person likely to succeed at Sun Life has changed. The stars of the future are likely to be innovative, customer-serving, and above all, flexible. Indeed, the company sees attitudes and behaviours as more important than academic qualifications. It can provide all the training anyone needs—but that's useless without the right approach!

Sun Life is well served when it comes to internal communications. It has its own communications manager whose team produces the company newsletter and other items.

The newsletter looks, feels and reads just like a newspaper and is printed as well as edited in-house. It recently won an award for in-house newsletters. There are also formal communications of business issues through briefing documents, together with lunchtime business sessions: two-way communication over buffet meals.

Each year, the company holds a Challenge Day under the aegis of its Community Partnership Co-ordinator. Over 600 people regularly take part, helping with community projects in and around its Bristol head office site: painting the homes of the old and infirm, making toys, clearing rubbish from sites and transforming them into play areas, and so on.

Human Resource Priorities

The company's human resources policy is embodied in its vision: a commitment to ensure that it has high calibre, motivated people with the appropriate skills to allow it to achieve its business objectives now and in the future. It has a detailed mission to help bring this about, best summed up in its objective to balance the needs of the business and the individual.

Considerable resources are devoted to human resources: a group HR department of around 40 people, as well as 50 dedicated training staff within the business areas. HR issues are regularly on the agenda at general management level, and the Corporate Plan has a section on HR. Each department then has its own plan to be implemented, arising out of the overall plan. Targets are set through the corporate planning process, published, and reviewed regularly. Staff are surveyed and the results published and followed up.

Career Opportunity and Development

Sun Life has no specific graduate recruitment programme; graduates are welcome to apply to the company and hard-working ones will move up quickly, but a degree in itself is no guarantee of promotion. Having said that, certain specialist areas look for graduate intakes: actuarial departments, for instance, want maths and science graduates, while IT graduates are sought for special projects. The company also recruited three MBAs this year, a trend likely to grow.

With the flatter structure, career development is fostered by moving within the company. Indeed, the current chief executive, Les Owen, has stated that he wants senior management to have had exposure to different parts of the business. This is good news for the customers as well as the staff of Sun Life. Another part of career development is to work exclusively on a special project, for three to six months. Such people are usually middle managers chosen for their ability and potential. Managers have their own Development Programme, run by a management development manager.

The company operates a 360 degree appraisal system. This means that your boss, your colleagues, your reports and your customers, as well as you, have an input into your appraisal that takes into account everything from competencies and behaviour to attitudes. This is obviously more time-consuming than some systems, but also seems to produce more constructive and balanced results.

The company recognises that the old 'jobs for life' adage has gone forever. Nevertheless, for those who want a long-term career (and the current average length of service is nine years), Sun Life offers plenty of career development and continual challenge. It's also quite possible to move through the ranks: chief executive Les Owen joined as an actuarial student at the age of 22, and is only 45 now. Michael Baker joined at the age of 16 and has worked in many areas—this is his second stint in HR! Indeed, of the 10 general managers, five started at the ground floor.

Training is taken seriously at Sun Life: £4 million was spent on training in 1995, 7.5% of the salary bill. Each of the 25 customer services departments has its own full-time trainer, as does every sales channel. There is a blend of internal and external training. People are also encouraged to enhance their professionalism by taking relevant insurance or actuarial exams. This takes the form of day release, paying examination fees and sometimes bonuses for passing.

Pay and Benefits

The company sees itself as a median payer—although in the upper quartile when it comes to total earnings. Individual salaries are in fairly wide bands: for instance, the average managerial salary is £32,000 while the highest is £51,600. These wide bands are in place throughout the organisation, and movement between bands is entirely performance-driven. Managers can award individual merit increases from 0–10% of salary, arising out of performance against targets. There are also team-related bonuses where the team makes savings against its budget while meeting its customer-service standards.

There is a wide spread of benefits. These include a recently introduced Employee Assistance Programme whereby employees can get independent, expert and confidential advice on anything from finance and law to personal health; a group-wide profit-sharing scheme; an SAYE scheme; a non-contributory pension plan; free life assurance cover; free private medical insurance; sports club membership; a season ticket loan; and a career break scheme.

Another benefit will be the brand new head office, planned for completion in 1996. This landscaped facility will bring everyone together in one area, and offer excellent sports, eating and entertainment facilities as well as a crèche.

The Future

The biggest challenge to any UK insurer is the competition. The company's objective is to continue to grow, but this can only be done by developing the skills of its people. Another pressure is to control costs by doing things smarter—without compromising the high service standards.

Traditional methods of distribution are also no longer enough. Sun Life has to ask itself how important newer channels, such as telephone selling, will become in the years ahead.

Another challenge is to operate more flexibly. As Michael Baker puts it, "We will be offering different types of employment packages in the future. I'm sure we'll be staying open for longer hours. Some people may work shifts, others will perhaps work from home. The changing needs of the business will continue to affect us here, as elsewhere. Our challenge is to stay on top of those changes."

Tesco

Tesco is the UK's leading food retailer. Employing over 140,000 members of staff across the UK, the company operates approximately 540 stores throughout England, Scotland and Wales.

Committed to delivering shareholder value, value for money and unparalleled standards of service, Tesco is currently engaged in a programme of expansion across Europe with significant outlets in France, Hungary, Poland, and the Czech and Slovak Republics.

Biggest Plus: A challenging, dynamic environment for ambitious professional staff

Biggest Minus: Demanding work and long hours typical of the retail industry

Tesco plc
Tesco House
PO Box 18, Delamare Road
Cheshunt, Waltham Cross
Herts EN8 9SL
Tel: 01992-632222
Fax: 01992-644283

The Business

Tesco was founded by Sir Jack Cohen. Cashing in a First World War gratuity to hire a barrow in the East End of London, Cohen's cut-price business took-off in the summer of 1924 when he met T.E. Stockwell, a partner in a firm importing tea. Agreeing to buy tea in bulk at ninepence a pound, the two men combined their respective initials to create the name Tesco. The new brand name was an instant success, and over the next 70 years, Tesco grew from its corner shop origins via supermarket outlets into today's food retailing empire.

Group turnover in 1996 exceeded £12 billion (an annual increase of 19.8%), with pre-tax profits soaring to £724 million (up 17.3%). Tesco's innovative reputation has been re-affirmed by the launch of Clubcard, a widely admired (and imitated) scheme that allows the company to communicate directly with over eight million members, and foster their loyalty in the process.

Company Culture and Style

Tesco offers a highly professional, energetic working atmosphere. The company is justifiably proud of its reputation for creativity, a reputation emphatically underlined by a series of customer service concepts over recent years including Cashcard and One-In-Front (opening more checkouts if any queue contains more than two customers).

Successful managers lead from the front. Executives of the future tend to be motivated individuals with an ability to coach and develop others, expressing a clear vision of where the business is going and how it can get there.

Teamwork is crucial. Staff are encouraged to eschew personal glory, thinking instead in terms of groups and team relationships. Fun at work is actively encouraged, esprit de corps counterbalancing the strain of working long hours.

In the past, Tesco has placed managerial emphasis on depth of experience in specialised disciplines. Now breadth of experience is also encouraged. The Career Management Programme is aimed at helping managers work across functions and locations, developing well-rounded individuals to meet the challenges likely to be posed in the new millennium.

Human Resource Priorities

Tesco's HR function is committed to developing the highest quality managers in the retail industry. In turn, those managers are encouraged to instil their own people with a significant degree of self-sufficiency, equipping teams for sustained performance.

HR priorities may be standard—recruiting, motivating and keeping the best people—but Tesco's ambitions run deeper. Beyond the customary HR remit, Tesco believes that staff should become partners in the long-term future of the business. The company also wants its managers, not the HR function, to look after people.

Most UK stores have their own personnel managers and many also have a training manager. Besides further professionals in a variety of head office positions, other members of the HR function operate with regional teams, acting as an interface between stores and head office. Each of the European businesses also has an HR director and teams of its own.

People are a priority at board level. Human resources director Lesley James is a member of the executive and Terry Leahy (who will become chief executive in 1997) not only regards HR as a leadership function but also has played an active role in past HR initiatives.

Tesco prides itself on listening to the needs of its customers and regularly consults staff on matters of internal concern. Attitudes towards jobs, training, management style, benefits, appraisals and terms and conditions are all carefully monitored and action taken to target improvements.

Career Opportunity and Development

Tesco has constructed a competency framework built around a series of factors identified as crucial to success, for example conceptual thinking, teamwork and drive. The business actively encourages self-development as well as supporting more formal development programmes.

The company is currently rolling-out a major career management initiative for senior managers, providing encouragement for executives to move across functions, locations and businesses. 50 UK managers are presently enjoying 'development moves' to European operations. Those embarking on spells abroad receive significant support and are welcomed back to the UK once their period of secondment comes to an end.

Tesco runs countless in-store programmes covering all aspects of store operations from slicing meat to operating a check-out. All such programmes are run on a needs-driven basis. Experience suggests that some members of staff may derive greater benefit from personal guidance by an appropriate mentor than being enrolled on yet another course.

Tesco's graduate recruitment scheme is branded 'Excel'. Designed to provide rapid career progression by offering a variety of process and management challenges, 166 graduates joined the scheme in September 1996.

Vacancies are advertised internally. Tesco has a long tradition of developing its own talent, although the company also recognises the value of importing recruits to provide a fresh injection of ideas. Many employees have risen through the ranks— Tesco's chairman, Sir Ian MacLaurin joined the company as a graduate.

Pay and Benefits

Tesco leads the way among food retailing companies, offering upper quartile rewards as a minimum. The company has moved firmly away from rigid pay structures dictating standard increases across the group. Rises are awarded according to performance, with staff being appraised against pre-determined objectives; reviews are conducted in April, with any pay increases implemented each July.

Although all jobs across the group are graded within pay bands, Tesco remains sensitive to market pressures. In certain key areas, the company is sometimes prepared to exceed pre-set targets.

Tesco provides a highly attractive basket of benefits. Staff with more than one year's service are automatically allocated shares—part of the overall strategy of encouraging staff to become partners in the business. Cars are provided on both a 'need' and 'status' basis. Each relevant grade has a car value attached, and staff are entitled to trade-up, down or take a cash alternative. Tesco's contributory pension scheme is highly regarded. Not only is the scheme open to part-time members of staff but it also provides life insurance cover.

The company has also negotiated a wide range of voluntary benefits with service providers, including optical and dental health care plans. Other perks include 25 days' annual leave, 10% staff discount in Tesco stores, and a generous maternity scheme.

The Future

Tesco sits proudly on top of the supermarket summit. Quality produce, customer care and unstinting staff effort may have enabled Tesco to overtake its long-term rival, Sainsbury's, but staying ahead of the pack demands equal resolve:

"When you're driving towards the top," suggests Deirdre Palin, European personnel and training controller, "it's easy to summon the ambition and commitment of everyone within the organisation. Staying there, however, presents even more of a challenge. The task is to keep driving the company forward, sustaining the same level of innovation and creativity."

In a fiercely competitive sector of industry, the need to recruit staff skilled at dealing with customers is paramount. "The challenge in that case," Deirdre suggests, "is to keep finding these people, hooking them into business success, and keeping them interested and motivated at work."

Although continuing to expand inside the UK, Europe offers a prime source of future growth. Working with staff in France, Hungary, Poland, Slovakia and the Czech Republic not only presents significant language barriers but—in the case of ex-communist countries—also means coming to terms with a traditional work ethic somewhat at odds with attitudes in the UK.

In Europe, as elsewhere, the seeds of Tesco's impressive endeavours have begun to bear fruit. A new 60,000 sq. ft. hypermarket in Budapest is the largest food outlet in Central Europe, offering a blueprint for other locations that potentially could incorporate non-food activities.

There lies the ultimate challenge. Sainsbury's partnership with the Bank of Scotland indicates one direction for supermarkets that is already common throughout the USA. Such radical developments hold few fears for Tesco, a forward-thinking organisation amply qualified to meet any challenge head-on.

Thames Water plc

Thames Water is the largest water company in the UK and one of the UK's top 100 companies by market capitalisation. As well as operating at a local level, the company is also an international operation. Its turnover exceeds £1,190 million and it employs about 10,500 staff, 1,200 of them overseas.

Biggest Plus: Great career opportunities and the chance to make a difference

Biggest Minus: Convincing people that water companies can be efficient

Thames Water plc
14 Cavendish Place
London W1M ONU
Tel: 0171-833 6121
Fax: 0171-833 6138

The Business

At a time when many privatised water companies are the target for widespread criticisms, Thames Water has an outstanding record. Its household bills are lower than for any other water company in England and Wales. Over the past five years it has invested more than £1.9 billion—£1 million a day—in modernising its infrastructure and systems to serve its customers and meet exacting regulatory standards. The advent of privatisation has allowed Thames Water to plan for the long term and raise the finance needed for major investment for the future.

This type of outlay gives the answer to those who believe that water is a free gift from nature and requires no management. In fact, supplying clean water and removing dirty water is big business. The company has 11 million customers in the UK that it serves with a network of 112,000 km of underground pipes. It is currently making the biggest improvement to the water and sewerage system since Victorian days.

Thames Water plc has three main operating divisions. The main subsidiary is Thames Water Utilities, which supplies water and collects and treats waste water throughout London and the Thames Valley. Thames Water International combines the company's contracting, consultancy and operational management services: providing water supply and waste water services to public communities, particularly in developing countries. And Thames Water Products and Services develops and manufactures a range of high quality products such as specialist water treatment equipment.

Company Culture and Style

So what is it like to work for Thames Water? Head of personnel Steve Jay: "Working here is fascinating because of the possibility of making a difference. We work with everyone: our customers range from single domestic customers to massive industrial complexes and even foreign governments; we interact with regulators such as OFWAT, the Environmental Agency, local communities and environmental pressure groups. It's vital to take all these groups into account and under-stand their needs."

This culture obviously spans a range of areas; an operational scientist works in quite a different culture to an engineer. Nevertheless, there is a Thames Water culture that is about freedom to contribute. The company has the refreshing approach of acknowledging that it doesn't know everything there is to know. As a result, people who join the company are not hidebound by restrictions but positively valued for their new perspectives and skills.

Interestingly, the company's dynamic approach pre-dates privatisation—which may go some way to explain its present success relative to other water companies. Change really began to take hold in 1986 when the chairman introduced a programme of embracing change.

Thames Water employs over 10,500 people. Nine years ago, the company employed around 9,000 people, most of whom were working in what is now the utility company. Now that company employs about 5,500 people: the remaining 5,000 or so employees work in new and diverse areas in the UK and overseas. This influx has boosted the sense of dynamism and excitement about the company. Thames Water today is a company on the move with an outgoing, hands-on attitude that is winning it a reputation for excellence both at home and abroad.

Internal communications are handled through *Thames Water News*, a monthly magazine for the entire group, and *Thames Water Views*, a video which appears four times a year. Both of these report on all the different companies and divisions at home and abroad. Each business unit will handle local-level communications in its own way. There are also bulletins, noticeboards and email.

A fundamental aspect of the culture is concern for the environment. The company has won an array of awards for its work, which can include greenery access schemes on company land, designing buildings to harmonise with the local community, care for fish and other wildlife, and providing sewage biosolids to agricultural land. The river Thames is now one of the cleanest metropolitan rivers in the world, with salmon and even otters returning to its reaches.

Human Resource Priorities

A major part of the Thames Water agenda is concerned with developing employee competence and capability at all levels. This is particularly true of the management team; turning managers into leaders has in turn enabled them to help their people develop more effectively.

The whole area of improving people's performance is seen at Thames to centre on five key areas: employee communications; performance management; improving people's ability to manage change in the organisation; involving people in their own target-setting and development; and sharing goals, aspirations and direction in a common mind-set. These initiatives have led to widespread shifts in the company's approach. For instance, there is a move away from formal organisational structures and job evaluations and towards having people playing a key part in de-fining their own roles.

Career Opportunity and Development

More and more graduates are finding that Thames Water offers them the chance for early opportunity and a stimulating career that can develop as they wish. Rory Channer joined the company with a degree in occupational psychology. "I joined Thames Water as a business analyst. Initially I was part of a small team, working on procurement systems. In my second week on the job I was asked to write one of the systems' user manuals. This is an important aspect to any system and I appreciated being trusted with that level of responsibility so early on."

Graduates join the Graduate Business Development Programme which is run in the form of several residential courses, typically lasting a week, during the first 15 months with the company. The courses develop business awareness, personal development and business skills, while graduates also do project work in groups, spend six weeks at the Customer Centre and often take part in an outdoor development weekend.

Each graduate is assigned a mentor, someone other than his or her line manager, ideally placed to offer practical advice.

Thames Water has a flat structure where people can develop across different jobs and functional roles. Everyone can take significant responsibility and development can be rapid. The growing number of international jobs offers new challenges and scope for experience; Thames has already landed half a dozen large contracts with partners such as the Dick Corporation of the USA. These can be in places as diverse as Turkey, Malaysia or China. In Malaysia, for example, Thames people are now helping to look after the State of Kelantan's water supply system.

There is a wide range of training available, including corporate training and local training programmes. Chief press officer Clare Bonney: "We have links with three business schools, IMD in Lausanne for top management development, Templeton College in Oxford, where about 400 of our managers have been through development programmes, and Henley Management College which runs DMS and MBA programmes, tailored to our needs."

Cross-skilling is important at all levels with about 70% of the technical workforce now cross-skilled. All operating staff are now being trained up to NVQ standards. Self-learning and needs-related training is supported and encouraged.

Pay and Benefits

The company is regarded as a fair payer, which it needs to be to attract the quality people it requires. Despite this, people are often not attracted so much by the remuneration as by the opportunities, scope and buzz about the company. Pay rises are part of a system whereby individual performance is related to reward.

Benefits include a profit-sharing scheme which allows people to take cash or shares—and typically over 50% now take shares. The company also operates sharesave schemes and has good pension arrangements.

The Future

Thames Water exists in an environment of constant change. As a result, one challenge is to handle the changing direction of the company. This may result in some types of job being shed and others created. In a climate where lifetime job security is no longer expected, employees are encouraged to develop their skills. The company is open about all employment changes and always seeks to redeploy people wherever possible.

The main challenge for the future, though, is to ensure that the company attracts and retains the right calibre of people to manage its future and that those people are developed to their potential. Given the blend of empowerment, responsibility and career development opportunity in place, Thames Water would look to be well placed to meet this challenge.

THE **600** GROUP

The 600 Group

The 600 Group is a UK-based international engineering business, with highly de-centralised global operations. The company's main business is the manufacture of high quality, precision machine tools that are marketed and distributed world-wide. In 1996, the group's annual turnover was £160 million. Of the 1,500 employees in The 600 Group, two-thirds are found in the UK, 11 at the company's lean head of-fice in Milton Keynes.

Biggest Plus: Determined company, bucking the trend in its industry

Biggest Minus: Always a cyclical business

The 600 Group plc
Witan Court
284 Witan Gate
Milton Keynes MK9 1EJ
Tel: 01908-234600
Fax: 01908-235600

The Business

The 600 Group once was as famous in Colchester as the local oysters. Producers of the Colchester lathe, the plant there once employed 3,000 people; now it is closed. It is not only a sign of the times, but a sign that the company recognised how close to death it was. Now The 600 Group stands as a business success, having turned it-self around.

The 600 Group came face-to-face with some hard realities. Orders had disappeared, the company was badly structured, having grown very quickly, and executives held responsibility for companies for no apparent reason. When the group began haemorrhaging money, its old paternalistic, autocratic style looked less appropriate than ever. New managing director Colin Gaskell realised it was time for drastic change.

As a result, the company trimmed its staff levels to produce a leaner, more focused work base, and began to change the culture. The large centralised corporate headquarters was broken up and operational responsibility was shifted quickly to individual subsidiaries that were far better placed to understand and respond to their markets. Sensibly, responsibility for developing business strategy was also shifted, to which was added the discipline of strong monthly financial reporting. These changes have returned The 600 Group to profit—£13.5 million in 1995—and the future trends look encouraging.

Company Culture and Style

The next task was to instil a new culture. "We had to understand how to engender a new style, one that would move us from survival mode to growth," says Ken Fowler, human resources director. "We wanted entrepreneurial behaviour and teamwork. What emerged were five core competencies that staff needed to acquire if the company was to thrive in the nineties."

The first competency was a fundamental requirement to understand the business. The company believed that it produced some of the best machine lathes in the world, but this had to be married to a sensitivity in meeting specific customer requirements, to make a quality product a profitable one.

Understanding corporate direction, including company structure and management processes, is the second competency, and thirdly, development orientation focuses on having awareness of each individual's needs and those of their teams. Organisation influencing recognises the importance of being aware of other elements in the organisation and having the ability to influence them. Finally, strategic perspective means thinking ahead beyond day-to-day issues to plan for what is at the same time a cyclical business, and one that needs to expand.

The response to the call for a new entrepreneurial spirit was tremendous, unleashing energies and attitudes that had obviously laid dormant. The 600 Group is characterised by open, honest, direct, hard-working employees who have dispensed with politics. These are people prepared to get things done and who have a sense of fun. Individuals have relished being given greater freedom, implicit in which is trust—mistakes are no longer criticised, support is integral, and people are more inclined to try things out without fear of having to cover-up any errors.

Human Resource Priorities

With this scale of restructuring and cultural change, HR's role was and is crucial. In closing its Colchester plant, The 600 Group showed simultaneously its new-found business decisiveness, and its caring attitude towards employees, helping them retain their dignity and self-esteem. Many took early retirement—whatever the stage of the business cycle or The 600 Group's financial strength, the company maintained a well-funded pension plan. And considerable support was offered to help displaced employees find employment, going beyond providing outplacement services for each single person.

"It is an important element in the way we would want to treat people," says Ken Fowler, "it also helped diffuse many of the difficulties we might have had. The added bonus was that it got everyone to focus on the future, instead of the past and present."

One important spin-off from change was the introduction of a flatter structure to the group. This helped create rapid communication and understanding throughout the organisation. People had to communicate laterally, which introduced informal teamworking with people having to depend upon each other more. HR took a positive role to support this new structure through training and communication.

Career Opportunity and Development

The 600 Group encourages managers who will take measured risks and be able to seize opportunities. In recruitment, these qualities are made quite clear. New joiners, unshackled by anything that has gone before, have a real opportunity to make a decisive impact on what is still a quality international company. The intake of new graduates has remained steady at around 12 each year. Incumbents benefit from a revitalised training and development process aimed at helping all staff acquire modern commercial, personal and communication skills.

There is plenty of opportunity at The 600 Group, but the company prefers to put round pegs in round holes. Dedicated computer freaks may not be given the chance to holler down customer service lines, nor will language specialists be charged with designing new generations of machine technology.

Historically, there has been little movement between the globally spread businesses, but this is changing. Cross-divisional work opportunities are likely to increase, and on a more informal basis, the company is keen to encourage its staff to network by means of overseas visits, and attending group conferences and development programmes.

The 600 Group is still small enough to factor-in the all-important personal touch to communications and development. The company runs a series of four-day courses for 12 people at a time, which consider the personal development goals of each individual; they are held in a relaxed environment and the chairman is there talking to everyone. One of the skills the course sets out to teach is people-handling.

Managers from around the world meet annually, to discuss the company's strengths and weaknesses. "At a recent meeting in Stratford upon Avon the managers were asked to think about the company globally. Working as a team, they were challenged by the chairman, Michael Wright, to come up with ideas for further improving the group," says Fowler. "A response was faxed to Wright and within 24 hours, three of the ideas put forward were in the process of being implemented."

The performance review process includes an assessment of individuals against key competencies, and an element of self-assessment, resulting in two-way feedback. These appraisals are held once a year formally, and informally at interim periods.

Pay and Benefits

Engineering has never been one of the highest-paying sectors, but the group pays competitively.

There is a management incentive plan and an SAYE share scheme for all employees that has been readily taken up; when this was first offered in 1992, 600 Group's share price was 34p—four years later it had increased eight-fold.

The Future

It gives Fowler great satisfaction to hear people "talk the language of an entrepreneurial growth-style culture," although he reckons the company is only half-way through its cultural revolution, and even then, cultural change often proves to be a continuous process.

In business, the company has raised its sights, and aims to double turnover over the next five years. The 600 Group believes that it has some great products coming out, and the internal debate rages around whether to pursue organic growth or synergistic acquisitions—or both. And although The 600 Group is already an international business, there remain a number of markets to exploit—the company is working out its best strategy to expand into the Far East, for example.

The 600 Group does have a certain reliance on the cyclical machine tools business, and this remains a potential source of weakness. "What happens in two or three years time is of concern," says chief executive Colin Gaskell. "That's when we are predicting the cycle will dip." The group should aspire by then to have its business revenues more evenly spread across geographic markets than they are at present. If one of the UK, the rest of Europe, North America or Asia suffers, the others could cushion the effects, but this balance is not there yet and needs to be reached quickly, hence the aggressive expansion plans for Asia.

"We know we can suffer a 30% downturn in orders and sales and still be profitable, which is something we couldn't have done five years ago. That's why we advocate being conservative with the amount of resource that we have." That this is possible underlines the progress 600 Group has made. If it carries on the momentum, downturns could become things of the past.

TOYOTA

Toyota Motor Corporation

Toyota Motor Corporation of Japan is one of the world's great car manufacturers. Famous for its reliable, and increasingly stylish, motor cars, it has been manufacturing in Europe since 1971. Toyota commenced production at its UK plant in Burnaston, Derbyshire, in 1992, producing variants of its Carina mid-class saloon. By 1996, annual production had reached 110,000 vehicles; 75% of this production is exported to mainland Europe.

In 1995, Toyota announced expansion plans to reach a target production of 200,000 vehicles annually, involving a further investment of some £200 million including an additional assembly plant. There is also an engine manufacturing plant in Deeside, North Wales, producing 1.6 and 1.8 litre engines. There are more than 2,100 employees at the Burnaston plant, and a further 200 at Deeside.

Biggest Plus: Treats people fairly, with trust and respect, to engender team working

Biggest Minus: The need to learn and train for new skills is continuous

Toyota Motor Manufacturing (UK) Ltd.
Burnaston
Derbyshire DE1 9TA
Tel: 01332-282224
Fax: 01332-282801

The Business

Since 1962, when Toyota shipped its first Europe-bound cars to Denmark, operations in Europe have grown significantly.

Today, Europe is one of the world's largest car markets with nearly 12 million automobiles sold in 1995. Projections for the turn of the century suggest this figure could rise to 15 million vehicles. Against this background, Toyota's decision to manufacture in Europe was an easy one to make, and based on a corporate philosophy of building cars where its customers are. Already selling 400,000 cars and trucks in Europe in 1989, Toyota Motor Manufacturing (UK) Ltd. (Toyota UK) was formed in the same year.

The attractions of the UK included a ready availability of an extremely large piece of land, a highly skilled and flexible work force nearby, good transportation links with Europe, and a supportive, encouraging government at both local and national level. The UK's large domestic market and strong traditions of vehicle manufacturing were also factors.

Toyota's European operations are fully integrated. At its heart is Toyota Motor Europe Marketing and Engineering (TMME), based in Brussels. As well as housing design, training and accessories development centres, TMME buys Toyota Motor Corporation (TMC) cars, and sells them onto distributors in individual countries. The distributor in the UK is Toyota GB, but it is not owned by TMC.

Company Culture and Style

The shared goal at Toyota is customer satisfaction, which reigns supreme. Customer satisfaction is at the heart of all Toyota activities, from research and development to manufacturing, retailing and servicing, and quality is central to achieving customer satisfaction. Total Quality is assured by following two basic principles: quality is built in at every stage; and quality is continually improved.

Toyota UK recognises that highly competent, motivated people who are treated with respect will show great commitment to the fulfilment of the company's objectives. Fundamental to this 'people' philosophy is a determination to provide the individual with both personal growth opportunity and stable employment. This is best achieved by securing long-term prosperity for the company.

The right people are vital. Previous motor industry experience takes a back seat to teamworking aptitude, and good communications skills; the ability to learn and the will to improve are also valued highly.

Much is said about the working practices introduced in manufacturing locations by Pacific Rim companies. The Toyota Production System (TPS) is a concept that strives for the absolute elimination of waste, overburden and unevenness in all areas. The aim of TPS is to provide the customer with the highest quality, at lowest possible cost, in a timely manner with the shortest possible lead times.

The process of continuous improvement is also known as Kaizen. And the two main pillars of TPS are Just in Time (JIT) and jidoka. JIT provides the right parts and materials in the exact amount needed, only when needed. This is sometimes referred to as a pull system, which works by use of a kanban. A kanban is a card or signal that carries production and delivery instructions from one process to an-other, automatically ordering parts as they are used up. Heijunka, or production levelling, is used to smooth out production in all departments over a period of time.

The second pillar of TPS is Jidoka, or 'automation with a human touch'. It is the ability of a machine or production line to stop automatically or be easily stopped when an abnormality occurs, highlight problems and contribute to the achievement of high quality. At the heart of TPS lies member initiative and creativity. Decision making involves the direct participation of those closest to the issue—the members.

Toyota UK's products have won many accolades, from the UK Consumer Association and in the 1996 JD Power/BBC Top Gear customer satisfaction survey, which named the Carina E as the best British-built car. In addition, Toyota UK has achieved recognition for its efforts in the form of ISO 9002 and ISO 14001 certification, a National Training Award, and Investors in People.

Toyota UK puts much store on being a 'good corporate citizen', in a manner that is socially responsible and contributes to the well-being of the communities in which the company operates. Creating a successful company is a fundamental part, but Toyota spends much time and money supporting a range of projects that address genuine social needs and deliver no direct commercial benefit.

Human Resource Priorities

A primary human resource objective is to improve the quality of working life for employees by ensuring that they are treated with dignity and fairness, and that they are provided with economic security and opportunities for advancement, in recognition of their contribution to the company.

Toyota UK's organisation is flat and the company likes to keep it that way. Flat structures make for ease of communications and flexibility. Divisions divide into departments, groups, and then teams. The team structure is a key element of the company's effectiveness, helping to build trusting relationships and flexible, co-operative teams with broad job skills.

A common term at Toyota is 'mutual trust and respect', between members, between management and members and between the company and its union.

The company has signed a Single Union Agreement with the Amalgamated Engineering and Electrical Union (AEEU). No other unions are recognised or represented. This agreement has helped support the company's philosophy. A joint commitment has provided an environment in which individuals feel that they can play an active role and grow as the company grows. Toyota UK offers shared success in return for shared responsibility.

The Toyota Members' Advisory Board is a forum where elected representatives and company executives meet together regularly to discuss matters of common interest. This Board supports Toyota's drive for success and supplements the day-to-day communication channels between members and the company. In all decision-making processes, Toyota aims to reach a consensus opinion wherever possible, and the Members' Advisory Board facilitates this goal.

Career Opportunity and Development

Toyota UK encourages its members to develop their skills to the utmost capacity, and views training as essential to the maintenance and improvement of the company's performance. Training is primarily directed towards skill development for specific job requirements.

Not surprisingly, real performance improvements in the work place are achieved and developed through on-the-job training (OJT). OJT encourages individuals to learn their own jobs to a such a standard that they are able to train others. All members are trained to be multi-skilled and by learning many jobs, Toyota staff find movement and rotation of jobs possible, even easy. While being better able to respond to the needs of production, employees probably enjoy more challenging, varied and interesting work.

In addition to ongoing structured and OJT, Toyota UK has two other programmes aimed at further developing the professionalism of shop floor members. The company also provides its members with opportunities to study for work-related qualifications financed by the company.

Pay and Benefits

Toyota treats everyone with fairness and respect to encourage company-wide teamworking. All members are, therefore, paid a monthly salary with the same terms and conditions—for example, one pension scheme, private health care for all members and their families, the same restaurant, car parking and work wear.

Fairness is also ensured by thorough systems for evaluating performance, deciding promotions and conducting salary reviews. All members have twice-yearly reviews of progress against set criteria and every member can progress up a salary band that recognises developing skills, capability and performance.

Each year the salary increase comprises two elements: a core increase that recognises the company's position and the members' contribution as part of a company team, and an individual appraisal-related increase which recognises individual contribution.

A key factor in 1996 was the company's desire to reward its members for their efforts in producing more than 200,000 high quality cars to date and ensuring the smooth introduction of the 1996 face-lifted Carina E. The award also anticipates their future contribution to successful growth.

The Future

Toyota UK is set to increase its production to 200,000 vehicles a year by adding a Corolla series vehicle in 1998. This will also mean increased production at the Deeside engine plant.

The expansion will create around 1,000 new jobs, with the majority of recruitment being local to the plants, beginning in mid-1997, so that initial training can start well in advance of Corolla production commencing. Training for phase two has already begun with a unique scheme to train experienced production members as maintenance members through a three-year off- and on-the-job training programme. As part of the phase two development, an all-purpose training centre is being built.

With Toyota's commitment to training and a highly skilled and motivated work force, this is a considerable task, but one that is integral to the company's continued success.

Unigate

Unigate is a European food and distribution group. Its fresh food division includes St Ivel products that produce yellow fat spreads, yoghurt, fromage frais, desserts, cheese, butter, milk powders, cream, savoury dips and fruit juices. Malton produces and exports pork and cooked meats. Unigate is the leading processor and distributor of fresh milk in the UK. Wincanton Logistics provides dedicated, shared and consolidated distribution services for major retailers and manufacturers. US Restaurants owns and operates 110 Taco Bueno Mexican restaurants in Texas and Oklahoma. Unigate plc has over 31,000 employees and an annual turnover of £2.1 billion.

Biggest Plus: A reshaped company with a new appetite for success

Biggest Minus: Not for you if you don't relish handling significant responsibility!

Unigate plc
Unigate House
Wood Lane
London W12 7RP
Tel: 0181-749 8888
Fax: 0181-576 6071

The Business

The last five years have been a period of transition for Unigate as the group has divested its non-core businesses to make it much more tightly focused. Today, the group consists almost entirely of food and distribution companies that work closely together to create mutually beneficial synergy's. Unigate sees this era of change as one of opportunity.

Giltspur, the exhibitions business, was sold for £40 million and Unigate's stake in Nutricia was placed with institutional investors. The US restaurant business, Black-eyed Pea, was also sold. The company ended 1995/96 with no debt, £171 million in net cash, and assets of over £530 million—the fifth consecutive year of profitable growth. As a result, Unigate is actively exploring opportunities to develop and expand its presence in Europe.

The rising cost of milk has hit profits. In response, Unigate is switching from doorstep sales to supermarket sales. As the company strives to increase its market share and profitability, its belief is that nothing is static and that it must constantly produce new and better products, new ideas, and new packaging. For the first time in 60 years, Unigate is buying milk direct from farmers. It has enlarged its marketing budget to increase consumer loyalty to leading brands and enlarge its share of the total chilled products market.

One of its main aims is to provide blue-chip companies in all market sectors with more cost-efficient and long-term solutions. Each of the main businesses within Unigate now has the scale to compete effectively as a low-cost producer. British Airways has recently appointed Wincanton to manage storage and distribution for its in-flight retail sales business.

Unigate companies have reduced the number of management strata. This has shortened the lines of reporting and enhanced decision making throughout the organisation. Employees now have much greater freedom to interpret instructions within a broad framework of corporate ideals.

Company Culture and Style

The company philosophy is that growth increases competitiveness and increased competitiveness creates growth. Success depends on the company's capacity to deal with change in the world, in the industry and in the economy. Unigate believes that its employees know that the only route to job security, competitive pay and a dependable pension is a successful business; the company also recognises that people make a company truly successful.

Unigate feels that it has developed a unique management style and culture that have fostered a great sense of corporate togetherness. This has provided employees with increased material benefits. Unigate believes that no company can respond quickly to change without empowering individuals to take decisions at every level.

At the St Ivel factories, teams of employees are regularly formed to resolve problems or identify ways of raising output reducing waste or cutting costs. Three teams at the Paignton plant identified cost savings in excess of £300,000 a year.

Hierarchical management is seen as a thing of the past. A flatter structure means that employees should be flexible, good at communicating, and possess excellent interpersonal skills. Candidates need to have stamina and resilience, resourcefulness and creativity. They also need to be pragmatic and have common sense, enthusiasm, commitment, motivation and vision, and hold at least a lower second degree or HND equivalent.

If they fulfil this brief, their talent will be recognised, appreciated and nurtured. They will be judged solely on their ability to perform and will be given considerable responsibility from early on. Many graduates are now senior managers in the group's main UK businesses.

Unigate puts money into new capital equipment—such as the £30 million invested over the last three years in the automation of production lines at three of its six manufacturing plants.

Human Resource Priorities

To foster good relations and employee participation, Unigate provides an annual report to employees that deals with group and divisional results. There is also an in-house newspaper. 4,000 employees participate in the SAYE share option scheme, and the group also operates a profit-related pay scheme called Paywise in which 95% of UK-based employees participate, holding options on 6.2 million ordinary shares.

Employees are encouraged to learn faster than their competitors, and to take ownership of their own careers. Commitment to equal opportunities is enshrined in the ethos of the corporation, which makes it clear that people from diverse backgrounds positively enhance the company and encourage creativity. Employees are selected, recruited, developed and promoted entirely on merit. Unigate wishes to maintain a work place free of sexual or racial harassment or intimidation. Anyone disabled during the course of employment knows that the company will try to retain their services.

Career Opportunity and Development

Investment in training is vital for Unigate. The company is keen that employees should build on and add to their skills. A wide variety of career development opportunities is offered, from the acquisition of professional and other nationally recognised qualifications such as NVQs, to bespoke in-house training courses.

All graduates enter the Unigate organisation at management level and are quickly asked to take on responsibility. They are given a great deal of support through automatic placement on a structured training programme called Management Development Programme, or MDP. This begins within a few months of joining and lasts from nine to 12 months. It consists of staggered three-day residential courses and associated ongoing commercial projects. Mentoring is also a key element of the training programme although this operates less formally in some parts of the organisation. It is seen as helping to further and shape careers.

An annual performance improvement review sets goals for the coming year and managers often identify areas in which further courses may prove useful. Work can pile up, so employees must be adept at managing their time!

Pay and Benefits

Rates of pay are competitive. The SAYE share scheme, which is open to UK employees generally, is linked to a monthly savings contract under which employees save tax free up to £250 per month over five years. Options are no longer granted by the company at a discount to the market price at the date of grant.

Pensions for executives are provided on a non-contributory basis through the Unigate Group pension scheme or where appropriate in individual cases through the use of an unfunded arrangement.

The Future

The challenges for the future are all about targeting growth markets, producing new products and services, managing change, increasing competitiveness and investing in people.

Unigate has a proven ability to manage far-reaching structural changes in the markets that its companies serve. Unigate's strong financial position means that it is well placed to make substantial acquisitions in either the UK or Continental Europe.

Unilever

Unilever

Unilever is one of the world's largest consumer goods businesses. A market leader in foods, detergents, personal products and speciality chemicals, Unilever generates sales of £31.5 billion and profits of £2.5 billion annually. Unilever employs over 308,000 people world-wide, 22,000 of whom work in the UK.

Biggest Plus: Outstanding opportunities for career development

Biggest Minus: Impossible to remember all those brand names!

Unilever plc
Unilever House
Blackfriars
London EC4P 4BQ
Tel: 0171-822 5252
Fax: 0171-822 5951

The Business

Unilever was founded in 1930 by the amalgamation of Lever Brothers in the UK and Margarine Unie in the Netherlands. The resultant company became one of Europe's biggest industrial organisations, and it has continued to build on that base ever since through international expansion. Today, Unilever manufactures products in over 90 countries and is the world leader in many of its markets. Its operating companies market literally thousands of household name products, including PG Tips, Batchelors soups, Flora, Oxo, Cornetto, Magnum, Lux, Persil, Jif, Dove, Pond's lotions, Timotei shampoo, Signal toothpaste, Obsession, Eternity and many more.

The organisation describes itself as international rather than global, since many of its products are specific to certain markets rather than sold world-wide. As a result, Unilever can be seen as a local company in all of its countries; many consumers world-wide regard Unilever's brands as local properties, because their mothers used those brands.

Expansion is very much a controlled and planned operation. The group's businesses tend to survive and prosper due to this long-term approach. The group now has 12 joint ventures in China, for instance, whereas there were none five years ago. But this is just the start of a policy of growth in the region that looks 10 or 20 years into the future.

Company Culture and Style

Many operating companies make up the Unilever Group, including such well-known names as Bird's Eye Walls, John West Foods, Van den Bergh Foods, Lever Brothers, Elida Gibbs, Calvin Klein and Elizabeth Arden. Unilever employees are employed by those companies, and as a result see themselves as part of their company. Conversely, managers are seen as a national common interest group. Their terms and conditions are the same, as are their appraisal schemes, pay scales and benefits.

Managers and employees alike nevertheless have a strong sense of belonging to the Unilever Group. This is aided by the fact that most of the factories and offices of the operating companies do not employ more than 500 people. This in turn makes for an open culture with good communications.

Unilever's ambitious goals of global business growth make the group an exciting and absorbing organisation to work for. These ambitions mean that change is constant, with the operating companies undergoing frequent restructuring and repositioning in order to build viable long-term businesses. People likely to do well at Unilever in the 1990s and the next century are those with an international outlook, open to diverse ideas, exceptionally bright, motivational and competitive.

Internal communication is handled through a group newsletter, individual company newsletters, and a great deal of team briefing, cascading and use of noticeboards. In addition, a large meeting of the top 300 managers is held each year. This takes the form of a 'State of the Nation' address which reviews Unilever's overall business and looks at next year's targets. This is used as a framework fordownward cascading throughout the group.

Human Resource Priorities

Each of Unilever's companies has always regarded people as a vital part of its business. Not surprisingly therefore, HR ranks highly at the group. At Unilever itself, and in all the main subsidiaries, personnel departments and agendas are represented at board level.

A planning system throughout Unilever incorporates people planning. At management level this system becomes highly sophisticated, devoting considerable time and energy to succession planning and identifying the stars of tomorrow.

Empowerment is well developed throughout the group, aided by a long-term commitment to Total Quality Management and team briefings. Demonstration that the systems really work is provided by the fact that Unilever companies hold no less than 32 Investors in People awards. The huge hierarchies once commonplace in some companies are gone, leading to more interesting jobs all round.

Career Opportunity and Development

A number of Unilever's UK companies are good medium-sized businesses in their own right with turnovers of £700 million or more. As a result, many people can build highly successful and rewarding careers without moving elsewhere. It is now unlikely, however, that people could rise to the top of a single company, let alone Unilever itself, without moving between companies. Of course, many people relish the opportunity to build their careers by taking on a series of challenges. At any time, 1,800 Unilever managers are working outside their home countries, of which 600 are British.

Hugh Stirk is Unilever's national UK personnel manager and has himself worked for the Group in detergents, packaging and food companies, in both factories and the head office. As he says, "Unilever provides an outstanding opportunity for managers wishing to grow and develop by changing responsibilities, both in the UK and internationally. Even in the individual companies this is now the case. Lever Brothers for instance, once seen as predominantly a UK business, now operates in 17 European countries."

All jobs are advertised internally before going outside in accordance with Unilever's policy of promoting from within—and indeed there is often no alternative to this thanks to the excellent and diverse opportunities for experience that home-grown candidates have. Recently appointed chairman of the group, Niall FitzGerald, has spent his entire career with Unilever companies—and in doing so has built up a fund of expertise an outsider would find difficult to match. In any one year, 30% of those appointed to their first managerial posts within Unilever have come up through the ranks.

The group has recruited graduates since 1945. Today, between 80 and 100 graduates come on board each year, most through the Management Development Scheme which combines formal training, progressive work experience and steadily increasing responsibility; a few science graduates are recruited as Direct Entrants, largely for Unilever's two UK research laboratories. Jane McKellar recounts her time in the Management Development Scheme: "Even though my training was based in the UK, I was in close contact with other operating companies throughout the world. As group product manager for the Beautycare Group, I was in charge of a fantastic portfolio of leading brands...such as Pond's creams, Cutex, Brut, Denim, Hero and Lynx, marketing them in regions as culturally different as the Far East and South America."

Training is taken very seriously at all levels. Indeed, Unilever claims to offer the best general management and development training available in the UK today, together with a well-established system of career guidance.

Pay and Benefits

The policy at Unilever is to be at least at the median level of other blue-chip businesses in the industries in which it operates. Overall, pay is regarded as above-average by outside observers.

Benefits include a first-class pension scheme which has four times salary payable as death in service benefit, five weeks' holiday, bonus schemes related to the performance of the operating company, family private health care for all managers and company cars for middle management and above.

Hugh Stirk believes that job security is greater at Unilever companies than elsewhere: "Over a long process of change, improvement and investment, we have built very efficient and effective businesses." If redundancies are unavoidable, the group minimises the sense of shock or surprise by giving long notice periods: a year's notice of a major change is not unknown, while six months is regarded as the minimum. This allows time for more effective outplacement, and in any case Unilever-trained personnel are often snapped up quickly when they become avail-able. However, given the number of people who have celebrated 25 years or more with the Group, this may not be often!

The Future

Unilever aims to turn its powerful market positions into those of leadership where this is not already the case, and continue its geographical expansion. The UK, Europe and the USA remain important markets, but have nothing like the growth potential available elsewhere in the world and particularly Asia. This expansion and growth therefore constitutes a considerable challenge, requiring the company to meld big business and global issues with local knowledge and flexibility.

Stirk: "Our mission won't be achieved unless we have the manpower, and particularly the management, to do it. We already have 20,000 managers world-wide and 2,000 in the UK, but we need more high-calibre men and women for the future. The related challenge of identifying the businesses, the products and the brands which can be truly successful is dependent upon getting the HR challenge right."

A final challenge is the problem typical of groups composed of operating companies. Unilever itself makes and sells nothing; all that work is done by its subsidiaries. The challenge is therefore to make Unilever itself well-known and exciting. If the group can raise its own profile while keeping its brands at the forefront, it really will have the best of both worlds.

United Biscuits

United Biscuits

United Biscuits is an international food business. It has leading market positions in the UK, continental Europe and Australia, and is building its presence in Asia. United Biscuits has an extensive portfolio of famous brands in biscuits, savoury snacks and frozen and chilled foods, including McVitie's Digestive and Penguin, KP Hula Hoops, Phileas Fogg, San Marco and Linda McCartney meat-free products. Employing some 27,800 staff world-wide (19,000 in the UK), United Biscuits is structured into three regional groupings with 46 manufacturing sites world-wide and products available in over 90 countries.

Biggest Plus: Great reputation as a people business with an informal, innovative style

Biggest Minus: The dazzling array of products are a fattening temptation!

United Biscuits (Holdings) plc
Group Headquarters
Church Road
West Drayton
Middlesex UB7 7PR
Tel: 01895-432100
Fax: 01895-448848

The Business

1995 was a watershed for United Biscuits (UB). A disappointing financial perform-ance triggered decisive action aimed at repositioning the business and improving results significantly. The company sharpened its strategic focus, disposed of burden-some operations, and committed to concentrating effort and resources in a drive for shareholder value.

UB enjoys a great reputation as a 'people organisation', where things get done because people know other people. This makes for a responsive business, which can put pressure on support processes and systems to keep pace with change. UB strives for a balance in working methods, making sure that it doesn't lose sight of the bene-fits that informal working relationships can bring.

UB's strengths include its flexibility in addressing problems and responding to changes in the marketplace. And the high public awareness of UB's products has enabled the company to build a strong base of customer loyalty.

A major organisational review at the end of 1995 resulted in UB revising its operating structure to strengthen control and reduce financial and management 'stretch'. The removal of a complete senior management layer has led to improved lines of reporting and quicker decision making.

There are many businesses within UB—and famous names at that. If in the past UB has tolerated a fairly decentralised structure, with operating companies forging strong individual identities, the company is going through more of a 'centralist' phase to reinforce some important corporate values.

International companies need to be selective, and UB is. Chairman Colin Short puts it this way. "We have many strengths—our brands, our leading market posi-tions, our manufacturing capabilities, the skills and commitment of our people. But to deploy them to best advantage we must concentrate our firepower, using them selectively in markets where we can compete most effectively."

Company Culture and Style

Key business principles of focus, rigour and delivery are intertwined with the com-pany's commitment to quality and innovation. UB is an environment where "naturally creative people are given a lot of responsibility early on in their career," according to Claire Dickson, UB's management development & training director. "You can take an idea and pursue it upwards, and translate it into action; the organi-sation is not hierarchical.

"The type of individual who flourishes at UB has excellent communication and interpersonal skills. You have to believe in what you do, and enthusiasm and tenac-ity are always welcome characteristics. Rank-pulling and status consciousness are virtually non-existent, and if we need information we tend to go to those who have it, be it a trainee or a senior manager."

UB is undergoing a major culture change, focusing minds on the paramount importance of creating value for its shareholders, and helping individuals to under-stand the levers they have within their control to achieve it. Training is crucial, be-ginning with managers. "We are committed to making managers financially aware of the business actions that affect shareholder value," says Sarah Abbot, HR & training manager. "At a time when we can least afford it, we are taking people out of their businesses for two to three days to give them shareholder value training. Additionally, shareholder value principles are now built into appraisals and objectives. Satisfying shareholders is critical and everyone has a responsibility."

The personal, interactive style at UB sees everyone working hard, but the company is rightly asking itself "are we doing the right things?" 'Being busy' sometimes makes people not feel personally threatened by change, but UB employees are now asked to analyse their work and methods, and be totally focused on whether they are doing the right things to meet these objectives.

Human Resource Priorities

UB enjoys healthy relations with its employees and trade unions. The group chief executive chairs the company's highly successful European Works Council, which provides a forum for the exchange of both information and views between management and employees. In 1994, UB became the first British company to establish a Europe-wide consultative council. Informing and consulting staff on matters of general concern is of prime importance to UB.

This commitment to employees also extends beyond when service has concluded, namely in the event of redundancy. UB assists the individual in finding a new job, providing new skills or outplacement help. "We stay in touch with former employees," adds Sarah Abbot. "We do not want their or our reputation to be tarnished and recognise that the jobs market is highly competitive and former employees need to be assisted as much as possible."

For employees taking maternity leave, UB exceeds statutory requirements to ensure that their female employees remain as in touch and informed as possible while out of the work place. UB provides three self-help manuals for expectant employees during different stages of pregnancy, offering practical child care advice and other matters relevant to working mothers. UB also maintains contact during maternity leave and chronicles the mother and new-born's development, while also keeping the mother updated on activities at the company.

Career Opportunity and Development

There is a big drive at present to emphasise—particularly to graduates—that you are not tied to one subsidiary company in UB. Believing that careers are more attractive if you can move across companies in the group, UB intends to back words with deeds, and such career development moves are likely to increase.

UB recruits approximately 60 graduates a year, all of whom attend the 'Management Essentials' programme along with other young managers with senior management potential. Management Essentials comprises three modules of four to five days management training, with an optional follow-up module. Additionally, all graduates are seconded into UB's sales force for their first six months to give them commercial experience. Graduates who are bilingual or trilingual are increasingly being hired to maximise the company's international opportunities.

International assignments number around 50 at any one time, and as UB sets about integrating and extracting synergys from its relatively independent European operations, such opportunities might increase. UB admits to not having 'grappled' with the area of European graduate recruitment, but it intends to, and has already introduced the Management Essentials programme in Europe.

With an HR manager and training manager at every site, UB conducts an annual review of senior management strengths, and the group chief executive chairs a strategy forum for management development. Managers have twice-yearly performance and potential appraisals with the line manager.

UB's top management team is relatively young—the average age of the Group Management Committee is 46 years. All except the most senior vacancies are advertised internally, and while there is no fast track scheme, there are many instances of employees rising through the ranks to the top management positions.

Pay and Benefits

UB's pay and benefits packages are highly competitive, aiming to attract and motivate the best employees possible. That means upper quartile in terms of pay. Belonging to the Review Club, UB targets its peer group as the leading UK food and drinks companies, but increasingly benchmarks other industries, particularly in graduate recruitment.

Graduates start at £16,000 and UB's overall remuneration policy is designed to provide arrangements which also reward high performance against short- and long-term business targets. Pay structure includes an incentive element for managers based on company (group or subsidiary) results.

Benefits are 'typical' although the company claims that its company car scheme is more generous than most. The company offers two pension schemes (defined benefit and defined contribution), and encourages employees to participate in share ownership via three different schemes including SAYE.

The Future

Attention is now focused quite firmly on delivering a vast improvement in financial performance and engendering a performance-dedicated culture while continuing to maintain supportive and developmental attitudes to employees.

UB's obvious business challenge is to leverage the potential synergys of its world-wide operations, and to share and translate the best practices across all businesses. This might see the company adopting a centralist stance for a while, but it is probably right for the company at this particular time.

UB needs to implement important changes without losing its commitment to innovation. It is vital that the company continues to originate new ideas, exploit new market sectors, launch new products and improve existing ones. The signs in the 1996 half-year results are that it is getting the balance right.

In driving a performance-based culture through the organisation, UB recognises that it still has very good people on its books, and must get the best out of them. Making employees also feel valued, and to continue their training and development, is a key challenge. It is a challenge that the company is meeting.

Virgin

Virgin is one of the UK's largest private group of companies, bound together by one of the most powerful brand names around and four core values—quality, competitiveness, innovation and fun. Virgin Group has grown in size 30 times over the last 12 years through a series of alliances, joint ventures and outsourcing. In this time it has catapulted from a modest music and entertainment company with revenues of £50 million to a diversified global conglomerate with revenues in excess of £1.5 billion.

The group of Virgin companies and their joint ventures currently employ over 10,000 staff, and operate in at least 22 countries with a mix of media, entertainment, retailing, publishing, merchandising and travel activities. There are now eight main divisions: Virgin Communications, Virgin Retail, Virgin Travel, Voyager Investments and Virgin Hotels Group, Virgin Radio, Virgin Cinemas and Virgin Direct, each of which operates autonomously.

Biggest Plus: Total belief in the company, the brand, the values and the leadership

Biggest Minus: Work hard as well as play hard

Virgin Management
Camden Hill Road
London   W8 7AR
Tel: 0171-229 1282
Fax: 0171-727 8200

The Business

Virgin is not really a 'group' as such, because the financial results are not aggregated centrally. Each business runs its own affairs. If there is a group, it is really a collection of shared ownership, shared leadership, and shared values. In many respects, Branson's business group resembles a *keiretsu*—a society of business. The Japanese think so anyway

The companies, which include wholly owned businesses, alliances, joint ventures and outsourcing arrangements, grow around a name that must stand for something. Anything which employees do must fit these corporate brand values, which is how the Virgin 'group' works. But Virgin is not a brand extension—as a 'house' brand, it adapts to diverse types of businesses and services.

Richard Branson's business style has sometimes been viewed as slightly eccentric, but few can deny his success. Virgin has a sizeable global presence, and incredible name recognition. It is profitable and growing fast, entering and claiming significant share in new markets. But all this has come about without most of the trappings of the multinational. There is no head office, little sense of management hierarchy, the minimum of corporate bureaucracy. This is the ultimate lean enterprise.

Company Culture and Style

The Virgin brand has a number of key values that must be instilled in any new business venture, and it is worth repeating them again: quality, competitiveness (or value for money), innovation and fun. How do these translate into corporate competencies across the different businesses, which might themselves have their own subcultures?

According to Will Whitehorn, Virgin's director of corporate communications and one of Branson's closest lieutenants, Virgin's core competency is the ability to identify relevant business opportunities, move quickly and manage the growth of new businesses. And of the hundreds of business proposals that Virgin receives, only a few pass 'Go'. These are always ones that will be faithful to the four attributes.

As Branson has explained: "If we launch a new product, people assume that we will come up with something a bit different. But it's also synonymous with fun and with entertainment in the broadest sense. The value of the name is enormous. We get asked to put the Virgin name to many things, but we say no to most of them."

Virgin focuses on businesses that can generate their own growth potential. In this context, it is easy to see why some of Virgin's target markets are those occupied by near-monopolies or where cartel-like behaviour is evident. Not only is there a fat margin to cut into, but you can be the people's champion while you are doing it.

The battle with British Airways is well documented and Virgin Atlantic Airways (with 5,000 staff the largest business in the group) has made considerable inroads to the airline market, picking up awards and accolades on route. Virgin Direct confounded the conventional industry wisdom that you cannot sell non-obligatory financial services over the telephone, by introducing its own PEP.

When Virgin decided to enter the cola business in a joint venture with Canadian partner Cott Corporation, taking on Coke and Pepsi in one of the world's most entrenched duopolies, a small team of Virgin managers was able to call upon a range of management talent in the group. After three months Virgin Cola had shifted £50 million of product with only four employees.

Working through joint ventures, alliances and outsourced operations is integral to Virgin's culture, and imbues the style in which managers and staff work. Employees of joint ventures—for example Virgin Direct is a 50:50 venture with AMP—think that they work for Virgin. Identifying with the Virgin group—or the Virgin name—instils confidence, a belief that they cannot fail to succeed, as well as helping to open doors.

People at the top must believe passionately in the Virgin values and in what they are doing. The top 100 or so managers do, and are convinced that together they can build a British, truly global brand name, something not achieved since the war. Realising this ambition is a great challenge, and a highly motivating one at that.

Human Resource Priorities

Virgin really has little need for central HR policies, although each individual business will have its own HR or personnel professionals to take care of the core tasks of recruitment, training, remuneration, and so on. HR at Virgin is more behavioural and instinctive, than written. If people are inculcated with the ways and values of the business, knowing that everything (including their livelihood) depends upon outside perceptions of the company brand name, motivations and behaviour happen almost instinctively.

Individuals are encouraged to speak their minds, however, and in the absence of hierarchies, managers are the first port of call. There is no atmosphere of retribution, and the system works well. The 'myth' of all employees having Richard Branson's home telephone number is actually true. Maybe 150 employees call each week and despite globe-trotting business schedules, Branson succeeds in answering around half of these personally. He talks to employees a lot.

Everything relating to employees and the company comes back to the brand. If employees have no confidence in the company, this soon works its way through to the customer. Virgin knows that employee perceptions are very important.

Do not conclude that a belief in fun and enterprise makes life one big party. Nor is there mayhem. People work very hard at Virgin. The airline and financial services industries demand minimum and consistent standards as the ante to doing business. At Virgin Atlantic Airways (VAA), some of these regimentation's (including the three allowable colours of nail varnish for stewardesses) are introduced on a six-week induction programme that everyone must attend.

Career Opportunity and Development

You are less likely to join Virgin Management, more probably one of the individual businesses. But Virgin people can and do move around a lot. Mark Furlong was a marketing services assistant at VAA—stagnating and unfulfilled, but able to pick up the telephone to Richard Branson. The company at the time was putting together its bid for running the Eurostar franchise, and Furlong now finds himself as marketing director of London & Continental Railways, the consortium running the Eurostar services and the Channel Tunnel link.

Virgin is not a good company to work for if you are disinclined to take the initiative. Failing to avoid the cliché 'self-starter', people typically stay for six months or for life, especially at management level.

One of Branson's philosophies in building the record business was instead of trying to make a good business even larger, he preferred to start a new one, and take the management team with it. A regular diet of fresh challenge is one reason why he has kept his management team together for so long. In a way, the *keiretsu* developed naturally, without anyone realising it was that.

Pay and Benefits

Pay and benefit will vary across the businesses, but Virgin generally pays around market levels. It is not a 'get rich quick' proposition, yet levels of employee satisfaction are usually much higher than in comparable businesses. Virgin Direct salespeople are paid a salary, not a commission.

The deep involvement and identify that staff have with the Virgin name extends into rewards. There is a central principle that people should share in the profitability of the business—VAA for example has a simple but valued profit share scheme. Virgin Direct staff receive a flat bonus based on the company's performance, not on their own individual 'book'.

All employees get other Virgin benefits—discounts at the Megastore or cheap flights, for example, and an invite to the famous Virgin annual party.

The Future

The biggest challenge for Virgin will be maintaining a flow of good management into the business. It has a good team, but it is not top-heavy. With the businesses diversified, it will need to find the thread through its people that provides intrinsic understanding and energy to take the company forward.

This dilemma is no more acute than in Virgin's quest to become a global brand. The company needs and wants to hire local people in new countries, but it also wants Virgin people, living and breathing the Virgin culture. Finding people with the skill and sensitivity to adapt and apply the Virgin brand to local cultures will not be easy.

Considering the business areas likely to grow the quickest, the 'people moving' businesses are important to Virgin, and watch out for it trying to build a world-wide transportation company. The Megastore/Virgin Retail concept is one that can be easily rolled-out around the world, maybe involving integrated multiplex venues, restaurants and megastores. Cola could be a very big business for Virgin, as could financial services. One thing is almost certain—the Virgin *keiretsu* will make an impact whatever.

WHITBREAD

Whitbread

Whitbread is a leading British retailer in drinks, eating out, hospitality and leisure. It also has interests in German and Canadian restaurant chains. In the year to 2 March 1996, its turnover was £2,750 million and its pre-tax profits were £283 million. Whitbread employs 70,000 people in the UK, approximately half of which are part-time workers.

Biggest Plus: A consensus-driven company where nice people finish first

Biggest Minus: No time to sit around and drink up the profits

Whitbread plc
Chiswell Street
London   EC1Y 4SD
Tel: 0171-606 4455
Fax: 0171-615 1000

The Business

Founded in 1742 as a family brewery, Whitbread is one of Britain's oldest-surviving beer producers. The Whitbread Beer Company markets such leading brands as Stella Artois, Heineken, Boddington's, Murphy's and Flowers. But outsiders are often surprised to learn that beer accounts for less than 15% of the group's profits. Today, Whitbread plc is an organisation with far wider leisure interests—and owns many well-known high street names.

The restaurants and leisure division includes the Beefeater, Pizza Hut and T.G.I. Friday chains. Also in this division are Travel Inn, the UK's fastest growing hotel chain, the UK hotels franchise of Marriott International, the Costa Coffee stores, and Thresher, a leading drinks retailing chain. The group is the premier operator in private health and fitness through its ownership of David Lloyd Leisure. Overseas, Whitbread is the leading steakhouse operator in Germany with its Maredo and Churrasco chains, and owns a restaurant chain in North America called The Keg.

In addition, Whitbread Inns is one of the UK's leading pub retailers with brands such as Brewers Fayre, Hogshead ale houses and Wayside Inns, while Whitbread Pub Partnerships leases 2,200 pubs to licensees.

Company Culture and Style

The group has a distinctive style which HR policy director John Shaw sums up as follows. "I'd describe us a very sensible company, one which anticipates market trends and consults internally before we make acquisitions. We believe it's important to get everyone on-side. As a result, we can look back on a successful history: even in recent recessions we've continued to do well." Latest figures back up this claim, with Whitbread enjoying five successive years of sales, profit, earnings and dividend growth to March 1996.

With so many well-established companies within the group, cultural differences do exist—but less so than might be imagined. A Whitbread tradition permeates the organisation that encourages people to feel free to make suggestions and talk openly. There is a definite feeling of pride in the Whitbread culture. There is also a friendliness and a respect culture often absent from large, successful companies. Nice people may finish last in the world of tennis, but at Whitbread nice people actually flourish in its consensus culture.

People work hard at Whitbread, but they also enjoy their work. There's a real sense of teamwork and lots of socialising between employees, even at weekends. Despite the hard work and long hours many put in, stress seems not to be a major factor in the group. A long-standing group football contest, the Brussels Trophy, is typical of the spirit at Whitbread; this year, 32 sides entered—a record!

Each of the operating companies has its own internal communications programme, but there is also a group-wide initiative. An excellent and lively newspaper, *Whitbread News,* runs news stories that are interesting to read as well as focusing on staff around the group. Strategic issues are covered in more detail in *Management Review,* which are then cascaded downwards. A Key Communicators Group ensures that these major messages are circulated efficiently and to a wider audience.

Whitbread takes its role in society seriously: its business in the community unit invests around £2 million a year and thousands of voluntary man-hours in charitable work.

Human Resource Priorities

Human resources is important at Whitbread, although much of the work that was once handled centrally has been devolved to the operating companies. The head office continues to address policy issues such as health and safety and equal opportunities, while the operating companies focus on specifics.

The essential Whitbread HR policy comes down to a firm belief that the way to get the best from its people is to manage them properly. One way this is checked is through analysis of turnover, sick absence, long-term sickness and access to health care. More sharply defined views are obtained through the group's quality of life survey. People are asked annually how they are treated, what they feel about company strategy, how satisfied they are with their benefits and so on. Where any problems emerge, senior management immediately addresses the issues.

Career Opportunity and Development

Structures across the group are becoming flatter and hierarchies less pyramidal. As a result, people are more empowered than ever before, allowing Whitbread to cut its number of senior managers from 250 to 140. This process has meant that promotions are fewer than in the past, although more meaningful when they do occur.

This means that the grades have very wide pay bands, which also overlap. The grades consist of A, B, C and senior management: grade C remuneration could vary from £35,000 to £55,000, and responsibilities increase accordingly. There are also opportunities to move between the operating companies to gain greater knowledge. There were 100 such moves in the management structure in 1996, and it is clearly becoming more important to have well-rounded experience when it comes to applying for the top jobs.

There are many examples of people rising through the ranks in the group. A sales assistant at Thresher rose to become its operations director, for instance. There are also lots of long-serving staff: dinners and awards are regularly held for both 20- and 30-year servers.

Each business recruits independently for its own needs. Some functions have formal graduate training and induction, but most graduates join on an ad hoc basis, many of them having already gained experience in one of the companies by working there in the kitchen or behind the bar during term evenings or vacation. Indeed, the group is now keen that graduates should have some practical knowledge before joining full time.

Similarly, each business has its own training functions. There is a great deal of in-house training, covering technical knowledge such as wines and spirits, hotel catering and so on. In-house trainers are employed by most of the businesses. There is also a range of specific training modules from outside.

Over the past ten years, group employees have risen by 10,000. Some redundancies have occurred, however, over this period, particularly in manufacturing and due to rationalisations. At Whitbread, every effort is made to re-employ the person;

if this cannot be done, there is a great deal of consultation, after-care and counselling. Help is provided with interview techniques and preparation of CVs.

Pay and Benefits

Whitbread acknowledges that it needs to offer top levels of pay to get the quality of staff it wants. Often, pay can increase as experience rises and the employee learns more about the job. At all levels, pay is reviewed annually, and discussions and consultations are held to explain the pay awards. Across the board, Whitbread is seen as competitive for pay in its industry sectors; senior management pay, for example, varies from £50,000 to £395,000.

Benefits include free shares to all staff after three years, a contributory pension scheme, an SAYE scheme after one year, subsidised meals, good sports and social clubs and a Whitbread card giving discounts across the group's products and services. There is also a free issue of products every month such as 24 free cans of Stella—although the keep-fit fanatics can choose to take the allowance in leisure vouchers! Holidays are an interesting benefit: the minimum is four weeks but five weeks is the norm. Some employees in Threshers can sell a week to the company or buy an extra week.

Managers enjoy a remarkably flexible car scheme that can be upgraded by 20% above salary level or downgraded and the difference taken in cash; a private health care plan for partners and family; and for senior managers an executive share option scheme.

The Future

John Shaw sees the challenge as being primarily about customer service. "In many areas of our operations, customer expectations are rising all the time. This means that what is seen as good customer service today will be only average tomorrow. We need to keep striding ahead in terms of what we offer, which in turn requires us to recruit, retain and develop the very best staff."

Another challenge is to manage the ever-growing portfolio of companies that is Whitbread today: introduce best practice procedures for each, benefit from economies of scale within the group, and foster the Whitbread culture in new acquisitions.

Finally, the employee group is likely to become ever more diverse, with more women and more ethnic minorities represented.

The future obviously holds many surprises as well as challenges; but Whitbread's long-term strategy looks like a strong asset in dealing with them.

WPP Group plc

WPP Group

WPP is the world's largest advertising and marketing services group. The 40 companies in the group offer clients—local, multinational and global—a comprehensive and, when appropriate, an integrated range of marketing services, including advertising, market research, public relations, sales promotion, direct marketing, identity and design, and specialist communications such as pharmaceutical, recruitment, and business-to-business communications.

The group's companies include some impressive names—J Walter Thompson and Ogilvy & Mather are two of the most powerful names in advertising; Hill & Knowlton is one of the few well-known global public relations agencies; Sampson Tyrrell Enterprise is a highly regarded creative design agency in Europe; Millward Brown International and Research International are leaders in market research; and the Henley Centre is well known in Europe for strategic planning and marketing consultancy. WPP employs more than 20,000 people in 786 offices across 84 countries. In 1995, the company had revenues of £1.6 billion.

Biggest Plus: Marvellous group of companies, professional approach to people development

Biggest Minus: No marketing business is for people who like lots of security

WPP Group plc
27 Farm Street
London W1X 6RD
Tel: 0171-408 2204
Fax: 0171-493 6819
http://www.wpp.com

The Business

WPP companies live by their wits. Clients come to them for intelligence, experience, inventiveness and imagination: all to be applied for competitive advantage. The management of its people and the harnessing of their talents is, therefore, central to the success of the company.

WPP aims to be the preferred provider of advertising and marketing services. Increasingly sophisticated clients are looking for a more co-ordinated, global approach, and meeting this need is at the core of WPP's strategy. The parent company's objective is to add value to clients' businesses and the careers of its people. Client lists are impressive. Between them, the group's 40 companies served more than 300 of the *Fortune* 500 companies in 1995.

There are different ways to look at WPP. As the sum of many individual operating companies; or as a parent company with a changing role to play in the business of the group. WPP has realised that in certain defined activities, it can be of even greater value to its clients and provide even greater opportunities and rewards for its people. Strict criteria are applied. If any activity is better undertaken by an individual company, or if centralising an activity threatens operating companies' autonomy or identity, it is better left decentralised.

Company Culture and Style

WPP recognises that it is a collection of individual companies with their own styles. It has no wish or intention to change these, and companies such as JWT and O&M must retain their own special identities. Instead, WPP has sought to overlay certain ideas and values that are part of its culture, and which it would like individual companies to *add* to theirs. The value placed on what individuals can deliver, what they can achieve, as opposed to the way they work, for example; the notion of ownership of the business that people work for; and working together in teams.

Chief executive Martin Sorrell has sought to improve the degree of co-operation among the many disparate parts of the WPP empire. Much effort has gone into helping individual operating companies improve the quality of their service offer, and facilitate cross-company partnerships where appropriate. The WPP Group has developed a programme of cross-company initiatives that includes training, recruitment, career development, incentive schemes, information technology, property, procurement and practice development.

WPP is full of talented people. It is another role of the parent company to help make group companies even more attractive to talented people throughout the world. Professional initiatives include the Atticus Awards (for original thinking in marketing services) and the WPP Marketing Fellowship programme, where newcomers are rotated through group companies as part of WPP's process of building a generation of multi-disciplinary managers.

Human Resource Priorities

The parent company takes an active approach to personal and professional development, to identify people with potential to take on leadership roles in the group.

This professional approach to human resources sets itself apart from most marketing services companies; WPP has tended to model itself more on clients.

WPP recognises that it is a commercial business, not a hobby or an artistic endeavour. Too many marketing services companies take a *laissez faire* approach to people development, relying on instincts and raw talent. "Without the strategic perspective," suggests human resources director, Brian Brooks, "talented people can easily fall through the cracks. It comes down to education and development. There really is no other way to help our people exploit their full potential."

Not that the company ignores the subject of financial reward. This is regarded as vital, but WPP defines remuneration strategy in terms of what it wants to accomplish as a business, and how it can help the business get there. HR focuses much effort on recruitment. Aware that much of the cream of universities and business schools is soaked up by investment banking and management consultancy, WPP has gone to lengths to promote the chance to work in a multi-disciplinary, creative environment. It hopes to develop people rapidly who can deliver integrated solutions to clients, leading to a fast-tracking management cadre within WPP.

WPP draws out its qualitative points of difference. It welcomes a diversity of viewpoint, and encourages openness. The group has many women in senior positions, with WPP only judging people on what they contribute. There is considerable flexibility in the work place, relating to hours, style of working and pace of career progression. Chris Jones, e.g. is CEO of JWT World-wide at just 41. Conversely, if people are happy at a middle level, and delivering, there is less pressure to continually move upwards.

WPP encourages a lot of internal communication. Martin Sorrell's monthly CEO Report goes out to 1,500 senior people, generating vital feedback, while *Network* is the Group's quarterly newsletter sent to 10,000 of its professionals worldwide. WPP is about to introduce its own Intranet and Web site, and already has a GIOTTO multimedia kiosk showcasing the group's work and services.

Career Opportunity and Development

Revenue growth is a critical ingredient in providing business and career advancement opportunities. Many WPP companies are growing fast, and offer a range of challenging, rewarding and exciting careers in all marketing disciplines. Individuals are more likely to apply to WPP's individual companies than to the parent company, but the latter increasingly plays a valuable role in recruitment.

The '100 Club' is identified as those people who are currently leading the business and delivering value to shareholders. The '300 Club' trawls for the highest potential people not yet in leadership roles. Business programmes, customised for WPP by the London and Harvard Business Schools, are aimed at both 'clubs'.

In addition to individual company's own training programmes, the parent company runs brand leadership courses and sector-specific workshops, bringing together professionals from different disciplines and different companies. Other initiatives are also aimed at developing competencies which people might not have, but will need—people management skills for instance. Increasingly, ambitious people in the group recognise that to gain valuable management experience, they will need to spend some time in the fastest developing markets of the world; this prospect is relished by many.

The group is embarking on an ambitious programme to introduce 360 degree performance appraisals in to each of its companies; this may take years, but this is a popular and relevant idea in a business like WPP, with its heavy emphasis on teams and interaction, making it critical to get a comprehensive view of performance including the *client* perspective.

Pay and Benefits

WPP applies the notion of fewer, better-paid people. Staff costs to revenue ratios have dropped by 7%, while margins were improved. Yet the top 400 people earned more, largely due to incentive remuneration. WPP spent $80 million on incentives in 1995, and prefers to reward senior people for performance instead of providing benefits, cars, and perks.

WPP is publicly committed to wider internal share ownership, and various programmes have been developed to enable a large number of WPP professionals to participate actively in the growing value of the company. Initially, only the senior group was targeted. Since then, share options were granted to 450 people in 1994/95 (the 300 as well as the 100 Clubs). In 1997, WPP is planning to introduce a world-wide Stock Ownership Program for all of its people. The group wants everyone to think and act like an owner, encouraging senior people to retain their shares and lead by example, rather than cash-in on good share price performance.

The Future

Marketing services as a sector has a reasonably bright future, and WPP is positioned well in it. The group has grown faster than the sector as a whole, gaining market share. The long-term trends in the marketing services industry indicate that the non-advertising areas are likely to grow the fastest, and that demand for services will grow faster in non-US markets.

WPP, with its geographical spread and breadth of services, is well placed to exploit these trends. Both JWT and O&M are well placed in growing regions such as Asia Pacific and South America.

Within the organisation, other important trends are emerging. The use of technology in terms of business, efficiency, ways of working, communications, knowledge sharing represents a major business challenge. Technology is invading the work place and needs to be related to clients and translated into the marketing context. WPP has recently hired an expert from Booz-Allen to head-up the group's IT function.

Restructuring the work place and transforming organisational structures is something which WPP has committed to, aimed at delivering the best client service in the industry and 'better work, faster'. The WPP Space Program that is concerned with 'redefining the office', has 14 test-bed sites across the group. The principal mission is to push accountability further down the organisation to more people. One benefit of greater accountability is that reward can be linked to it, enabling the group to extend performance-related pay to more people.

WPP believes strongly, and has challenged itself to prove, that the value of the group to client companies can be a great deal more than the sum of its parts.

ZENECA

Zeneca Group

Zeneca is a British-based group of three international businesses: pharmaceuticals, agrochemicals, and specialties. In its mission statement, Zeneca describes itself as, 'a leading international bioscience group which creates new products and services to improve human health and nutrition and the quality of life.'

Over 30,000 people are employed by Zeneca in researching, manufacturing and selling its products, including 12,000 employees in the UK. In 1995, Zeneca achieved sales of £4.89 billion, on which it made an operating profit of £894 million.

Biggest Plus: Young exciting company, all the advantages which go with a fresh start

Biggest Minus: Not yet a famous name

Zeneca Group plc
15 Stanhope Gate
London   W1Y 6LN
Tel: 0171-304 5000
Fax: 0171-304 5151

The Business

The opportunity to create a company the size of Zeneca was virtually unique. Zeneca was launched when the bioscience businesses were demerged from ICI in 1993. Starting almost with a clean sheet, the company brought with it the history and values carefully cultivated over the years at 'old' ICI.

This presented a superb opportunity to look at everything afresh—an opportunity that the company grasped. There is an ethos in the company of business primacy, but also a desire to give strategic business units significant freedom to make their own way, without 'throwing the baby out with the bath water'.

The business values of the company transcend business boundaries, which is right for the style of company Zeneca wishes to be, and the type of person it wants to employ. The corporate head office is very small (around 90 people) for the size of company. Empowered managers in the divisions, challenging the norms and doing things differently, refer to the 'power of Zeneca' in breaking new ground in time scales unthinkable at 'old' ICI.

Zeneca has been very, very busy as a result, and this is shown in its strong financial and share price performance. Zeneca may be a lesser-known name, but it is one of the largest UK companies by market capitalisation.

Company Culture and Style

At the time of demerger, the company expressed value statements with respect to employees. But it also spent a lot of time emphasising the needs of customers and of shareholders. Realising that emphasising these parts of the stakeholder package might bring the danger that others (i.e. employees) might feel neglected, Zeneca has been doing some thinking about the people in the organisation.

Chief executive David Barnes says, "Zeneca's people are the ambassadors of the company in the business world in which they work and the community in which they live...Let there be no doubt about the importance of people in Zeneca. They are the source of our future prosperity, growth and renewal; it is their knowledge and capabilities that are the intellectual assets of the company and they must be developed and nurtured accordingly."

Group manager for human resources David Hyde suggests, "the market capitalisation of Zeneca, at £17 billion, is well above the fixed asset value of the company. The difference is traditionally explained away as 'goodwill'. I prefer to think that it represents the intellectual capital behind our current and future product base, which is absolutely essential to the future of the organisation."

Zeneca is conducting a world-wide corporate values survey among 4,355 employees, seeking their views on what the company's values are and should be, and how important they are for business and personal success. Zeneca is only three years old, and a new culture will emerge that reflects cultural values that the company wishes to express, and which employees fundamentally support.

Zeneca is already 'freeing up' the organisation, encouraging its people to aspire to be the best and recognising that they need to be given freedom to achieve it. This is all about behaviour, about encouraging and supporting people all the way. David Hyde is in no doubt that the key driver of this is 'trust'.

Diversity is valued at Zeneca, appreciating the creative potential that men and women with differing backgrounds and abilities bring to the company while reflecting the group's values of being open, honest and worthy of trust and respect.

Successful people at Zeneca have imagination, drive, a 'can do' attitude, and the aptitude to work across boundaries, functions and in teams. The central theme is about setting realistic and challenging goals, and then delivering.

Human Resource Priorities

David Hyde's group HR department contains a number of specialists, but there is no separate HR strategy. "It's more about the alignment of people resources to business strategy, with each area working together to make sure that everything fits." HR's central goal is to get the best out of all Zeneca's people, and stoke up the value of the 'intellectual capital' on the balance sheet.

Planning senior management development and succession planning means providing development opportunities for people identified as having the potential to make it to the top. Group HR is also addressing its remuneration systems, to develop competitive salaries that link reward with sustained performance.

Career Opportunity and Development

Zeneca companies are all leaders in their fields and consequently, the group offers interesting and challenging careers. Being a science-based company, Zeneca historically has recruited more technical and science graduates. It is now doing more in commercial jobs, and is also taking a few MBAs (a relatively new development). The company has just about every job, discipline and function you can think of or, as David Hyde puts it "with over 30,000 employees, there are a lot of career opportunities".

Zeneca subscribes to the increasingly popular 'self-managed career' approach. Employees who take an equal share of their own development and seek new challenges will be offered support, and the company will sometimes 'punch holes' where there is advantage to the business and to the individual.

Promising UK employees have plenty of opportunity to gain international work experience. As a global company, Zeneca is likely to encourage a more international flow of people within all countries in which the group has operations.

A significant amount of promotion is internal, which is likely to continue. But the company recognises that certain specialist expertise and experience must be recruited externally to achieve business objectives and create a healthy range of views throughout the company.

Pay and Benefits

Zeneca is market-competitive on salaries, and for most employees, the annual rise is linked to performance. Increasingly, employees are able to see clear results of their endeavours and be rewarded accordingly.

A bonus system is also in place for everyone; 75% of the bonus is based on the contribution of an individual's business unit, and 25% on the performance of the company as a whole. Bonuses can be taken in company shares instead of cash, the uptake of which has resulted in 75% of employees becoming shareholders.

Zeneca has revamped its pension scheme to feature choice, portability and flexibility. The 'best of both worlds' includes a money purchase scheme for employees under 45, and the choice of a final salary scheme for employees over 45.

All employees have access to an SAYE share option scheme and higher up the management leader board, executive share options come into play. Company car benefits are very flexible, including a cash option.

The Future

Sir David Barnes wants all Zeneca's businesses to be upper quartile performers, through innovation, effective marketing, and best customer service. He also aspires to Zeneca delivering average five-year earnings growth of 15% per annum.

Zeneca's pharmaceutical and agrochemical businesses have the best new product pipelines they have ever had and, while the company is resourcing up, it will inevitably be a little stretched. Meeting this peak level of activity is challenging for all employees and a great deal of effort is being spent on looking at 'improved ways of working' through re-engineering.

Zeneca's specialties business has suffered some necessary downsizing of underperforming operations, but remaining employees may want some reassurance that the group is now focused firmly on the core activities, which are performing well and look to have a promising future.

Press speculation has suggested that Zeneca's performance could attract an aggressive bid, which only makes the company a victim of its own success. Zeneca's employees know from newspapers reporting Sir David Barnes that the company has 'a rosy independent future' with plenty of organic growth ahead. It is unlikely that the people who write the take-over stories, however, spare a thought for the unsettling effect this can have on employees. But as Sir David Barnes puts it: "I'm not going to stop being successful."

The international basis of Zeneca's business is being increasingly reflected at senior management level, and in the future this should be reflected at board level, which presently is made up exclusively of British executive directors, four of which are 'home-grown'.

Zeneca enjoys an excellent reputation with its shareholders, customers and opinion formers, but its image is less strong in the minds of the general public. Zeneca got the fresh start, but ICI kept the name. Employees who were mightily proud to work for ICI, the bellwether of British industry, now need to feel proud all over again, of Zeneca. David Hyde says that in the local communities in which it operates, people are very familiar with Zeneca, but admits to occasionally, when visiting a Zeneca facility, having to concede defeat to taxi drivers—"OK then, take me to ICI".

But Zeneca's excellent reputation continues to grow, and if this marvellous success story continues, Zeneca will no longer need to announce itself as "you may not have heard of us..."

A view from the Association of Graduate Careers Advisory Services

The labour market for new graduates in Britain is becoming increasingly complex and competitive. Students completing their degree and postgraduate studies face an apparent maze of options, a far wider range of opportunities than those entered by graduates 20 and more years ago. The need for good, clear and accurate information and for professional careers guidance has never been greater. Job applicants need to consider many issues both about themselves and about their potential employers. This book provides valuable information about those companies in Britain that have made a clear commitment to staff training and development, to good human resource management and to equality of opportunity. As such, it enables job seekers and those planning a career change or developmental move to identify those companies that offer what they are seeking.

This volume focuses mainly on large private companies and provides some excellent company profiles for those considering their next career move in this direction.

Careers advisers working in higher education institutions in Britain have a wealth of information and contacts across the whole spectrum of graduate employment opportunities including public sector organisations and small- and medium-sized enterprises. The companies listed here have demonstrated how they meet the exacting criteria of the publishers in relation to their policies and practices for employee development. Their size, national and international profile, and range of activities clearly have an impact on the career development opportunities available. Large, blue-chip companies continue to attract high fliers and this publication will help ambitious new graduates and finalists find out how such companies compare.

Inevitably, however, the list has to exclude employers, large and small, which are making considerable strides in the area of human resources development and management. Small, regionally based companies that are growing fast, are innovative and committed to staff training and development, or newly privatised parts of the public sector, finding new ways of meeting public needs, may provide similar challenges and opportunities but on a lesser scale. New graduates need to recognise that 'best' is a relative term and that the old cliché 'horses for courses' applies in graduate recruitment as it does elsewhere. Job seekers and job changers will find much in this volume to help them consider which companies they might wish to apply to and what they might be looking for in a potential employer.

Margaret Dane
Association of Graduate Careers Advisory Services

Skills for graduates in the 21st century

The world of work continues to change profoundly and so do graduate careers. To deal successfully with these changes, graduates will need a new set of skills—those of self-reliance. They are the skills to manage a lifetime's progression in learning and work, rather than to do the work itself. As process rather than functional skills, they enable people to utilise and transfer skills and knowledge. This differentiates them from the other attributes that graduates need in the work place.

The Association of Graduate Recruiters (AGR) recently examined the changes taking place in graduate careers in order to predict the kinds of skills that will be required. Self-reliant graduates need to take responsibility for their career and personal development, and to manage their relationship with work and learning. AGR's report suggests how these skills can be developed, especially within the context of higher education. The pace of change in business, with global competition, deregulation, and new technology means organisations must respond rapidly to market demands. 'It is impossible to imagine that the skills needed in the work place will remain the same in the 21st century,' the report says.

The changes facing organisations have an effect on careers and on the skills required. In the past, self-reliance skills have been assumed—or neglected—by both employers and higher education. These skills are now to the fore because career transitions are more frequent and people need to be flexible and adaptable. Academic knowledge rapidly becomes obsolete, supporting structures have disappeared and people have to manage uncertainty and change.

In the new world of work, careers are very different. Gone is the job for life with its planned career structure and company training scheme. Gone are the clear functional identity and the progressive rise in income and security. Instead there is a world of customers and clients, adding value, lifelong learning, portfolio careers, self-development and an overwhelming need to stay employable. The self-reliant graduate is aware of the changing world of work.

Simply asking employers what they need from graduates is not enough to predict the skills that they will need in the future. Employers have different requirements, often based on past, or at best, current requirements. They are also unlikely to take account of the need for graduates to have the skills to know when and how to get a better job with their competitors, not just how to find and keep one.

AGR summarises the skills needed for self-reliance as: self-awareness, self-promotion, exploring and planning opportunities, action planning, networking, matching and decision making, negotiation, political awareness, coping with uncertainty, development focus, transferring skills and self-confidence.

Traditional graduate jobs are the most vigorously promoted but routes into employment are changing. Many graduates will now join small- or medium-sized enterprises or larger organisations outside formal graduate training schemes. However, in the opinion of AGR, graduate-level skills are not being effectively applied in these sectors.

Mary Wilson
Association of Graduate Recruiters

The international perspective

There may be a tendency to see careers as being confined to our own shores, unless we are offered a secondment to the Bahamas one day, when we might think again. Such a view would be a mistake for several reasons.

First, it has become a truism that the world is shrinking and that markets and labour supplies have become global. Countless firms now see their best prospects of growth as taking place in overseas markets. Rapid developments in communications and ease of travel have played a major part in this opening up of new markets, as have economic growth and political change.

Secondly, working overseas now has more advantages in terms of career acceleration than snags. In the past one suspects the occasional instance of the firm despatching a problem person to an exotic location where they can be conveniently forgotten for a while and can do less harm than in the UK. Today, employers use overseas postings not as a dumping ground, but rather as concentrated development for the rising manager who can gain a breadth and concentration of experience in a smaller overseas operation much faster than at home. The primary purpose is not of course the individual's development but the firm's. There is a two-fold benefit: exporting expertise from the UK operation and learning from the host country and business environment.

I mentioned snags: the number and importance depend on where you go and at what stage in your life. Disruption of schooling may be a concern with some locations and an advantage in others. Similarly facilities and creature comforts aren't the same everywhere, although the more austere the environment, the stronger seems to be the expatriate community. The worry used to be "will they forget me while I'm away—will all the good opportunities pass me by?" Ungrounded fears, I suggest, where good employers are concerned. These fears can be reduced or removed if the organisation designates a 'mentor' who will watch out for the assignee's career prospects.

In our work as career counsellors we meet many instances where international experience is a major asset, or its absence a disqualifier for some jobs. Recently a 30-year-old had two long stints abroad for his employer including the experience of setting up a high-tech production facility in Africa and making it profitable within six years of joining as a graduate. Obviously, this stood him in very good stead relative to his peers in the UK.

The final argument for the international dimension is that work isn't only about making money for our employer and ourselves. We often work with people in mid-career, who are not necessarily in crisis, but who are stalled and dissatisfied. Our emphasis is on achieving the right combination of use of abilities and interests; blurring the distinction between work, leisure and learning. We suggest that employment is about self-development, learning, enjoyment and personal growth. I rest my case.

Robin Alcock
KPMG Career Consulting

Corporate Culture: the fit between the individual and the company

This article aims to provide you with a few basic guidelines on how to fit your personal culture with that of an employer— which type you are likely to be happiest with, and therefore most productive in.

1. Know yourself.

A good occupational psychologist can administer numerical and verbal reasoning tests. These form part of many employers' test batteries, and doing these tests in advance can help you to know better where you stand. Analyse the type of people you feel comfortable with.

2. Know your work culture.

Consider your own values and beliefs in deciding your career direction. Assess yourself honestly. Do not aim for a fashionable, highly paid job that, deep down, you are not going to be happy with. Establish your views on public service versus public sector, your views on being a clever 'doer' versus a 'seller', (i.e. which are you going to like best—selling the work or doing it?)

3. Establish your core skill.

Personal fit with a corporate culture is important, but not nearly as important as your personal fit with the core skill you choose to develop. Your choice of that skill is the single most important selection you will make. Aim for what you are likely to be best in, even if this may not seem to be what the market currently demands.

4. Set your objectives.

Look at the career patterns of those working within your core skill. What career steps have they taken, at what age, and what experience have they gained? Importantly, what organisations have they been with? Contact the relevant industry association and talk to somebody who knows the career patterns within that calling. Again, aim at what you believe your personal best can be.

5 Draw up your shortlist.

Prepare a list of the employer cultures into which you are most likely to fit. This book will help you to do that. Establish the real level of internal respect that an organisation will have for your skills. A major retailer may need architects, surveyors and the like, but are people in these occupations really 'family' to the company? Try to establish the Employer Brand of each of your chosen organisations. What is their reputation internally, and among their suppliers? What are the key factors in people's development there?

6. Check references.

Check out a specific employer during the recruitment procedure as carefully as they will check you out. Be tough-minded about this. Ask to meet some senior people, or the heads of the functional skill you are targeting. When you are their age, do you want to be like them?

Finally, a message for employers reading this. Apply the same rigour, honesty and sensitivity in your recruitment procedures as you expect from the talent facing you. Describe your culture, warts and all. It will not be everyone's ideal, and being clear about your corporate culture from the outset will save both sides time and money.

Simon Barrow
Chairman of People in Business

406

Pay and benefits

Recent evidence shows that pay increases have been low and are staying low—the current average is 3%. This is astonishingly stable and indicates a complete change in thinking on pay increases. There are a large number of organisations that would like to stamp out the concept of the annual pay round, which only became part of the British psyche in the 1960s. However, the reality is that annual pay increases normally will take place. With inflation and pay increases so closely linked, and the need to maintain the UK's global competitiveness, maintaining low pay rises is important and this would appear to have been achieved.

There is also a general feeling that the 'feel good factor' is now improving.

Differing economies within the country and industry groupings naturally have different pay levels that translate into regional pay differences. Percentage pay differentials for management jobs between the UK national median and the regions show the following pattern: Eastern Counties: −4.8%, London: +19.2%, North East: −4.7%, Northern Ireland: −4.8%, North West: −2.6%, Scotland: +7.1%, South East: +4.9%, South West: −3.6%, West Midlands: −6.3%.

When we speak of pay and benefits, we are considering the total package that comes with a job. A list of pay and benefit related items that could be included in the total package follows–other items may also feature.

Pay: Basic pay, bonus, commission, performance-related pay, profit-related pay, overtime, shift allowance, call-out allowance, market supplement.

Benefits: Holidays, sick pay, pension, company car, private health insurance, long-term disability insurance, life assurance.
Clearly not every package would include all of these items, but a remarkably large number would be included and are often disregarded by the employees.

If a value is placed on each of these, it can be seen that the typical package can be quite substantial and can cost the employer a large additional amount on top of the basic salary. When this is added to employer's National Insurance contributions (currently 10.2%), the total costs of employing an individual are often between 50% and 60% above the basic salary.

As might be expected, as seniority increases so does the level of benefits: a graduate trainee's typical package might be basic salary, company pension and life assurance, possibly with profit-related or performance-related pay. A middle manager would normally have private health insurance and performance-related pay, plus life assurance increasing to about three times annual salary and perhaps long-term disability insurance. For a senior manager, a company car would typically be around 1800cc and above, but more organisations are offering contract hire and leasing arrangements giving the individual more choice. Health and long-term insurances would increase.

The way forward over the next few years appears to be low economic growth, an improvement in the 'feel good factor', small rises in inflation and pay levels and a drifting upwards of benefit packages

Steve Flather
The Reward Group

Changes in career patterns and job security

Change and flexibility have become the watchwords of management in the 1990s; the organisations that will succeed beyond the millennium will be those that adapt and change in response to the economy and the needs of the global consumer.

Successful organisations must perform a delicate balancing act to ensure that their most important assets—their people—remain motivated when job security is increasingly lacking. The concept of a 'job for life' is truly dead and buried.

One of the major changes affecting recruitment patterns is the use of fixed-term contracts. These allow companies the flexibility to meet short-term employment needs but have led to a rising sense of insecurity among employees. A survey recently carried out by Sanders and Sidney revealed the increase in such contracts: 20% of jobs on offer were on a fixed-term basis, compared with only 3% five years earlier. Over three quarters of the employers surveyed said that fixed-term contracts were likely to become a permanent feature of the UK job market, with over half believing they could become as prevalent as traditional open-ended contracts. However, although job seekers were willing to accept fixed-term contracts, they did so with considerable reluctance. Their greatest concern was the potential impact on their financial situation. Other concerns were possible adverse effects on a company's culture and that team building could be made more difficult.

Even in today's fast-changing environment, job security is valued higher than personal fulfilment, promotion prospects and even salary.

However, our survey also highlighted the positive aspects of short-term working, particularly the increase in personal freedom and the combination of long-term flexibility with short-term security. Some employees valued the opportunity to undertake a variety of jobs with different industries—now called 'serial employment'.

Linked with this is the phenomenon of a 'portfolio career', whereby a number of jobs are undertaken, possibly interspersed with periods dedicated to training and development, leading to a person working in different fields and pursuing two or three jobs in tandem. This, I am convinced, will become more common in years to come.

So what does the job market hold for the future employee? The fact that more and more women are embarking on or returning to careers, combined with changing working patterns and the increase in part-time jobs, will lead to a marked reduction in full-time employment. Alongside it will co-exist many different forms of flexible working, be they home-based or from a neighbourhood office, on a fixed-term contract or in a part-time job. Individuals will move through periods of employment, self-employment, serial employment and even unemployment with greater ease and acceptance.

Once employees have overcome their initial reluctance and gone through the inevitable transition curve, they may begin to enjoy the freedom to re-engineer their lifestyles to suit the changing business environment. They may even benefit from the change and their careers may take on a new lease of life.

Frances Cook
Sanders and Sidney